I0755894

The Marquess of Granby

The Marquess of Granby

The Marquess of Granby

The British Army's Great Commander of Cavalry During the Seven Years' War

ILLUSTRATED

Walter Evelyn Manners

With a Short Biography of the Marquess of Granby

by G. P. R. James

The Marquess of Granby
The British Army's Great Commander of Cavalry During the Seven Years' War
by Walter Evelyn Manners
With a Short Biography of the Marquess of Granby
by G.P.R. James

ILLUSTRATED

FIRST EDITION

Leonaur is an imprint of Oakpast Ltd

ISBN: 978-1-916535-18-3 (hardcover)
ISBN: 978-1-916535-19-0 (softcover)

http://www.leonaur.com

Publisher's Notes

The views expressed in this book are not necessarily those of the publisher.

Contents

CHAPTER 1

1740-1745: Early Days

The courtesy-title borne by the eldest sons of the Dukes of Rutland had, prior to 1888, been for thirty years in abeyance in consequence of there being no heir-apparent to the dukedom. In that year the succession of the seventh duke brought the distinction "Marquess of Granby" once more into use and notice.

Journalistic comments to which this circumstance gave rise served only to show how little was remembered of the Marquess of Granby whose name, four generations ago, was a household word throughout England—a name respected, honoured, and beloved by all classes of the community, rich and poor, to an extent to which history provides but few parallels.

History enumerates, or, it may be said, consists of, myriads of names that have attained to fame; but fame and popularity, in popularity's best and highest sense, are neither synonymous terms nor necessarily combined qualities. On the whole, instances of men to whom this "double-first" has been freely accorded by the sympathies of their contemporaries by no means fall with broadcast profusion from recording pens.

A scrutiny of what modern biographical notices hitherto existed concerning John Manners, Marquess of Granby, suggests their authors' opinions to have been that he was, contemporarily, an overrated, though an eminently popular man. On the other hand, it is plain that not one of them was ever at the pains of doing more than repeat opinions derived almost exclusively from two sources, *viz*. the writings of "Junius" and of Horace Walpole—sources about equally tainted when matters of personal character are at stake.

The first was a literary buccaneer, eager to lampoon the Archangel Gabriel himself, had he, instead of Granby, been a member of the Grafton Administration: the second out-Heroded Herod in vindictiveness towards those upon whom his adverse and peevish prejudices fastened.

"Junius," there is no difficulty in seeing, had no personal animosity whatever against Granby; Walpole most distinctly had "Junius" practically withdrew all his libels on the marquess; Walpole did not; and remains in this instance, as in many others, a far more damaging libeller than the former, because his motives are less obvious, and his statements are consequently more attractive of belief.

Of the extraordinary interest and value attaching to Walpole's *Letters and Memoirs*, all who have dived deeply, or merely dipped superficially, into eighteenth-century records are well, and gratefully, aware The everlasting pity is that one as conscious as Walpole most surely was of the far-reaching results of his written experiences and opinions, should have been so devoid of the judicial sense, and so incapable of any attempt, even, at acquiring it. What he said, and equally what he left unsaid, concerning John, Marquess of Granby, has had the effect of misrepresenting and obscuring a man who, in Walpole's own significant phrase, "*sat at the top of the world*," and in the good company of William Pitt, Earl of Chatham

The result of this blighting monopoly which Walpole has exercised over Granby's character has been that historical writers have for the most part, labelled the marquess with the one empty word "popular," and have then cautiously passed by on the opposite side of the literary highway. And, although such writers have continually warned us against Walpole's unreliableness, they have as continually served up his mere opinions as facts often without owning from whence they derived their authority. No one has more frequently done this than Macaulay in the course of those Essays in one of which he holds up Walpole's writings to our special obloquy.

That Walpole knew an exceptionally great deal of what was going forward in his day is not disputed by anyone; the whole contention concerning his attitude towards Lord Granby (among many others) is that he deliberately refrained from saying *all* he thoroughly well knew, or that he misstated his knowledge in order to indulge his prejudices. Walpole placed public affairs, in the abstract, upon no higher platform than he allotted to those of society; and, in the concrete, he used precisely the same instruments of personal defamation and skilful satire to assist his partisanship concerning both. Frederick the Great wrote:

"Political intrigues, if they conduce to no result, deserve no more consideration than society squabbles."

But Walpole was incapable of rising, controversially, above the intrigue political or the squabble social, and therefore remained a slave—a very witty and brilliant slave—to the violent rancour and spiteful personalities incidental to either.

Since the publication of Walpole's *Memoirs*, records have come to light (some recently, some many years ago) which better tend to prove upon what foundations Granby's popularity was based. He was esteemed and respected by the sovereign as a brave and brilliant soldier, a most loyal and chivalrous subject, and disinterested public man: he was beloved and—as the phrase runs—worshipped by the nation at large, especially by that section called "the people," although he never pandered to it, and disclosed no infinitesimal trace of the agitator or the demagogue; on the contrary, he was foremost in the cause of authority, law, and order.

To gather the full significance of such a popularity it is necessary to realise that it flourished in a transition period when the sovereign was yet unidentified with entirely British interests and sympathies, and the relation of the Throne to the nation was not unattended with a large element of friction and incoherence. It was in an age of flagrant corruption, when the aristocracy, among which Granby was high-placed, strove to subordinate both Throne and people to its own political interests, that the name of "Granby" became a synonym for all that was loyal and respectful to his king, and for all that was noble, just, generous, straightforward, brave, and unselfish as regarded his fellow-subjects.

This popularity, in spite of having been so flippantly touched upon, appears to have been one of the most moving and intensely real influences of George II.'s reign, as well as of the opening years of that of George III.; while on more than one occasion Granby was certainly looked to as holding what journalists call "the situation" in the hollow of his hand; and on these occasions he steadfastly opposed all encroachments upon liberty, whether originating on the part of king, ministers, or people.

To attempt to write a *memoir* of Lord Granby now, when masses of documents are, apparently, lost, and traditions obliterated, is to approach that most thorny of tasks a literary reconstruction. The writer has attempted it solely because no other, let alone some more properly qualified, person has thought it a sufficiently alluring task; and the part enacted by him pretends to nothing beyond that of a humble *chiffonier* wistfully searching for scraps of fact carried upon fitful gusts of disquisition into archival nooks and corners, and there left derelict and forgotten. The little thus acquired has been grafted upon a familiar historical epoch.

A very frequent citation and traversing of Walpole's statements may prove tiresome to those unversed or uninterested in the celebrated *Letters and Memoirs*; but Walpole's portrait of Granby still practically "holds the field." The only course open to any modern inquirer after truth is to keep that portrait plainly in view, to accept those features and characteristics which are supported by corroborative evidence; and emphatically to discard those that are proved to be incompatible with authenticated facts—an incompatibility sometimes made clear by Walpole himself, through his proneness to lapse into direct self-contradiction.

The third Duke of Rutland succeeded his father in 1721, having married in 1717 the Hon. Bridget Sutton, daughter and heiress of Robert Sutton, Lord Lexington. Upon the death of this last, in 1723, his estates in Nottinghamshire, comprising the manors of Averham, Kelham, Rolleston, and Syerston, together with the residences of Averham and Kelham, passed to his daughter, the Duchess of Rutland, having previously been settled by Act of Parliament upon her younger sons, should such be born to her.

Of this Duchess of Rutland nothing important is known. In the course of seventeen years, she presented the third duke with eleven children, of whom eight died too young to render their names worth recording. The rate of infant mortality then ruled very high; smallpox ravaged the higher as well as the lower class, and was the cause of the death of one at least—Lady Leonora Manners—of the above eight little mortals.

★★★★★★★★★★

The second Duke of Rutland and his daughter, Lady Rachel Manners, and son, Lord Thomas Manners, died of smallpox in 1721-3; and in 1757 the third duke announced another outbreak of the disease (at Rutland House), and asked for leave of absence from Court and his duties as Lord Steward.—*Historical Register* and *Newcastle Papers.*

★★★★★★★★★★

The three children who arrived at maturity, and with whom we have to deal, were—

John Manners, Marquess of Granby, born in 1721, who forms the subject of this *memoir*;

Lord Robert Manners, born in 1722;

Lord George Manners, born in 1728, for whom George II., and Frederick, Prince of Wales, stood godfathers.

The Duchess of Rutland died in 1734, aged thirty-five, at Kelham, whereupon the Sutton estates devolved upon Lord Robert Manners; and, by Act of Parliament, he assumed the name of Sutton in addition to his patronymic of Manners. He was henceforward known as Lord Robert Manners Sutton, (often simply known as Lord Robert Sutton), and later took up his residence at Kelham, where he became actively associated with Nottinghamshire.

Of the third Duke of Rutland frequent mention will be made, since he survived his famous son, the Marquess of Granby, by nearly a decade of a long life of eighty-three years. Many testimonies remain on record to the duke's qualities as a devoted father, a loyal subject, a good patriot, and as a liberal landlord and neighbour. Highly educated and cultured, he *understood*, and from love of them, patronized literature as well as art; while in his several homes he maintained his family reputation for a genial hospitality which, practically, knew no limits.

Unambitious, and devoted to the life of a country gentleman at Belvoir Castle, and occasionally at Haddon Hall, (he was the last duke who resided there), he occupied such official positions only, during the reigns of the first, second, and third Georges, as did not involve him in the intrigues of the various family factions, which in his day complicated and frequently shifted the "landmarks" of the two great political parties. Born in 1696 (William III.), he became successively a Lord of the Bedchamber to George I.; Chancellor of the Duchy of Lancaster from George II.'s accession (1727) till 1738; Lord Steward of the Household from 1755 till 1761; and Master of the Horse from 1761, shortly after George III.'s accession, till 1766. He was one of the Lords Justices of Great Britain appointed during George II.'s absences in Hanover; bore the Queen's sceptre at the coronations of George II. and George III.; and was a Knight of the Garter for more than fifty years.

In 1727 he was appointed Lord Lieutenant of the County of Leicester, a position which involved considerable administrative activity, and the highest responsibilities. A lord lieutenant was then, in effect, the viceroy as well as military head of his county, and in that honourable post the duke evidently found his keenest interests. Thoroughly conversant with militia details, and devoting much attention to the army, he was resorted to for advice and information in times of national danger. Such officers in the regular forces as possessed his friendship found in him a ready champion when, as was common in that age of corruption, their due claims to promotion were set aside in favour of some Court *protégé*.

A politician without prejudice, and a courtier free of certain undignified characteristics which have become identified with the term, the duke was in every way fitted to inspire those qualities of intrepidity, simplicity, honesty, and generosity which found such a notable exponent in the person of his son, the Marquess of Granby.

Even spiteful, detractions Horace Walpole throwing stones from behind the safe wall of his private correspondence—many of which missiles were levelled at Lord Granby—alluded with kindly feeling to the Duke of Rutland. He even once described him as "a nobleman of great worth and goodness," (*Memoirs of Reign of George II.*) a high encomium (from Walpole, that is to say) upon one with whom, from difference of social tastes and political sympathy, he possessed no intimacy.

Playfair, in *British Family Antiquity*, thus epitomised the duke's character—

> His Grace in public and in private always displayed the goodness of his heart, his parental affection, and a zealous regard for His King and Country. Esteemed and loved by his relations and friends, revered by his neighbours and tenants, and honoured by the world at large, the Duke of Rutland will ever be remembered as an ornament to the Peerage of England.

Such was the father who, according to Sir William Draper's testimony, ("Junius'" *Letters*), steadfastly impressed upon Lord Granby the necessity of never doing, or suffering, a mean action.

Of Lord Granby's childish and boyish days no details have been sought, for all such—without exception—constitute the most insipid reading. But to stray for one moment into those fields of imagination which are otherwise left untrodden, it may be surmised that the story of William, Lord Russell (the Patriot), and of his wife, Lady Rachel, formed an important factor in Lord Granby's nursery traditions.

The stern tragedy, the romantic devotion, and pathos surrounding the memory of those great-grandparents of Granby can scarcely have failed of impressing one so little remote from their influence as he was. At the time of Lady Rachel's death, he was two years old, so that no very definite personal remembrance of her could have remained to him.

> I hope while I live you will always think of your old Grandmama as a friend that wishes you all the good qualities makes one useful to his country and happy to himself, and then he can't be only wise but a good man too, which is true wisdome.

So wrote Lady Rachel (Rutland MSS., vol. ii.) to one of her grandsons, "Master Manners." She was eighty-seven years old at the time of her death, having been born in 1636, during the reign of Charles I. This fact is interesting, in what is termed the perspective of history, as showing how one long life, by overlapping another of only forty-nine years, formed a connecting link between the period of Charles I. and that of Lord Granby, which extended into the reign of George III.—a space of time involving nine reigns and the Commonwealth.

Besides his father and mother Lord Granby's elder relations consisted of two dowager duchesses, Katherine and Lucy, relicts of the first and second dukes; and the following uncles and aunts, all prominent figures at Court and in society: Lord William Manners, a noted patron of the turf, a mighty fox-hunter, and successful gambler; Lord Sherard Manners; Lords Robert and Charles Manners, both in the Guards; Lady Katherine Pelham; Lady Frances Arundel; Lady Galway; Lady Caroline Harpur; and the Duchess of Montrose, all *née* Manners, and frequenters of the circles which Horace Walpole has immortalised.

★★★★★★★★★★

Lord William was killed by a fall from his horse in 1772. In 1755 he alludes to having started from Stroxton before sunrise and arriving home after dark, and a twenty-mile ride following on "a very long chase."—*Newcastle Papers.*

★★★★★★★★★★

Lady Katherine Pelham was the wife of Henry Pelham, the Prime Minister, whose brother, the celebrated Duke of Newcastle, was thus brought into close relationship with the Rutland family. Lady Katherine was by way of being a politician, and dabbled industriously in the streams which flowed towards office and preferment. (She died, aged eighty, in 1780, at her house in Whitehall.) She herself was many years Ranger of Greenwich Park, and Housekeeper of the King's Palace there, and kept her brother-in-law, the Duke of Newcastle, frequently employed upon what he styled "my Lady Katherine's jobbs." *(Newcastle Papers.)*

Before going to school Lord Granby's education was pursued under different tutors, among them Mr. Malachi Postlethwaite, author of the *Universal Dictionary of Trade and Commerce*, in recommending whom to a place in the Salt Office the Duke of Rutland described as one "whose works published his merit." Lord Granby then proceeded to Eton, where his tutor was Mr. John Ewer, a gentleman who afterwards owed all his promotion to the Belvoir interest, which finally landed him on the episcopal bench.

Of Granby's Eton career nothing is known, except that it was contemporary with that of Henry Seymour Conway and William Draper; but of the Eton of his day something may be gathered from some school accounts of his brother, Lord George Manners, who followed him there, and who was also confided to John Ewer's care.

These accounts show that, excluding such luxuries as "alterative electuaries," "purging draughts," "doses of tincture of rhubarb" at 2*s.* 6*d.* the dose, "pots of bumattem" (*sic*), tips to Mr. Ewer's servants, and occasional bottles of port and mountain, the total yearly expense of Eton College was covered by a sum of £100.

The modern Eton boy may be interested in knowing that his proverbial smartness extends back at least to 1740. Lord George's accounts show that he indulged in a lavish supply of clean linen per week, in addition to sundry white waistcoats. Items of gloves, hair-ribbon, hair-powder, ruffles, shoe-buckles, etc., embody the requisites of the dandy of that day—the hair-powder explaining the *raison d'être* of the "bumattem."

Another set of Eton bills, twenty years later in date, show that a private servant was allowed to be kept, for whose lodging £2 10*s.* per half-year was charged.

At the age of seventeen Lord Granby left Eton, and proceeded to Trinity College, Cambridge, where he was admitted July 3, 1738, his tutor being Mr. Young. His residence at the university is also unmarked by any recorded events, and he quitted it too early to take a degree, and prepared for the extensive Continental tour which then formed an integral part of the education of every important member of the aristocracy, or landed gentry. Such tours were infinitely more fruitful in the lessons of life then than now, when transit has become so uniformly easy, cheap, and expeditious.

★★★★★★★★★★

Edward Gibbon, before starting on his travels, wrote to his father that £1,000 a year was an ordinary allowance for that purpose; and £700 was eventually fixed as the most economical yearly outlay upon which his tour could be made. See his *Letters*.

★★★★★★★★★★

The *Sturm und Drang* commenced with the start from, and ended only with the return home. Roads in England were infested with highwaymen, and the Channel-crossing was effected in distressingly inadequate sailing-boats, whose departure, leave alone their arrival, was dependent upon favourable winds and tides. Lady M. Wortley Montagu describes (*Letters*), how, after being tossed about all night in midchannel, the master of the packet-boat warned her that they were in danger, and eventually transhipped his mail and passengers into "a little fisher-boat," in which the journey was completed.

Crossings between Dover and Calais occupied *ordinarily* from five to seven hours, and passages of twenty-four hours are recorded. Lord Frederick Cavendish related (*Newcastle Papers,* August 30, 1764), how, while accompanying his dying father—the Duke of Devonshire—to Spa, they were, after a prolonged passage, prevented by a low tide and heavy sea from entering Calais harbour. In consequence, they had to take to their small boat and row through the surf some two miles to land, on gaining which they had a mile to walk before reaching Calais. Yet we grumble at the luxury of being sick during a paltry hour and a quarter!

Lord Granby was accompanied by a doctor, and his whilom Eton tutor, John Ewer.

★★★★★★★★★★

Mr. William Hewett, of Stretton Magna, is said by Bigland to have accompanied Lord Granby on the Italian portion of his tour. A small portrait of Mr. Hewett used to hang in the hunting-lodge in Croxton Park.—*Beauties of England and Wales* (Bigland).

★★★★★★★★★★

Granby kept a journal, a portion of which remains, (at Belvoir Castle), entitled, *A Spasso to Broussa, Cuzicum, Troy, Macedonia, Thessalia, and some Islands of the Archipelago. Annis*, 1741-1742.

The journal proclaims in every line that the schoolmaster was, indeed, abroad; in fact, it is a sort of holiday-task replete with quotations from Strabo, Pliny, and appropriate works of reference wherewith Mr. Ewer was equipped for travel, in default of "Murrays" and "Baedekers." Of Granby's future character, the only signs afforded are through references to certain charitable institutions; and he commends very much the founders "of such necessary charities as had for their object the feeding of the hungry." These institutions were connected with the *mausoleums* which Granby visited, concerning which he wrote—

And now that I have seen all these *mausoleums* wherein the

> Turkish *sultans* lie above ground, I can't help observing that every particular *mausoleum* makes a much greater shew than Westminster Abbey, or the Chapel of St. Dennis, where many of the English and French kings are to be seen. Moreover, the provisions made for the poor of all sorts, who may freely call for the necessaries of life at any of these convents, have escaped the Charity of the *Christians*.

Many inscriptions found upon walls and columns were copied into the journal.

At "Troiaci, or Giaurkoe," Granby appears to have got quit of the Rev. John Ewer for a short time.

The marquess wearily wrote:

> It is said, that there are many vaults and cisterns in this village, but I had not time to look after them because I was engaged in a Greek dance with all the women of the village, who pass their Sundays very merrily dancing in a circle after the Greek manner.

As an antidote to this relaxation a comparison is next entered upon respecting the probable extent of the country of Troy according to Homer, Damastes, Charon of Lampsacus, and Seylax!

Although so much of this tour was accomplished by sea, in a large Turkish boat called a *volique*, and much rough weather encountered, it did not make a good sailor of Lord Granby, who complained in later years of invariable sea-sickness when crossing to and from the Continent during the Seven Years' War.

They started from Constantinople on November 3, 1741, and the journal ends thus—

> On the 13th of June (1742) we were to the Northward of Lesbos, or Mytilene, with a high sea, and contrary wind at N.E. Next day we got into a bay opposite to Tenedos, where we came to an anchor and stayed all night. We sailed next morning early, and got through the Hellespont with a fair wind. We were all next day becalmed near Marmora, and on the 17th of June we got to Constantinople with the wind at North East.

Lord Granby's tour occupied a considerable time. The above diary finishes in June, 1742, and His Lordship's portrait is recorded as having been executed by Liotard, at Constantinople, in 1740. The feeling induced by the journal is one of regret that it does not record the unfettered impressions of the writer from the very moment of leaving Belvoir. So healthy a young mind in so strong a body would have produced something infinitely more readable and instructive if left to follow its own impulses, instead of the beaten track laid down for it by good John Ewer's pedantic scholarship.

During Lord Granby's absence upon his travels, his name was put forward in connection with the parliamentary representation of the borough of Grantham. In April, (*Rutland MSS.*, vol. ii.), 1741, the Duke of Rutland was informed that Lord Tyrconnel had declined standing, in consequence of which Lord Granby would probably remain unopposed; and, in June, (Granby was elected May 4, 1741), the duke was congratulated upon his family's success both at Grantham and Newark, which latter borough elected Lord William Manners, the duke's brother.

In politics the duke was a Whig, tolerant and moderate for the most part, though sternly opposed to the Stewarts, and confident that the country's best interests were safeguarded by allegiance to the House of Hanover. But of factions among the Whigs, or of participation in those family cabals which for their own small ends opposed Administrations devoted to the principles of the Revolution of 1688 and the exclusion of the Stewarts, he would hear nothing.

After George I.'s accession, history says that the Tory Members of Parliament scarcely numbered fifty—contemporary Toryism being identified with Jacobitism. The Whig party was numerically omnipotent, and was directed by a *phalanx* of "governing families" of Bentinck, Campbell, Cavendish, Fitzroy, Grenville, Lennox, Manners, Pelham, Russell, and others, who had established the Hanoverian dynasty, and intended to maintain it; but, as the greater contains the less, so the strength of the Whig party embodied its own poor weakness of internecine family jealousy.

An early opportunity for the outbreak of schism was afforded by the first two Georges themselves; firstly, by their tendency to subordinate British interests to those of the Electorate of Hanover; secondly, by their quarrels with their respective heirs.

The misunderstandings between George II., when Prince of Wales, and his father, do not relate to Lord Granby's period; but others arose, directly after George II.'s accession, with his son Frederick, Prince of Wales, and reached their climax in 1737, in which year George II. dismissed the prince from St. James's, and intimated that those who sympathized with him would not be welcome at Court.

★★★★★★★★★★

> Pope, writing from Twickenham to Lady Mary Wortley Montagu, said: "Our gallantry and gaiety have been great sufferers by the rupture of the two Courts, here: scarce any ball, assembly, basset-table, or any place where two or three are gathered together."

★★★★★★★★★★

The Prince of Wales soon after established himself at Leicester House, which Thomas Pennant called "the pouting place of princes," since George II. had bought it when in a similar situation of disgrace and chronic opposition. (Frederick, Prince of Wales, also purchased Carlton House, which he used for purposes of ceremony.)

Not being in sympathy with Court squabbles, factions, or intrigues, the Duke of Rutland resigned his office of Chancellor of the Duchy of Lancaster in 1738, and for seventeen years devoted himself exclusively to his county duties at Belvoir Castle. Horace Walpole incidentally referred to him as politically "attached to the prince," who certainly fostered at Leicester House many views with which the duke sympathized—*viz.* that English interests should be considered before those of Hanover; that "party" should be as far as possible sunk; and the government entrusted to the best men obtainable from all quarters which espoused the cause of the Hanoverian dynasty at large.

These articles of political faith gained William Pitt to the "Leicester House" Court; and between Pitt and the Rutland family a long political and personal sympathy endured, which was only once in any danger of rupture.

Such, briefly, was the position to which Lord Granby returned from his foreign travels, welcomed by all on account of his charm of manner, good looks, and open-heartedness, which invested him with a natural faculty of ingratiation, whether at St. James's, Leicester House, or at the various lesser rallying-points of political hair-splitters.

There was one potent element which from time to time had rallied, and thus saved, the Whig party from its own dissensions. The Jacobite party was not yet annihilated, and had made a threatening appearance several times during the third Duke of Rutland's life. In 1701 Louis XIV. had formally acknowledged the claims of James Edward, the Old Pretender, to the English throne; and in 1715 the third duke, at nineteen years of age, was well able to realise the Jacobite Rebellion of that year, the camp formed in Hyde Park, and how his father, the second duke, as Lord Lieutenant of the Comity of Leicester, was called upon (*Rutland MSS.*, vol. ii.), to seize the persons and arms of all Papists, Non-jurors, and others suspected of being disaffected to His Majesty George I.

****

"The tents are carried thither this morning; new regiments, with new cloaths and furniture. . . . You may soon have your wish to enjoy the gallant sight of armies, encampments, standards waving over your brother's cornfields, and the pretty windings of the Thames stained with the blood of men."—Pope to Mrs. Theresa Blount, 1715.

****

Jacobite activity was again rife in 1721, the year of the Marquess of Granby's birth, promoted by two causes—the universal social ruin and disorganisation arising out of the collapse of the South Sea Bubble, and the birth of Charles Edward, known later as the Young Pretender.

****

In reference to Alexander Pope's speculations, Dr. Johnson alluded to this period as one "when the contagion of avarice tainted every mind, and even poets panted after wealth." See *Lives of the Poets,* under Pope.

****

Behind all these Jacobite plots and threats skulked France, ready to second any promising scheme against England; or, the scheme being successful, to invade her. On the Continent, another opportunity had arisen for France to push her interests and those of the Bourbon House by aiding the Elector of Bavaria in his claim to the Austrian Succession, which had been nominally secured to Maria Theresa by the Pragmatic Sanction; an arrangement which Prince Eugene had pithily said would have been far better guaranteed by 100,000 men than 100,000 treaties.

France adopted her established plan of frightening George II. by menacing Hanover; and in order to obtain the neutrality of the Electorate, George withdrew his active support of Maria Theresa. Sir Robert Walpole's similar, and traditionally consistent, desire for peace was largely based upon the patent certainty that a Continental war meant for England a revival of Jacobite troubles.

However, England sympathized with Maria Theresa, and clamoured for war, upon which Sir Robert Walpole retired, as Earl of Orford, and was succeeded, after a brief interval of no special incidental interest, by Mr. Henry Pelham, who had married Lady Katherine Manners, Lord Granby's aunt.

Thus began the reign of the "Pelhamites," whom for reasons—mainly of jealousy begotten of his father's fall—Horace Walpole so heartily hated, and so unscrupulously reviled. The new Ministers voted money and men for the creation of a diversion in favour of Maria Theresa in the Netherlands, under Lord Stair. He was joined later by George II. in person, and the Duke of Cumberland; and the Battle of Dettingen, remarkable as the last at which a British king was present, was fought and won.

Events in other parts of the Continent secured the Austrian Succession to Maria Theresa and her husband; but George II., as a German potentate, wished to assert himself among the other Electors, and England was itching for direct war with France. The Jacobite "bogey" was once again utilised, and France collected a fleet and an army, under Marshal Saxe, for the invasion of England in support of the Stewarts. The invasion was abandoned, chiefly owing to stress of weather, and Marshal Saxe, who said "the wind was decidedly not Jacobite," repaired to the army in Flanders, where the English forces and their Hanoverian, Austrian, and Dutch allies were commanded by the Duke of Cumberland, with General Sir John Ligonier, and the Prince of Waldeck.

The Battle of Fontenoy ensued, in which the French were victorious, at a cost which left them small ultimate advantage. Meanwhile, Prince Charles Edward, the Young Pretender, remained in France; and though active French co-operation with him had for the moment ceased, he was determined to turn to account the scare which the threatened invasion had aroused in England, as well as the reverse which she had sustained at Fontenoy, and at which battle he was rumoured to have been present. Thus began the Rebellion of the Forty-Five, to repress which energies were awakened in England which met with prompt and substantial sympathy from the Duke of Rutland, the Marquess of Granby, and other members of their family.

MARQUESS OF GRANBY

CHAPTER 2

1745-1746: The Jacobite Rebellion & Culloden

History repeats itself, and the third Duke of Rutland, Lord-Lieutenant of the County of Leicester, received notice, September 5, 1745, from the Lords of the Council, of the landing in Scotland of Prince Charles Edward, in the same terms as were addressed to the second Duke in 1715.

The time was propitious for this, the last of the Jacobite attempts upon the throne of Great Britain. Owing to the gradual establishment of a standing army, the older and more representative force of the Militia had sunk into desuetude, and the people generally had become unaccustomed to the use of arms, or the idea of defending themselves, since a permanent force was maintained for that purpose at their expense.

George II. returned from Hanover on hearing of the rebellion, and landed at Margate. A considerable portion of the army was engaged in the operations in Flanders against France, so that the news that Prince Charles had landed, in spite of the reward of £30,000, (*London Gazette*, August 6, 1745), offered for his person, spread considerable excitement throughout England.

★★★★★★★★★★

Mr. H. Pelham wrote to R. Trevor (September 20, 1745): "We have scarce any regular troops in the country, and, between you and I, I don't find that zeal to venture purses and lives that I formerly remember."—MSS. of Earl of Buckinghamshire (*Hist. MSS. Com.*, Rep. XIV. App. 9).

★★★★★★★★★★

The *London Gazette* held out inducements to recruits, and a bounty of £6 per man was offered to all who should enlist in the four battalions of Guards, the minimum height for which was fixed at 5 ft. 7 in. without shoes.

The Lords Justices had taken measures pending the king's return, and Sir John Cope, with a small force, was despatched to Inverness. A movement, by which he thought to lure the Pretender's army from a strong position, laid open the road to Edinburgh towards which Prince Charles at once hurried. On his march he encountered some cavalry which Cope had left behind him, and a skirmish known as the "Canter of Colt Brigg" was fought, and won by the Highlanders, before whom two dragoon regiments fled, without halting, to Dunbar.

None of the clans would rise for the government; the Dukes of Argyll and Athol came post-haste to town, having failed of raising a man for King George, and Horace Walpole "looked upon Scotland as gone." (*Letters*, September 6, 1745.)

Of considerable Scottish sympathy with Prince Charles there was no doubt, though the extent of English sympathy was so far unascertained. Prince Charles established himself at Holyrood House, and, after refusing to set a price upon the king's head as an offset to that placed upon his own, he reluctantly offered the small sum of £30, saying, he felt sure no follower of his could be capable of winning it.

Troops were recalled from Flanders, but before they could arrive, three battalions of Dutch Auxiliaries landed at Gravesend, and enthusiasm "to venture purses and lives" having at last kindled, the Dukes of Bedford, Montagu, and Devonshire obtained leave to raise regiments for the king. These volunteer regiments were to be enrolled for a period of 122 days. (Coxe's *Memoirs.*) Yorkshire was especially active, and the Archbishop of York took a leading part in the defence of that county, where 4,000 men were raised, and a body of fox-hunters, under General Oglethorpe, was converted into a regiment of hussars. At a meeting held at York, the archbishop made a most stirring speech, concluding with the words:—

> May the Great God of Battles stretch out His all-powerful hand to defend us; inspire a union of hearts and hands among all ranks of people; a clear wisdom into the counsels of His Majesty; and a steady courage and resolution into the hearts of his generals. (*London Gazette,* September 26, 1745.)

The meeting drew up an Address to the king, signed by all the leading men of the county, denouncing "the Popish Pretender," an example quickly followed by the corporate bodies of London and the provinces. The London Addresses contain a remarkably large proportion of foreign names; in one from Spitalfields, they are in a decided majority, the district having been colonised by the French Huguenot silk-weavers some sixty years previously.

Among the rest were (*London Gazette*)—

An address from:
the county of Leicester, presented by the Duke of Rutland.
the borough of Newark " " " Lord William Manners.
the borough of Grantham " " " the Marquess of Granby.
the county of Nottingham " " "the Duke of Newcastle.

The last includes the names of Lord Robert Manners Sutton and Thomas Thoroton, a name of frequent occurrence later.

Zeal continued to spread, and the further raising of regiments was undertaken by the Dukes of Rutland and Kingston, Lords Herbert, Halifax, Falmouth, Cholmondeley, Berkeley, Derby, etc.

★★★★★★★★★★

The Duke of Kingston was a fine, handsome man. of "sketchy" education and weak character, who fell a victim to the charms of Elizabeth Chudleigh, otherwise Mrs. Hervey, or the Countess of Bristol.

★★★★★★★★★★

The Duke of Rutland's was a foot regiment, of which the colonelcy was bestowed upon the Marquess of Granby (October 4, 1745), who thus, at the age of twenty-four, first became associated with the service of which, in after years, he was the idol as well as the head. No exasperating examinations preceded his commission; all that was necessary was his re-election for the borough of Grantham, which took place, unopposed, October 31, 1745. In September he had been appointed a deputy-lieutenant for the county of Derby. Possessed of nothing yet, save an already notorious reputation for courage, and power of attracting devotion, to fit him for the command of a regiment in the held, the marquess's mentor must be sought in the person of his lieut.-colonel, a soldier of experience, named Stanwix, who afterwards distinguished himself in Canada under Wolfe. (Afterwards Colonel of the 8th Foot, and Governor of Carlisle. Drowned in 1766 while crossing the Irish Channel.—*Rutland MSS.*, November 12, 1766.)

The Duke of Rutland was an honorary captain in this regiment of his own raising, and Lord George Manners served in it; whilst Lord Robert Manners Sutton obtained a troop in his relative's, the Duke of Kingston's, Light Horse which rendered most signal service throughout the rebellion, and practically originated the reinstatement of light dragoon regiments in the British Army. (Chiverton Hartopp, afterwards Lieut.-Governor of Plymouth, was a captain in this regiment, and Richard Sutton clerk-chaplain.)

Besides the duke's three sons—aged respectively twenty-four, twenty-three, and twenty-two—their uncle. Lord Robert Manners, served against the Pretender.

In spite of this respectable quota supplied by one family, the duke, then aged fifty, appears to have had misgivings whether his own presence in the field was not expected, for a friend wrote to him:—

"As you have elsewhere an avocation, (Lord Lieut. of Leicestershire), of infinitely more consequence to the public, surely your attendance in quarters could never have been expected, nót mentioning the subscription you have already made to His Majesty's service of three of the most gallant youths in the whole Kingdom."

Poor Sir John Cope, sent, as Walpole wrote, with "no experience and no force, to fight for a Crown," was completely defeated at Preston Pans, September 21, 1745, an event which hastened the completion of the new regiments.

★★★★★★★★★★

Mr. J. Erskine, of Preston Pans, writing, September 30, 1745, to the Rev. Charles Wesley, said: "The dragoons behaved abominably. Col. Gardiner, finding he could not stop the flight of his regt. of dragoons, put himself at the head of the foot forces, and was so mortally wounded that he dyed."—MSS. of J. Elliot Hodgkin (*Hist. MSS.* Com., Rep. XV. App. 2).

★★★★★★★★★★

On November 7, 1745, (*Marching Order Books*, Record Office, ten companies of the Marquess of Granby's regiment were ordered into quarters at Leicester, Loughborough, and Harborough. From thence they were marched (November 12, 1745) to Nottingham, and (November 19, 1745) to Warwick, and the camp which had been formed near Lichfield.

To this camp the Duke of Cumberland and Sir John Ligonier, just arrived from Flanders, were hurrying with some regular troops seasoned at Dettingen and Fontenoy, besides three battalions of Foot Guards, and some of the new regiments.

A large camp of Train-bands and Guards was formed at Finchley, of which George II. declared he would take command. "The March of the Guards to Finchley," painted by Hogarth, was considered by the king such a gross and undeserved libel, that he refused to accept the dedication of the print of that picture, which was thereupon transferred to the King of Prussia. (*History of the 1st or Grenadier Guards.*)

Arrived at Lichfield, the Duke of Cumberland was joined by Granby's, Gower's, Halifax's, Cholmondeley's, and Montagu's Infantry, together with Montagu's and Kingston's Horse.

The rebels were now in England. Outflanking General Wade, they entered *via* Carlisle, and pushed on towards Lancashire, demanding money, food, and especially hoots, of the districts traversed. Wade pursued them south with 12,000 men, and Cumberland awaited them at Stow; but the Pretender's small force of 5,000 outflanked the duke, and actually penetrated to Derby, which was requisitioned for the sum of £19,000. (A gentleman writing from Derby assured a friend that "the Highlanders said grace, with great seeming devotion, both before and after meals, just like any Christian."—*Memoirs of Sir Robert Murray Keith.*)

Nothing but the Finchley camp now remained between Prince Charles and London, but, against his own convictions, he took pause. Lord George Murray (commander of the rebels after they entered England), earnestly counselled retreat, for Cumberland and Wade were in hot pursuit in rear, and the Finchley camp lay before. Any of these three was numerically superior to the Pretender's whole army, and no encouragement had reached him of the least sympathy in England. On the other hand, a dash through, or past, the Finchley camp, would have placed London at Prince Charles's mercy, while such a stroke might have aroused the English Jacobites to action, and brought aid, presently, from France. London was panic-stricken on the "Black Friday" which brought the ominous news from Derby.

★★★★★★★★★★

Horatio Walpole (uncle of Horace Walpole) wrote: "The Rebels after having got as far as Derby, with a design and expectation of coming near this great city in concert, as I imagine, with the French, who were to have succoured them by an invasion from Dunkirk." December 18, 1745.—*Hist. MSS. Com.*, Rep. XIV. App. pt. 9.

★★★★★★★★★★

To oppose any Jacobite rising in London, alarm posts were advertised, (London Gazette), at which the six regiments of City Militia were to assemble upon the signal of seven cannon shots, fired alternately from the Tower and St. James's Park.

Divided counsels engendered hesitancy among the Pretender's

followers, which grew into absolute panic, and a precipitate retreat was commenced, the success of which afforded an early proof of the sorry strategic qualities of the Duke of Cumberland, and of the excellent use made by the Highlanders of the boots collected during their southward march.

Unable to outmanoeuvre and open up the small fugitive army, the duke, for all his numerical superiority, merely acted the part of "the puss'd pursuer," and such skirmishes as occurred ended chiefly in favour, of the rebels.

On December 1745, the "Georgia Rangers" and a detachment of the Duke of Kingston's Horse, under the command of Lieut.-Colonel Mordaunt, and Captains Lord Robert Manners Sutton and Lord Byron, arrived at Preston, and the King's Regiment of Dragoons suffered severely in a skirmish at Clifton, near Penrith, the rebels shouting, "No quarter! Murder them!" as they despatched the wounded English officers lying on the ground.

After dislodging a party of Highlanders from Lowther Hall, which the Pretender had taken on his march south, the Duke of Cumberland got on terms with his foe at Penrith, and was worsted in a skirmish; but, continuing the pursuit, retook Carlisle. By incredible marches the rebels held on their way until Glasgow was reached, where recruits, including some French officers and men, increased their numbers to about nine thousand; and Prince Charles commenced the siege of Stirling Castle, garrisoned by a force under General Blakeney. ("One would really think these Highlanders had wings to their feet, like so many Mercurys."—*Letters* of first Earl of Malmesbury, December 19, 1746.)

Encouraged by the partial success of the Jacobite rising, France was again bent upon invading England. In consequence, the Duke of Cumberland was summoned south to meet this fresh emergency. Before leaving the north, he superseded old Marshal Wade by General Hawley, and, among other dispositions of troops, Lord Granby's regiment was ordered to Newcastle and Gateshead. (*Marching Order Books*, Record Office). With misplaced contempt of his adversary, General Hawley advanced carelessly to the relief of Stirling Castle, amusing himself en route. He took up a weak, undefended position at Falkirk, which Prince Charles outflanked and attacked, inflicting a crushing defeat (January 17, 1746) upon Hawley, many of whose soldiers bolted outright, in the manner so inexplicably prevalent during the Rebellion.

So important a reverse brought the Duke of Cumberland back to the north. His army, according to the Chevalier de Johnstone, (*Memoirs of the Rebellion*), now consisted of the infantry regiments of Ligonier, Richmond, Sinclair, Albemarle, Howard, Skelton, Bland, Sempill, Bligh, Douglas, Leslie, Bernard, Roper, Sowle, Johnson, Gower, Montagu, Halifax, Granby, Cholmondeley, and the cavalry of Montagu and Kingston, with a thousand additional Horse under General Oglethorpe.

Abandoning Stirling, Prince Charles marched to Inverness, which town he took; and the Duke of Cumberland proceeded north by the east coast, in order to obtain his supplies by sea. The Marquess of Granby, finding his own regiment was to remain in garrison at, and about, Newcastle, volunteered to accompany the duke, to whose staff he was forthwith attached.

Lord George Manners remained with Colonel Stanwix at Newcastle, of which town he soon wrote they were all tired, "as the inhabitants were not over civil."

Immediately after leaving London, the Duke of Cumberland wrote to the Duke of Rutland—

> I hope the next news you will have in town from these parts will bring you the account of success against the disturbers of our peace and tranquillity; at least I believe we shall do our utmost. (*Rutland MSS.*)

During the march towards Inverness, some operations took place in the district of Strathbogie, where Colonel Roy Stuart was with a body of Highlanders. Roy Stuart tried to lure Lord Granby, when on outpost duty, into an ambush, an attempt in which Granby succeeded in entirely outwitting him, and the Duke of Cumberland sent Colonel Conway with orders to General Bland, commanding the vanguard, to advance and surprise Roy Stuart's camp. (Stuart, formerly in the Scot's Greys. He entered the French service, and afterwards that of Prince Charles Edward. See Lord Tweedale's letter, September 14, 1745, Jesse's *Pretenders.*)

General Bland marched, Lord Granby being among the officers who accompanied him; but Roy Stuart, getting wind of his danger, retreated precipitately to Keith, his men leaving a good hot dinner ready in their quarters, which Bland's troops later discussed. General Bland pursued until nightfall when, the weather turning very wet and hazy, he deemed it prudent to halt until daylight. The Marquess of Granby, Colonel Conway, Captain Halden, and others, with Kingston's Horse, a few Heavy Dragoons, and Campbell's Regiment continued, however, to drive the rebels for some two miles further towards the Spey, for which service they were mentioned in the *Gazette*.

The Duke of Cumberland occupied Nairn, April 14, 1746, and on the ensuing night Prince Charles installed himself at Culloden House, the residence of President Duncan Forbes. (President of the Court of Session at Edinburgh. He was an ardent supporter of the reigning Family, and his example prevented large numbers from joining Prince Charles.)

★★★★★★★★★★

After Prince Charlie's flight the Duke of Cumberland occupied Culloden House. The prince left his walking-stick there, and the duke his box of dominoes. These relics were dispersed, among many others, at a sale at Culloden House in July, 1897. The walking-stick is now (1899), in the possession of H.M. the Queen, and the domino-box in that of the Mackintosh of Mackintosh. The original Culloden House was destroyed and rebuilt, about 1780, in the Georgian style.

★★★★★★★★★★

A night surprise which the prince had intended upon Cumberland's position was abandoned, and the prince fell back upon Culloden Moor. The next day (April 16) the Battle of Culloden was fought, the Young Pretender was disastrously defeated and put to flight. The Rebellion of the Forty-Five was over, and Walpole wrote (to Sir H. Mann, April 25, 1746), that London was blazing around him with fireworks and illuminations. The Duke of Kingston's Horse, Lord Robert Sutton's Regiment, greatly distinguished itself, and three troopers in it, Nottingham butchers by trade, were credited with killing fourteen of the enemy. (*Annals of Newark-on-Trent.*)

Though defeated and dispersed, the hills were full of the fugitive Highlanders, invulnerable—so the Scottish leaders had boasted—once they gained the fastnesses which were inaccessible to any but their own people. Establishing himself at Fort Augustus, the Duke of Cumberland commenced harrying the surrounding country, employing especially Kingston's Horse, and severities occurred which added to Cumberland's name the epithet of "Butcher," from which it has never since got free. Whether deserved or not, we have no need here to inquire. Suffice it to say that much has been urged in his defence, as well in his accusation; and that the fact holds that he put a final stop to the Jacobite risings whose chiefest cause of danger to England was that they brought France sniffing like a jackal for an opportune moment of attack upon her when engaged with other foes.

Two months after the victory of Culloden, Lord Granby, who, though brave to heroism, was the personification of clemency and compassion, thus wrote to his father from Fort Augustus, where he remained with the Duke of Cumberland—

> We have been at this place about a month, and I believe we shall stay here some time longer. The duke (Cumberland), since he has been here, has sent out several detachments to drive in all the cattle belonging to the rebells, and to destroy and burn all their country, which they have performed with great success, having drove in several head of cattle, and burnt everything they came near, without the least opposition. The duke sent a detachment of an hundred of Kingston's horse, 50 on horseback and 50 on foot, into Glenmorrison's country to burn and drive in cattle, which they executed with great expedition, returning in a couple of days with 1,000 head of cattle, after having burnt every house they could find.
>
> The duke has now shown the Gentlemen of Scotland, who gave out that the Highlands were inaccessible to any but their own people, that not only the infantry can follow rebel Highlanders into their mountains, but that horse, upon an occasion commanded by him, find nothing impracticable. Captain Chadwicke, who commanded, says he was surprised to see the boldness of the men, who galloped up and down mountains that he thought was impossible to have walked down. I hear some of our new raised regiments are continued; if mine should be continued, I'll get to Newcastle as soon as possible, for Stanwix writes me word that our men begin to be uneasy and want their discharge. (*Rutland MSS.*, vol. ii.)

The uneasiness existing among some of the men of Lord Granby's Regiment, due to inaction and unhealthy quarters, increased to actual mutiny, which Lord George Manners hoped would tend to bring the rest to their senses. He reported to his father his capture of thirty-nine deserters at Boroughbridge, adding that "it was too hard to keep them among a parcel of rebells, where there was a very bad distemper." Later he wrote that Colonel Stanwix had ordered the prisoners to be confined in York jail, and that he himself was starting for Belvoir to consult the Duke of Rutland on the matter. Mr. Henry Fox, Secretary at War, informed Colonel Stanwix that, in answer to a petition from "his mutinous prisoners in York jayle," the king had consented to pardon them under such circumstances as Lord Granby, the Duke of Rutland, or the commanding officer should think fit.

From Fort Augustus, Lord Granby wrote further to his father—

> I desired Col. Stanwix to acquaint Your Grace with His R.H.'s orders about a general court martial, but I suppose as we shall be broke immediately it will not be put into execution. I see by the newspapers that the king allows 6 days' pay to each soldier to defray his expenses home, and the same paper mentions that Lord Berkeley has given his men 4 days' pay per man over and above the king's allowance. I hope Your Grace will pardon the liberty I am going to take in desiring a gratuity of half a guinea a man may be given to our soldiers when they are dismissed, as it will be an encouragement to them to enlist again as soldiers, if any unforeseen accident should require any more regiments so to be raised, which I think not impossible, for, untill a peace is concluded, France will no doubt try to keep up the Rebellion in the Highlands, which will be no difficult matter, if he will venture a little more money and men, for the spirit of rebellion still prevails among the greatest part of the clans, for numbers still remain in arms lurking among the hills, and those that have submitted, have brought in nothing but old rusty firelocks and pistols, and I don't doubt every man of them, upon the landing of a few men and a little money—if the Pretender was to set up his Standard again—would join him.

This letter, together with that previously quoted, affords strong proof that, though the victory at Culloden had scattered the Highlanders, the final quelling of them was effected by Cumberland's subsequent operations—"butcher" or no; and recent literature has shed an unbecoming light upon that erstwhile romantic and chivalrous character, the Scottish Jacobite.

Lord George Manners arrived at Durham, on his journey south, in time for the races. At the Assembly there he danced minuets and country-dances, and invited Colonel Stanwix to accompany him to Belvoir. He had just met, he wrote to his father, "four of his grenadiers (each infantry regiment comprised a certain number of grenadiers), mounted on horseback, with their bayonets fixed, escorting Secretary Murray (Sir John Murray, Secretary to Prince Charles Edward), to the South. They seemed in high spirits; he very dejected and talks little." No wonder! They were sure of reward; whilst their important prisoner was contemplating death on the scaffold, or the alternative which he adopted, of turning King's evidence.

Of Lord Granby's regiment two more entries occur in the *Marching Books:* one when it was ordered to furnish a guard to receive from "the jaylor of Newcastle" one John Dawson, a deserter from Major-General Wolfe's Regiment of Foot. (The 8th Regiment.) This prisoner was to be delivered to the next regiment of Horse or Foot on the road to London; and thus, be passed on till he was handed over to the keeper of the Savoy prison. The second entry records the march of the regiment south, resting every fourth day, to Leicester. It was soon afterwards disbanded; the marquess receiving a letter of thanks for his services and those of all ranks of his regiment, coupled with the hope that many of the rank and file would re-enlist in the army.

"Kingston's Horse" was disbanded at Nottingham, September 15, 1746, and the Duke of Kingston received a similar letter to the above. Nearly the whole of his men re-enlisted in a new light cavalry regiment, sanctioned by the king, called the "Duke of Cumberland's Dragoons." The Duke of Cumberland was appointed Colonel, and Lord Robert Manners Sutton Lieut.-Colonel, with thirteen of the former officers of "Kingston's" under him. This new dragoon regiment soon distinguished itself brilliantly in Flanders under Lord Robert's command.

With the summons issued to the Duke of Rutland, by Lord Chancellor Hardwicke, to attend the House of Peers for the trials of Lords Cromarty, Kilmarnock, and Balmerino the scene of the Rebellion closed, so far as the Belvoir family was concerned. The first of those peers was acquitted, and the two last may be dismissed in the brief language of the *Gazette*:—

> Aug. 19th, Whitehall. Yesterday, William, late Earl of Kilmarnock, and authur, late Lord Balmerino, condemned for High Treason, were beheaded on Tower Hill.

****

Lord Lovat was also beheaded, mainly through the evidence of Secretary Murray, whom some of Granby's men brought south as a prisoner. An interesting epitome of Lovat's career occurs in Burton's *Reign of Queen Anne*.

****

The circumstances of the private raising of regiments were not unattended by adverse comment and criticism. Horace Walpole, who had quaked in Arlington Street when the rebels were at Derby and threatening London, denounced the movement, after the danger was past, with his usual emphasis of style and disregard of accuracy. He accused the noblemen, who raised the regiments, of the sheerest jobbery and self-interest, stating "that not 6 of the regiments were ever raised, nor 4 of them employed." This astounding assertion is refuted by records of the Rebellion.

In a Committee Report issued early in 1746 a return was made of the number of effectives in each of the thirteen new regiments of foot, and two of horse. The full strength of the former was fixed at 780, the same as in the battalions of the regular army. Of the thirteen, three were over 100 short of their full strength, (these deficiencies were about on a level with those of the regular army), and the rest showed various smaller deficiencies, *excepting* the Marquess of Granby's Regiment. This, owing to the popularity he thus early won, attained to the total strength of 780 effectives, while none, even, of the regular infantry battalions reached that number.

A motion was proposed in the Commons, by Sir W. Yonge, to the effect that the fifteen new regiments should be placed upon the regular establishment for so long as they might be required. The raisers, he said, (Almon's *Debates*), "desired nothing for the expense of recruiting, mounting, or clothing. All they desired was that the regiments, when raised, might be paid by the public."

And why these regiments, which were raised with much trouble and at great cost, should have remained a burden upon those whose example and influence produced so fine a body of men at a critical juncture, and for a national cause, it is impossible to understand. The opposition to them was principally based upon the idea that they might give a dangerous influence to the aristocracy who raised and commanded them; an idea which was vehemently deprecated by Mr. Henry Pelham and Mr. Pitt.

The bounty alone, of 10*s.* 6*d.* per man, asked for by Lord Granby on the disbandment of his regiment, amounted to some £400, in addition to the original heavy outlay for recruiting, clothing, and feeding these 780 soldiers.

★★★★★★★★★★

The arms and tents for all these regiments were issued from the Ordnance Department. On October 12, 1745, a first issue was made to the Marquess of Granby's Regiment of 390 carbines, new pattern; 402 pairs of pistols, carbine bores; 202 broadswords; 12 drums; 390 cartridge-boxes and belts. On November 9, following, 165 tents were issued.—*Military Entry Book* (Record Office).

****

Of the colonels and other officers of these regiments Walpole also fell foul, saying they would interfere with "the brave old part of the army who had served all the war," (i.e. in Flanders). A more genial and intelligent estimate of the former is afforded by a letter among the correspondence of the first Earl of Malmesbury, which says, (November 12, 1745)—

> The Duke of Kingston, Lords Gower, Granby, Halifax, and other lords will on this occasion march at the head of their respective regiments; and though you cannot imagine that any of these lords are much skilled in military matters, and consequently no great feats can be expected of them in that way, yet their personally appearing shows a true attachment to the cause they are engaged in, and will certainly emulate the soldiers they command.

A somewhat romantic story remains to be repeated in connection with Lord Robert Manners Sutton. Four years after the Rebellion, Horace Walpole visited Arundel Castle and, in describing it to George Montagu mentioned a gloomy gate-way and some dungeons in which he (Walpole) surmised was still kept an old woman who, during the "Forty-Five," offered to disclose to Lord Robert the spot where some arms were hidden at Worksop, in Nottinghamshire.

> The Duchess of Norfolk (Worksop Manor then belonged to the Duke of Norfolk), complimented Lord Robert into dining before his search, and in the meantime the woman was spirited away—and *adieu* to the arms!

The anecdote does not explain itself so fully as could be wished. Various plots were known, or suspected, to be on foot involving concealed depots of arms, and advertisements were printed in the *London Gazette,* notably with reference to Norwich, (October 19, 1745), and that neighbourhood, in which free pardons were offered to any informers. The Norfolk and Rutland families were connected both by remote and subsequent marriages. The former partly resided in Nottinghamshire, but their implied sympathy with the Rebellion does not tally with a contemporaneous announcement that they had arrived from that residence in town, and had been graciously received by the king at St. James's. The upshot of the matter was, however, clear that

Walpole believed the old woman to be still, in 1749, detained in custody at Arundel, as the surest way of impressing her with the golden attributes of silence.

The "Forty-Five" called into existence various effusions, poetical and otherwise, of which was the *The Heroes* by Sir Charles H. Williams. Its author was a friend of Horace Walpole, and an admirer of his father. Lord Orford. Its allusion to Lord Granby's hair, and his likeness to Charles XII. of Sweden, arose from the fact that the former was completely bald at the age of twenty-four. Voltaire thus describes Charles XII.:—

> He was possessed of a superior and noble figure, a fine brow, large blue eyes, filled with softness, and a well-formed nose, but the lower part of his face was not agreeable . . . he had hardly any beard or hair.

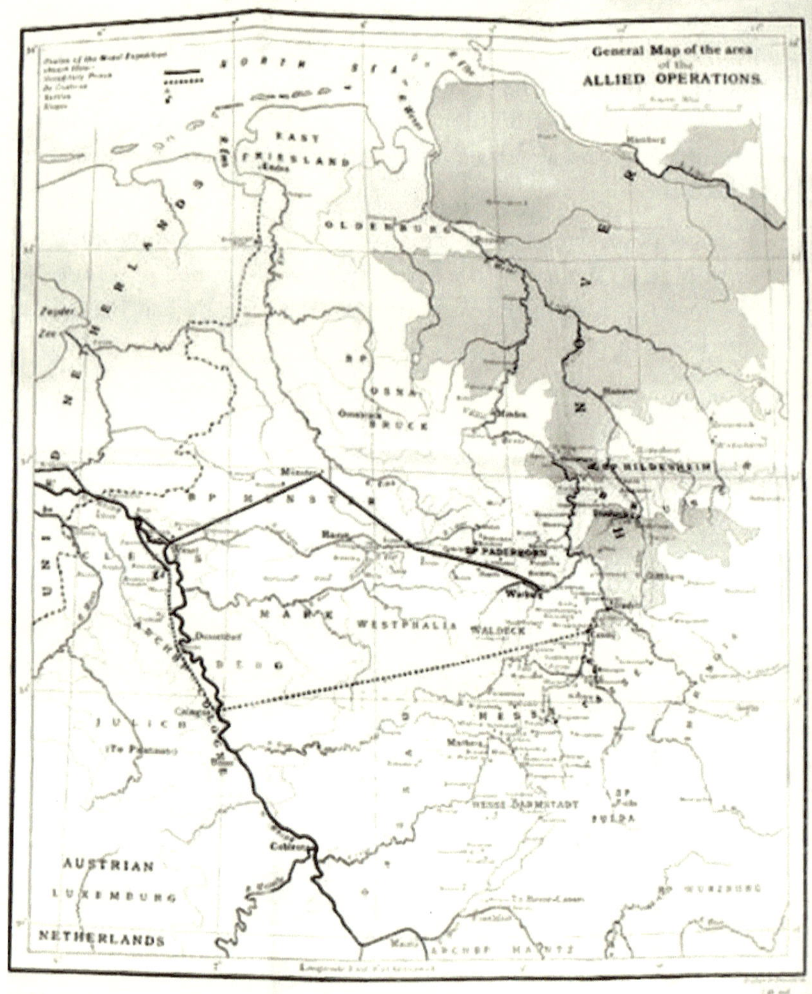

In the text, pp. 74, 135, 163, Westphalia is used as a geographical term for the whole of the country between the Netherlands and Rhine as far south as the Moselle on the east, and the Weser on the west.

In the same sense, at p. 75, Lower Saxony is used to designate the country between the Weser and the Elbe.

The names are survivals of the older appellation of the circles of Westphalia and Lower Saxony, and must not be confused with the small Duchy of Westphalia, belonging to the Elector of Cologne, marked on the map as the grand Duchy of Saxony, of which Dresden was the capital

William Augustus, Duke of Cumberland at Lauffeldt

Chapter 3

1746-1747: Flanders, Lauffeldt & Leisure

Having crushed the Jacobite Rebellion, England was able to resume her operations in Flanders against France, who had meanwhile proved too strong for the Austrians. After the victory of Culloden, the soldiers greeted the Duke of Cumberland with the cry, "Now, Billy, for Flanders!" and he sailed, February 1, 1747, for Holland, and assumed command, together with the Prince of Orange, of an English army strengthened with foreign Allies. Sir John Ligonier also returned; and the duke was accompanied, among others, by the Marquess of Granby, Lord Robert Manners Sutton, and Lord George Manners.

No regular sequence of Army Lists exists prior to 1754, and available documents do not show clearly in what capacity Lord Granby and Lord George made the campaign of 1747. (Their names do not occur in the *Ledger of Commissioners* and *Military Entry Books* for 1747-8). Lord Robert commanded the Duke of Cumberland's Dragoons, but his brothers were apparently acting as volunteers on the duke's Staff. Lord George informed the Duke of Rutland that he, Granby, and Colonel Barrington were in camp six miles from Antwerp, quartered about a mile from the Duke of Cumberland, in a pretty house with a fish-pond and gardens—just such a place as he, Lord George, "could wish for about 4 or 5 miles from Belvoir."

Lord Granby furnished considerable details of camps and military dispositions. The French position he described as most difficult to ascertain, from their constant marches and counter-marches. They were threatening to attack the Duke of Cumberland's camp, which was so strong Lord Granby feared they would never be such fools as to make any real attempt upon. Bob was well, and with Hawley's detachment; George desired his duty; and the Duke of Rutland was to tell Lord William Manners, (brother of the third duke), that Granby would write to him touching their "next winter campaign at fox-hunting."

As for Lord Robert Sutton, he pronounced himself forbidden to stir out of Westerloo camp, where he was with 15,000 infantry and 4,000 cavalry under Generals Somerfeldt and Hawley. He therefore knew nothing of general affairs, but understood his two brothers were well.

Reverses were sustained by the Allies at Hulst and Roucoux; and a series of operations took place in the neighbourhood of Maestricht, culminating in the Battle of Lauffeldt, or Val (July 2, 1747), an affair richer in casualties than in decisive results on either side. The French gained the advantage, but the Duke of Cumberland took four standards and four colours, and avoided a total defeat through the promptitude of Sir John Ligonier, who led a magnificent cavalry charge which enabled Cumberland successfully to retire his troops.

Sir John Ligonier, then hard upon seventy years of age, had his horse shot under him, and was taken prisoner by a French *carabinier*, to whom he instantly offered his ring and purse. The *carabinier* gallantly declined the booty, and said that all he required was Sir John's sword. Louis XV. later received the anglicised Frenchman, John Ligonier, with the greatest distinction, and, on hearing the above story from him, rewarded and promoted the *carabinier*.

Besides Sir John, his two *aides-de-camp*, Captains Keppel and Campbell, were taken prisoners, as were also Colonel Conway, (Henry Seymour Conway, Horace Walpole's cousin), and Lord Robert Manners Sutton, who with his regiment of dragoons rendered signal service in the charge, together with the Scots Greys, and each lost a standard. Lord Robert, who was wounded, wrote that, on the evening of the battle, he supped with Marshal Saxe in his tent, and upon remarking that the French loss had been very great, the marshal replied, with the greatest indifference, "Not above 11,000."

Besides Lord Robert Sutton, five officers of the Duke of Cumberland's Dragoons were reported "missing." (Report issued from Whitehall by authority).

The reverses of France at sea, and in Italy, outweighed her advantages in this desultory campaign in Flanders, and she looked eagerly for peace. Louis XV. sent Sir John Ligonier back, on parole to the Duke of Cumberland, with pacific proposals which took definite form, in 1748, as the Peace of Aix-la-Chapelle.

The Duke of Cumberland arrived home in November, 1747, and the Marquess of Granby, Lord George, and Lord Robert in due time found their way back to Belvoir. The last was doubtless released on parole soon after his capture, as in the recorded case of Colonel Conway.

Records afford more evidence of Lord Robert's doings, in this campaign of 1747, than of Lord Granby's, because the former was regularly appointed to a command, while the latter had still remained somewhat of a freelance, performing Staff duties. His desire for an active military career was now interrupted by the period of peace, some ten years, which followed the Peace of Aix-la-Chapelle.

The marquess remained a colonel on half-pay, and was promoted to the brevet rank of major-general in 1755. Upon his return home from Flanders he resumed his parliamentary life, and his name occurs very frequently upon committees, especially those appointed to consider the making of roads, in which the country had been found very deficient for strategic purposes during the Forty-Five. One of the most urgent was soon completed between Newcastle and Carlisle.

Though we learn that in Uncle Toby's days our armies swore terribly in Flanders, Lord Granby's vocabulary appears to have acquired no expansion in any direction owing to his later campaign in that country. Public speaking, especially, he disliked with intensity; it was the one thing in life of which he was genuinely afraid. But his short, unadorned, and infrequent utterances in the House of Commons carried that conviction with them which is inseparable from a combination of strong common sense with generous, tolerant methods of judging men and measures, irrespective of "party," or of self-interest. Lord Robert Manners Sutton also entered Parliament as member for Nottinghamshire in 1747, and his regiment (Cumberland's Dragoons) was disbanded in 1748, after the Peace of Aix-la-Chapelle.

Besides their parliamentary and county duties, the three brothers were much addicted to sport. The Marquess of Granby, from his earliest years, was an ardent and accomplished performer across country in pursuit of either stag, fox, or hare. Anything approaching to an adequate account of the marquess's sporting doings would now be scarcely possible; but, as illustrating one side of a many-sided character, a few details happened upon during an examination of his period may not be out of place; especially at that point of his career, lying between the Peace of 1748 and the outbreak of the Seven Years' War, when he had most leisure to devote to amusement.

He was one of the finest riders of his age—not merely to hounds, but in the "all-round" sense, having been known to have accomplished 120 miles in the saddle at a stretch. Hunting was his favourite pastime as much as soldiering was his ideal of a profession. The wild stag was, principally, hunted in England till about the middle of the eighteenth century, of which sport the vale of Belvoir supplied an unlimited amount, being unenclosed as far as Newark, and abounding in deer. Granby's father sang the praises of "stagghunting," from Lord Lexington's seat at Kelham in 1719, to the Duke of Newcastle, offering him, on Lord Lexington's behalf, fifteen to twenty brace of fallow-deer "to stock Haughton Park."

The same (third) Duke of Rutland built the hunting-lodge in Croxton Park, in 1730, portions of which remain. (Lord Granby often resided there. In the part that remains the widow of the famous huntsman, Will Goodall, lived until her death, in October, 1898). Of the Belvoir hounds the history is traced to 1730, and they appear to have been first entered solely to fox at a date slightly prior to that usually adopted (1750) when the practice became general throughout England. In 1747, while serving in Flanders, Lord Granby sent a message to his uncle, Lord William Manners, concerning "their next winter's campaign at fox-hunting," and the marquess is assumed by the *Badminton Library* volume on hunting to have been the first Master of the illustrious Belvoir Fox-hounds. At any rate he shared that office with Lord William Manners, his uncle.

In the hunting world Lord Granby was associated with the Marquess of Rockingham, Lord Darlington, and Lord Byron, sometime Master of His Majesty's Stag-hounds north of the Trent; and in 1754 his brother, Lord Robert Sutton, was appointed Master of His Majesty's Harriers and Fox-hounds. Letters here and there to Mr. Thoroton prove that hunting was never far from Lord Granby's mind during the tedious campaigns of the Seven Years' War, at the close of which he hunted regularly in the Belvoir country, and at Scarborough, where he built some kennels. Scarborough was a favourite resort of his, with which he was politically connected, and a year before his death one John Chamberlayne wrote—

"Agreeable to your commands I have bought a pack of hare-hounds, and have sent them to Scarborough as you directed. There is 26 couple of fine, healthy hounds, boney and well mixed."

★★★★★★★★★★

When the Allies were retreating before De Broglie and Contades, after the Battle of Bergen, Granby wrote (May 19, 1759) to Thoroton from Lippstadt: "Give orders to Robin to deliver the hounds I promised Walsrode to the bearer."

Mr. John Cradock relates meeting frequently at Scarborough, at the table of the celebrated physician Sir Noah Thomas, the Duke of York, the Marquess of Granby, Sterne, Mr. and Mrs. Gibber, and Colonel Sloper,—*Literary and Miscellaneous Memoirs.*

Scarborough was represented in Parliament by Captain George Manners, who died in 1772; by Lord Robert Manners, 1802-7; and by Charles Manners-Sutton (the Speaker), 1807-31.

★★★★★★★★★★

Though a patron of the turf and liberal subscriber to many sweepstakes, of 100, 500, 1,000, and 1,200 guineas, run for during a series of years at Newmarket, Ascot, and York, Lord Granby apparently took more interest in hunters and cavalry chargers than in racehorses. His grandfather, the second duke, and his uncle. Lord William Manners, maintained extensive racing studs; but he personally appears to have had only an occasional horse in training between 1750 and the commencement of the Seven Years' War. In 1751 he ran a horse called "Chance;" in 1752 "Rib" and "Brisk" at Huntingdon; in 1753 he was represented at Newmarket and Odsey by "Rib;" in 1754 by "Dwarf;" and in 1755-6 he won, with an unnamed colt, two matches against the Earl of Northumberland's "Beacon." In the same last-named years, he ran "Chance," "Whitefoot," and "a black filly" at Ascot, Grantham, and Hambleton.

★★★★★★★★★★

One of the second duke's most celebrated racers was "Bonny Black Mare," by "Black Hearty," by "Brierley Turk." She won at Hambleton as a three-year old, and again as a five-year-old. As a six-year-old she beat Lord Hervey's "Merryman," conceding three stone, and "Hackwood," after which she was backed to run four times round the King's Plate course at Newmarket, without rubbing, against any horse or mare in the kingdom. A portrait of "Bonny Black Mare" is contained in the *Sportsman's Pocket Companion.*

★★★★★★★★★★

At "Cocking" he found a frequent antagonist in Mr. Edmund Turner, of Stoke Rochford, with whom in 1751 he fought a main of sixteen battles at Grantham, of which Mr. Turnor won eleven and the marquess five. In 1753 this match was repeated on June 20 and following days, when the marquess won ten battles to Mr. Turnor's six; the latter being again defeated in 1754, in a main of nine, by five battles to four.

Besides his own brothers and uncles (Lord Robert Sutton, Lord George Manners, Lord William, and General Lord Robert Manners), Lord Granby's racing associates were the Duke of Cumberland, the Marquess of Hartington, the Marquess of Rockingham, Captain R. Shaftoe, Captain Jennison Shaftoe (of the 1st Foot Guards), Mr. Thomas Shaftoe, Mr. Fisher, and many others.

In the domain of sport Lord Granby was, therefore, as well-known as in that of war, politics, or society; and in 1749 the last was much excited by his engagement to Lady Frances Seymour, daughter and co-heiress of the stately Duke of Somerset, who had lived in such regal pomp at Petworth. Walpole surpassed himself in gossip concerning this match: he estimated the lady's fortune at over £130,000, and Lord Granby's allowance from his father at £6,000 a year.

The fickle attention of London society might have been diverted from Granby's matrimonial prospects by considerably less than several alarming shocks of earthquake such as, in April, 1750, caused a general exodus. Within three days 730 coaches laden with patrician fugitives were counted passing Hyde Park Corner. Night was the time, as usual, most feared; and Walpole described a party composed of Lord Granby's aunts. Lady Katherine Pelham, Lady Frances Arundel, and Lady Galway, who, with the latter's husband, left town one evening for an inn ten miles out, where they intended playing "brag" till five the following morning, then to return "to look for the bones of their husbands and families under the rubbish." (To Sir H. Mann, April 2, 1750).

This story, coupled with Lady Katherine's busy pursuit of the sweets of office, presents her in a somewhat hard and worldly light. But human nature is complex, and her maternal instincts were of the strongest. Near Claremont, the Duke of Newcastle's seat, Mr. Pelham and Lady Katherine had a residence called Esher Place. Here their two sons were taken ill, dying eventually within twenty-four hours of one another, and to it Lady Katherine (who caught their complaint in nursing them) could never afterwards bear to go, or to any place which she specially associated with her dead boys. Their disease was an ulcerated sore throat, which, becoming prevalent, was called "the Pelham fever." The Duke of Rutland lost a son from the same cause.

London soon forgot the earthquake, and Walpole airily described a party at Vauxhall Gardens at which Lord Granby was present. For the entertainment of George Montagu, Walpole on this occasion invests with the manners of a drunken lout the same Granby whom he elsewhere describes as "affording a shining example of the idea that noble blood diffuses an air of superior excellence over the outward form, and refines the qualities of the mind." Under careful scrutiny, the whole tone of this letter throws doubt upon its veracity. Walpole sets forth what he asserts was passing in Lord Granby's *thoughts* about his approaching marriage, and attributes to him ideas and motives the existence of which is founded solely upon Walpole's imagination.

This feat of thought-reading invariably bears the same flaw, no matter whether performed by Walpole a hundred and fifty years ago or by the Society chatterbox of our own day: the thoughts supplied always coincide surprisingly with the prejudices of the purveyor, and in ninety-nine cases out of a hundred have never even crossed the brain of the individual upon whom they are fathered. Walpole added that Granby's temper had been previously ruffled by the prince, (Frederick Prince of Wales, died in the ensuing year, 1751), who had won of him, and Dick Lyttelton, £1,900; after which H.R.H. had declined to play any longer.

Lord Granby's wedding-day, September 2, 1750, is described as "a mighty topic of conversation." Walpole said that the bride's guardian. Lord Winchelsea, had tied up her property so tightly that the Duke of Rutland had endeavoured to break off the match; and her income was now estimated to be only £4,000 a year, and Lord Granby's the same. Further, they were each in debt for the sums of £7,000 and £10,000 respectively.

This indefatigable Paul Pry then assures Sir Horace Mann that Lord Granby had offered his bride presents to the value of £12,000, and desired that she should pay for them! The taunt implied in this statement is, once again, scarcely compatible with Walpole's own declaration that "generosity was not only innate in Lord Granby's breast, but was never corrupted there," and that "he seemed to conceive no use of money but to give it away."

But no matter; any stick was good enough wherewith to belabour the "Pelhamites," with whom Walpole insisted on classing the Rutland family, despite the fact that it followed—though always independently—the policy of William Pitt, whose Alliance with the "Pelhamites" was a mere political *mariage de convenance.* Lady Katherine was the only member of the family to whom the term might apply as the wife of Henry Pelham; but even she, too, was intimate with Pitt, and at Leicester House, where the "Pelhamites" were never welcome. Her influence and persuasion was, to a large extent, the cause of the Duke of Rutland now being pressed to leave his retirement, and his name was put forward as likely to succeed that of the Duke of Richmond as Master of the Horse. Nearly four years were, however, yet to elapse before the Duke of Rutland resumed any office.

In August, 1751, the arrival of a son and heir. Lord Roos, was announced in the Granby family, which was subsequently increased as follows:—

Lord Charles Manners, born 1754, who became fourth Duke of Rutland, 1779.

Lord Robert Manners, born 1758, who died of wounds received while commanding the *Resolution* in Lord Rodney's action in the West Indies, 1782.

Lady Frances Manners, born 1753, married firstly to Lord Tyrconnel, and secondly to Philip, second son of Lord Newark.

Two other daughters were born, who died in extreme infancy.

In the October following Lord Roos's birth, Lucy, Duchess of Rutland, died. She lived at Beaufort House, Chelsea, and a quaint characteristic of her survives. When she heard of a specially incredible incident from some gossiping visitor, she used to request her daughter to step into the next room and write it down. "Lord! madam," Lady Lucy Manners would reply, "*it can't* be true."—"No matter, child, it will do for news into the country next post"! Walpole was fond of quoting this saying, in his letters, as a justification of any improbable statement.

An important event of the year 1754 was the death of Henry Pelham, First Lord of the Treasury, Lord Granby's uncle by marriage. His death severed ties with which the cohesion of the various Whig factions had been satisfactorily secured; and he was succeeded at the Treasury by that interesting and astonishing personage, his brother, the Duke of Newcastle—"Holies Newcastle," as he signed himself.

In the changes that occurred pressure was again brought to bear upon the Duke of Rutland to return to Court, he having been promised, according to Walpole, the Privy Seal in the room of the moribund Earl Gower, then "inarticulate with the palsy." The Duke of Rutland had also been very ill at Belvoir, and reported dead, when he suddenly came to town; and his brother—

> A Lord William Manners, better known in the groom-porter annals than in those of Europe, together with the whole Manners family, intimated to the Duke of Newcastle that, unless Lord Gower was dismissed in a month and the Duke of Rutland installed in his place, they would oppose the prosperous dawn of the new Ministry.

The determination of Walpole to be, at any cost, sparkling, effervescent, and above all things entertaining in his letters is here fully illustrated. Macaulay has severely attacked him for attempting the role of a historian; but his more chastened style, and, at least, greater attempt at exactness in that capacity is patent to anyone who reads his letters side by side with his *Memoirs* of George II. and George III., in which latter works Carlyle pronounced him to be "unusually accurate, punctual, and lucid."

On the face of it, it does not seem probable that the Duke of Rutland, who hated London life and Court ceremony, should have been a party to, or the subject of, the "job" set forth by Walpole, as above, concerning an office to which the duke did not succeed after all. Turning to Walpole as a historian one finds the incident thus described:—

> The Duke of Marlborough succeeded Lord Gower in the Privy Seal, and the Duke of Rutland, a nobleman of great worth and goodness, returned to Court which he had long quitted, (since 1738, or for seventeen years), yet *without enlisting in any faction*, though governed too much by a mercenary brother, and was appointed Lord Steward.

Such were the true facts, and great stress should be laid upon the circumstance that the duke resumed office without enlisting in any faction: it explains much, hereafter, concerning both the duke's and Lord Granby's political conduct.

As Lord Steward of the Household, in which office he continued until 1761, the duke became responsible for all expenses and wages connected with the king's household, as well as for the good government of the same. In the Counting-House sat daily, under the presidency of the Lord Steward, one of the most ancient Courts of Justice in England, known, from the covering of the table, as the "Board of Green Cloth." This Board, according to Edmund Burke, originated in the principle that the king's household was a body corporate possessed of a Government, Magistrates, Courts, and Bylaws within itself.

★★★★★★★★★★

Mr. Levett Blackborne, whose letters of 1770-1 (*Rutland MSS.*) afford some interesting details of Charles Yorke's acceptance of the Great Seal, and of Lord Granby's last days, was Steward of this Court under the Duke of Rutland.

★★★★★★★★★★

It had jurisdiction over all offences committed in the king's palaces, and verge of the Court; and without the Lord Steward's Warrant none of the king's servants could be arrested for debt.

Walpole's reference to the "mercenary brother," and the "groom-porter annals," pointed to Lord William Manners, and his frequent presence in the apartments of the Groom-Porter (an office which still survives in name), whither the Court gamblers frequently resorted to play cards. The Groom-Porter had the privilege of supplying chairs, tables, cards, etc., to the king's lodgings; and to him were referred all disputes arising from cards, dice, and bowls. During the New Year festivities at Court in 1728, Lord William (*London in Jacobite Times*), in one evening won 1,200 guineas, and the king and queen lost 500 between them. Early in George III.'s reign gambling at Court was forbidden, but any effect of this example upon society at large was imperceptible.

Chapter 4

1754-1755: Minorca Falls

Among the many duties of the Lord Steward was that of swearing in, personally or by his appointed deputies, the members of a new Parliament. Upon the list of those deputies in 1754, and on many other occasions, the Marquess of Granby's name appeared; and upon the assembling of the newly elected Parliament of that year he was selected to move the re-election of the Right Hon. Arthur Onslow to the Speaker's chair.

On this occasion Lord Granby made probably the longest speech he ever delivered. He addressed Mr. Dyson, Clerk of the House of Commons, as follows, (from the *Journals of the House of Commons,* 1754, the use of capital letters is preserved just as they appeared in the report, according to the custom of the time):—

> Mr. Dyson, As it is necessary, before we proceed to business to make choice of a proper person to preside in our future deliberations and debates I rise, if the House will give me leave, in order to propose one. The chair is not a post of ease and repose, but of great labour and activity: it requires a person of a distinguished character, whose authority may the better support the dignity of this House.
>
> It is of the greatest consequence that we chuse the most able person we can find to supply this important office; for the qualifications of a speaker must necessarily have great weight and influence in our proceedings; and the public business, as the person we shall fix on may prove more or less expert, will accordingly be either facilitated or obstructed, expedited or perplexed. That honourable chair, Sir, demands in the person who shall be destined to fill it, many talents and many virtues: it requires, in general, great abilities, it requires in particular an exact skill in

the orders, rules and methods of Parliament; it requires a perfect knowledge of all the powers and privileges of this House and a consummate Experience in the infinite variety of business necessarily to be transacted within these walls. Besides these great talents, the greatest integrity and impartiality, an unshaken resolution and steady firmness of mind are virtues that ought to be eminently conspicuous in the character of the speaker of this House.

Very difficult indeed. Sir, it is to find so many great qualifications united in any one person; yet we have the happiness of having one gentleman amongst us whom experience has shewn us on many occasions to be equal in every shape to this important office; one whose great ability and integrity has appeared in innumerable instances through the course of several successive Parliaments; one whose zealous attachment for our present happy establishment, and for the whole constitution of this nation in general, is well known; and who has a heart warm with that zeal and affection which is the proper character of a speaker of this house, a zeal and affection for the right and liberties of the Commons of Gt. Britain. I perceive every gentleman's eyes are already fixed on the Rt. Honble Mr. Onslow; I don't doubt therefore but I shall meet with the unanimous approbation of this House when I move that Mr. Onslow may be desired to accept of this important trust, and that he will again take possession of that chair which he has filled in four successive Parliaments with the greatest ability and integrity, with so much honour and reputation to himself, to the satisfaction of former Parliaments and to the advantage of the kingdom.

There can but one doubt occur in the choice of Mr. Onslow, and that is how far he himself can be induced to accept of this important and laborious office; and yet I flatter myself there is one argument resulting from his own virtue, and love of his country which will be able to over-rule this difficulty. There is no man whose long and faithful services give him a juster title to repose and dignity than Mr. Onslow. No man has a stricter or more indisputable claim to every argument of self-defence that can possibly excuse his embarking again on this laborious office; no man can forego the arguments with greater grace and dignity; no man so likely to sacrifice every consideration of personal ease and advantage to the interest of the public and to

> the importunities of this House than himself. I therefore move, That the Rt. Honble Arthur Onslow, Esq., be desired to take the chair as speaker."

Mr. Thomas Pelham seconded the motion, which was carried unanimously.

The transfer of the Premiership from the Commons to the Lords occasioned difficulties as to the leadership of the Lower House. Henry Fox, Secretary at War; William Pitt, Paymaster of the Forces; and Murray, Attorney General, were all potential occupiers of that position; but each embodied some disagreeable possibility of factious combination against the Duke of Newcastle, who was not less nervously than eagerly fingering the reins placed in his hands through his brother's death.

A time-honoured custom, which under parallel circumstances we still follow, was adopted of selecting for the post a man possessed of no claim to it at all—a respectable, colourless nonentity named Sir Thomas Robinson. Forthwith Pitt and Fox, under a careful exterior semblance of supporting the Duke of Newcastle, sank their own differences for the moment and applied themselves to heckling Robinson on every possible opportunity.

Occasion for the shifting of this disagreeable position for poor Robinson soon arose. Though nominally at peace, England and France were gradually drifting into very strained relations respecting their rivalries in India and America. Frederick the Great was, moreover, suspected of designs upon Hanover; and this fact, coupled with the sustained dread of a French invasion, reduced England to a condition of alarm and depression which was unrelieved by the slightest confidence felt in Newcastle's ability to deal with the threatened Continental war.

To distract England from pressing her claims in America, France sought aid in Europe for an attack on Hanover, a policy which was distinctly unjust, since George II. had stipulated for the neutrality of Hanover, as regarded France, during the dispute of the Austrian Succession. George II. consequently, repaired to Hanover, and, without the knowledge or sanction of Parliament, concluded some private subsidiary treaties with Hesse and Russia for a supply of troops to be paid out of the British Exchequer.

Hints were thrown out in the King's Speech in 1754 of the need of supplies "for the protection of British rights in America;" and in 1755 Parliament was informed of French preparations for war. On this occasion the Marquess of Granby, and George Townshend, moved the Address and a vote of credit, which resulted in the sum of £1,000,000 being granted for the purpose of "protecting and regaining the king's violated dominion in America."

The money obtained, the king's treaties were disclosed, and the cost of the subsidized Hessian and Russian troops was proposed to be met out of the vote of credit.

Here, at once, was the signal for the re-sorting of factions in the Commons. Fox, who had already been intriguing with the Duke of Newcastle against Pitt, supported the treaties, and was in consequence made a Secretary of State. Pitt vehemently opposed them on the grounds that we had no direct interest in these schemes for the good of Hanover, which were un-British, irritating to Prussia, and provocative of war. George Townshend, who had seconded Lord Granby on the vote of credit, was "shocked to see such a gross misapplication of it;" likewise his brother Charles, who said the Address of the previous year had only mentioned America and Great Britain—not Hanover. He appealed to Lord Granby whether such was not the case, declaring "that His Lordship's answer would be a full reply to the boldness or preciseness of *any* minister!" (The importance attached to Lord Granby's Parliamentary utterances is reflected in this declaration made when he was about thirty-four years old).

Faction, not patriotism, was at the bottom of all this noise; and Lord Granby's conduct affords an excellent example of the level, impartial course he always strove to adopt. An opposer of Hanoverian preferences he was known to be; and, as such, had been in sympathy with the Prince of Wales, and Pitt, at Leicester House. But in this case the danger to Hanover had arisen out of George II.'s support of purely English interests in America, and Lord Granby dissented from Pitt's indiscriminate disregard of the king's German dominions.

Walpole, who also spoke in this debate, wrote:

> With great decency, Lord Granby said that, if anything had been done contrary to the Address, the House must judge of it; yet he was not such an enemy to Hanover as to let the French satiate their rage on Hanoverian subjects, because their Elector had acted the part of a British king." (*Memoirs of the Reign of George II.* J. West, in a letter to the Duke of Newcastle, said Lord Granby spoke with great warmth and clearness to the effect that so long as ministers pursued the true interests of their

country they would receive his support.—*Newcastle Papers,* December 13, 1755).

Lord George Sackville, an individual who will absorb our attention presently, supported this view also; and the treaties were approved by 289 votes to 121. Mr. Pitt's opposition occasioned his dismissal from office.

The national disquietude which had thrown a gloom over the year 1755 was still as strongly marked in the ensuing year. Menaces of invasion by France kept the government and the public in so trying a condition of nervousness that 6,000 Hessians and 9,000 Hanoverians were brought over, much to Pitt's disgust, for the augmentation of the home garrisons. It is to the credit of these subsidised troops that they behaved quietly and well, though exposed by the neglect of the military authorities to much privation, which was principally alleviated by the kindness of private gentry. (R. Glover's *Memoirs*).

France, however, was only massing troops on her northern coast for us to stare at while she slipped away, unobserved, to the south for the purpose of attacking Minorca, then under the veteran Governor Blakeney, who made a brave defence. Admiral Byng was despatched to the rescue with a fleet which, on arrival, he considered so unequal to that of the French that, after fighting an unsuccessful action, he withdrew—and Minorca fell. (Minorca then represented to us what Malta does now).

Upon this disaster the humiliated English public broke into angry clamour against Byng and the Duke of Newcastle's Government. Newcastle fell into one of his attacks of political hysterics at the prospect of losing power; a prospect made more probable by the astute Mr. Fox, who enacted the part so graphically styled "ratting," and escaped from the foundering Ministry. Newcastle clutched at every floating straw, but, deserted and despairing, he soon resigned likewise.

The Duke of Devonshire, supported by the Grenvilles, succeeded Newcastle at the Treasury, and the king had, perforce, to consent to Pitt's return to office as Secretary of State, a circumstance which naturally entailed his being the *esprit fort* of the Cabinet. Distasteful as this situation was to George II., it was soon fated to disappear. Pitt boldly defended Admiral Byng, but both were objects of the Royal antipathy. Lord Granby was equally energetic in Byng's defence, and was to have proposed a vote of acquittal in the House of Commons in conjunction with Lord George Cavendish, but the government did not, at the last, dare to press it.

"Unheard and untried," says Glover in his *Memoirs*, "Byng was devoted to destruction by king, ministers, and people;" and his trial and hearing did not alter their determination. The admiral was shot on the quarter-deck of the *Monarque*, and Pitt was once more dismissed owing to the king's persistent dislike of him. He had, however, carried some of his points; the Hessian and Hanoverian mercenaries were decently got rid of, and a bill was passed for embodying a large force of militia by means of the ballot. This course had been put forward at the opening of Parliament in the King's Speech, and the Marquess of Granby was one of the Committee appointed to consider the Address.

With this raising of the militia, the Duke of Rutland, as Lord Lieutenant of Leicestershire, was of necessity much occupied, and was energetically helped by his sons. The scheme was highly unpopular with the country people; and Lord Robert Manners Sutton, who was actively identified with the Nottinghamshire Militia after leaving the army, is said by Walpole to have been even in danger of his life in the town of Nottingham. Lord Granby was similarly engaged in Yorkshire (with which county the Duke of Rutland was connected), and wrote from Scarborough to the Duke of Newcastle as follows:—

> I am sorry the Militia Bill has occasioned such discontent; the country people in these parts have been very riotous; they have visited every gentleman's house and forced them to give them money. We have just heard that they have demolished several houses at York. Our friend, Mr. Osbaldeston, (Member for Scarborough), has been visited by them, his house very much damaged, and been obliged to send them money. May this spirit of sedition soon be quieted. I hope Your Grace will excuse this paper and scroll (*sic*), as it is writ in haste.

★★★★★★★★★★

"On Sunday ye 15th after trenity, and on the 13th of Sept., Esquier Duncombe desired all his tenants to come and assist him against the mob that was resen about the Meleatey that was loted (raised)—1,420 men with armour. Esquier Duncombe gave them drink at his own house, and at nit he gave them meat and drink at Helmsley Blakeymour ale houses."—Pape's *Diary*, 1757. "Esquier Duncombe" was ancestor of Lord Feversham, of Duncombe Park, Yorks.

★★★★★★★★★★

The Duke of Devonshire's Cabinet soon fell after Pitt's dismissal, and the only possible solution of the deadlock was to reconcile the

Newcastle and Pitt interests, to which end Lord Granby's conciliatory powers and popularity with all parties were much in request. Walpole alludes to him as "the mock champion of the people, who was negotiating to unite the Patriot Minister (Pitt), with the late Chief of the Criminal Administration," (Newcastle).

George II. was still obdurate against Pitt, and encouraged Fox to attempt to form a Cabinet. The result was that "it rained resignations," (Walpole to Sir H. Mann, June 9, 1757), actual or threatened, on the part of the "Pelhamites" and the supporters of Pitt. Lord Rockingham informed Newcastle that he was dressing for Kensington to tender his resignation, and that Lord Granby had just told him the Duke of Rutland would resign that day also.

An awkward and threatening pause followed, during which the country unequivocally showed its preference for the guidance of Pitt. The king at last gave way, and Mr. Fox's stillborn Administration was hustled out of sight to give place to a Coalition Ministry, with the Duke of Newcastle at the Treasury, and William Pitt as Secretary of State for the Southern Department, and Leader in the House of Commons.

★★★★★★★★★★

The Northern Department comprised the Low Countries, Germany, Denmark, Sweden, Poland, Russia, etc. The Southern Department comprised Home affairs, and France, Switzerland, Italy, Spain, Portugal, and Turkey. These Departments were changed in 1782 into the Home and Foreign Secretaryships.—Hadyn's *Book of Dignities.*

★★★★★★★★★★

This strong government included Lords Holdernesse, Granville, Temple, Barrington, Halifax, and Anson; Henry Fox, George Grenville, and Legge. The Duke of Marlborough (the second duke), was Master General of the Ordnance, the Duke of Devonshire Lord Chamberlain, and the Duke of Rutland retained his office of Lord Steward.

So considerable a struggle had not settled itself without friction, and the king had taken steps to try and coerce into obedience some of Pitt's most formidable supporters. To this end a gentleman, whose name is immaterial, had been nominated to a place under the Board of Green Cloth without the Duke of Rutland's knowledge, and which he had intended to bestow upon Mr. Thomas Thoroton, who is described in the next chapter. When the government was fairly established the duke wrote to His Grace of Newcastle about the desirability of some equivalent being made to Thoroton, saying—

> I am the more earnest in this request as His Majesty's coldness towards me renders it daily more requisite, for, although I could support my spirits in the disagreeable situation in which I find myself so long as my honour and character are untouched, it is too much to submit to be both frowned upon and dishonoured.

Lord Granby said that his father had been very much displeased, but "was then easy," and inclined not to further dispute the affair.

Although the dates of the letters do not point to any connection with the above dilemma, several had passed on the propriety of bringing Mr. Thoroton into Parliament. Lady Katherine Pelham advised the Duke of Newcastle to offer him the vacant seat for Boroughbridge. She had been characteristically busy: Walpole included her in "the private chorus that had not the less part in the drama for being cyphers" which had strongly dissuaded Newcastle from coming into power without an understanding with "Leicester House."

Since the Prince of Wales's death in 1751, his widow, the princess dowager, and the notorious Earl of Bute were elaborating, at Leicester House, the schemes which were to take definite shape so soon as the prince's son should succeed to the throne as George III.

Newcastle had already offered the Boroughbridge seat elsewhere, but now asked to be released from the engagement, owing to the:

> . . . .great obligations I have to the Marquess of Granby (as well as to all the Duke of Rutland's family, which is very numerous in the House of Commons) for his uncommon behaviour in support of me in the Commons, where he is at the head of my friends, and where his personal credit and influence are much greater than any other person's.

★★★★★★★★★★

Newcastle is universally allowed to have been second to none in knowledge of the value of the various factions, and prominent men in Parliament. Lord Granby at the date of the above tribute to his influence in the Commons was only thirty-six, and exercised it through his character alone. He held no office, and belonged to no faction.

★★★★★★★★★★

Newcastle was deeply intent upon establishing a right to lay exclusive claim to the Rutland interest, which was in reality devoted towards establishing and maintaining an *entente cordiale* between him and Pitt. As an old friend and relation, the Belvoir family regarded the Duke of Newcastle with much affection and esteem, for in his private life he displayed excellent and attractive personal qualities. Newcastle received a very biting letter from the rejected nominee for Boroughbridge, and then offered that borough to the Duke of Rutland for Thoroton, to whom "the election would not be one farthing expense, nor put him to the trouble of a journey unless it were agreeable to him." The duke accepted the offer, and Thoroton was introduced to the bailiff and *burgesses* as "a gentleman of great consideration in Lincolnshire, and of known zeal for His Majesty, the Royal Family, and the interests of his Country." Lord Granby being unable to do so. Lord Robert Manners Sutton accompanied Thoroton to Boroughbridge, and he was duly elected.

When the composite Administration, known as Pitt's Ministry, started upon its career no possible combination could have exceeded it in strength. Pitt relegated with relief to the Duke of Newcastle all the inner wire-pullings, the patronage, the packing of Parliament, and the general party-management in which His Grace was as proficient as Pitt was maladroit.

Fox was kept quiet by being made paymaster, in which lucrative office he at once commenced to repair his straitened means by utilising to the utmost the privilege enjoyed by that official of investing, for his own profit, the large balances which lay in his keeping. This privilege Pitt, when paymaster, had consistently refused to exercise: Fox amassed a huge fortune.

Pitt was allowed his own way in respect of the national policy, and became paramount in our Continental affairs as well as in the virtual management of both army and navy. Besides the embodiment of the Militia, he revived a previously mooted scheme (originated in Duncan Forbes, of Culloden), of raising some Highland regiments for King George's service, thereby creating an element of trust in Jacobite districts and circles by extending towards them a show of confidence. (Scottish regiments existed before this date, considerably; and served at Dettingen and Fontenoy).

The proposed force was to consist of two battalions, each of a thousand men, commanded by Montgomery, Lord Eglinton's brother, and the Master of Lovat, son of Lord Lovat who was beheaded on Tower Hill. The Master of Lovat had been attainted after the Forty-Five, but pardoned upon condition of never re-entering the Highlands. In a debate which arose, some had deprecated Lovat's appointment on the ground of inconsistency, and that he was "a disaffected Highlander who had gained what military experience he possessed in rebellion." On the other hand, it was argued that under Lovat alone would his clan, the Frasers, enlist. Lord George Sackville (son of the Duke of Dorset), defended the appointment, choosing sarcasm, as was his wont, to point his arguments. He asked why rank should not be allowed to these "extemporaneous officers" as it had been to the colonels of the new regiments raised during the Forty-Five? This sneer, which was directed pointedly against several men then sitting in the House, did not pass unnoticed. The Marquess of Granby rose and remarked that he "was sorry to hear rebels compared to those who had taken up arms to crush the Rebellion." (*Memoirs of the Reign of George II.*, vol. ii.)

To this little passage of arms may be due the fact of Walpole's subsequent conviction that the greatest enmity prevailed between Sackville and Granby in Germany—a conviction which is proved, by the strongest evidence, to have existed in Walpole's mind alone.

Chapter 5

1756-1757: The Third Silesian War

Uninteresting as European politics may be, from their staleness acquired in a hundred and forty years or any ineptitude with which they are here dealt, they cannot be entirely passed over if Lord Granby's period is to be even superficially described.

The Peace of Aix-la-Chapelle (1748) had concluded the War of the Austrian Succession, but had not quelled its bitternesses and jealousies. One of the chief of these arose out of the regret felt by Maria Theresa that, following the advice of England, she had ceded Silesia to Prussia in exchange for the support of Frederick the Great. In short, she wanted Silesia back.

She thereupon commenced some secret understandings with Essie, Saxony, and Poland that, should Prussian aggression again threaten those countries or her own, they should make a concerted effort to crush Frederick, and divide his territory quietly among them. Agreed upon this, they then offered a share in the scheme, and contingent spoil, to Louis XV. through Madame de Pompadour.

Louis XV., in an evil day for himself, relinquished an Alliance which was open to him, or rather had not yet expired, with Prussia in favour of that offered him by Maria Theresa, (Voltaire said that this Alliance with Austria cost France more in men and money than two hundred years of previous wars with that country), whose traditional Ally was England. But the whole order of European sympathies were complicated, or changed, by the results of innumerable treaties of Aix-la-Chapelle, Versailles, Breslau, Dresden, the Barrier Treaty of Utrecht, and yet others which need not be discussed.

Frederick the Great, suspecting what had been done by Maria Theresa, challenged her in 1756 to show her hand. The colloquialism must be pardoned, for it exactly applies to the circumstances. The empress refused to comply; and, without more ado, Frederick marched into Saxony, penned up the Saxon Army like sheep in a fold, and defeated the Austrian Army under Marshal Browne at Losowitz. The Saxon Army capitulated; Frederick took Dresden, and demanded the production of the secret treaties. Maria Theresa had left these in the archive-room at Dresden under the care of the Queen of Poland, to whom Frederick sent Marshal Keith to treat for their surrender. (Attainted for complicity in the Jacobite Rebellion of 1715. He was son of William, ninth Earl Marischal of Scotland, and was killed at the Battle of Hochkirchen in 1758. Another account names Major von Wangenheim as the envoy).

Humour, that salt and solace of life, is to be found even attending international crises of the highest import, and Lord Dover describes how, as a last resort, the queen sat upon the chest containing the most compromising documents. Keith bluntly explained that, voluntarily or under forcible compulsion, from off that chest Her Majesty had got to come! Finally, the papers were obtained, which Frederick published as proving his suspicions up to the hilt.

Frederick spent the winter in Dresden, and, "Protestant hero" though he was dubbed, exacted the most crushing contributions from Protestant Saxony for the support of his troops.

Thus commenced the Seven Years' War or, as the German portion of it is also called, the Third Silesian War.

Louis XV.'s mistake constituted England's opportunity. Louis' one paramount aim should have been to escape from all quarrels in which France had no direct interest, in order to devote her last man and her last *sou* to defend her colonial position against England.

★★★★★★★★★★

Sir Horace Mann echoed the opinion he heard expressed by many European envoys at Florence, thus: "One cannot account for the perseverance of the French in Germany, which exhausts them of money and reputation at the time that their affairs go so ill everywhere else."—September 29, 1759, to Horace Walpole, *Mann and Manners at the Court of Florence* (Doran).

★★★★★★★★★★

England at first drifted into hostilities with France without any formal declaration of war; nor must the original inception of the war ever be attributed to William Pitt. He, many years after (when Earl of Chatham), disclaimed responsibility for what "it had been the fashion to call his German war," whereas he had not taken office until it was commenced, and the first treaty signed (January 16, 1756) between

England and Frederick the Great. Finding the war an accomplished fact Pitt, seeing his opportunity, pursued it with all the vigour of his nature. Frederick himself pointed to the Duke of Cumberland as having precipitated hostilities by steadily fanning the flame in London when France and England first commenced bickering. Cumberland's motive was to make himself master, through military renown, of the next reign so soon as his father, George II., should die; and to place Henry Fox in the Duke of Newcastle's shoes.

The rumours of French aggression, and designs for an invasion of England, were so thoroughly believed in that Frederick the Great said the mere name of "Frenchman" was sufficient to lash the people of London into fury, and that there were moments when England, who passed for being so sensible, believed herself lost beyond recovery. In such a condition of European affairs, the prestige attaching to the sword of so magnificent a soldier as Frederick the Great was not likely to go long a-begging. France, when too late, tried to retrieve her position, and sought to renew the treaty about to expire between herself and Prussia; but Frederick's answer was to show the Duc de Nivernois the treaty which he had just signed with England. And thus, England and Prussia tumbled in haphazard fashion into an Alliance which was fraught with the most momentous issues for both of them; and eventually tumbled out of it again in precisely the same manner.

George II. and Pitt both welcomed this Alliance, but from different motives: George, as of old, was actuated solely by fears for Hanover; but Pitt saw a brilliant advantage to be won by joining Prussia in a struggle in which England had no direct interests whatever, and which Alliance would indubitably entail an attack on Hanover by France.

In adopting such a course Pitt revolutionized his own former policy, in which his sincerity and single-heartedness have, in consequence, been pertinently questioned by his critics. Ignoring his old antipathy and opposition to Hanoverian interests, he now stoutly declared any menace to Hanover to be a menace to England; for he saw that by employing Hanoverian and other subsidized troops against France, he, with the addition of a very small English force, could keep a principal portion of the French Armies and resources concentrated on German battlefields whilst he put the main strength of England into the Colonial War. He would win America in Germany!

This was a grand conception, but its development soon exceeded the limits which even Pitt had set to it, and the patience of the English people, who did not understand the scheme, nor the object of sacrificing thousands of men and millions of money which brought no obvious, direct result of territorial conquest such as dazzled their eyes in the colonial section of the war. The aid to the colonial conquests afforded by the German operations was little recognised in Pitt's time; it may now be said to have vanished out of the national memory. They became unpopular from the first, and it was mainly owing to the Marquess of Granby's position in the hearts of the public at home, and of the troops in Germany, that Pitt was enabled to continue that phase of the war even so long as he did.

The Duke of Cumberland, then Captain-General of the British Forces, was appointed to the command of the Hanoverians, Hessians, Brunswickers, Saxe-Gothans, etc., with whom he engaged one French Army, under Maréchal D'Estrées, Contades, Chevert, and De Broglie. Frederick the Great was opposed to the Austrians and Russians, to co-operate with whom a second French Army presently proceeded eastwards, under the Prince de Soubise, after first driving the Prussians from Cleves, Emmerich, and various posts north of Cologne.

To Frederick's operations occasional reference, only, need be made: they are recorded in some tons of literature, and the main intent of these pages is to plead for the forgotten portions of the war on the side of England. Purely English action, at the outset, was confined to isolated expeditions of combined naval and military forces directed against the French coasts. These were of Pitt's own planning. He was strangely enamoured of them in spite of their non-success; his object being to prevent by these diversions a concentration of the enemy's forces.

Of these expeditions that upon Rochefort, under Admiral Hawke and General Mordaunt, was abortive. Attached to this was Conway, Horace Walpole's cousin and favourite; and, in the subsequent inquiry into its failure, Conway narrowly escaped being "broke," and his name was removed from the King's Staff. He had been up till then senior to Lord Granby in rank, as he was in age, but, in the years during which Conway was refused further military employment, Lord Granby passed over his head. (Conway was not employed again until April, 1761, when he was sent to serve under Lord Granby in the German War). To this circumstance the jealousy with which Walpole viewed Granby's successes was palpably due. (Walpole considered Conway to be Sackville's sole rival in military capacity.—*Memoirs of the Reign of George II.*, vol. iii.) Conway was undoubtedly hardly used; he was brave, high-minded, and moderately talented; but fatally wanting in decision and the power of inspiring sympathy. (His friend Sir Robert Murray

Keith said, *Memoirs*: "Conway is of a very cold disposition." Walpole himself alluded to the "disgusting coldness" of Conway's manner).

A great and devoted affection for him was the most graceful trait of Walpole's life. This digression will explain itself in many later pages.

Another expedition against St. Malo, under the Duke of Marlborough and Lord George Sackville as regarded the military force, succeeded only in destroying some French shipping and naval stores. (Charles Spencer, second Duke of Marlborough, succeeded to the title through his mother, daughter of the celebrated duke). A third expedition was made later against St. Malo, under Commodore Howe and. General Bligh. Cherbourg was first taken, and a military force landed in the Bay of St. Cast. After destroying some shipping, etc., the troops were surprised, in the act of re-embarking, by the French and terribly worsted, many being drowned in attempting to regain the ships.

Before the date of this last expedition, there occurred a crowning disaster. The Duke of Cumberland's army was forming a barrier before the King of Prussia's provinces on the Elbe, by defending the River Weser against the French, under Marshal D'Estrées. By outmanoeuvring Cumberland, the marshal succeeded in crossing the river, and defeated the duke at Hastenbach. Cumberland retreated towards the sea and his transports, lying in the estuary of the Elbe, but was surrounded at Stade, where he surrendered to the Duc de Richelieu, who was sent to supersede Marshal D'Estrées in spite of his recent victory. Presently Cumberland was compelled to sign the Convention of Klosterseven. By this Convention the duke undertook that the Hanoverian troops should be disarmed, sent into cantonments, and the Auxiliaries dismissed.

A defeat sustained by Frederick at Kolin aggravated the effects of Cumberland's disaster; for the latter released the French Army from Hanover and enabled it to add its weight to the odds against which Frederick was contending. Marshal the Duc de Richelieu ordered certain French detachments to join Prince de Soubise's army, and the whole entered the King of Prussia's dominions, penetrating to Halberstadt and Brandenburg. Equal to the occasion, Frederick marched westwards to meet this new foe, which he defeated at Rossbach, November 5, 1757. In his absence the Austrians possessed themselves of the coveted Silesia, but returning, Frederick gained Silesia once more by the victory of Leuthen.

These battles, like most fought in the German portion of the Seven Years' War, were advantages snatched breathlessly here and there by either side, at a mutual cost that deprived the victors of power to retain the foothold gained.

The Duke of Cumberland returned home—with what feelings may be guessed, if Frederick the Great is to believed—and was received with sullen indignation by the nation; by the king with the words, "Here is my son, who has ruined me and disgraced himself." He resigned all his commissions and military distinctions, including the grand old title of "Captain-General" of the British Forces, to which, from dynastic reasons rather than from any military fitness, he had been appointed, following closely upon so illustrious a soldier as John, Duke of Marlborough. The title "Captain-General" was then placed in abeyance, to be revived, if necessary, as George II. thought to do in 1760, and George III. in 1765; but it never was revived.

Sir John Ligonier, then colonel of the Royal Horse Guards, or "Blues," succeeded to the duke's colonelcy of the 1st Regiment of Foot Guards (the Grenadiers), and to the supreme position in the army under the title of "Commander-in-Chief," which first appeared in the *Army List* of 1758.

John, Marquess of Granby, now re-entered upon active service, after eleven years of peaceful avocations, and was appointed to the colonelcy of the "Blues," *vice* Ligonier. This regiment was, on its original formation, commanded by Aubrey, Earl of Oxford, whose colours it embodied in its uniform, and during whose career the name of the "Oxford Blues" became customary for the purpose of distinguishing it from a blue regiment of dragoons brought by William III. from Holland. Its ordinary title, previously, had been the Earl of Oxford's Horse.

These changes were anticipatory of the increased assistance which Pitt saw was necessary to Frederick the Great, if America was to be won by sharing his quarrels in Germany. Since his victory at Rossbach Frederick, and Pitt, became the idols of the English nation. A yearly subsidy—such as Pitt formerly thundered against—of £670,000 was voted to Frederick; the Convention of Klosterseven was repudiated; Hanover was to be re-armed, and 12,000 British troops despatched to defend her—but where was the general to command the whole? At the moment, excepting veterans, England possessed none of tried experience. Sir John Ligonier, then about eighty years old, was relegated to departmental duties at home; Amherst, James Abercrombie, and Wolfe, all young, were engaged in the Colonial War.

Frederick the Great was applied to in consequence for a commander, and he, delighted thus to gain control of the Hanoverian side

ROYAL
HORSE,Gds

of the war, supplied one in the person of Prince Ferdinand of Brunswick, (brother of the reigning Duke of Brunswick, and "a soldier of approved excellence, and likewise a noble-minded, prudent, patient and invincibly valiant and steadfast man."—*History of Frederick II. of Prussia*), who had won the first advantage in the Seven Years' War as general of one of the three Prussian Armies. Prince Ferdinand was thirty-six, exactly the same age as Lord Granby, but, since the age of nineteen, had served, and studied war, under Frederick the Great in the first and second Silesian Wars.

Prince Ferdinand entered at once upon his task, and proceeded to remobilise the Hanoverian Army, finding in Stade 30,000 troops which the French had omitted to disarm. To assist him he employed his nephew, the Hereditary Prince, son of the reigning Duke of Brunswick, who much disapproved the whole scheme, having hoped Hanover might have remained neutral after the Convention of Klosterseven, to which end he had negotiated with France. (See the Duke of Brunswick's letter, November 27, 1757, to his brother Prince Ferdinand, assuring him his action would disgrace his family, and bring a stain upon his country which he pretended to serve.—Hume and Smollett, vol, xii.)

So quietly was Pitt's repudiation of Klosterseven effected, that the first intelligence gained of it, on the part of France, was that Hanover was actually again under arms, with Prince Ferdinand in command. The Duc de Richelieu was recalled by France, and replaced by the Comte de Clermont.

Prince Ferdinand began by driving the French garrisons out of Hanover. He gradually manoeuvred them westwards across the Rhine. The Hereditary Prince, then twenty years of age, dislodged the French, under De Chabot, from a position at Hoya on the River Weser, across which the prince had patiently transported his troops, in a gale of wind, by means of a single raft.

Ferdinand followed De Clermont over the Rhine and defeated him severely at Crefeldt, June 23, 1758; but, too weak numerically to hold his ground, the prince retired to his former position east of the Rhine, on the River Lippe, to await the arrival of the English Army. At Lippstadt, on the Lippe, he established one of his principal garrisons.

The victory of Crefeldt at once established Prince Ferdinand's popularity in England, where his reputation had been pushed by Major Grant (a Scotchman, whom Frederick the Great had sent to London with the news of his victory at Rossbach), and London rang with eulogies concerning Ferdinand of Brunswick, who had struck such an important blow in the interests of George II. on the Continent.

After Cumberland's recall, the French, quite unjustifiably and by stratagem, possessed themselves of the neutral imperial city of Frankfort, where they established a large garrison and magazine, which they maintained until the close of the war.

Goethe, then a child, describes how this circumstance converted, in a moment, a peaceful town into a scene of war; and how his father hated the French deputy-governor, the Count de Thorane, who was quartered upon him, and invested his house with all the clatter, bustle, and unrest incidental to an important military office. Goethe had many opportunities of seeing the French officers of high rank. He describes the fine-looking Prince de Soubise; the Duc de Broglie, a middle-sized, well-made young man, keen of eye, and resolute of countenance which, no more than his manner, ever betrayed the least mental agitation.

The city of Bremen had surrendered to the Duc de Broglie in January, 1758; but Prince Ferdinand retook it, and established there his principal base of supply in March, 1758. Minden surrendered to him in the same month, and was garrisoned with a force under General Zastrow.

The English military preparations were pushed forward rapidly, and with an enthusiasm which attracted many patrician volunteers who eagerly seized the opportunity which ensured them both fun, and fighting. Those of them who had no military status were granted some nominal rank to invest them with the privileges of *cartel* in case of becoming prisoners. Among these volunteers were Sir James Lowther, "master of £40,000 a year," Sir John Armytage, the Duke of Richmond, Fitzroy, (afterwards Lord Southampton), and Lord Downe who was later shot to pieces, and died almost simultaneously with receiving the Colonelcy of the 25th Foot, which his services and gallantry won for him.

Emden, at the mouth of the River Ems, was taken by Commodore Holmes (March 18, 1758), and was used as the port of disembarkation of the British Army until the mouth of the River Weser was substituted for it later at the Marquess of Granby's request. Frederick's original wish was that the Rhine should have been the line of defence; but in this he was overborne by George II. and his Hanoverian Ministers, (mainly by Baron Münchhausen), to comply with whom the more easterly line was adopted of the River Weser which was almost anywhere fordable. Frederick consequently withdrew his garrison and artillery from Wesel on the Rhine, partially dismantling the fortifications there; but these were presently repaired by the French, and Wesel occupied by them.

The Commander-in-Chief of the English Army was Lieut.-General the Duke of Marlborough, (Master-General of the Ordnance), who had returned home after the second attack upon St. Malo. Lord George Sackville, after that affair, had declared (in contempt of Pitt's expeditions) that "he would no longer go buccaneering," and joined Marlborough's army after its arrival on the continent, without having presented himself in due form before the king, who threatened to recall him. However, seasoned officers were scarce, and Lieut.-General Lord George Sackville was permitted to remain, and as second in command. (Lord George served in Flanders, and was wounded at Fontenoy; afterwards he fought against Prince Charles Edward in the Forty-Five, and made the campaign in Flanders of 1747).

Third in rank came Major-General the Marquess of Granby, after eleven years of retirement, commanding a brigade of cavalry, which included his own regiment, the "Blues." Besides these were Major-General Mostyn, originally of the Foot Guards, *A.D.C.* to the king, and now, (1899), Colonel of the 5th Royal Irish Dragoons; Major-Generals Waldegrave (afterwards third Earl of Waldegrave), and Kingsley, and others of lesser degree whose names will figure presently, such as Edward Ligonier, (nephew and heir of Sir John, created Viscount Ligonier 1757), Lord Brome (or Broome as it was then spelt), and William Faucitt.

Jack Mostyn, as General Mostyn's friends called him when they did not use his *sobriquet* of "Noll Bluff," was younger son of Sir Roger Mostyn, Bart. Brilliantly witty, genial, gallant, and good-humoured, he was universally popular in his profession, and at Court where he was a constant member of George II.'s evening party. Albeit a dashing soldier he was extremely modest, and had refused the command of an expedition to Quebec on the grounds that he professed to be no more than a simple cavalry officer.

★★★★★★★★★★

Walpole, in his *Memoirs*, characteristically asserts that Mostyn sought to curry favour at Court by serving under a Brunswick prince in Germany. Respecting the chief command, Walpole wrote (February 10, 1758): "The Duke of Marlborough commands, and is in reality commanded by Lord George Sackville. We shall now see how much greater generals we have than Mr. Conway, who had pressed to go *in any capacity*, and is not suffered."

★★★★★★★★★★

He became a devoted friend, and companion in arms, of the Marquess of Granby, who took great interest in Mostyn's career as will be shown, by one incident especially, in describing the progress of the war.

Even at this moment, the very outset of his career as a commanding officer, the Marquess of Granby's popularity was such that fifty-two young officers applied to serve as his *aides-de-camp*. Of these, Lord Brome was first selected; and, though the number of applicants might excite no comment in these days when the size of the army has so greatly increased, it was then thought very remarkable, as Walpole has recorded on more than one occasion.

Before commencing the events of the war, the indulgence of the reader is appealed to respecting all military details and technicalities. The history of the British Army employed in the German portion of the Seven Years' War, treated by a competent professional hand inspired with British sympathy, remains unwritten; such an attempt is not aspired to, or possible, in these pages." All that has so far been published is really due to foreign chroniclers, professionally competent, but who have not recorded all that might be said of the English officers and men who bore the brunt of the fighting during the German campaigns, as much as their countrymen at home bore the brunt of the expense.

Frederick the Great, in *Memoires de la Guerre de Sept Ans*, treated Prince Ferdinand's operations as the merest details of his own, and wasted no time, even, over the circumstances which balked the prince of a crowning victory at Minden, saying, "*Le prince n'eût pas le temps de soutenir l'Infanterie Anglaise par d'autres brigades.*" It is scarcely surprising, therefore, that Frederick should have made perfunctory reference only to a certain "Milord Granby" and the troops which he commanded, especially as, at the time of writing the *Memoires*, Frederick had quarrelled irrevocably with England, as he did soon after with Prince Ferdinand.

J. W. Archenholz (*Geschichte des Siebenjährigen Krieges*) treats the war entirely from the German standpoint, though with occasional references to the English troops, their splendid equipment, and the horses of certain cavalry regiments, respectively bay, roan, black, and grey. Colonel J. de Mauvillon (*Geschichte Ferdinand's Herzog's von Braunsch-*

weig) is more graphic and more generous. He awards high praise—the first rank, in fact, in the Allied Army—to the English troops; and equally high praise to Lord Granby, especially to his power of controlling the difficult and heterogeneous materials of which his infantry was composed. ("I really believe all the oddities of the three kingdoms and Germany are met in this army."—Earl of Pembroke to Lord Charlemont, July 16, 1760). But in his natural zeal for the service to which he belonged, De Mauvillon asserts that Prince Ferdinand employed the English mostly under the Hereditary Prince.

English regiments were detailed, and for obvious reasons, to serve under the Hereditary Prince in some of his dashing, "wild-cat" operations up to the siege of Wesel; but he was subordinate in rank to Lord Granby, and no more commanded the British Army than did Colonel de Mauvillon himself.

★★★★★★★★★★

In June, 1700, Lord Granby himself applied for permission for Captain Ainslie to serve as *A.D.C.* to the Hereditary Prince, as the latter sometimes had English troops under his command, and an officer speaking English was essentially necessary to his Staff.—*Newcastle Papers.*

★★★★★★★★★★

Nor is it certain that the English officers who most frequently acted with the Hereditary Prince—notably Major-General Griffin—received their just share of recognition.

De Bourcet (*Memoires sur la Guerre de Sept Ans*) does not tend to throw much light upon the general details of the war, which he treats from the French point of view, and not in a very kind manner.

Tempelhoff, Lloyd, Von Retzow, etc., all deal principally with phases of the war other than those in which the British were concerned; and though several eighteenth-century writers expressed their hopes that posterity would one day do substantial justice to the British operations in Prince Ferdinand's campaigns, those hopes remain unfulfilled, for Carlyle's allusions to them are limited to translations from the above foreign authorities in his magnificent *History of Frederick II. of Prussia*. ("The history of those brilliant years is not, surely, forgotten by Military men."—*MSS.* of the Duke of Roxburghe, who as Sir J. Innes Norcliffe served under Lord Granby in Germany).

A work entitled *Operations of the Allied Army,* 1757-1762, compiled in 1764, by "An officer who served with the British Forces," affords but the baldest details of that portion of the Allied Army with which the writer's sympathies might have been most naturally concerned. It contains a number of plans of the battlefields, and valuable maps of the different areas of the campaigns; excepting for the compilation of these the British Army is little indebted to it individually, and it bears evidence in the text of having also been chiefly derived from foreign sources.

As Pitt's public never entirely mastered the plot of his German War, there is perhaps no ground for surprise that the English participators in its triumphs, reverses, and the exceptional hardships which the circumstances of the war imposed upon them, should have failed to attract an appreciative recorder while facts were still easily accessible, and tradition was yet green.

Chapter 6

1758-1759: Bergen and Minden

Lord Granby embarked at Harwich in July, 1758, and duly arrived at Emden, where he received orders from the Secretary of State, Lord Holdernesse, to start for Prince Ferdinand's camp as soon as possible with the "Blues," and the rest of his cavalry.

By the 25th of July the transports arrived off the Ems, and one man-of-war, a yacht, and thirteen transports entered the river with great difficulty, owing to lack of pilots, which reslted in one transport going aground; but Lord Granby obtained a number of large boats, by means of which the horses were landed without any casualties. For this circumstance the king signified his approval of Granby's activity.

****

> The first force despatched to Germany comprised Napier's Regiment (12th), Kingsley's (20th), Welsh Fusiliers (23rd), Home's (25th), Brudenell's (51st), and Stuart's (37th); and the following cavalry: Blues, Bland's (1st K.D.G.), Howard's (3rd D.G.), Inniskillings, Mordaunt's (10th Dragoons), and Greys.

****

Having landed his contingent. Lord Granby commenced his march without awaiting the rest of the army. From Jemmengum, twelve miles from Emden, he wrote to the Duke of Rutland, after which the traces of his march cease.

A fortnight later the Duke of Marlborough wrote to Mr. Pitt of an uncomfortable progress to Coesvelt (or Koesvelt, due west of Münster)—

> We came here by excessive long marches, and 4 days such a heavy rain without the least intermission as I never saw before. The Foot were obliged to march all the way up to their middles in water, and not a dry spot to lie on at night.

Prince Ferdinand's position was still some twenty miles distant, and the Duke of Marlborough on arrival found the former divided by the River Lippe from the French Army, which was withdrawing towards Wesel on the Rhine.

Prince Ferdinand's task was now, with 12,000 English, 30,000 Hanoverians, and some Brunswick, Hesse-Cassel, and Saxe-Gothan subsidiaries, to drive 80,000 French out of Westphalia, and Lower Saxony.

The first survey of affairs was not pleasing to Marlborough. He found that not only had two Hanoverian lieut.-generals been made senior to Lieut.-General Lord George Sackville, (Lieut.-General January 27, 1758), by ante-dating their commissions; but that Lieut.-General Spörcken, who was junior to, and had served under the duke previously, was now made a general, also with an ante-dated commission, which placed him between Prince Ferdinand and the Duke of Marlborough.

Here was another instance of Hanoverian preferences, and the duke, who had often opposed English subservience to Hanover, immediately wrote home, desiring that a general's commission dated prior to Spörcken's might be sent him, or else His Majesty's leave to retire from the service. He promptly received the commission, (dated July 10, 1758); his objection to the English being, in his words, made "cleavers of wood and drawers of water to the Hanoverians" having had the desired effect with the king.

Almost immediately after the arrival of the English troops at Münster they were attacked by fever and dysentery. The Duke of Marlborough was one of the victims, and he died in that town on October 28, 1758, much regretted throughout the army and in England.

****

> Smollett wrote of him: "Though he did not inherit all the military genius of his grandfather, yet he far excelled him in the amiable and social qualities of the heart: he was brave beyond all question, generous to profusion, and good natured to excess."—*History of England.*

****

This event rendered Lieut.-General Lord George Sackville, (Lieut.-General of the Ordnance), Commander-in-Chief of the English Army, with Major-General the Marquess of Granby as second in command; while, at home, the Master-Generalship of the Ordnance was bestowed upon Lord Ligonier.

According to the testimony of Lord Fitzmaurice,[1] then serving with the British forces in Germany, Lord George at once began the same tactics which he had adopted previously against the Duke of Marlborough, in the St. Malo expedition, of endeavouring to assume personal credit for all that went well, and to create a popularity for himself at the expense of his chief, Prince Ferdinand, who, in the long run, proved himself more than a match for Lord George.

In December all was quiet with the armies, and Sackville returned to England on military business. The troops, since November 15, had been in winter quarters, Granby being at Paderborn, whence he wrote to the Duke of Newcastle, begging also to be allowed leave on account of his private affairs, and Lady Granby's ill state of health. He also vehemently urged the reinforcement of their army by a brigade of guards, another of foot, two regiments of dragoons, and from 6,000 to 8,000 foreign infantry.

> I do from my soul hope it is the intention of the government to augment Prince Ferdinand's army. I think it impossible to defend such a length of country with an army so much inferior to the enemy's. . . . I own I sincerely dread a defeat, or a retreat to the Weser, either of which, in the light I see things, must be fatal to the common cause.

As Granby was temporarily commander-in-chief, his application for leave was not very convenient; but, hearing from the Duke of Rutland how urgent the reasons were, the king consented, expressing himself "extremely well pleased and satisfied with Lord Granby." The latter wrote, saying that possibilities of an action had arisen which, after all, forbade his coming, and again entreating reinforcements.

****

Major Keith, of the Highlanders, also abandoned his leave to serve "his honest general, to whom both his duty and inclination engaged him" (December 15, 1758). The editor of these *Memoirs* wrongly explains the honest general to be Conway (see Keith's *Memoirs*, vol. i.)

****

Lord George Sackville joined the army March 16, 1759, accompanied by General Mostyn, the Duke of Richmond, and Colonel Fitzroy, of whom the two last were appointed *aides-de-camp* to Prince Ferdinand; and the Allies left winter quarters to march southwards.

The French forces, divided into two armies under Marshal Contades (who had superseded De Clermont) and De Broglie, were looming formidably, one in Westphalia, and the latter in the neighbourhood of Frankfort. Upon gaining this important position, which commanded the navigation of the Main and of a portion of the Rhine, Prince Ferdinand early set his hopes. With this intent, and leaving Sackville and Spörcken, with 25,000 men, near Münster to watch Contades, he attacked De Broglie (April 13, 1759) at Bergen, to the north-east of Frankfort, but was repulsed, and Prince Ysenburg, who led the Hessians, was killed.

★★★★★★★★★★

Goethe listened to the cannonade from the roof of his father's house. The Frankfort inhabitants were full of expectancy of deliverance from the French. The Count de Thorane, after the repulse of the Allies, spoke of it in a congratulatory vein to Goethe, senior, who lost his self-control, and retorted, "Would to God, they had sent you to the Devil, even if I had gone in your company."—*Aus meinem Leben.*

★★★★★★★★★★

We did not call it a defeat, but one of those "strategic movements to the rear" resulted from the engagement; and Prince Ferdinand had to fall back upon the Weser—just as Lord Granby had feared might occur. The two French Armies then joined, and the superiority of their numbers made any immediate resistance indiscreet.

Lord Granby wrote from Alsfeld, regretting that he could not substitute "Frankfort," and announced this reverse to the Duke of Newcastle. The Allied Army had lost 2,000 men; but they were not dispirited, and the British cavalry had escaped well. The "Blues" had one officer, and four troopers, wounded, seven horses killed, and four wounded. He thought they would remain that night only in their cantonments; but Prince Ferdinand "kept all his movements secret, and marching orders never came out till late in the evening."

Captain G. L. Hall, (June 5, 1759), drew a plan of the affair at Bergen, saying "we don't allow it the name of a battle," and sent it to Thomas Thoroton, at Rutland House, for the Duke of Rutland. He put the Allied strength at 24,000, and that of the French at 30,000, with great superiority as regarded artillery which was well served, but "luckily every ball was buried where it struck, the ground being extremely soft and marshy." Their loss, including deserters, did not exceed 2,400, but all accounts placed that of the enemy at near 7,000 in killed and wounded.

The results of this "skirmish," "affair," or whatever it might be called, were sufficiently grave to warrant its being termed a battle outright. Prince Ferdinand's retreat by Ziegenhayn, Lippstadt, and Osnabrück towards Minden, on the River Weser, laid Münster, Cassel, and Göttingen at the mercy of the French, who at once garrisoned those places. In the east, affairs were even worse: defeated at Züllichau and Künersdorf, Frederick the Great's fortunes were reduced to so low an ebb that he meditated suicide. Dresden was in the hands of Marshal Daun; Saxony swept clear of Prussians; and only the dilatoriness of the Austrians in following up their successes prevented an end being put to a struggle which might have been known as the Three, instead of the Seven Years' War.

De Broglie ousted General Zastrow, and, intending to cut the Allies off from the Weser, possessed himself of Minden as Ferdinand approached from Osnabrück. Prince Ferdinand, outnumbered as he was, decided that a battle was inevitable if Hanover were to be saved. He advanced to Stolzenau on the Weser, which he bridged, and then encamped on the heath of Petershagen. Contades, on arrival, had placed his army with Minden on his right, a stream called the Bastau in front, while a morass protected his left flank. De Broglie crossed to the east side of the River Weser. Between the French camp and that of Prince Ferdinand lay Minden Heath, which was destined to become classic ground.

To attack a superior force in so naturally strong a position was a hopeless task, so Prince Ferdinand sought to lure his enemy to ground where the numerical inferiority of the Allied Army would be somewhat less important. Ferdinand's inspiration was to offer to the enemy an apparent chance of cutting off a large Corps, under General Wangenheim, which he left by the Weser, at Todenhausen; while he, with the main army, withdrew westwards towards Hille, out of sight of the French.

The ruse was successful; Contades left his camp and made for the bait, advancing (August 1, 1759) on to Minden Heath—a battlefield of Ferdinand's own choosing.

Wangenheim—the bait—remained in his position (in front of Todenhausen), rendered very strong with two batteries erected by Count La Lippe Bückebourg; but a rapid concentrative movement suddenly displayed, advanced to within touch of his right, the compact front of the whole Allied Army, whose left was thus covered by Wangenheim's Corps against De Broglie's operations, who re-crossed from the east bank of the Weser, and formed Contades' right wing. An ineffectual cannonade upon Wangenheim's batteries was all that De Broglie had to do with the Battle of Minden—the real struggle lay between Contades and Prince Ferdinand.

The order of battle on either side was exactly reversed. Contades placed his cavalry in the centre, flanked right and left by infantry: on the side of the Allies an infantry centre was flanked by cavalry, that on the right commanded by Lord George Sackville—"mark the sad name of him!" ejaculated Carlyle.

The French cavalry made several ineffectual charges, after repelling which the offensive was assumed by the English and Hanoverian infantry centre upon the French cavalry, and with such impetuosity that the latter was at once broken and disorganised.

The English "Minden" Regiments, "the unsurpassable six," (Kausler, quoted by Carlyle. The 12th, 37th, and 23rd Regiments suffered most, Newcastle Papers), were—

"Napier's,"	the 12th,	now the	Suffolk Regiment.
"Kingsley's,"	" 20th,	" "	Lancashire Fusiliers.
"Huske's,"	" 23rd,	" "	Royal Welsh Fusiliers.
"Home's,"	" 25th,	" "	King's Own Scottish Borderers.
"Stuart's,"	" 37th,	" "	1st Battn. Hampshire Regt.
"Brudenell's,"	" 51st,	" "	1st Battn. King's Own Yorkshire Light Infantry.

They advanced owing to a mistaken order, but once started nothing could equal the *élan* of their attack. As Lord George Sackville said in his evidence later, these six regiments, "it would scarcely be credited in future ages, by a single attack put to flight 40 battalions and 60 squadrons."

For a moment the French cavalry rallied, charged, and the Allied infantry, raked by a harassing cross fire, lost ground; but, supported by some artillery, the gallant infantry held their own, and the whole French Army retired in confusion into, and beyond, the town of Minden.

****

The French Army was estimated at 50,000; that of the Allies at 36,000. The Hereditary Prince with 10,000 men had been detached to attack a French post at Gohfeld, on the Werre. Not to be confounded with the River Werra.

****

As the infantry, under Generals Waldegrave and Kingsley, commenced their attack. Prince Ferdinand sent his *A.D.C.*, Captain Witzingerode, to Lord George Sackville with orders to advance with his cavalry towards the left and there form one line, on the fringe of the heath, in support of the infantry. The sudden collapse of the French cavalry centre, its recovery, and final retreat, caused Prince Ferdinand to send off in quick succession Captain Edward Ligonier, and Colonel Fitzroy with renewed orders to advance, and to profit by the opportunity of pursuing the retreating enemy.

Lord George argued, hesitated, and split hairs with these *aides-de-camp,* finally saying that their orders were conflicting, and that he would repair personally to Prince Ferdinand for instructions. He found the prince, unruffled and courteous, who merely repeated his original order which, in despair, he had just sent by Wintzingerode and Fitzroy to the Marquess of Granby, remarking: "I know he will obey me!"

Lord Granby, commanding the 2nd Line of the cavalry of the right wing, had all this while been sitting impatient for action, but out of sight of what was going on, and ignorant of Sackville's conduct. With him were Mostyn and General Elliott. (Not the General Elliot of "Elliot's Light Horse.") As Lord George returned from Prince Ferdinand's presence, he saw the 2nd Line of cavalry advancing under Lord Granby, whom he twice halted. Another message partially informed Lord Granby of the state of affairs, and he at once galloped on with the 2nd Line, but it was too late. He never got near the enemy, who was thus enabled to retreat under the ramparts of Minden, and all chance was lost to the cavalry leaders of carrying disaster beyond retrieval into the French Army, or of seeing themselves in the *Gazette.*

The Hereditary Prince successfully cut out the French post, at Gohfeld, which he pursued hotly to the Weser; so, abandoning Minden and Cassel, De Broglie and Contades retreated southwards, having sustained a loss of 6,000 men in killed, wounded, and prisoners, thirty pieces of cannon, ten colours, and seven standards. Hanover was saved; but England's whole object in the war ought to have been at the same time won.

Sismondi wrote:

> Contades' Army should have been annihilated: men, horses, cannon, colours—all should have fallen into the hands of the enemy.

Archenholz declared that:

> The greatest defeat of this century seemed certain, when the faithlessness of an English general saved the French from com-

plete destruction.

The Marechal de Contades, who commended his wounded, left in Minden, to Ferdinand's charity, was recalled in consequence of this defeat: De Broglie was made a Marshal of France and Commander-in-Chief of the Army in Germany. Among Contades' captured papers were instructions of the cruellest description issued by the French Government for the devastation of the districts involved in the war. To reinforce De Broglie the Comte de St. Germain, with 80,000 men, was sent to the Rhine.

The Allies encamped on the battlefield, and, on the evening of Minden, Lord George Sackville, with the utmost composure, took his place among the general officers that dined with Prince Ferdinand, who exclaimed in blank astonishment: "*Voilà cet homme autant à son aise commc s'il avait fait des merveilles!*"

The "Orders of the Day" issued the day after the battle embodied Prince Ferdinand's thanks to the whole army, and especially to the English infantry and artillery, to whom the chief honours were due, and who had sustained the main share of the losses.

★★★★★★★★★★

Prince Ferdinand wrote personally to Captain Macbean: "It is to you and your brigade that I am indebted for having silenced the fire of a battery of the enemy, which extremely galled the troops, and particularly the British infantry."

★★★★★★★★★★

Upon the Marquess of Granby, who happened to be general of the day, the duty devolved of conveying the prince's thanks to the British troops.

The "Orders" continued:—

> His Serene Highness further orders it to be declared to Lieut.-General the Marquess of Granby that he is persuaded that, if he had had the good fortune to have had him at the head of the cavalry of the right wing, his presence would have greatly contributed to make the decision of the day more complete and more brilliant.

An intimation followed that in future the most implicit obedience to orders was demanded.

Lord George Sackville at once wrote to Prince Ferdinand, demanding a withdrawal of the compliment to Lord Granby, which was an indirect censure upon himself. The prince emphatically refused;

and Lord George, on August 3, 1759, laid the matter before Lord Holdernesse, Secretary of State, and requested his own recall from the German command.

Until August 13, nothing had been officially reported home, concerning Sackville, from the Allied Headquarters; but, in consequence of the attitude he was assuming, and the statements he was circulating among the troops. Prince Ferdinand, on that date, requested that Lord George might be recalled.

His Majesty replied that Prince Ferdinand's application had been anticipated by Lord George's wish to return home *on leave.* An announcement (*London Gazette*, August, 1759), followed that His Majesty had been pleased to appoint the Marquess of Granby, Lieut.-General, (Lieut.-General, February 5, 1759), of His Majesty's Forces, to be Commander-in-Chief of all His Majesty's British Forces then serving under the command of Prince Ferdinand in Germany.

On signifying this to the prince the king wrote:

"*J'espère que ma nomination du Lord Granby pour commander mes troupes Britanniques vous a été agréeable.*"

And the prince answered:

"*Je ne saurais me loner assez du zêle, et de l'empressement que Mylord Granby témoigne pour concourir à tout ce que le service de Votre Majesté exige.*"

Lord Granby duly received his official appointments, and instructions to take over from Lord George Sackville's secretary all his cyphers and papers.

The same *Gazette* contained the promotion of Major-General Mostyn to be Lieut.-General; and he thereupon succeeded to the position of second in command vacated by the marquess.

Lord Granby's own letter (to the Duke of Newcastle. August 3, 1759), concerning Minden must now be recorded; it was written two days after the battle, when the indignation in camp was at its height, but it avoids all allusion to that, or to any disappointment, whatever, having befallen him.

> My Dear Lord,—I take this opportunity of my friend Col. Fitzroy's setting out for England to congratulate Your Grace on the compleat victory gained by Duke Ferdinand: all the troops engaged behaved with the utmost bravery; the British infantry and artillery have gained the greatest honour. General Waldegrave's (Lieut.-General, April 10, 1759), behaviour has merited the ap-

plause of everybody in the army and deservedly. General Kingsley, (Lieut.-General, December 13, 1760), behaved likewise with the utmost gallantry. Your friends Jack Mostyn and John Granby were not engaged, yet don't think they behaved ill.

You will have much better accounts of the battle than I can give, from many hands. I shall end therefore with my sincere wishes of happiness to my dear friend Lincoln (Lord Lincoln. Granby's cousin, and nephew and heir of the Duke of Newcastle), and to Your Grace.

Not a syllable in this letter suggests the furious indignation which was then raging throughout the British cavalry division, and the whole Allied Army.

The Duke of Newcastle replied:—

I had in Sussex your short, proper, and manly letter so becoming yourself, your high rank, and superior way of thinking. I little thought I should so soon have an occasion of congratulating Your Lordship upon the greatest distinction which a soldier can, at this time, have—I mean the command of all H.M.'s troops under Prince Ferdinand. I am truly sorry for Lord George Sackville whom I have long known. I don't trouble him with a letter upon this occasion, neither do I know whether it may be proper for you to say anything from me to him upon it. I must leave that to Your Lordship's discretion and judgment. . . . I believe His Majesty never conferred a command with more pleasure and more confidence than he did this upon Your Lordship; I don't mean to plead merit, for the whole was over before I came to town.

A letter has gone astray from the *Newcastle Papers* which would have been most interesting as expressing Jack Mostyn's opinion of Sackville in his "slap dash," picturesque style.

Newcastle replied to it:—

I don't wonder that you were vexed at not being engaged, but no mortal can blame you, and by what I heard by chance, in a little closet at Kensington, you will I believe soon see that the king is as gracious to you as ever . . . above all be well with Granby and I think nobody can be ill with him.

A second letter of Mostyn's affords some idea of what pungent matter his first contained:—

> .... Knowing how things of this sort are taken up and handled in England I could not but look upon myself as unlucky to have had ye chance of 2 battles in one campaign without a right to be mentioned in a *Gazette*. No more mention made in those damned newspapers of your humble servant than as if 'Noll Bluff' had not been in the land of the living.... Our present commander told me how kindly Your Grace mentioned me in your letter to him and at the same time expressed himself very kindly to me from his own acquaintance, and good opinion of me. I have no doubt of maturing it: we are very happy under his command.

The Marquess of Granby acknowledged the Duke of Newcastle's congratulations, and said he had desired Lord Holdernesse to convey his grateful and dutiful thanks to His Majesty.

At home the Duke of Rutland addressed the following very considerate letter to the Duke of Newcastle:—

> Belvoir Castle, Aug. 20, 1759.
>
> My Lord,—His Majesty's great goodness to Lord Granby and the height to which he has raised his reputation by the confidence he hath reposed in him determined me to repair to London purposely to return my most dutyfull and grateful thanks to His Majesty for this transcendant mark of his gracious favour to my son. But the apprehensions I labour under that it may carry the appearance of exulting over the misfortunes of an unhappy person to whom I am also related determined me to defer executing this my purpose untill length of time might free me from the censure of disregarding the sorrows of others provided their affliction turned to the honour and credit of my family. If Your Grace is of opinion that in this point I reason right, I must sollicite the continuance of your goodness to me and mine by representing at a proper opportunity to His Majesty this my reason for continuing at this place: for it would prove the most penetrating affliction to lye under the suspicion of ingratitude, or that His Majesty should conceive that I wanted that high sense I ought to have of this distinguishing mark of favour to my son.
>
> I am, &c., &c.,
>
> Rutland.

★★★★★★★★★★

> The connection between the Rutland and Dorset families was but a remote one. Lord John Sackville (brother to Lord George) having married into the Bedford family of which Catherine (daughter of Lord Russell and Lady Rachel Russell was the first wife of the second Duke of Rutland.

★★★★★★★★★★

Newcastle acquainted Granby (August 24) with having received his father's letter, and in reference to the late appointment said—

> It pleases me to hear what universal satisfaction it gives; . . . and delighted me to see the Dutchess of Somerset, (Lady Granby's mother), and Lady Granby at Court to make their compliments to His Majesty. I hear Your Lordship is to have the honour of investing Prince Ferdinand with the Garter.

Granby's next letter to Newcastle (August 29) announced an affair at Wetter, from which camp he dated, and De Broglie's retreat to Marburg. He had appointed Lieut.-Colonel Browne to be his secretary, and hoped the king would allow Browne to remain in that capacity, as he was useful to him; more especially as familiar with the arrangements for the large number of French prisoners then on their hands.

A long private letter was enclosed, which is too interesting to abridge, written after the Allies had started in pursuit of De Broglie—

> Wetter Camp.—I can assure Your Grace our friend Jack never signed any paper, (in allusion to a report that Mostyn had signed a paper exonerating Lord George Sackville), he even contrived not to read any. The night the duke's orders came out Lord George desired me to come to his quarters, when after complaining at the duke's cruel treatment of him he shewed me a paper which (as he believed I knew it to be true) he hoped I would sign; I answered there were many things in it I was quite ignorant of—orders delivered to him that I had never heard of till after the battle, and therefore did not know the time he received them, or how he put them into execution. In regard to what I knew myself of matters of fact I differed with him in several things, and therefore could not possibly sign the paper. He then proposed to me to write a letter to the duke to clear him of some particular things relating to myself that he said was laid to his charge in regard to his halting the 2nd Line.
>
> I told him I had already repeated to him several times all I could say in regard to matters of fact concerning the orders for

> halting which I received from him: that he was the best judge in regard to his own affairs; if he thought those facts could be of any service to him in regard to his conduct on the day of battle, I should truly declare to the duke, if he called upon me, everything I knew, but I did not understand French enough to explain myself in a letter. I was then desired to let a letter be indited for me which I might sign if it pleased me—a letter was begun and almost finished, but it was so contrary to my inclinations and way of thinking that I stop't it by declaring I could not sign it; His Lordship has shewn a paper to most of the field officers of cavalry none of whom, I am almost confident, have signed any paper, nor, as I know, in any shape given their opinion of it.
>
> In regard to Lord George's conduct and behaviour that day the First Line are the best judges of, as they saw how he acted on his receiving his orders to advance; I never saw him but once, never knew of the orders he had received from Ligonier and Fitzroy, never received any orders from him but those for halt. Your Grace will excuse me if I remind Your Grace of my friend and lieutenant-colonel, (Lieut.-Colonel Johnston, of the Royal Horse Guards): it was unhappy for him that the Blues had not an opportunity of shewing that the pains he had for so many years been at in disciplining them was not thrown away, and I flatter myself this unfortunate affair will not prevent his succeeding in the purchase of General Brown's Regiment.

The above letter, written by this "young man of no capacity," (Walpole so described him), Newcastle later acknowledged, and said he had read it to the king, who was extremely pleased with it, especially that part relating to Jack Mostyn.

Upon hearing of the victory of the Allied Army, Sir Edward Hawke, who was watching the English Channel for the French fleet destined for the invasion of England, drew up his fleet before Brest and indulged in a tremendous *feu de joie.* He then sent a polite message by a Dutchman who was putting into Brest, explaining that the demonstration was in honour of Prince Ferdinand's glorious victory!

Lord Granby, who now led the 1st Column of the Army, consisting of both lines of the cavalry of the right, next wrote (to Lord Granby), from the camp at Niederweimar. He said the good news received of successes in other parts of the world had put everyone in the highest spirits—with the invariable, eighteenth-century consequence that "a Bumper to the good news went about."

Attention must now be directed towards London, where the first news of Minden was received with an acclamation untempered by any reservations. Lord Holdernesse assured Prince Ferdinand "*ce n'étoit qu'illuminations et Feux de Joye, et Vive le Prince Ferdinand!*"

Horace Walpole described how every house in London was illuminated; every street had two bonfires, and every bonfire had two hundred squibs. Then his ill-nature crept in, and, little knowing of Lord Granby's own modest and unresentful disclaimer of any share in the Minden glories, he wrote to Sir Horace Mann—

> We conclude Prince Ferdinand received all his directions from Lord Granby, who is the Mob's hero. . . . Lord Granby has defeated the French! The foreign *Gazettes*, I suppose, will give this victory to Prince Ferdinand, but the mob of London, whom I have this minute left, and who know best, assure me that it is all their own marquess's doing!

The first despatches had been brought by the prince's English *aides-de-camp*, the Duke of Richmond and Colonel Fitzroy, and contained no allusions to Sackville. But rumours began to spread that something was wrong in Germany. Doubtless the two *aides-de-camp* let fall some whispers concerning the cavalry of the right wing. At all events the whispers increased in scope and volume until they grew into a roar of indignation which rivalled that directed against Admiral Byng, and the facts one by one crept out. The Sackville topic entirely engrossed society and the general public.

Walpole, as usual, knew everything—or thought he did. To his deservedly favourite cousin Conway he wrote—

> You have heard, I suppose, of the violent animosities that have reigned for the whole campaign between him (Lord George) and Lord Granby, in which some other warm persons, (in allusion to Prince Ferdinand), have been very warm too.

And elsewhere, relevant to this period and episode, Walpole placed the following upon record, in considering which it must be distinctly remembered that the removal of Lord George Sackville from the Army secured the advancement of Granby, not Conway, whom Walpole held to be Sackville's only rival:—

> Lord Granby. . . . .was an honest, open-hearted young man of

> undaunted spirit and no capacity, and of such unbounded generosity and good nature that it is impossible to say which principle actuated him most in the distribution of the prodigious sums which he flung away. If he wanted any recommendation to Prince Ferdinand besides these ductile qualities, he drank as profusely as a German. Lord George's haughtiness lost him this young man, as it had lost him the Duke of Marlboro'. Between these two Lords (Sackville and Granby) a coolness soon ensued, and divided the army—if it can be called 'division' where almost every heart sympathized with Lord Granby.

This allegation of "violent animosities" having existed between the two British commanders has been repeated, upon Walpole's authority, in various works relating to the time, though it is uncorroborated, and easily refutable. The Duke of Newcastle, notwithstanding all his shortcomings as a statesman, was at that date certainly among the best *informed* men in Europe—using the word "informed" in its strict sense. He knew what was going on in every department of the State; he had his correspondents and confidants in every Court and camp in Europe; and, above all, there was scarcely a back-staircase that did not harbour one of his dependent listeners. In his encyclopaedic correspondence there is no mention of this raging "animosity"; and, that he was ignorant of any is plain in that he delegated to Lord Granby's discretion and judgment any expression, on His Grace's behalf, of sorrow or condolence with Lord George after his supersedure in the command.

Major-General Yorke, through whose hands all the war news passed, wrote that neither Prince Lewis of Brunswick nor himself had ever heard anything, at the Hague, of any disputes, or bickerings, having occurred between the generals prior to the Battle of Minden. (General Yorke was Minister at the Hague).

Next, to whom did Lord George, the day after Minden, turn for countenance and assistance in the strait in which he found himself, but to the Marquess of Granby himself?

Further, when the court martial at length was summoned. Lord George objected to one or two of the men selected to try him—notably to a General Belford, (Walpole called him Colonel Balfour), of the artillery, and he was withdrawn. Had there been "animosities," would not Sackville have objected to Granby's uncle, General Lord Robert Manners', presence as a member of the Court? Yet Lord Robert sat unchallenged throughout the trial.

Last, and as usual, not least, we have the testimony of a man who had nothing to learn from Walpole in any department of life, and who at this particular juncture was serving with the Allied Army, and was an eye-witness of the facts in dispute. Lord Fitzmaurice, afterwards Lord Shelburne, says in his autobiography—

> Lord Granby took decidedly the line of Prince Ferdinand from *no motive of jealousy or ill-will to Lord George*, to whom he always behaved with more than respect, and a degree of honour which went the length of delicacy on all occasions, and refinement upon some (in reference to Lord Granby's conduct at the court martial); but from motives of probity, generosity of nature, and a laudable ambition.

★★★★★★★★★★

Lord Shelburne, later first Marquess of Lansdowne and Prime Minister. The secret of the identity of "Junius" is said to have died with him.—*Life of Lord Shelburne*, by Lord E. Fitzmaurice

★★★★★★★★★★

The question may arise in the reader's mind—why this flogging of a horse dead since 140 years? The answer is because the episode affords a typical specimen of Walpole's inaccuracy, of which he has been found guilty by a long array of commentators and editors, as well as by all who study his pages for information as apart from merely reading them for amusement. Lord Granby's character chiefly rests, historically, upon what Walpole wrote concerning him; and the same looseness of statement which marks this Sackville episode should be carefully borne in mind in relation to more important events in Granby's life hereafter dealt with.

Chapter 7

1759: Münster and Quiberon Bay

After the Battle of Minden, the French Army remained for some time at Giessen, south of the River Lahn; and Prince Ferdinand fixed his principal headquarters at Osnabrück. He began at once to besiege Münster, which the French governor declared he would defend to the last, in spite of the protests of the unfortunate inhabitants. The success of the Allies had enabled Prince Ferdinand to detach the Hereditary Prince with 15,000 men to the assistance of Frederick the Great, in Saxony; and meanwhile Ferdinand gradually crept nearer to De Broglie's camp.

On his arrival home, Lord George Sackville met the storm of execration and abuse which awaited him with the most perfect *sangfroid*, and at once demanded a court martial. Old Lord Ligonier, who had probably keenly envied Sackville's brilliant, but neglected, chance of as nice a ride after Frenchmen as a dragoon could wish, bluntly declared that if Lord George desired a court martial "he had best go seek it in Germany."

Both the king and Lord Barrington, the War Secretary, preferred that Sackville should voluntarily sink into oblivion; but, as he persisted in asserting himself, the king gave him another earnest of His Majesty's opinion by stripping him of all his military employments. Sackville so far had merely resigned the German command, and was home, nominally, on leave.

The Lieutenant-Generalship of the Ordnance was promptly bestowed by the king upon the Marquess of Granby, and the Colonelcy of the 2nd, Queen's, Dragoon Guards upon General Waldegrave.

The Duke of Newcastle acquainted Lord Granby of his promotion, and volunteered some hints respecting the Ordnance department which would require a great deal of attention so soon as a peace should afford the necessary leisure.

Lord Granby's news was now dated principally from Kroffsdorf, about two miles from, and in easy sight of, the enemy's position at Giessen. A draft of 432 men had reached him, *via* Emden, to partly repair the Minden casualties, but in future he desired that the mouth of the Weser might be adopted, instead of that of the Ems, as the point of disembarkation. Münster was partly in flames; Marburg and Cassel were gained to the Allies by the Prince of Bevern; the Hereditary Prince and General Wangenheim had defeated a large body of "Fischer's Irregulars," (a Free Corps in the service of France), thus clearing the heights near Wetter. Granby was in great hopes of hearing that these successes were to be followed by better news of Frederick the Great's struggle with the Russians. The marquess' due acknowledgment was made, through Lord Holdernesse, for the confidence the king had shown in him—

> . . . . a confidence I shall try to deserve by strictly attending to the great trust reposed in me, and by zealously, as far as depends on me, promoting on every occasion the good of the Service in which I have the honour to be engaged.

The Duke of Rutland left Belvoir for London to thank His Majesty, of whom he received an audience, together with leave to return at once to Belvoir. The duke wrote his thanks, from Rutland House, to the Duke of Newcastle, whom he begged to excuse him from calling at Newcastle House, as it would oblige him to make other visits instead of returning directly to the country.

★★★★★★★★★★

Newcastle House (formerly Powis House) still, (1899), survives at the north-west angle of Lincoln's Inn Fields; here the Duke of Newcastle transacted most of his multifarious business and held his levees. His hospitality at Newcastle House, as well as at Claremont, was conducted on a magnificent scale.

★★★★★★★★★★

In France great preparations were at this time being made in fitting out "*la Grande Expédition*" which was to invade England—weather, and Sir Edward Hawke, permitting—under the command of Conflans, and Prince Soubise.

Granby wrote:

> I find, that the French are determined to risk an invasion. If they do, I hope our ships will give a good account of them; for though I should not be very apprehensive of the consequences

> were they to land, yet I can't help saying that if our troops should be deprived of the pleasure of drubbing them on land by our ships sinking them at sea, it would save some trouble and a great deal of hurry—so I shall not be sorry.

News of the fall of Quebec, General Wolfe's death, and Monckton's wounds, reached Granby at Kroffsdorf. His friend George Townshend had also distinguished himself, to whose uncle, the Duke of Newcastle, Granby wrote his congratulations. A *feu de joie* was ordered at Kroffsdorf, and during its course the French camp kept up a continual "opposition" beating of drums, and firing of small arms.

To the Duke of Newcastle Lord Granby, expressing great sorrow for the loss of General Wolfe, and for Monckton's condition who was said to be mortally wounded, wrote:—

> If the French really intend making a great effort to get once more into Hanover, considering the superiority of their numbers and without an augmentation of our army here, I can't help being apprehensive of the consequences, notwithstanding the bravery of our troops and the great abilities of the wise and good prince who commands them.

★★★★★★★★★★

Newcastle wrote of Monckton as "Granby's cousin." John Monckton. first Viscount Galway, married Lady Elizabeth Manners, daughter of the second Duke of Rutland. Monckton figures in West's picture, "the Death of General Wolfe," and in sundry Wedgwood cameo-portraits.

★★★★★★★★★★

> What may be the consequence should we be obliged to retire towards the Weser, and Hesse again fall into the hands of the French, I shall not pretend to determine; but during my stay in that country after the affair of Bergen, on the appearance and rumours that we should march soon to Lippstadt, I found great discontent among them, and, on our quitting Cassel, bitter complaints on their being abandoned again to the enemy. These reasons made me earnestly wish to be strong enough to act with two armies—an offensive and defensive one; 60,000 effectives for the offensive and 30,000 for the defensive would make me easy about the event, though the enemy would still be much superior to us.

As the probability of winter-quarters, for both the Allied and French Armies, increased, Lord Granby began to talk of returning to

England, where he could the better expedite many matters of consequence. The weather in November became very rainy—

> Our camp is in a very terribly dirty condition: we comfort ourselves the French are quite as badly off. They have marched some troops into cantonments on the road to Frankfort, and we are in hopes their whole army will soon take the same road. Our whole army forages today round the country for 6 days; there is no mention yet of where our winter-quarters are to be.

The *Rutland MSS.* contain little at this period (August to December, 1759) save official letters concerning artillery, pontoons, horses, military-train, etc., and Lord Granby's life is chronicled much more fully in the *Newcastle Papers*. Forgetting, nevertheless, that Granby now had to write officially to Lords Holdernesse, Barrington, and Ligonier, the Duke of Newcastle began to complain of the infrequency of Granby's private letters to him. Newcastle's thirst for news was unquenchable, and his tendency was always to suspect people of want of recognition, of ingratitude, and general neglect towards him, unless they assured him repeatedly to the contrary. The mails were unpunctual, and the duke would write and upbraid Granby for his silence, and then acknowledge, a few hours later, the simultaneous arrival of two or three letters from him.

The Marquess of Granby, in a sense, was a bad correspondent. He hated writing, a feeling which he shared in good military company, (the Duke of Marlborough detested writing), and indited his despatches and letters in as weak, colourless, and characterless a hand as could, by some queer psychological freak, have become evolved from so spontaneously energetic and masculine a nature. In composition his letters were clear, easy, and concise; and he had a conspicuous faculty of expressing himself in direct, unconstrained language upon difficult occasions, when a nature less frank would have sought refuge in platitude, and the commonplace.

In October the Duke of Newcastle had querulously complained of Granby's neglect, and was plainly hungering for gratitude concerning the Ordnance appointment; and then, in a postscript, acknowledged two letters both of which expressed Granby's cordial thanks, and modest pleasure at the honour done him. These the duke read to the king, "who promised himself everything that could be expected from Lord Granby's zeal and affection." People in England, the duke suggested, would be easier could they hear that Dresden was once more in the hands of the Allies, and that General Imhoff was master of Münster. In extenuation of his shortcomings as a correspondent, Granby wrote:—

> When I first began to be a man of business, I forgot to set down the dates of letters received and answered, with many other things that a real man of business would be astonished at; but I find I begin to improve, though it has cost me many a headache.

All being quiet. Lord Granby now applied for leave of absence, should the king approve; but heard through the Duke of Newcastle that His Majesty expected a winter campaign, and was afraid of too many officers being absent from the seat of war. As Granby "was so deservedly high in His Majesty's favour," Newcastle dissuaded him from leaving until the campaign was obviously closed, and thus summed up the situation:—

> We all here see the necessity of an augmentation to Prince Ferdinand's Army, but in our present circumstances it is impossible to send any troops from hence. Monsieur Conflans is sailed with his whole fleet to invade this country or Ireland, and our best intelligence tolls us that the great expedition is still behind: that the regiments detached from the French Army in Germany (of which we have no account from Prince Ferdinand or Your Lordship) and the troops now in the Low Countries are all designed to make an attempt on England in the month of December under the Marshal Soubise. Our fleets, thank God, are strong and numerous.
>
> Prince Ferdinand will receive a letter by this post desiring and authorising him to get any troops he can—Swiss, German deserters, or Regular German troops—in order to augment and strengthen his army. . . . But English we have not to send. I have now, my dear Granby, told you the state of our case. I see plainly your situation. You want and you ought to have 2 armies, but the question is, Where to get them? . . . And now to the agreeable side of our present situation.
>
> Sir Edward Hawke, with a great superiority of force (strengthened since by the most manly resolution of Admiral Saunders, who is gone to join Hawke with the ships returned with him from Quebec), is in full pursuit of Monsieur Conflans, and there is the finest prospect that the whole navy of France may, by the Blessing of God, have before this time received a most fatal blow. What a most glorious end of this most glorious war

would that be! . . . I drink your health almost every day. . . . Lord Lincoln is shooting. My love to Jack Mostyn. . . . Lord Robert, Lord George, and Thoroton are all pure well. (*Newcastle Papers*, November 23, 1759).

Upon assuming the Command-in-Chief, Lord Granby was at once confronted with what was to become his *bête noire* in the form of commissariat estimates, and dealings with the Hanoverian Chancellerie in respect of maintenance of the subsidised troops, and the French prisoners in the hands of the Allies.

Of the commissariat difficulties Lord George Sackville had already complained. The king had decided that his Hanoverian provinces should pay contributions in specie in lieu of providing the Allied Army with corn, etc., at reasonable prices fixed by the commanders-in-chief. The result was that the British Exchequer reaped no benefit from the contributions, since it paid three times the proper value of the corn supplied.

Newcastle, on behalf of the Treasury, and always fearing the enmity of Baron Münchhausen and the Hanoverian Ministers, urged Lord Granby to lose no time in giving the necessary certificate for the sum of £20,000, which should then be remitted to the Hanover *Chancellerie* for the maintenance of the French prisoners. These were some 38,000 already. (*Newcastle Papers,* October 19, 1759. Granby to Newcastle).

In October and November, 1759, Granby wrote 2 concerning the claims of the *Chancellerie*, but without showing the slightest intention of passing them without thorough investigation, in spite of Newcastle's hints that such a course would be agreeable in high quarters. It was not until January, 1760, that Granby concluded the claims then pending, in spite of Newcastle's exclamation of, "Have done with the *Chancellerie*, and pay it!"

On the 16th of January, Granby informed His Grace that he had received the thanks of the Regency of Hanover, embodying those also of the King of England, for the manner in which he had conducted the negotiations to a close. The utter absence of a proper British department to organize the supply of the army caused the occurrence of a period of chaotic confusion, and resultless expenditure, which will be alluded to later.

George II. having bestowed the Garter upon Prince Ferdinand for his services at Minden, the arrangements were made for the Investiture. (Besides the Order of the Garter Prince Ferdinand received £20,000, a large portion of which, Archenholz says, he distributed among his officers and men). The Marquess of Granby had written to congratulate the prince on this honour, the nature of which he explained in August (1759); and in November, Mr. S. M. Leake, Garter King of Arms, was sent over with powers appointing the Marquess of Granby First Plenipotentiary, and himself Second, to carry out the ceremony. A large and a small tent were prepared at Kroffsdorf, impudently placed within full view of the French Camp. Prince Ferdinand, escorted by a detachment of the Blues, was met by a procession consisting of—

The Marquess of Granby's Secretary, (probably Colonel Browne, but he employed more than one), carrying the hood;

Colonel Fitzroy, A.D.C. to Prince Ferdinand, carrying the collar;

Colonel Ligonier, A.D.C. to Prince Ferdinand, carrying the cap and feather; and,

The Marquess of Granby, First Plenipotentiary.

Arrived at the smaller tent, Prince Ferdinand sat down with the Plenipotentiaries on either side. The bands played while the Investiture was proceeded with. The Marquess of Granby then rose and made a short speech in French, to which the prince responded. A roll of drums ensued, and the trumpets sounded, while the procession adjourned to the large tent in which a great dinner was given by the Marquess of Granby.

****

"The ceremony and feast of conferring the Order of the Garter upon H.S. Highness was performed and kept by the Marquess of Granby in the grandest manner upon a hill within sight of the French Army" (G. A. de Reiche, October 26, 1759, *Newcastle Papers*)

****

Prince Ferdinand dined in the habit of his Order, his cap being held behind his chair. At the second course the prince rose, assumed his cap, again removed it, and drank—

Firstly, the British sovereign's health.
Secondly, the rest of the royal family.
Thirdly, the Knights Companions of the Garter.

The Marquess of Granby rose, and in return drank—

Firstly, Prince Ferdinand's health.

Secondly, the rest of his family.

Thirdly, the King of Prussia.

Since it may be confidently assumed that all these healths were pledged in bumpers, they constituted a formidable beginning to the evening which was yet "young." Next day Prince Ferdinand gave a return banquet, and both (the *Gazette* discreetly remarks) were conducted "with as much order and splendour as the circumstances of the camp would permit."

Lord Granby announced the fall, on November 20, of Münster, which, with the arrival of any good news from Saxony, would soon give them winter-quarters, he hoped, at Frankfort, where the joining them of 20,000 Prussians would end the campaign happily. They heard that Marshal Daun was retreating fast with the King of Prussia at his heels, and meantime the Allied Army was gradually going into cantonments.

The king consented to Lord Granby's return home as soon as winter-quarters were definitely assumed, and, in his absence, the command was to devolve upon General Mostyn. Newcastle wrote:

> Give my kindest love to him, and tell him I know he can *follow*, when you are gone we shall see whether he can *lead*.

As to the reinforcements, desired so strenuously by Lord Granby, both the king and Lord Ligonier said it was impossible to spare a man from England, which they were assured was shortly to be attacked by the "*Grande Expédition,*" consisting of 30,000 or 40,000 men under Prince Soubise.

These fears were finally put a stop to by Sir Edward Hawke's splendid victory over Admiral Conflans' Fleet at Quiberon Bay, the news of which Newcastle sent to Granby in a most exultant letter. The total destruction of the French fleet put Granby and the whole army in the best spirits; he was full of hopes that Admiral Saunders and George Townshend had arrived in time from Quebec, in making which attempt his "friend George had acted with his usual spirit." Lord Granby was still quartered at Kroffsdorf, and the king might be assured, he wrote, that all home-coming that winter would depend upon affairs in Germany.

At Fulda the Hereditary Prince had, by one of his daring adventures, surprised and made prisoners three battalions of Wurtemburg Grenadiers on November 30. The Duke of Wurtemburg, with 10,000 men was then serving, with a sort of roving commission, in the French cause, and—

> . . . .the grenadiers were powdered for a *feu de joye* that was intended the morning they were surprised, and the Duke of Wurtemburg was to have given a great dinner, ball, and supper at night to the ladies—but the Hereditary Prince very uncivilly spoilt their sport!

★★★★★★★★★★

Frederick the Great said the Duke of Wurtemburg foraged and ravaged the country without distinction between friend and foe, and was followed by "*toute une Synagogue de Juifs,*" to whom he sold his booty.

★★★★★★★★★★

Following upon his complaints of Granby's correspondence, the Duke of Newcastle assured him that he had most quickly become a "man of business," and that with perseverance none would do better than he. Granby acknowledged the compliment, saying—

> I am afraid I am but a Jade, and that I shall 'train off;' however if I keep in any form above an hackney I hope Your Grace will not strip me and turn me out of the string, but give me another year's training. I send this by my honest friend Ned Harvey whom I strongly recommend to Your Grace as a man I most sincerely love and have the greatest confidence in.

The victory of Quiberon Bay caused an immediate relaxation of the strain upon England's resources, and peace was even talked of as a probable result of France's disaster. A meeting of "the King's Servants" was at once held to consider the augmentation of the Allied Army, and the result of their deliberations sent direct to Prince Ferdinand.

Newcastle was in high feather at the collapse of Admiral Conflans—

> Last year England was to be invaded, our fleets destroyed, etc., at present I hear they intend to turn their whole force against your army, and the king's Canadian dominions. Give a good stroke during the winter, and I will engage they give you no further trouble.

A hard frost succeeded the wet weather which had made the camp at Kroffsdorf so wretched, and Lord Granby sustained an accident. His horse fell on the slippery ground, and a blow on His Lordship's eye culminated in a severe inflammation, for which, according to the habit of the day, he "was twice blooded." This trivial accident is only mentioned in order to note that the king heard of it with much regret, saying, "how remarkably satisfied *all* his people were with Lord Granby," who he hoped would be able to regulate all there was to be settled before coming home. During his absence, the Treasury thought the power of issuing money to meet current expenses would have to be vested in the Commander-in-Chief *pro tem.*, General Mostyn.

However, Granby's departure was still impossible. He sent his congratulations on New Year's Day to the Duke of Newcastle. A visit from the enemy had been expected for several days, and the troops had passed one entire night under arms, and in line of battle. De Broglie was plainly meditating some stroke, and probably wished to try conclusions with the Allies before the Hereditary Prince rejoined them with his 15,000 men:—

> . . . If fight should be Monsieur de Broglie's intention, though our army may not perhaps be quite so numerous as the enemy, we doubt not of success, as our troops are in great spirits and wish nothing better than to fight the French for winter-quarters.

De Broglie gradually retired from the Lahn towards Frankfort, and the Allied camp was moved northwards, and the headquarters established at Marburg. Granby had quite recovered from his accident, and said he had "the pleasure of living in the greatest harmony and friendship with good General Spörcken, and Count Kilmansegge; Mostyn and Waldegrave the same."

He was much concerned to hear that the king had seemed displeased at the presence, at a levee, of so many officers holding cavalry commands in Germany. Prince Ferdinand had authorised Lord Granby to send home all the recruiting parties, or officers whom he deemed should go; and Harvey, of the "Inniskillings", Johnston, of the "Blues", Preston, of the "Greys" and Sloper of the 1st King's Dragoon Guards, were all sent on account of the necessity of buying horses for their regiments.

The king was greatly pleased with Granby's letter of New Year's Day, and with his eagerness to fight the French for winter-quarters. Newcastle wrote—

> Lord Robert Sutton has been most obliging to me and has taken our militia in Notts: this will have the best effect here. . . . It is the greatest satisfaction to me to hear that everybody who

> comes from the army is equally full of Your Lordship's praises. The king is satisfied with you beyond measure, and that makes my business go on very comfortably.

The campaign was now over. De Broglie established himself in Frankfort; the Allied Army had marched northwards, and was comfortably settled in winter-quarters in Cassel, Paderborn, Münster, and Osnabrück, and Lord Granby's thoughts were turning with relief towards his wife and children, towards Belvoir, and the hounds and horses from which he had so long been separated. Mr. Pitt was seriously at work upon the reinforcements, the Hanover Chancellerie was settled with for the time being, and everything promised a pleasant holiday. But a shadow was stealing over this fair prospect of which Lord Granby was totally unaware until it assumed, in a moment and without warning, a darkness as of night. The Marchioness of Granby was taken suddenly ill, and, after two or three days, died on January 25, 1760.

Lady Granby, who was thirty-two at the time of her death, succumbed to an attack, in the head, of what was then known as "St. Anthony's Fire," or *erysipelas*—"a St. Anthony's Fire which struck in, and seized her brain," as Mrs. Grenville wrote in allusion to the event.

★★★★★★★★★★

Lady Rachel Russell, writing July 1, 1686, to Dr. Fitzwilliam, alluded to her eldest girl being ill of "St. Anthony's Fire, as we call it." In 1089 an epidemic of, supposed, *erysipelas* prevailed, especially in France. Public prayers were instituted for the removal of the pestilence. Some miraculous cures were announced as due to the prayers to St. Anthony, and the disease was named "St. Anthony's Fire."—*Lives of the Saints* (Rev. A. Butler).

★★★★★★★★★★

Walpole wrote:

> There has been cruel work among the ladies; My Lady Granby is dead, and the famous Polly, (in allusion to the part played formerly by the duchess, *née* Lavinia Fenton of "Polly Peachum" in the *Beggar's Opera*), Duchess of Bolton, and Lady Bessborough.

A very unreliable authority, (Mrs. George Anne Bellamy, in her *Apology for her Life*), in allusion to the same circumstance, says that Lord Granby was devotedly fond of his wife, and a false report of his having been killed in Germany brought on the attack which so soon proved fatal. As this rumour is stated to have arisen out of the circumstance of Lord Downe's death, which did not occur until eleven months later, the story can hardly be accepted in its entirety. Lady Granby was the eldest daughter of the Duke of Somerset by his second wife, Lady Charlotte Finch; and her portrait, painted by Hogarth, is at Belvoir Castle.

The Duke of Newcastle wrote to Lord Robert Manners Sutton—

> I cannot trouble Your Lordship with a letter without most sincerely condoling with you upon the great loss which Lord Granby has had. I have not had yet the courage to write to him, as I am uncertain whether he will come over or not. . . . I saw Mr. Thoroton on Tuesday, from whom I had the satisfaction to hear that the Duke of Rutland was as well as could be expected.

Newcastle's doubts were removed by Lord Granby himself, who had arrived back at Osnabrück prior to leaving the army—

> I shall set out tomorrow, or next day, for England, when in person I will assure my dear duke of my sincere regard and friendship for him. Oh! My Dear Lord, how happy was I a few days ago in my thoughts of soon being in England. The Duke of Newcastle, I am sure, feels for the cruel misfortune that has happened to his most faithful, and obliged friend.
>
> Granby.

Lord Granby arrived home, and nearly the whole of his leave was absorbed by matters relating to his troops, whose health was already distressing him, to the reinforcements, and to the trial of Lord George Sackville.

Chapter 8

1759-1760: Home Politics

Before proceeding to the events following upon Lord Granby's return from Germany, a glance must be thrown over his family's doings at home, where, to repeat Chesterfield's oft-quoted and graphic sentence—

> The Duke of Newcastle and Mr. Pitt jogged on like man and wife; that is, seldom agreeing, often quarrelling; but, by mutual consent, upon the whole not parting.

The ceaseless energy displayed by Pitt in opposing France in her colonial schemes, as well as in her threatened invasion of England, was communicated, throughout the country, by a reciprocal enthusiasm which the Duke of Newcastle had been incapable of arousing. The Duke of Rutland was unable, through ill health, to attend a county meeting respecting the Militia in Leicestershire, concerning which Sir Thomas Cave informed him—

> The spirit of the people to oppose the natural enemy of this Kingdom is so great, that I had a roll of 50 volunteers offered me, every one a man of considerable property. It is to be wished that every gentleman of larger fortune had the same zeal, though, as to subaltern commands, there are many gentlemen, I believe, who will chearfully undertake the duty when they find it neglected by those who have large properties to defend. (*Letters to his Son,* May 18, 1758).

Of colours to choose from, for the Leicestershire uniform, there still remained to the duke those of buff, white, and yellow; the latter "not a pleasing colour to the eye, or cleanly in the wear."

Volunteers from the militia to the regular army were urgently sought, to which intent the Duke of Newcastle consulted Lord Robert Manners Sutton in Nottinghamshire, saying that the king was much pressed for the want of 2,000 men to be drafted immediately into the ranks. Upon this topic Newcastle applied to the Dukes of Rutland, Kingston, and Devonshire.

The Duke of Rutland replied—

> I fear the levying of men to compleat the regiments will be an arduous piece of work, and in this county impracticable, where from the scarcity of men labour is raised to a high price; moreover the turnpike-roads now making in this county, Nottinghamshire and Derbyshire will so effectually (even when the harvest is over) employ the labourer and find him subsistance that I see little hope of collecting men in these parts, almost on any terms, to answer the emergency. Could a method be found out to render practicable the scheme I proposed of annexing to each battalion of foot now in England one or two companies of the unemployed militia, to serve with these regiments until the danger of invasion was over, I think it might very well answer the purpose of compleating the marching regiments for present service, as most of the militia are acquainted with the manual exercise. . . . However, I foresee difficulty, and that it is a work of great delicacy, but in difficult times, difficult things must be attempted—nor can we hope to surmount dangers without braving them.

A letter upon the same topic was addressed by the Duke of Rutland to the High Sheriff and Grand Jury at Leicester, which was published in the *Gazette*. Lord Robert Manners Sutton attended a large meeting at Mansfield, and afforded great assistance both in Nottinghamshire and Sussex, of both which counties the Duke of Newcastle was Lord Lieutenant, and where he said "the militia went down heavily." Lord Robert, as already noticed, undertook the Colonelcy of the Notts Regiment. In reference to the latter he communicated the following serio-comic episode to Newcastle:—

> Mr. Martin Bird wants his name scratched off the *Militia List*, as his wife, on hearing he had taken a commission, was so affected he thought she would have died! I suppose the lady's condition will be sufficient plea with Your Grace to let this gentleman off.

Lord George Manners was equally busy, and acquainted the Duke of Rutland with a difficulty which had arisen concerning the Colonelcy of the Leicester Militia for which the Marquess of Granby's name had been put forward. There was a doubt whether the marquess could serve in that capacity for two counties; but the *Lists* do not show his eventual appointment to any.

Two circumstances occurred in connection with the Church and the army which testify to the loyalty maintained by the Duke of Rutland and Lord Granby towards their friends. The Duke of Newcastle made Church preferment his own special province, and he had long promised a bishopric to the Rev. Dr. John Ewer for whom, since his school days, Granby had shown great affection. In 1759 the See of Llandaff had become vacant, but Ewer was passed over; shortly after that of Gloucester was available, and of this Ewer was considered certain. However, with the artfully worded preamble, "I know how well Your Lordship wishes the most perfect and cordial union and friendship between me and Mr. Pitt," Newcastle informed Granby that Pitt was recommending a King's Chaplain to the vacancy at Gloucester, and that the king was unfavourable to Dr. Ewer because he was not a Royal Chaplain, and was consequently unknown to His Majesty.

Poor Newcastle was between the devil—for to him Pitt was the *very* devil—and the deep sea of the displeasure of the Rutland family: all he could do was to plead the king's insistence on a Royal Chaplain, and point out that Granby was endangering his own prospects by teasing the king who had lately shown him so much favour. That Newcastle really did his best for Ewer his correspondence proves; and seeing the matter was hopeless he wrote on one of his *Memoranda for the King*, "I give up my recommendation of Dr. Ewer for the king's service." Both Granby and his father were seriously hurt at this disappointment, and the former wrote to confront Newcastle with his repeated promises of "the next bishopric" for Ewer—

> My dear Lord, my heart was set upon it—nothing can make me more unhappy than his being laid aside; if nobody can be made a bishop but a king's chaplain, the chamberlain makes all the bishops. I am certain Your Grace will do all in your power for Dr. Ewer, for you know my affection for him . . . and I hope that I shall soon have the occasion of assuring Your Grace that you have made John Granby the happiest of men.

The Duke of Rutland was more emphatic, and likewise scouted the non-eligibility of Ewer—

> . . . .for the ridiculous reason that he was not a king's chaplain, as

if all merit was confined to that appellation, or that no one person had either merit or understanding sufficient to recommend to a bishopric but a Lord Chamberlain! If this be laid down for doctrine and practise in the present case, whatever may be Lord Granby's resolution I have taken mine, and although it will never change the sentiments I shall ever entertain of Your Grace's goodness, nor I hope deprive me of the continuance of your friendship, it must necessarily make an alteration in my situation.

Lord Granby's good nature as usual prevailed; he saw Newcastle's uncomfortable predicament, and waived his claim, for which courtesy Newcastle thanked him handsomely. But the Duke of Rutland, who liked to see "the next man "get his promotion instead of being passed over owing to a job at the last moment, was still further incensed by two officers, Captains Burton, (then one of Lord Granby's *A.D.C.*s, and later Deputy Quarter-Master-General in Germany, and who had served in the "Forty-Five"), and Spike (respectively the senior Captains in Conway's and Lascelles' Regiments), being unjustifiably superseded in the vacant majorities of both regiments.

Both were friends of the duke and Lord Granby, on whose staff Burton then was, while Captain William Spike had served in Granby's Regiment in the "Forty-Five," and was an officer in whom the duke said he had been interested "almost from his entrance into the army," and that he was "determined to relieve the injured, or relinquish his credit at Court." This furnished a fresh cause of anxiety to Newcastle concerning his support from Belvoir. In the end Captain Burton got his step, but Captain Spike did not, and retired from the army. Dr. Ewer was positively promised the next vacant bishopric, which proved to be the See of Llandaff, and which he held from 1761 until 1768, when he was translated to that of Bangor.

In connection with the German War a commendable tide-mark in the growing current of sympathy, flowing from easy home-dwellers towards those who had too long been considered only as appropriate food for powder, was indicated early in 1760. Ligonier informed Lord Granby of a gift, to the British troops in Germany, of flannel waistcoats and other comforts, from the merchants of the City of London. The distribution of these welcome presents, as well as money destined for the relief of widows and orphans of deceased soldiers, fell to the lot of General Mostyn after Lord Granby's departure for England.

Mostyn wrote word to the marquess that he was endeavouring to do the most good with these gifts that was possible; but added that there was no confining the relief to widows only. A soldier's widow rarely remained so above twenty-four hours; and a wife, or any woman following the army, might be as necessitous and fit an object for charity as any other.

As the Marquess of Granby's charity was of the rare order which "thinketh no evil," and which relieved misery as soon as witnessed, without demanding certificates of character, marriage "lines," or the profession of any prescribed orthodoxy of belief, it may be taken confidently for granted that Jack Mostyn's administration of the clothing and funds met with his complete approval.

General Mostyn also informed Granby that the health of the army had improved since its settlement in winter quarters; although, in spite of wholesale shooting, glanders still prevailed among the horses. Mostyn wrote:

> I am very tired of correspondence with '*Mon cher Rheden*,' (Adjutant-General of the Hanoverian Army), and I sicken at the sight of pen, ink, and paper.

Here was another good soldier upon whom writing-materials had a demoralising effect!

It will be remembered that General Mostyn was empowered to draw warrants upon the Treasury during the commander-in-chief's absence: forthwith he commenced, in the words of a well-known banker to an active customer, to draw like a dray-horse. From Osnabrück he advised some preliminary drafts of £5,000 in a highly official letter to the Duke of Newcastle, accompanied by a private letter in his more natural style:—

> Ye twin brother of this letter (for they will both be laid at Your Grace's door in the same envelope, both of ye same date, and both be delivered into Your Grace's hand, as one may say, at the same birth, will inform you that I have (during ye, I hope, short time of my having ye command of H.M.'s British Forces here) more business than I believe any man in Europe, except Your Grace. And, what is the worst of it is, that it is all in the writing and reading way—two things I never had patience to bear, and that I am afraid I do very ill. I like my quarters very well in ye main, and I take all ye pains I can that they may not dislike me; but however impartial and general one may be in

> one's disposition, there is always some one body that wins one's heart, and takes up more of one's attention than the rest. This is exactly my case with regard to Madame Ammeling, the lady who keeps the post office here, and with great dignity presides over that business.
>
> She is not of ye first *noblesse*, but she is ye best creature in ye world. She loves ye king, and toasts (for she has done me ye honour to dine with me) Your Grace, and says on your subject with a warmth as if it came from her heart, '*Das ist ein Prave Kerle!*' (The Duke of Newcastle had made her acquaintance in accompanying George II. on his Hanoverian journeys.—*Newcastle Papers*).

Mostyn continued to draw, and entered with great seriousness into some Hanover *Chancellerie* affairs, with the result that he overdrew the account, and the Duke of Newcastle and Mr. Samuel Martin from "Treasury Chambers" both hastened to cry, "Hold, enough!"

Newcastle informed Mostyn that it was his terrible misfortune, both in his public and private capacity, "to draw for money when his banker had none," and Mr. Martin, in the more severe style of a Treasury official, admonished the temporary commander-in-chief, who thus excused himself to the duke—

> I have just received a letter from Mr. Martin which I don't say puzzles the cause, but am very much afraid will puzzle me damnably; however, I will answer it with as much form as I am master of. . . . I never drew a warrant in my life, or saw one, till now, and being once engaged, I shall never be able to hold my hand till directed by, what shall always direct both my hands, Your Grace's commands.

The Treasury Account was adjusted after the strain put upon it by Mostyn, who said he only wished the duke could *raccommode* his private credit as easily as his public. He had come to the conclusion during his brief authority that he loved private friendships better than public honours—

> Here am I, Lieut.-General *des Troupes Britanniques; Commander-in-Chief and Ministre Plénipotentiaire de Sa Majesté,* prodigiously honoured, damnably harassed, and very ill paid.

Altogether Mostyn was glad to hear that before long Lord Granby would be returning; and from the above correspondence the inference may be drawn that, good, cheery fellow as he was, Jack Mostyn's estimate of himself was a true one—to wit, that he pretended to be nothing more than a simple cavalry officer.

★★★★★★★★★★★

In relation to the poor of Ireland, General Mostyn once said that until visiting that country he never knew what the English beggars did with their old clothes (Lord Carlisle to George Selwyn, *Hist. MSS.* Com., Rep. XV., App. 6). Walpole mentions a mad Lord Pomfret whose habit was to call out individuals (selecting safe ones) on imaginary pretexts of insult. He once unluckily entered General Mostyn's lodgings at an early hour, drew his bed-curtains aside, and desired him to rise and repair to Hyde Park to afford satisfaction for an insult given at Court. Mostyn denied ever having set eyes on him. "Oh, then," said Lord Pomfret, "it is all very well—" "No, by God, it is not!" replied Mostyn; "you have disturbed me when I had been in bed but three hours, and now *you* shall give *me* satisfaction." The earl, however, begged to be excused (Letter to Sir H. Mann, November 11. 1780).

★★★★★★★★★★

Chapter 9

1759-1760: The Lord Sackville at Minden Scandal

Upon the Marquess of Granby's return home, and from the consequent shrinkage in his correspondence, his doings for a time are not so clearly traceable. The *Memoranda for the King,* which it was the Duke of Newcastle's' custom to draw up previous to his audiences with His Majesty, are, however, full of references to Lord Granby—

> Lord Granby's account of Prince Ferdinand—his manner—his diligence—his ability. Not extremely well served by the (Hanoverian) generals. Lord Granby's character of the Hereditary Prince—his discourse about Lord George Sackville. Granby perfectly informed of the State of the Army. Wish the king would talk to him. . . .

. . . . .and so on; but, as we cannot listen at the door while Granby is closeted with the king and his various ministers, the subjects of his conferences must be sought presently in results.

First, Lord George Sackville has to be dealt with. He addressed a letter, which embodied his defence, to Colonel Fitzroy, Prince Ferdinand's *aide-de-camp*; and he wrote to Mr. Pitt, besides sending his own former *aide-de-camp.* Captain Smith, with an account of his (Sackville's) conduct at Minden. Pitt, it will be remembered, had been a staunch champion of Admiral Byng; but in his queer, laboured style, he expressed to Sackville his infinite concern at not being able to find—

> . . . .either from Captain Smith's conversation, or Lord George's own statement of facts, room—as he wished—to offer his support with regard to a conduct which, perhaps, his incompetence

to judge of military questions left him at a loss to account for.

This would have been a "damper" to most men, but a little later Pitt commented on Lord George having shown his face at the Opera: "the event is hardly worth mentioning, as nothing was wanting to complete that great man's heroic assurance!" (To Lady Hester Pitt. November 19, 1759). In vain was Lord George assured of what sentence an adverse verdict would bring. The Law officers of the Crown tried to hatch some quibble about a Court Martial having no jurisdiction over Sackville, who was no longer in the army, but he persisted in his demand for a trial. Finally, February 20, 1760, he was put under arrest for disobedience of orders, and the preliminary steps made towards investigating his case.

Prince Ferdinand was requested to send over certain officers, whose evidence was necessary, as well as all the Orders issued to the troops; and he was desired to explain what he had meant by the expression used in his letter of August 13, 1759, "this officer (Lord George), through his conduct, might have brought the battle within an ace of being lost." (Prince Ferdinand's words literally translated were: "might have placed affairs within two fingers of their loss.")

The officers wanted were, so it transpired, all in England on leave; but Prince Ferdinand, from Paderborn, stated his intention of sending over, in addition, his German *aides-de-camp* De Derenthal and De Wintzingerode; he also addressed to the king a *Relation de la Bataille de Minden*. A translation of this appeared in various papers, and, as an instance of the smallness and conceit of human nature, it may be remarked that a passage in the original, describing how the English infantry was for a time in trouble, and almost losing ground before the French cavalry and artillery, is studiously omitted—bowdlerised, in fact, out of the English edition.

Ferdinand's letter is somewhat long, and its contents are embodied in the description of Minden, and in the account of the court martial. He charged Lord George with not having the cavalry saddled at the proper hour, and with being late in his own arrival on the scene of the battle. These charges were both disproved at the court martial.

The prince also stated that the cavalry of the left wing (which consisted of Hessian, Holstein, and Hanoverian Dragoons) attacked with great vigour. This attack seems to have happened prior to the final stage of the battle, for no cavalry pursuit occurred at all, and Lord George most pertinently asked *why* the cavalry of the left was not ordered on, separately and at once, without waiting for him.

Prince Ferdinand then went on to substantiate his compliment to Lord Granby which, one cordially agrees with Walpole, had better never have been made. (Walpole repeatedly remarked that Lord Granby was commended and promoted for what he would have done at Minden, not for what he did). Ferdinand had far better have openly censured Lord George than have done so covertly under praise to the marquess.

The prince owned he was vexed at the fiasco:—

> I could not help asserting the good opinion I had of Lord Granby from the good spirit in which he had endeavoured to execute my orders, which left no doubt but that he would have made the victory one of the most completely decisive if Lord George had not halted him, or if he had been at the head of the cavalry following only the promptings of his courage.

It must be borne in mind that this compliment to Granby did not stop, in effect, at him; but that it implied, besides his willingness to lead, an equal eagerness to be led on the part of the Blues, Bland's, (1st King's Dragoon Guards), the Inniskillings, the Horse Grenadiers, Howard's, (3rd Dragoon Guards), Mordaunt's, (10th Dragoons), and the Scots Greys, which regiments formed the right cavalry wing on the day of Minden, and were deprived of all chance of mention "in those damned newspapers," as Jack Mostyn phrased it.

The court martial assembled, and in Walpole's opinion Lord George would have been in far less danger leading up the cavalry at Minden than in every hour that he went down, a criminal, to the Horse Guards.

George II., Prince Ferdinand, Pitt, and the Duke of Newcastle were all dead against him. Newcastle's letters prove him to have been beset with fears that Sackville might escape, and during the trial he complained that the court martial was biased in Sackville's favour. The proceedings of the court martial held at the Horse Guards lasted, with adjournments, from March 7 to April 5, 1760; the Court was composed of the following general officers:—

Lieut.-General Sir Charles Howard, President.

<table>
<tr><td>Lieut.-Gen. Campbell.</td><td>Lieut.-Gen. Earl of Ancram.</td></tr>
<tr><td>" Earl of Barrington.</td><td>" Abercrombie.</td></tr>
<tr><td>" Earl of Delawarr.</td><td>" Leighton.</td></tr>
<tr><td>" Cholmondeley.</td><td>Major-Gen. Earl of Effingham</td></tr>
</table>

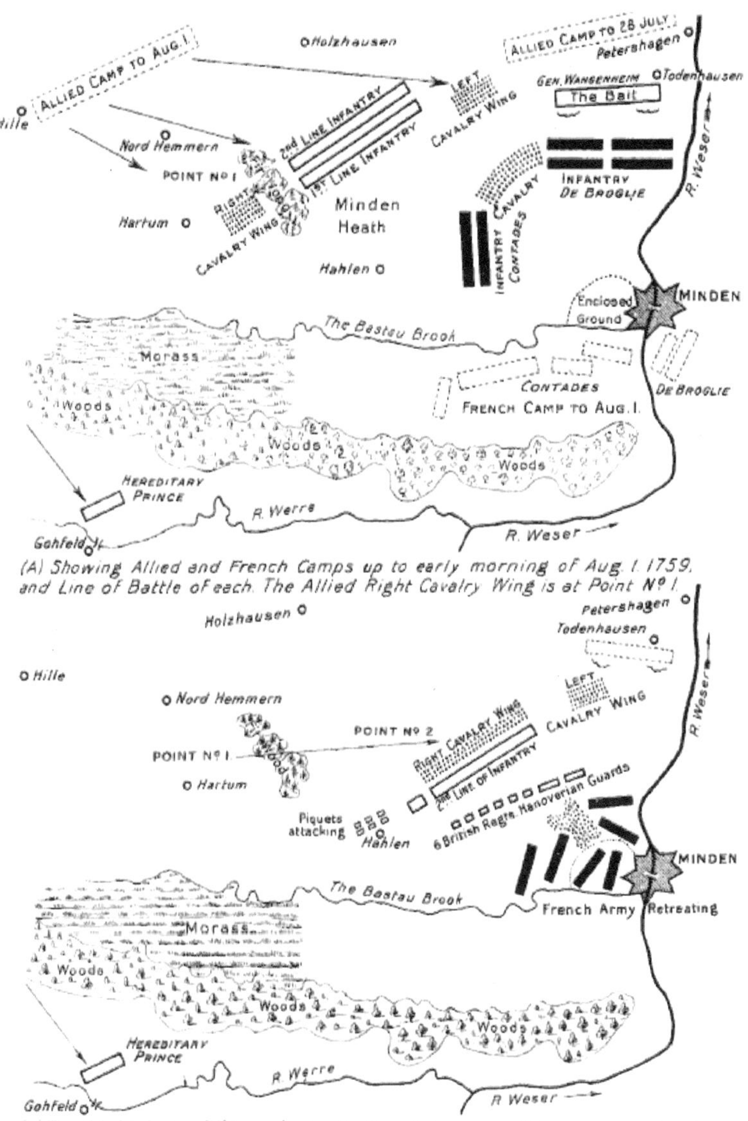

(A) Showing Allied and French Camps up to early morning of Aug. 1. 1759, and Line of Battle of each. The Allied Right Cavalry Wing is at Point No 1.

(B) The Allied Infantry (1st Line) driving the French Army into Minden. Right Cavalry Wing at Point No 2. (From Map and Drawings in British Museum, and Royal United Service Institution)

THE BATTLE OF MINDEN

" Earl of Albemarle. " Caesar.
" Stuart. " Car.
" Earl of Panmure. " Lord Robert Bertie.

Lieut.-Gen. Lord Robert Manners.

Deputy Judge Advocate, Dr. Charles Gould.

The evidence is arranged so as to constitute, as far as possible, a consecutive and succinct account of the proceedings, to understand which the reader's attention is directed to two important points on the battlefield: the point to which the cavalry of the right was first ordered, by a little wood between Hartum and Hahlen, which shall be called Point No. 1; and another, on the edge of Minden Heath, called Point No. 2.

In general terms. Lord George Sackville was accused of disobeying Prince Ferdinand's orders; but, in detail, he was charged with not having his cavalry ready to march by 1 a.m. on the morning of Minden; with having lost time in marching to Point No. 1; with directly disobeying orders before marching to Point No. 2; and with having been prompted to disobedience by motives of cowardice.

Lieut.-Colonel Sloper, commanding Bland's Dragoons, proved that the horses of the cavalry of the right were saddled, and the troopers lying down booted in their tents before 1 a.m. on the 1st of August. Sloper, upon all the other issues, was Sackville's most damaging and vehement accuser, but upon this question of the saddling, *etc.*, Prince Ferdinand was misinformed.

Some French deserters brought news to Prince Ferdinand's quarters, at Hille, that the enemy was in motion; upon hearing which the prince despatched every *aide-de-camp* he could find to place the army in motion: the cavalry of the right was ordered to Point No. 1, and Lord George was charged with being late at this post.

Captain Smith, his *aide-de-camp*, deposed that the cavalry marched to Point No. 1 at a proper pace; that he was the only officer who saw the whole column pass out of camp; and that he noticed the rear squadrons were hurrying to keep up with the head of the column. He owned he was not a cavalry officer, when questioned as to the pace at which the column should have proceeded.

The cavalry of the right must now be imagined as having arrived at Point No. 1, by a little firwood. The attacks of the French cavalry having been repulsed, Prince Ferdinand first directed some operations against a French detachment which was holding the village of Hahlen, (the French set fire to Hahlen before retiring), and sent orders to the infantry to march at beat of drum. These orders were misunderstood to mean that the infantry was to march at once with drums beating, and forthwith it advanced upon the French cavalry centre with the astonishing result that is a matter of history. The Hanoverian Infantry followed the English in the 2nd Line; the Hanoverian Guards and Hartemburg's Regiment alone sharing the British attack. Prince Ferdinand, seeing this, sent his *aide-de-camp,* Captain Wintzingerode, to order Lord George Sackville to march the right cavalry wing, by the left, to Point No. 2, at the edge of Minden Heath, and there form one line in rear of the infantry to support its gallant attack.

Captain Wintzingerode delivered this order in French. The French cavalry was now giving way before the English infantry, and, as Wintzingerode returned. Captain Edward Ligonier (1st Foot Guards, and *A.D.C.* to Prince Ferdinand), reached Sackville, informing him that Prince Ferdinand said the enemy was retiring, and he desired His Lordship *to profit* by that circumstance (*et il vous prie d'en profiter*).

Lieutenant Bisset, Captain Smith, *A.D.C.*, Lieutenant Whiteford of the Inniskillings, and Captain Hugo, *A.D.C.*, all deposed that Lord George Sackville at once drew his sword and marched the 1st Line of the cavalry of the right wing; but he sent no orders to the same effect to the Marquess of Granby, commanding the 2nd Line, and who was out of sight of Sackville.

Several commanding-officers of the 1st Line stated that they understood the second order, brought by Ligonier, to mean that a cavalry charge was intended, whereupon they ordered their men to throw away their corn, "picket-poles," and other dispensable encumbrances. Majors Marriott and Hepburn both deposed that they gathered from Ligonier's shouts, as he galloped past, that the enemy was giving way, and the cavalry was ordered up to charge.

Now ensued the moment when the French cavalry, reinforced and supported by artillery, rallied considerably, and by a determined effort placed in difficulties the English infantry, "which almost lost ground." (*Rélation de la Bataille de Minden*).

Prince Ferdinand, eagerly awaiting the aid of the cavalry, despatched Captain Fitzroy, *A.D.C.* (who arrived while Ligonier was still at Sackville's side). Fitzroy was somewhat breathless, and gave the same order, but used the words "British cavalry." Lord George Sackville directly halted the 1st Line (which was composed of British regiments only, while that under Lord Granby comprised a few Hanoverian) and told Fitzroy not to be in a hurry, and to give his orders distinctly.

Granby and an Infantryman on the Road

★★★★★★★★★★

> It must be observed that Sackville's conduct was all the more unaccountable as, so far, he had moved British cavalry only, and had sent no orders to Lord Granby, whose command included both British and Foreign cavalry.

★★★★★★★★★★

Fitzroy explained he was breathless from galloping, but both he and Ligonier maintained that the difference in their orders as to the "Cavalry of the Right" or the "British cavalry" was a detail of numbers only, but that the order was in the main the same, "to advance," also the destination—"to the left." Colonel Sloper, who was near, advised Lord George that the orders could only mean an advance of the cavalry to the left, Lord George retorted that the *aides-de-camp* did not understand their instructions, and galloped off to Prince Ferdinand to receive his orders personally, leaving the cavalry halted. Meantime the infantry, unaided, was achieving the victory of Minden.

Captain Fitzroy had preceded Lord George, and reported the facts to Prince Ferdinand, but found that the latter, weary of waiting, had sent Wintzingerode with a separate order to the Marquess of Granby to march the 2nd Line of Cavalry. He sent Fitzroy also to Lord Granby, saying, "I know he will obey me."

The prince merely delivered to Lord George, personally, the original order to advance to Point No. 2, on the edge of the heath; and; as Sackville returned, he saw Lord Granby already advanced clear of the fir-wood with the 2nd Line of cavalry: Lord George then marched the 1st Line. The Duke of Richmond and Colonel Webb presently brought orders that the cavalry should be formed in one line.

Thus, the cavalry of the right wing, with the 2nd Line in front of the 1st Line, had at last reached Point No. 2; but even these last movements were not carried out without delays, which are fully described in the Marquess of Granby's evidence, to which we now turn. His evidence is also arranged in the order which constitutes the best narrative.

Between four and five o'clock on the morning of August 1, Lord Granby was already up and dressing when he heard three or four cannon shots, at intervals, towards the right; he at once ordered his horse, and sent a servant to Lord George Sackville's quarters to see if anything sudden had occurred.

The servant returned saying all was quiet there, and the sentinel did not know what the firing was. The marquess got on his charger and rode off alone towards the right, (towards Hille), to a point whence he could see the tents of that flank of our camp. Seeing that the firing was directed against Prince Ferdinand's quarters and the two British battalions covering them, and seeing and hearing nothing to the left, he "very unhappily for himself rode on to the right, thinking to find an attack there." On arriving he found the camp empty; the troops having been cannonaded and drawn off their ground.

He then met Colonel Fitzroy and the Duke of Richmond, (English *A.D.C.*s to Prince Ferdinand), who told him the prince had already left, and all three galloped back to the main encampment. Owing to the tremendous dust caused by the troops placed in motion during Granby's absence, he and his companions missed a little lane they should have followed, and he only came up with the rear column of the cavalry of the right as it entered the North Hemmern Field, near to Point No. 1. (The Duke of Richmond and Colonel Fitzroy joined the prince.) (Prince Ferdinand's letter to the king, said he sent every *aide-de-camp* he could to place the army in motion.) The marquess took up his position with the 2nd Line, at what we know as Point No. 1, by the wood, and to the best of his belief he thought they remained there from twenty to twenty-five minutes before starting for Point No. 2, by the heath. He could see nothing of the enemy, nor did he see it all day, nor could he see what was going on with the 1st Line of Cavalry, and Lord George Sackville.

When Captain Wintzingerode was carrying his first order to Lord George, he had to pass the 2nd Line, and in so doing he stopped and asked Lord Granby where Lord George was. Lord Granby directed him, and understood him to say he was carrying some order, about advancing the cavalry, to Sackville; but no consequent instructions ensued from the latter to Granby.

A little later Wintzingerode came again in a great hurry, and asked, "Why, for God's sake, the cavalry of the right had not marched," on his bringing the first order, to form one line behind the infantry, at the same time saying that Prince Ferdinand wished Lord Granby to advance with the 2nd Line. Granby speedily put the 2nd Line in motion, but on condition that Wintzingerode should proceed to inform Sackville of the fact, and to say that no confirmatory orders had reached Granby from the latter. Before leaving, Wintzingerode led the Hanoverian regiments through the wood, while the Marquess of Granby led the "Greys," and without noticing any important obstacles either from the trees, the formation of the ground, or any troops on their front. (Sackville's witnesses, and he himself, alleged the existence of these obstacles). This movement was to the left and towards the heath.

General Elliott, of the 2nd Line, who had just previously been sent for by Lord George Sackville, now returned to Lord Granby, informing him Lord George would send him orders immediately, but meanwhile he must wait where he was until the 1st Line got up to him. In consequence Granby halted, well clear of the wood, having reached the spot where, as shown by the wounded on the ground, the action had first begun.

As Granby waited. Colonel Fitzroy arrived with the prince's second message previously described, and Fitzroy's evidence is for the moment pursued: he said he found Lord Granby on the enemy's, or Minden, side of the little wood, alone, and about forty yards in advance of his troops.

On receiving this order, Lord Granby asked him why it was brought to him instead of to his commanding-officer. Lord George Sackville, who was not far off. Fitzroy replied that the order had been sent repeatedly, but ineffectually, to Lord George, and the prince's instructions now were to deliver it to Lord Granby.

In consequence. Lord Granby advanced the 2nd Line sharply at the trot, and remarked to Fitzroy that the right cavalry wing was still not so far forward as the left. To resume the marquess' evidence, he stated that soon after, he, with the 2nd Line, arrived at Point No. 2, Lord George followed with the 1st Line. Granby at once rode up to explain why his advance had been made without Lord George's orders, whose command to halt had been obeyed as soon as received.

Lord George explained that the halt had been made for the sake of adhering to Prince Ferdinand's orders to form the cavalry in one line, and this Lord George proceeded to do at the edge of the heath. This done, he showed no sign of any further advance; so, Lord Granby, saying the prince's orders were plainly to advance on immediately, gave the word through General Elliott, to the cavalry under his (Granby's) command, to follow him.

Lord Granby himself galloped on some fifty or sixty yards in advance, but, after going some four hundred yards, he found the troops behind him had been again halted. He again ordered them on, and was informed they had been halted by Lord George; whereupon Lord Granby repeated his command, and enjoined them not to halt at all except by his, or General Elliott's, orders.

In spite of his efforts, we learn from Lord Granby's evidence and letter that he "never saw the enemy all day." The battle was declared to be won; the 2nd Line received orders to rejoin the 1st, after which the men were dismounted.

Replying to questions, put through the Court at Lord George's request. Lord Granby said he received no instructions from Prince Ferdinand on the day preceding Minden, nor did he know the position of the infantry when the cavalry first formed. Before the Battle of Bergen Prince Ferdinand sent for all the lieutenant-generals, (Lord George Sackville was not present at Bergen), to receive his orders, and explanations of his disposition of battle, which he could convey very clearly, and distinctly.

After the General Orders of August 2, and the *feu de joie,* Lord George Sackville went to Granby's quarters and asked him to make a written statement concerning Minden. Lord Granby declined to write a letter in French, or in fact any letter, but offered to accompany Lord George to His Serene Highness's quarters, and say what he had now done in the course of his evidence. Lord George particularly pressed him to say that, after the 2nd Line of Cavalry had passed the 1st, Lord George followed at the same pace adopted by Lord Granby. Granby replied that he really could not say, as he was fully occupied in *looking out in front*—it was a point upon which Lord George, and the 1st Line of Cavalry, were the best judges.

While being very explicit as to facts, and what actually took place, the Marquess of Granby showed a marked disinclination to give opinions as to what might have occurred had circumstances been different. On being pressed, he said he considered they might certainly have pursued the enemy had they marched as soon as the cavalry was first formed: they might have been up some twenty minutes earlier without blowing the horses, and keeping a proper line enough, without being as exact as if on parade. He galloped, and the 2nd Line came after him at a full trot, some galloping; and the infantry could obviously have been joined much sooner had the pace been maintained—whether the cavalry would have been able to do much execution he could not say.

On being much pressed as to whether he had shown any impatience, Lord Granby replied he believed he was vexed, and might have found fault with Lord George's manoeuvres, which, in his opinion, lost time.

Corroborative evidence was called proving that Lord Granby passed the 1st Line of Cavalry with the 2nd. Colonel Sloper said when he (in the 1st Line) got through the wood he saw the 2nd Line considerably in front, moving on fronting the enemy. When Lord George overtook the 2nd Line by halting it, and resumed command of the whole, they advanced slower than the 2nd Line had done when alone.

Lieut.-Colonel W. A. Pitt, 10th Dragoons (2nd Line), said he received an order from Lord Granby to follow him with his brigade. This was done at a trot until stopped by an *aide-de-camp* from Sackville. He told the *A.D.C.* as the first order was Lord Granby's His Lordship must be informed of the halt ordered by Lord George Sackville. The *A.D.C.* went on to Lord Granby, and, in consequence they were all halted for a quarter of an hour. He, Colonel Pitt, saw no difficulties in advancing, beyond avoiding treading on the wounded: at the front he saw no general officers save Lord Granby, and General Elliott.

Lieutenant John Walsh, Adjutant of the Blues (1st Line), said Lieut.-Colonel Johnston commanding the Blues sent him to Lord George Sackville to say "the 2nd Line was advancing and might the Blues follow?" (The "Blues," it will be remembered, was Lord Granby's Regiment, and though not on this occasion commanded by him, was eager to follow him when he passed the 1st Line).

Lord George said "No," and instantly ordered Lieutenant Walsh to go and halt the 2nd Line.

Lord George Sackville's defence was as follows:—

On July 31 Prince Ferdinand did not acquaint him with the probability of fighting a battle on the ensuing day, nor afford any idea of the intended plan of action. The order that the cavalry should be ready by 1 a.m. on the morning of August 1 was obeyed, as it had been for several days previously.

Between 5 and 6 a.m. on that morning, Lord George was awoke by cannon-shots on the right; but receiving no orders he took no steps individually. Soon after, General Spörcken, (Hanoverian Army), sent word that the troops were getting under arms.

Lord George directly rode out, without awaiting his *aides-de-camp*, and was the first general officer of the cavalry division who joined it: "this was good fortune, as it might have happened to him not to be so early as it had to other persons."

No orders had as yet reached him, but he marched the whole cavalry of the right wing (1st and 2nd Lines) in the direction which he assumed he was to follow.

On the march he was joined by the other generals and the *aides-de-camp*; while his orders and a guide also reached him later. The guide conducted him to Point No. 1, by the wood, towards which he proceeded at a proper pace, in order not to blow the horses, and arrived on his ground in as good time as the infantry.

He reconnoitred the ground so far as time permitted, but in consequence of having received no premonition of the battle he had not examined the ways leading from the camp to Minden Heath.

★★★★★★★★★★

After Minden, Prince Ferdinand, in his Standing Orders (August 16, 1759), desired that the generals and field officers would in every camp make themselves acquainted with the roads, avenues, and environs, in order to be able to execute any sudden orders.

★★★★★★★★★★

He did not approve of the position indicated to him by the guide (Point No. 1). The fir-wood, which he had not reconnoitred, was dense, and lay more or less on both sides of him, obstructing his view of the rest of the army and the enemy. Moreover, the position was exposed to the fire of several batteries, and, though under no personal anxiety whatever, he objected to exposing the cavalry before it was required.

On receiving the first order, to advance by the left to Point No. 2, from a foreign *aide-de-camp of no status as regarded the British Army,* he at once marched with the 1st Line; but to the front instead of to the left on account of the fir-wood, which appeared to be impassable. He was soon approached by another *aide-de-camp* bearing a contradictory order; in consequence of which he halted the 1st Line, and rode off to receive Prince Ferdinand's order personally.

As he galloped, Lord George noticed that the fir-wood was more open than he imagined, and he instantly sent his *aide-de-camp* Captain Smith back (as Fitzroy continued positive as to his order) to bring up the rest of the cavalry of the right wing, including General Mostyn and his brigade. (There is not a word about this order in Lord Granby's evidence. He acted on the independent order sent through Wintzingerode and Fitzroy by Prince Ferdinand.)

On reaching the prince, Sackville found him quite calm, and indicating, by his manner, no hurry or annoyance (of this Sackville made a great point): the prince merely ordered the advance of the cavalry of the right wing to Point No. 2, adding nothing which could be construed as implying an attack on, or pursuit of the enemy.

★★★★★★★★★★

This assumption of Sackville's, that he possessed no independent initiative, could not have been genuine. Prince Ferdinand's tactics were those of his master, Frederick the Great, and in *Operations of War* Sir E. Hamley writes: "In Frederick's battles, while the king directed all the movements of the infantry, we find the chief of the cavalry selecting his own time for the attack; and it was necessary in supporting offensive movements that the immediate commander should be left to his own inspirations." This remark also applies to Lord Granby's subsequent career in the Seven Years' War.

****

Sackville returned, and saw Lord Granby with the 2nd Line advancing; he at once marched the 1st Line, and halted Lord Granby in order to dress both lines. If this was what Lord Granby had disapproved of as "Sackville's manoeuvres," Lord George flattered himself his lordship would not have done so had he understood them to have been the outcome of Prince Ferdinand's explicit orders.

Upon reaching Point No. 2 Lord George again halted to dress the line, and made no effort at pursuit; firstly, because none had been ordered; secondly, because none was possible. The battle was over, and the enemy had retreated under the shelter of the Minden guns, and the British infantry had halted on the confines of the enclosed ground around Minden.

****

The infantry followed the French into the gardens round Minden, which circumstance originated the custom still observed by the 20th Regiment of wearing roses on the anniversary of the battle, at the close of which the infantry thus decorated themselves.

****

Had a charge been practicable, why was not the cavalry of the left ordered on, during the alleged delay, independently of the cavalry of the right?

"The glory of the day belonged to the six brave regiments of foot." The real question of the day was not who was to be blamed for what the cavalry had not done, but who was to be praised for the extraordinary intrepidity of the infantry.

After the battle Lord George heard, among the general congratulations, not one single word of censure; but on the succeeding day the unprecedented course was followed of censuring him, unnamed, in the General Orders. In doing this Prince Ferdinand "was uninformed of our manners, ignorant of the effect the orders would produce here, and unacquainted upon those points with the sensibility of Englishmen."

As to Colonel Sloper, Lord George stigmatised his conduct and evidence as false and malicious throughout. He was not even near when the conversations between Lord George and the *aides-de-camp* occurred. His statements were not made until after the issue of the General Orders of the 2nd of August, and he afterwards knew he must either persevere in the strongest accusations or be punished at Lord George's desire.

In support of Lord George's impeachment of Colonel Sloper's evidence, Captain Smith, *A.D.C.*, deposed that—besides the fir-wood—a Saxe-Gotha Regiment was impeding Lord George Sackville's advance from Point No. 1 to Point No. 2. Directly the Saxe-Gotha Regiment was cleared out of the way Lord George gave the word "March;" but Colonel Sloper, in Captain Ligonier's hearing, asked for time to get rid of picket-poles and encumbrances, and halted his squadron, although Lord George had replied that he must throw away his picket-poles as he advanced.

In consequence of this impeachment of Colonel Sloper's evidence the Judge Advocate decided upon re-examining some witnesses relative to this point. Sackville objected, but the Court permitted the Judge Advocate to proceed. Then, and not till then, was the question of cowardice specifically touched upon.

Lieut.-General the Marquess of Granby was consequently recalled, and asked whether, soon after the battle, Lieut.-Colonel Sloper had made any communication to him.

Lord Granby replied that a day or two after the battle—he could not pledge himself; he thought it was on the morning of the 2nd of August—Lieut.-Colonel Sloper told him that Wintzingerode, Fitzroy, and Ligonier had successively gone to Lord George with orders to march, which he did not obey. To the best of his belief Colonel Sloper added that Lord George was confused, or in a hurry—something to that purpose.

Lieut.-Colonel Edward Harvey, of the Inniskillings, said that Colonel Sloper, on the 2nd of August, made a similar statement to him respecting "the misbehaviour of Lord George Sackville."

Captain Ligonier, re-called, said that, directly after delivering his order to Lord George, he (Ligonier) not only spoke to Colonel Sloper, but that officer leant on his arm and said—

> For God's sake, Sir, repeat your orders to that man, that he may not pretend to misunderstand them; for it is near half an hour ago that he received orders to advance, and we are still here—but you see the condition he is in!

Lord George Sackville here, through the Court, asked for an explanation of these words. Ligonier replied that Lord George, for reasons which he (witness) could not explain, was perplexed, confused; but he could not answer for Colonel Sloper's meaning.

The Rev. John Hotham, Chaplain to the Staff, deposed that he was with Lord George by the wood (Point No. 1) when a cannonball fell near them. Lord George remained perfectly calm, and said, "You have no business here, fare you well, we shall soon be engaged."

Lieut.-Colonel Hotham, Lieut.-Colonel Bisset, Lieutenant Sutherland, Captain Lloyd, *A.D.C.*, Lieut.-Colonel Preston, Captain Williams, Captain Hugo, *A.D.C.*, and Captain Brome, *A.D.C.*, all deposed that they saw nothing unusual, or having the appearance of fear in Lord George's manner. Captain Smith, A.*D.C.*, said that Lord George would have gone to his death that day had it been necessary.

The Judge Advocate then, at considerable length, commented on the evidence. He said that Colonel Sloper's evidence rested, in the main, unshaken, in spite of Lord George Sackville's impeachment; also, that the evidence tended to prove that Colonel Sloper's remarks had been made prior to the issue, on August 2, of the General Orders.

Lord George's avowal that the prince received him civilly, and without censure, during the action proved nothing but that the prince maintained his calmness, after having sent an order to Lord Granby which Lord George had failed of carrying out.

The orders carried to Lord George had been, with an unimportant exception, clear and identical. This had not only been proved by several witnesses, but by Lord Granby's actual conduct in explaining to Lord George his reading of the orders which he proceeded to carry out, without finding any impediments offered by the fir-wood, obstructing regiments, or impracticable ground.

Evidence had amply proved that, far from being an *aide-de-camp* of no *status* in the British Army, Captain Wintzingerode had been regarded as a reputed *aide-de-camp* throughout the Allied Forces, and—as such—Lord George had previously recognised orders brought by him, and other foreign *aides-de-camp*.

Lord George had, with great minuteness, endeavoured to prove that, if any time had been lost, it was of quite unimportant duration.

★★★★★★★★★★

It would appear that Lord George suggested that the whole, and only, delay occurred while he was galloping to Prince Ferdinand. Lord Pembroke (Lieut. Colonel of Elliot's Light Horse) about a year later

> rode over the ground. He said "This I can swear, that my horse, without trotting a yard, walked from the extremity of the right wing of the cavalry to where the duke was, and there is no possibility of mistaking the place, in six or seven minutes and a half—I can't positively say which."—*Hist. MSS. Com.*, Rep. XII. App. pt. 10.

★★★★★★★★★★

This, at so critical a juncture, was not the point: if any time whatsoever had been needlessly wasted by Lord George, he was guilty of disobedience—if not, he was entitled to acquittal. The verdict was—

> That in the opinion of the Court, Lord George Sackville is guilty of having disobeyed the orders of Prince Ferdinand of Brunswick . . . and that he is hereby adjudged unfit to serve His Majesty in any military capacity whatsoever.

By the king's special command this rider was added—

> It is His Majesty's pleasure that the above sentence be given out in Public Orders, that Officers being convinced that neither high birth nor great employments can shelter offences of such a nature, and that seeing they are subject to censure much worse than death to a man who has any sense of honour, they may avoid the fatal consequences arising from disobedience of orders. (Officially sent to Lord Granby, April 25, 1760.—*Rutland MSS.*, vol. ii.)

The sentence was received throughout England with intense interest, and with varying impressions, and was read later at the head of each line of the troops in Germany, drawn up under arms with all the generals present. The king's expression of "censure much worse than death" bears out Walpole's opinion, that His Majesty considered the sentence inadequate, as the Duke of Newcastle most assuredly did.

With Lord Granby's presence in England, we have not yet done; but it must be understood that he had started back to Germany on the conclusion of his evidence, and before the issue of the sentence. The Duke of Newcastle wrote to him—

> I send Your Lordship in confidence, by the king's order, a copy of the very extraordinary sentence by the court martial; so short of what we had a right to expect, and, I may say, of the merits of the question. It is, however, a full condemnation of Lord George's behaviour, and a full justification of the king and Prince Ferdinand, and what they had done.

Guesses were made at the possible motives which had influenced Sackville, (Archenholz suggests that Sackville sought to ruin Prince Ferdinand in order to supersede him)—that he had, for example, wished to balk Prince Ferdinand of a signal and crowning victory; or, believing him beaten, to have sought the credit of saving the British cavalry. Stories were raked up that the late Duke of Marlborough and Admiral Howe had previously imputed cowardice to Sackville in connection with the attack on St. Malo.

The truth is to be sought in the fact that Sackville was an ambitious, scheming politician first, and a soldier only in a secondary sense, at a date when military and political power could be held simultaneously. He was a superficially clever, accomplished man whose actions were far less prompted by any honourable ambition to render public service than by an intense appreciation of his own value and importance; the furtherance of which engrossed, and encouraged, the crafty bent of his intelligence.

After Lord Ligonier, the Command-in-Chief of the Army would almost certainly have devolved upon him; or political developments might have easily brought him the Premiership. Without being in the least degree guilty of cowardice as a soldier, it is quite possible that he thought to reserve his important self for a greater political future, sooner than heedlessly risk his life in what he contemptuously called Pitt's "buccaneering expeditions," so fruitlessly directed against the French coast.

As to what actuated him at Minden—jealousy, pique at receiving no notification of Prince Ferdinand's plan of action—who shall say? But, were he a mere coward, why should he, possessing commanding position and interest, sufficient talents, perfect aplomb, and fair capability of winning "the bubble reputation" in any other profession, have sought it even as near "the cannon's mouth" as he attained to at Minden; and in the course of a war to which he repaired from nobody's initiative save his own, a circumstance which nearly entailed his recall? (Archenholz describes him as an Englishman unworthy of his country, but neither wanting in talent, nor in personal courage).

The court martial found him guilty only of disobedience to orders; and, at this distance of time when the enmities and prejudices, aroused in the hearts of many gallant but disappointed soldiers of 1760, he buried with them a hundred, or more, years deep in the past, we may safely concur in that verdict. All imputations of cowardice should be dissociated from the memory of Lord George Sackville's name: the

Marquess of Granby long since led the way in that direction. Commenting upon his conduct during the trial, Horace Walpole wrote—

"Lord Granby showed the same honourable and compassionate tenderness as Conway. So far from exaggerating the minutest circumstance, he palliated or suppressed whatever might load the prisoner; and seemed to study nothing but how to avoid appearing a party against him—so inseparable in his bosom were valour and good nature." (Lord George Sackville repaid this by writing some detractious things concerning Lord Granby and his family in after years).

Such unqualified praise from Granby's chief detractor should perhaps be gladly accepted without comment. But it is significant to mark how, even in this praise, Walpole must needs award an equal share to Conway! Except for what he may have said in private conversations Conway should scarcely have been quoted, for he was not engaged in the German War until long after Minden, neither did he sit on the court martial, nor play any part but that of the merest spectator in respect of the Sackville drama. To compare him therefore, in the matter, to Lord Granby who played so eminently an important part in it, was vicariously to inflate Conway after the fashion of the fabled frog. Providentially the frog's fate did not overtake Conway on the many occasions when Walpole thus fondly tampered with his moral dimensions.

The particular copy of the *Proceedings of a General Court Martial* (published by Authority: London, 1760) which was used in compiling these pages, formerly belonged to "Mr. Wm. Bateman, F.S.A., of Middleton by Yolgrave in the County of Derby." He carefully annotated the volume, and amplified it with newspaper cuttings relative to the after lives (chiefly the deaths—if the Irishism be permitted) of many of the men who figured in this historic trial. On the fly-leaves Mr. Bateman recorded that he took the book, in 1817, to read to a veteran named James Fisher, then aged eighty-two, who had served in the "Greys" at Minden.

The old dragoon was intensely interested, and remembered many of the circumstances cited of the day, which he said was so intensely hot and dusty that, added to the severity of the action, the faces of the infantrymen became almost black. He was especially interested by the evidence concerning the 2nd Line of Cavalry, in which he served; and, in regard to the order brought by Captain Wintzingerode, Fisher said he was close to the Marquess of Granby when he received it, and observed His Lordship remove his sash and bind it tightly round his waist as he prepared to lead the Scots Greys through the fir-wood for the expected charge.

One more matter concerning the marquess is suggested by Walpole's estimate of the material loss sustained by Lord George. (Sackville's name was struck out of the Privy Council Book by the king himself, and appearance at Court forbidden him.—Duke of Newcastle's *Memoranda for the King.* April 23, 1760—*Newcastle Papers*). Walpole states (letter to Sir H. Mann), the regiment to have been worth £2,000 a year, the command in Germany £10 a day, and the Lieut.-Generalship of the Ordnance £1,500 a year. (The salary was £1,100, but all offices carried profits in addition to the actual pay). Allowing for the superior pecuniary value of the Blues to the 2nd, Queen's, Dragoon Guards, Lord Granby's military and official income must at this period have amounted to close upon £8,000 *per annum.*

CHAPTER 10

1760: Return to the Continent

Shortly before the date of the marquess' return to Germany, some letters afford a clue to what had resulted from his conferences. Lord Robert Manners Sutton, in consequence of Prince Ferdinand's deficiency of Light Cavalry, forwarded to the Duke of Newcastle a proposition which had already been sanctioned by Mr. Secretary Pitt. (March 1, 1760).

> The Marquess of Granby ventured to flatter himself that many tenants and people of the counties where the family estates lay would eagerly enlist in a corps under his command. The corps was to constitute a Light Dragoon Regiment consisting of 6 troops, each comprising 2 sergeants, 2 corporals, 2 drummers, and 60 effective privates. . . . Lord Granby to be colonel, without pay. Lord Robert Manners Sutton (proposed) colonel-commanding, with a lieut.-colonel, a major, and 6 captains. Lord Granby and the captains to find the men and horses without any expense to the publick, and Lord Granby engaged to raise them within two months of the beating order. Should Lord Robert Sutton be appointed to the head of it. Lord Granby thought that fact might also induce many of the old soldiers to return again to the service. (*i.e.* those who had served under Lord Robert in Kingston's Horse and the Duke of Cumberland's Dragoons.)

On the 28th of March Newcastle wrote to Jack Mostyn that he had that day obtained the king's sanction to Granby's Regiment, and supposed "that Bob Sutton must have the charge of it." The king's approval of the scheme was officially conveyed to Lord Granby by the War Secretary, Lord Barrington.

The recruiting for this new regiment soon bore out Lord Granby's sanguine forecast, and the regiment was called the "21st Light Dragoons, or Royal Forresters" (*sic*). Its motto was *Hic et Ubique*, and it obtained, during its short existence, the character of being one of the finest regiments in the service. Critics of the stamp of "Junius," and of Horace Walpole, doubtless at the time complained of the conspicuous Manners component among its officers, but none had a better claim to the commissions. Lord Granby relied upon his family influence to enable him to raise the regiment in a time of universal war, when the authorities could scarcely enlist another man, and the compulsory Militia Embodiment by ballot had been met by violent resistance on the part of the country people, who believed that it rendered them liable to foreign service.

The 21st Light Dragoons included the following officers:—

Honorary Colonel—John Manners, Marquess of Granby.

Colonel—Lord Robert Manners Sutton, of Kingston's Horse and the Duke of Cumberland's Dragoons, and who served with distinction through the "Forty-Five," and the Flanders Campaign of 1747.

Lieut.-Colonel—Russel Manners, a cornet in the Blues, and captain in the 7th, Cope's, Dragoons, during the early portion of the Seven Years' War.

Among the other officers were John Holroyd, (later first Earl of Sheffield, Gibbon's great friend), Charles Harpur, and Edward Manners, who had not seen active service.

Mr. Thomas Thoroton actively assisted the marquess' practical scheme, especially in the obtaining of suitable horses. Recruiting Orders were issued impressing upon the officers that the men enlisted must be "light and straight, and by no means gummy." They were not to be under 5 ft. 5½in., or above 5 ft. 9 in. The uniform was scarlet with blue facings, trimmed with silver lace and buttons. The band wore black velvet hunting-caps. White bearskin horse furniture, with a silver cypher of "R.F." on blue cloth holster-caps, was used by the officers.

Mr. Pitt bestirred himself to the utmost in endeavouring to supply Lord Granby with the necessary reinforcements; and His Lordship was furnished with full powers to sanction, at discretion, anything His Serene Highness should deem necessary for the conduct of the war.

Granby, who had been appointed a D.L. for the county of Leicester, and a Governor of Christ's Hospital, returned to Germany between the 10th and 15th of April. He left a paper with the Duke of

Newcastle with the following recommendations:—

"To give Lord Broome (Granby's *A.D.C.*, afterwards Marquess of Cornwallis the best character to the king—the best and most admirable of men. Mr. Ambler (afterwards represented Bramber, with Thomas Thoroton, in Lord Granby's interest), for King's Council. A pension for General Elliott's (General Granville Elliott died in Germany soon after Minden), widow. Mr. Storer, (Lord Granby's Chaplain, occasional Secretary, and devoted friend), for King's Chaplain. Captain Hall for Deputy Adjutant General at home, (the Captain Hall who wrote the account of the engagement at Bergen. Granby thanked the king for giving Hall this appointment, May 14, 1760—*Newcastle Papers*).

Major-General Joseph Yorke, British Minister at the Hague, reported Granby's arrival at that place, and he reached Paderborn April 23, just in time to dine with Prince Ferdinand who was celebrating St. George's Day. A ball followed which Granby, naturally, did not attend owing to his recent bereavement.

The Duke of Newcastle's first news from home was that a proposal for a Congress had been coldly received by France, and as peace was improbable he hoped to hear of a speedy commencement of operations—"the first stroke, it is said, is half the battle." "Their great friend" (Mr. Pitt), considered that keeping the militia in good order afforded the only prospect of obtaining further reinforcements. Owing to Granby's position at the head of the British Army the period is now entered upon.

Both French and English were as yet unable to move, from the lack at that season, of green forage. De Broglie was riveted to his magazines in Frankfort; and Prince Ferdinand had to keep in touch, by the Elbe and the Weser, of supplies from Bremen and Hamburg.

General Mostyn subsided into ordinary military duties, saying that, as Newcastle had divided him into two personalities, "ye publick and ye private Mostyn," he could not quit the first without thanking His Grace for the honour done him. He likewise devoutly hoped the coming reinforcements would not be accompanied by an older lieut.-general than himself, as such an arrival "would hurt him more than the whole French Army."

These reinforcements included three regiments of Dragoons, the Carabiniers, "Waldegrave's," or the 2nd, Queen's, Dragoon Guards, and six battalions of Foot, under Major-General Griffin. ("Prince Ferdinand will be in raptures with the fine reinforcements you send him", May 13, 1760, General Yorke to Duke of Newcastle. Major-

General Griffin was afterwards fourth Baron Howard de Walden, and first Baron Braybrooke).

"This unanimous support of Parliament cannot but be a great encouragement to the King's Allies," wrote Lord Holdernesse; but, unfortunately, in the matter of numbers France could always outdo us. Frederick the Great had been able to send Prince Ferdinand some 2,500 cavalry at this date, which were very soon recalled. Newcastle assured Granby that, counting the above cavalry, the Allied Army amounted to 95,000 effectives—"a force more than sufficient to deal with M. de Broglie; but for God's sake Begin!"

The German historians, quoted by Carlyle, say that Ferdinand commenced this campaign with 20,000 English troops, which, with Hanoverians, etc., amounted to 70,000 as his total army. The force of 30,000 French, which under the Count of St. Germain was moving from the Rhine to join De Broglie, brought his grand total up to some 130,000 men.

★★★★★★★★★★

A return of the French Army in June, 1760, made out in French, probably copied from captured papers, represents it as numbering—

	97,315	on the Upper	Rhine—	*i.e.*	De Broglie
and	30,560	" " Lower	"	"	St. Germain
	127,875 (*Newcastle Papers*).				

★★★★★★★★★★

Both totals are stated in round numbers. The English Treasury remitted £150,000 monthly, and the Marquess of Granby had additional power to raise money upon warrants, drawn on the Treasury, should circumstances require it. A tremendous dispute arose soon after Granby's arrival. Mr. Michael Hatton, Commissary-General in Germany, told Baron Münchhausen that Prince Ferdinand's operations were being delayed by the Duke of Newcastle's dilatoriness at the Treasury, which prevented the completion of the magazines at Cassel, etc., without which the army could not march.

Munchhausen laid this complaint before the king and Pitt, which incensed Newcastle to the verge of frenzy; he being desperately jealous of Munchhausen, and afraid of him into the bargain. Newcastle fell upon the commissary-general tooth and nail. Everybody's wig was on the green both in England and Hanover, excepting Granby's; and that for the good reason that he never wore one, and always maintained his coolness and fairness on such occasions. Notwithstanding his advice, and tactful intervention, Newcastle succeeded in inflaming the king: Hatton was to be recalled—

> . . . he must forgive the Lords of the Treasury if, in an affair of such expense, they had more confidence in the Marquess of Granby, General and Commander-in-Chief, than in a Mr. Hatton!

Granby was "to ascertain the facts;" "undeceive Prince Ferdinand;" "justify the Duke of Newcastle;" but above all "to avoid offending Munchhausen." The air was full of hurtling vituperations concerning "the intolerable plague of this fellow Hatton." "My good friend Mr. Pitt is not always proof against such insinuations as have come from Hatton," wrote Newcastle, nervously, to Granby. During his long correspondence and political relations with the marquess, Newcastle never learnt that Granby's ideas of justice were not modified to suit circumstances. For Baron Munchhausen favours, or for Newcastle's private spites, Granby did not care so much as was conveyed in the Duke of Wellington's favourite expression of contempt—"a twopenny damn."

In January, 1759, he had already defended Mr. Hatton, whom, with customary self-effacement. Lord Granby had represented as deserving any credit due for the safe disembarkation of the British troops; and Hatton was pronounced from other quarters to be an honest man, and an able officer.

At the outset of this altercation Lord Granby was in bed at Paderborn with a violent fever—being bled, of course; and his letters were written by the Rev. Bennet Storer. Storer wrote again from Osnabrück. Lord Granby's fever had been—

> . . . very smart, attended with violent pains in all his limbs and an inflammation on his breast for which—and for the third time, he had been plentifully blooded.

In May, 1760, the troops were beginning to move towards Fritzlar, but His Lordship could not accompany them. In spite of his illness Granby did what he could for Hatton, in whom he had complete confidence, and who was most laborious.

In the end Newcastle, in a fine Pharisaical spirit, said "he thanked God he could forgive:" if Hatton was agreeable to Prince Ferdinand and Lord Granby, *they* could employ him; but Newcastle refused to have anything to do with him personally.

One temporary advantage accrued to Granby through Newcastle's determination to humiliate Hatton, though the commissariat in the end very much suffered. It was determined at home to send out Colonel Pierson, (1st Foot Guards), to relieve Lord Granby of the responsibilities of the Commissariat Department. Pierson was, of course, subordinate to Lord Granby's orders, but he was put over the heads of the civilian commissaries—Hatton to boot.

★★★★★★★★★★

> The Treasury desired that upon some points Lord Granby should maintain his supreme authority, especially in regard to the Secret Service Fund of £1,000 per month.—*Newcastle Papers.*

★★★★★★★★★★

Granby had already stated the utter inability of the general commanding to see to the minutiae of supply. He was on horseback, often from break of day till night, engaged in his purely military duties, and on regaining his quarters all remaining time was absorbed in necessary correspondence with Lords Holdernesse, Ligonier, and Barrington.

Newcastle's nervous temperament was further wrought upon by Granby's illness—

> My dear Lord, you must take care of yourself for the service of the public; in our present circumstances your absence for one day is a loss.... For God's sake don't throw yourself away, which you will do by going out too soon. The king, the public, and your friends want you.

Newcastle, further, enjoined Granby to postpone the society of "his jolly companions" until the campaign was closed by the winter.

When convalescent, Granby wrote, from Paderborn, his first letter to the Duke of Newcastle, which bears traces of great weakness. He had been excessively ill, and "blooded" four times; the fever was still upon him, and his uneasiness at this enforced inaction was increased by the duke's letters. The troops were marching on that day; but, under doctors' orders, and the prince's positive injunctions to obey them, Granby was remaining another day or two at Paderborn, but firmly resolved to arrive at Fritzlar in time to see the troops march in.

His eventual quarters at Fritzlar were two miles distant from Prince Ferdinand's, and he wrote to the duke—

> I assure you I am a very obedient patient to the physicians; at the same time I assure Your Grace that my fever was not

> in the least owing to any irregularities, and my dear Duke of Newcastle may likewise be assured that I will not let 'my jolly companions' (that I think Your Grace calls them in one of your letters) occasion a return of my old fever or create a new one. The great obligations I owe His Majesty will insure my not doing anything that may possibly put it out of my power of doing my duty. . . . I have lately got a commission in the Inniskillings for Cornet Turton, who is now in my family. . . . Nothing can make me so happy as that my friend Colonel Pierson should come over to me. ("Family" signified personal Staff).

The better news of Granby's health conveyed much relief to Newcastle and the king, "who had been in greatest pain about him."

> The king is extremely pleased with you, and has desired the Duke of Rutland to tell you to have your letters wrote in a larger hand, and blacker ink; and I have given Thoroton a specimen. I desire those to me may be in Turton's or Storer's hand, and a little blacker. (Both George II. and George III. were very particular about the calligraphy and style of official correspondence).

Thoroton had meantime been sending equally anxious inquiries on behalf of the Rutland family:—

> Lord Robert Sutton is labouring most assiduously to complete your Light Dragoons. The regiment is half complete, and the men are all most extraordinarily fine. . . . The king yesterday put an end to the Session of Parliament, and the town empties apace.

In pursuance of an inquiry of the king's respecting "the Royal Forresters," Thoroton sent the following memorandum to the Duke of Newcastle:—

> Lord Granby's Light Dragoons—230 strong; not a man under 5.5¾; near 300 horses, none under 14 hands, and the greater part above 15 hands.

Colonel Pierson arrived in Germany, and Thoroton told Granby that his friends at home were much pleased that His Lordship, by this change, was relieved of all troubles and vexations arising from army accounts, and Treasury details. Granby assured Newcastle that Prince Ferdinand fully confided in His Grace's zeal for the cause, and hoped for speedy successes which would soon dispel all memory of the late worries; the magazine at Cassel was fast being completed to two millions of rations.

Colonel Pierson's hand first appears June 5, 1700, in a letter from Fritzlar camp:—

> Lord Granby is perfectly well, and as much beloved as he deserves. The duke's (Prince Ferdinand), expression of him to me, amongst other compliments, was, '*Qu'il avail sûrement la plus belle âme du monde.*'

Directly following upon Lord Granby's recovery came another announcement of sorrow to him, and his family. The *London Chronicle's* report of the event ran—

> On Monday, 2 June, 1760, died at his grandmother's, the Duchess of Somerset, in Hill Street, after eating a hearty dinner, the Hon. Lord Roos, eldest son of the Marquess of Granby.

In a somewhat querulous letter, complaining of the non-receipt of news from Germany, the Duke of Newcastle wrote—

> I don't mention the last loss in your family. I pray God preserve you the two charming boys which are left.

Lord Granby's reply is missing, but he acknowledged a very kind letter of condolence from Lord Holdernesse, saying he "should always remember it as a mark of His Lordship's friendship."

England having no more fears of invasion, the king announced his intention of sending to Germany "Honywood's" (the 4th Horse), and "Elliot's," cavalry regiments, under General Elliot. Elliot's Light Horse" (now the 15th, King's, Hussars) had been quite recently embodied, light cavalry having been during a considerable time out of vogue in the British Army. A light troop only had been latterly attached to certain heavy dragoon regiments, but the services of "Kingston's Light Horse" during the "Forty-Five," and the "Duke of Cumberland's Dragoons" during the Flanders Campaign of 1747, had proved the efficacy of this arm. "Elliot's" was a sort of lineal descendant of both of the above regiments; it was recruited from a superior class of man to that ordinarily available, and, strange to say, included a large body of *ci-devant* tailors.

★★★★★★★★★★

A number of journeymen tailors and clothiers, who had come to

> London to petition Parliament to redress some grievance, enlisted in Elliot's." Charles Lamb refers to this in his Essay on "the Melancholy of Tailors": "Valiant I know they can be," etc. General Elliot was later created Lord Heathfield. and a portrait of him as Governor of Gibraltar, by Reynolds, is in the National Gallery.

****

A *Gazette* to it as "the 15th Dragoons, late Cumberland's broken," and it was the first of the resuscitated light dragoon regiments of which Lord Granby's, the 21st, formed one.

Granby was delighted to hear of this reinforcement and of General Elliot's appointment:—

> I am sorry my regiment is not ready; but I hope as soon as it is that His Majesty will be graciously pleased to add one more favour to the many His Majesty has already bestowed on me by indulging my brother with an opportunity, at the head of my regiment, of showing his zeal for His Majesty's service here in Germany.

The *Newcastle Papers* at this date contain many allusions to the commissariat difficulties, concerning which Horace Walpole has furnished a comparison between Lords Granby and George Sackville. Commissariat details are not interesting enough to be dealt with exhaustively, but it is necessary to notice Walpole's assertion in reference to them that—

> Lord Granby was tractable, unsuspicious, and not likely to pry into the amazing impositions of the German agents which Lord George had insultingly let Prince Ferdinand see had not escaped his attention.

Unsuspicious Lord Granby undoubtedly was—it is a common practice of men of single-hearted purpose and lofty sense of honour to attribute corresponding integrity to those with whom they are brought in contact; and they usually suffer for it. But that Granby was tractable, or likely to tamely submit to "amazing impositions," would scarcely have been asserted had Walpole been able to examine the Duke of Newcastle's correspondence, which is now public property.

That he was specially well fitted to cope with contracts, and the contractors—mostly Jews—who submitted them, would be foolish to assert; but that he worked assiduously and conscientiously to safeguard the public interests is proved. (See Granby's letter, in which he alludes to the hesitation he was held to have shown about drawing for money). And his endeavours were maintained in face of Newcastle's repeated injunctions to "have done with the Hanover *Chancellerie*," and of the king's evident wish that the expenditure should be controlled by the Hanoverian officials and Prince Ferdinand alone.

Soon after returning (with his "full powers"), Lord Granby was apostrophised by the Duke of Newcastle for having refused to draw for some forage accounts:—

> Your Lordship had, has, and shall have, full power to grant warrants upon the deputy paymaster for any money you may think necessary for the service of the army . . . for God's sake, my dear Lord, let us have no more doubt or difficulty on this point.

Granby replied that, on the latter point, he had no doubts whatever; but the *Chancellerie* having submitted to him some old forage debts, he had flatly refused to pay them, as pertaining to a period before he held the command, and as having no claim upon his monthly remittance of £150,000. However, should the Treasury wish it, he would gradually discharge these debts out of any surplus he might find himself possessed of after providing for current needs.

That influences were at work which Granby proved powerless to oppose there can be no question. As will be seen, no sooner had Colonel Pierson arrived as "Commissary General," than George II. insisted on his commanding the battalion of the 1st Foot Guards (in which regiment he was major); and Prince Ferdinand attached him to his personal Staff. Pierson was too keen a soldier to resist these arrangements which absorbed all his time, and the commissariat soon fell into a condition of hopeless confusion, and deadlock.

CHAPTER 11

1760: Corbach, Emsdorff and Warburg

The advance of the Allied Army, about May 5, 1760, into Hesse was effected under circumstances, roughly, as follows. General Spörcken was left with a detachment in the bishopric of Münster to watch the approach from the Rhine of the French Army of Reserve under the Comte de St. Germain. The towns of Cassel, Dillenburg, Marburg, and Ziegenhayn were garrisoned by Prince Ferdinand, and General Imhoff was placed in advance upon the River Ohm, near Kirchain, to hold the passes of that river against the main French Army advancing from Frankfort under De Broglie. Lord Granby remained with Prince Ferdinand and the main Allied Army (from which Frederick the Great had recalled his detachment of Prussian Cavalry), which Ferdinand was now marching, by Fritzlar and Ziegenhayn, intending for the heights of Hombourg, near the River Ohm. The Duke of Newcastle, from the safe neighbourhood of Lincoln's Inn Fields, made light of the withdrawal of the Prussian contingent, and assured Granby the Allies *must* number 92,000 well-conditioned, well-supplied troops, which "should give a good account of the enemy, with the Blessing of God."

The French main Army advanced northwards to Grünberg, and was reported to be in bad spirits notwithstanding its numerical superiority; Marshal de Broglie declaring that he should endeavour not to survive a defeat. A mistaken movement on the part of General Imhoff, permitted De Broglie to cross the River Ohm, an advantage which gave the French the command of that river, the possession of Amöneburg and Marburg, and enabled them to occupy the heights of Hombourg, which Prince Ferdinand had not nearly reached. (General Imhoff's instructions are stated to have been confusing, but Prince Ferdinand blamed him so relentlessly that Imhoff shortly afterwards resigned). Ferdinand in consequence halted, retreated from Ziegenhayn, and presently formed his camp at Sachsenhausen.

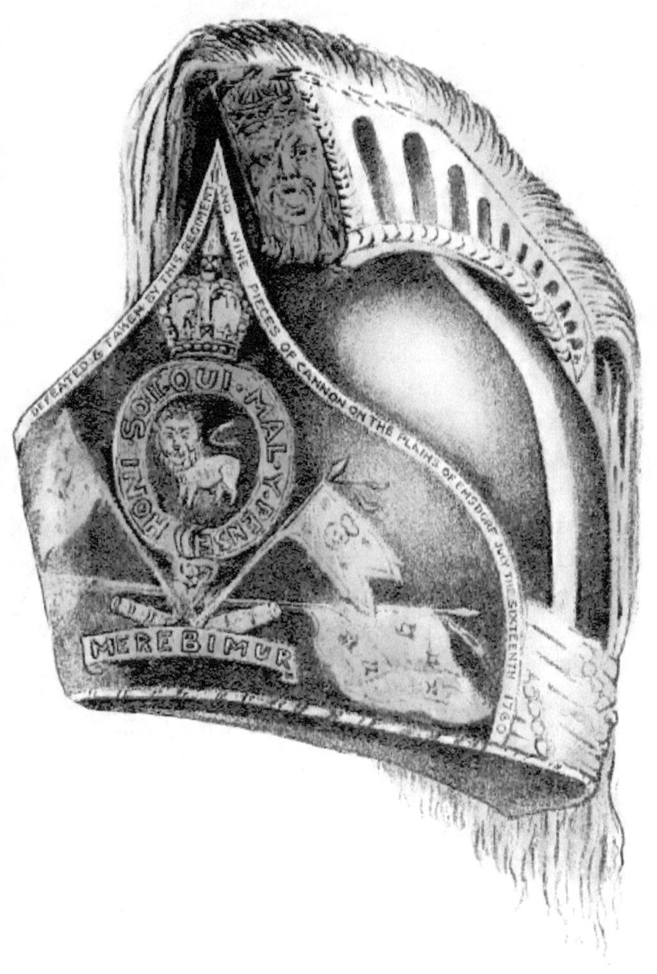

Helmet issued to Elliot's Light Horse after the Seven Years' War, and bearing the inscription: "Five Battalions of French defeated and taken by this regiment with their colours and nine pieces of cannon on the plains of Emsdorf July the sixteenth 1760."

Facsimile of a sketch by Captain L. Kennard, 15th Hussars, of the specimen belonging to the Officers' Mess of that Regiment, formerly "Elliot's."

At a Council of War held June 27, 1760, it was agreed to change the infantry to the 1st Line of the Allied Army, and the cavalry to the 2nd Line in consequence of the unfavourable nature of the country for cavalry tactics. Lord Granby remained with the 1st Line. De Broglie was pressing on via Neustadt, Rosenthal, and Frankenberg to the Heights of Corbach which General Lückner was holding. The opposing armies were soon only divided by a march of about three hours, and Lord Granby described the Allies as "under arms every morning by daylight, the infantry gaitered, cavalry saddled and bridled, and artillery horses harnessed, ready to march and form line of battle at the firing of 3 signal guns,"

In the interim the Hereditary Prince had been detached on outpost and reconnoitring expeditions; his command including two squadrons of the Scots Greys, and two of "Mordaunt's." (10th Dragoons). In an affair resulting from one of these, near Zielbach, the Hereditary Prince owed his life to an act of chivalry on the part of an officer of the French cavalry regiment of Berchiny which was badly cut up in the skirmish. The Frenchman had his pistol at the breast of the prince whom he suddenly recognised by the ribbon of an Order, and he dropped his hand sooner than take the life of a man whose gallantry had won the hearts of the French Armies. In another De Bauffremont's Dragoons, under M. de Poyanne, were almost annihilated by "Lückner's Hussars," and the 87th (Keith's) Highlanders—the Highlanders returned to camp riding the captured French horses.

★★★★★★★★★★

The Highlanders had only just joined at Fritzlar and Ziegenhayn; they were known as the 87th and 88th Highland Volunteers—the 87th under Major Robert Murray Keith, the 88th under Lieut.-Colonel Campbell.

★★★★★★★★★★

Meanwhile the Comte de St. Germain with the French Army of Reserve was rapidly advancing from the Rhine towards Corbach, and, though Ferdinand's position at Sachsenhausen was intrinsically a strong one, it was in continual danger of being outflanked owing to the detached operations possible to De Broglie with his two armies, and his vast superiority in numbers. On the 10th of July the Hereditary Prince, with a mixed German and English force, was ordered from Sachsenhausen to Corbach, which St. Germain had occupied with his van-guard after driving out General Lückner's small detachment there.

★★★★★★★★★★

The mixed force consisted of twenty-one battalions and nineteen squadrons, among which were Carr's, Brudenell's, Hodgson's, Cornwallis'; and three squadrons of Bland's Dragoons and two of Howard's, under Major-General Griffin.

★★★★★★★★★★

On the arrival of the Hereditary Prince, with whom were Major-Generals Griffin and Oheim, at Corbach, he is supposed to have under-estimated his opponents, and not to have realised the proximity of St. Germain's main army; at any rate, he attacked with his customary dash, and a ridiculously inferior force. He soon found himself not only opposed by St. Germain in force, but threatened on his rear by reinforcements from De Broglie's army, which were moving to join St. Germain, on the heights of Corbach, from Frankenburg.

Placing himself at the head of two squadrons, each, of Bland's and Howard's Dragoons, commanded by Major Mills and Lieut.-Colonel Moucher, the Hereditary Prince led an effective charge which enabled his infantry to retire creditably; but he lost nearly the whole of his right brigade of artillery under Captain Charlton. Major-General Griffin eminently distinguished himself, both in the attack and retreat.

The outposts of the camp at Sachsenhausen, where Lord Granby was in command during Prince Ferdinand's absence (who had moved to Wildungen with a large force), were threatened during this engagement, and Colonel Pierson described Granby's mortification at hearing the cannonade while not being able to stir to the Hereditary Prince's assistance; and Granby apologised to Newcastle for a short account of this affair: "being much tired with having been on horseback since 2 in the morning, owing to several alarms on the outposts."

Prince Ferdinand returned to Sachsenhausen camp, recalling thither the Hereditary Prince; and the latter's defeat, which entailed a loss of eight hundred killed and wounded, and eighteen pieces of cannon, decided George II. in sending to Germany one battalion of each of the three regiments of Foot Guards, which reinforcement sailed for the Weser, from the Nore, July 28, 1760, under the command of Major-General Julius Caesar, (died in Germany from the effects of a fall from his horse in 1762).

An attempt of De Broglie's on Fritzlar was repulsed without loss to the Allies, except a serious personal one to Lord Granby. The French Hussars captured sixteen of his horses, turned out to grass, together with two which Lord Fitzmaurice had procured from England as an intended present to Marshal de Broglie. It would be interesting to know whether his just share of this loot ever reached the marshal.

On the 14th of July the Hereditary Prince avenged his repulse of Corbach. He was sent south, on a secret expedition, to dislodge General Glaubitz who was maintaining the communications between Amöneburg and Marburg (from whence De Broglie was drawing his supplies), and with whom he came on terms near Emsdorff. Glaubitz's force consisted of five battalions of infantry, the Berchiny Hussars, and some *chasseurs*; his principal camp was behind the village of Exdorff, his right lying towards Allendorff, his left at Emsdorff.

The Hereditary Prince commanded six battalions of German infantry, and Lückner's Hussars.

★★★★★★★★★★

"Lückner's Hussars" (a Free Corps) were formed in 1757 by Oberstwachtmeister Nicolaus v. Lückner, and disbanded after the Peace of Hubertsburg. They wore a white uniform, trimmed with gold braid; and a gold-laced, scarlet pelisse edged with black fur. The busby was black, with a scarlet busby-bag. Sabretache and shabraque were both scarlet, trimmed with gold lace, and bearing the White Horse of Hanover surmounted by a crown.—*Uuiformenkunde* (Richard Knötel), IV. Band, No. 24.

★★★★★★★★★★

"Elliot's Light Horse," which were nearing the Allied headquarters after their long march from the coast, were ordered to proceed to a given rendezvous where they should join the expedition. General Elliot and Lord Pembroke (the colonel and lieut.-colonel) had already left the regiment for headquarters, and it was commanded by Major William Erskine.

Having arrived near Exdorff, after a march considerably delayed by the great heat of the weather, the Hereditary Prince sent his infantry (the men stripped to their waistcoats) to get round the enemy's left. Upon the firing of a signal gun by the infantry, the cavalry, led by the Hereditary Prince, attacked the front at a gallop, upon which Glaubitz's Cavalry, taken unawares, retreated towards Kirchain, leaving the infantry to follow as best they could. Lückner now made for the camp at Exdorff; but Major Erskine, leaving Exdorff on his right, pursued the French cavalry, and formed on the heights between Kirchain and Langstein, thus cutting off the retreat of the infantry.

★★★★★★★★★★

Lord Pembroke wrote: "Those rogues of Hussars ran at once for plunder into the enemy's camp, and, without striking one blow or firing a single shot, got everything, became rich, and doubtless will be soon all barons."—*Hist. MSS.* Com., Rep. XII. App. pt. 10

★★★★★★★★★★

Erskine then sent detachments to chase the straggling bodies of hussars who were crossing over the River Ohm for Amöneburg on the further bank. About sixty or seventy of the fugitives were captured. Meanwhile, the French infantry finding their retreat by Kirchain cut off by "Elliot's," made for Amöneburg by way of the bridge called the Brücker-Mühl (which became so famous as the last scene of the war in 1702). The Hereditary Prince's infantry and Lückner's Hussars were following the French and firing on their rear; but, for the moment, both horses and men of "Elliot's" were too blown after their exertions to charge. The Hereditary Prince rode up to them, thanking them for their brilliant conduct, and placing himself at the head of the regiment, asked them to make one more effort against the still retreating French infantry, which could now be seen marching in one column, headed by their grenadiers, for Nieder-Klein.

"Elliot's" answered gallantly to the prince's call, and approached the French column, forming in four squadrons on its right flank; when within some thirty paces of them the French faced about, and poured a withering fire into the Light Horse, who charged with two squadrons on the French centre, and one on each wing. The wings were broken, but the stronger centre offered more resistance, until, discharging their carbines almost in the enemies' faces, "Elliot's" rode clean through their ranks. About 400 or 500 of the French surrendered, while the rest continued a broken retreat, this time making for a wood on the road to Hombourg (on the Ohm).

Major Erskine again advanced on either flank of the French who, as he was preparing to charge, beat a parley and, to the number of 1,655, laid down their arms. Glaubitz himself was taken with all his tents, and nine cannon.

The casualties on the prince's side were very serious: he himself was wounded in the shoulder, and Elliot's Light Horse, which went into action 450 strong, lost in killed and wounded 4 officers, 125 men, and 168 horses—a grim baptism of fire, the memory of which is perpetuated by the word "Emsdorff" on their kettledrum-banners, and on the officers' full-dress pouches and sabretaches.

★★★★★★★★★★

Captain-Lieut. Basil, and Cornet Burd, of "Elliot's," were killed. Of Cornet John Floyd Lord Pembroke wrote: "Little Floyd whom you have seen at my house, just past 12 years old, behaved most gallantly, which I was very glad of. I could only have wished he had not had his horse shot under him, for it was an exceeding pretty one I had lent him."—Hist. MSS. Com., Rep. XXL App. pt. 10.

****

As a record of a first service by a new regiment this is hard to beat. The ground covered between the first attack and the point of the surrender extended over six miles, and the prisoners taken by "Elliot's" amounted to more than four times the total of their own strength.

Marshal de Broglie sent his own surgeon to assist attending the Hereditary Prince, on his return to Kalle camp, who enthusiastically exclaimed to Prince Ferdinand—"*Les Anglais ont fait des merveilles!*"

Lord Granby wrote to the Duke of Newcastle a high encomium on these exploits of Elliot's Regiment, and eagerly repeated his request that his own regiment might be sent out:

> Send us the 'Royal Forresters,' I'll answer for them that they will do themselves the honour of showing their zeal for His Majesty's service.

The Hereditary Prince's wound proved to be trivial; his complete recovery was shortly afterwards commented upon in a letter to Granby from one of the Secretaries of State, (Holdernesse), and the prince was able to play an important part in the last of the three actions belonging to this group of operations.

De Broglie's and St. Germain's armies were now joined at Corbach, where, finding that he was to act subordinately to De Broglie, St. Germain (who was De Broglie's senior) retired from his command, which devolved upon the Chevalier de Muy. (The Duke of Wurtemburg, about this period, withdrew with his 10,000 men to Saxony to take part in the Austrian section of the war).

****

"St. Germain has left the French Army in a pet with Broglie, which we are not sorry for, though we have a miracle at our head, for he was clever—consequently troublesome."—Earl Pembroke to Lord Charlemont, July 16, 1760.

****

The Chevalier de Muy was ordered, with the French Army of Reserve, to the River Dymel, which he crossed, and presently encamped with his right at Warburg, and his left on the heights of Ossendorf, his army being between 25,000 and 30,000 strong. Marshal de Broglie remained at Corbach, and Prince Ferdinand's position at Sachsenhausen became every day more critical. (The armies were so close to one another that "the advanced posts heard one another's conversations."—Earl of Pembroke to Lord Charlemont, July 16, 1760). His flanks were, both right and left, incessantly harassed by De Broglie, whilst De Muy's advance to "Warburg threatened his communications with Westphalia and Hanover. He resolved upon a retreat towards Cassel, which he effected on the night of July 24-25, Lord Granby commanding the rearguard with Major-Generals Schlüter, Griffin, Honywood, and Elliot. The Allied Army accomplished its retreat, unmolested, by the heights of Freienbergen, to the plain of Kalle, ten miles north-west of Cassel, where it encamped; the Hereditary Prince continuing on to Wilhelmsthal.

The restless manoeuvres entailed upon the Allied Army at Sachsenhausen had proved very wearing to both men and officers; and after its retreat to Kalle camp, Lord Pembroke, Lieut.-Colonel of Elliot's Light Horse, wrote that, were it not for their confidence in the extraordinary ability of Prince Ferdinand, they should consider themselves in a very serious strait, threatened on all sides as they were by—

"De Broglie with an incredible mob full double ours, whatever political falsifiers might say in England. . . . We have too many perpetual rouses for correspondence, and very little rest or belly-provender in return . . . for never poor devils lived harder, or earned their pay more than we all do . . . lying on one's arm night after night in damned bad weather, sleeping and starving au Bivouac, or on a stone under a hedge. Notwithstanding all this, as poor beggars generally are, we are vastly jolly and happy." (July 28-29, 1760, to Lord Charlemont).

Lord Pembroke had been recently appointed Lieut.-Colonel of Elliot's Horse from the 1st Foot Guards, but was scarcely associated with the exploits of the former regiment, as, immediately after arrival in Germany, he was given the command of a cavalry brigade, consisting of the Scots Greys, Cope's, and Ancram's, acting as a major-general. As he said, "I had the misfortune not to be then with, or see, our friends (Elliot's Light Horse) make so excellent a beginning."

Prince Ferdinand's aim was, with Cassel in his rear, to cover Hesse and keep the River Dymel open, upon which depended his communications with the bishoprics of Münster, Paderborn, and Osnabrück. He is assumed to have intended to cut off the Chevalier de Muy on the Dymel, whilst maintaining the appearance of remaining in force before Cassel. But this scheme, threatened as the right of the Allied Army was by De Broglie, and its left by Prince Xavier (the Comte de

Lusace), prompted a prophecy on the part of Major-General Yorke, Minister at the Hague, which was fulfilled to the letter. Yorke assured the Duke of Newcastle that the crossing of the Dymel, as Prince Ferdinand apparently intended doing, must involve the loss of Cassel.

Ferdinand left Generals Lückner and Count Kilmansegge to cover Cassel, instructing them to retire upon Münden if attacked in too superior force. General Spörcken's Hanoverian Corps, which had rejoined the main Allied Army, was ordered to Liebenau, on the Dymel, followed by the Hereditary Prince with the British Legion, two battalions of British grenadiers, under Maxwell, the Highlanders, and four squadrons of "Cope's" and "Conway's" Dragoons.

★★★★★★★★★★

The British Legion must not be supposed to have consisted of Englishmen; on the contrary, it comprised Continental nationalities of all sorts.

The grenadier companies of several regiments were formed into a battalion under Major Maxwell; later, another battalion was similarly formed. They are often alluded to as the British grenadiers, and must not be confounded with the 1st Foot Guards.

★★★★★★★★★★

Chance, in the shape of a dense fog, favoured these movements on the morning of July 29, 1760, as the troops crossed the Dymel, and formed between Liebenau and Korbeke. Prince Ferdinand marched from Kalle camp at eleven at night, Lord Granby leading the right wing, consisting of the British cavalry and the 1st, 2nd, and 3rd Brigades of artillery: they likewise crossed the Dymel, and the whole finally formed on the heights above Korbeke at 5 a.m., July 31. The Hereditary Prince and Spörcken were then instructed to advance by Dinckelburg, with their left towards Dossel, to turn De Muy's left at Ossendorf.

The Allies were again assisted by a thick fog, under cover of which this corps left its camp and gained a valley, along which its advance was unperceived by De Muy until it suddenly debouched upon him at about 11 a.m. Prince Ferdinand and Lord Granby followed with the Main Army—Lord Granby still remaining with the 1st Line—the English Cavalry being led by General Mostyn, in the 2nd Line.

The preliminary attack was successful, even to prematurity, upon De Muy's left, which began to collapse upon his centre and right; but Prince Ferdinand was still some five miles distant from Warburg. Ferdinand remained with the infantry, which made dogged efforts to get up in time, and detached Lord Granby with the British cavalry and artillery. Granby took on the cavalry at a full trot over the intervening five miles. Arrived at a point called Meine, he formed in line of battle, the enemy commencing to waver as soon as Granby's Cavalry appeared, and which soon decided the day. The French rapidly broke before successive charges; Granby, at the head of the Blues, personally breaking the French lines three times.

A fine effort was made on the part of three French squadrons, which rallied and took "Bland's" regiment in flank, but Lieut.-Colonel Johnston with one or two squadrons of the Blues rescued "Bland's," and what was left of the gallant French squadrons had to join the prevailing movement in the direction of the River Dymel. "Irish" Johnston (Lieut.-Colonel James Johnston of the 1st Dragoons, not to be confounded with Lieut.-Colonel James Johnston of the Blues), with "Conway's" took an entire regiment, with Major-General Sockman, prisoners; the British Legion carried the town of Warburg, and a precipitate retreat of the enemy commenced across the Dymel, in which many of the fugitives were drowned.

An attempt at forming on the southern bank was disposed of by Captain Phillips with the English Heavy Artillery, and the Chevalier de Muy was soon in full flight towards Wilda and Volksmissen, thus escaping Prince Ferdinand's intention (of cutting him off from De Broglie), but signally defeated.

Prince Ferdinand, and the main body of infantry, did not arrive until the battle was over: he ordered Lord Granby to cross the Dymel, with 12 British battalions and 10 squadrons, in pursuit of De Muy, who continued his retreat towards Wolfshangen. Granby bivouacked for the night at Wilda, and, on August 1, as Marshal de Broglie advanced in force from Corbach towards the Dymel, Granby rejoined the Main Army at Warburg.

The main losses of the Battle of Warburg fell upon Maxwell's grenadiers and the Highlanders, who shared the principal honours of the Hereditary Prince's attack.

The Blues' loss was slight. Cornet Cheney and 6 non-commissioned officers were wounded, 2 non-commissioned officers killed, 7 troopers taken prisoners, and 23 horses killed or missing. The Chevalier de Muy left 1,500 on the field, besides 2,000 prisoners, 10 pieces of cannon and his papers, of which a trophy remains, annexed to Prince Ferdinand's despatches, in the form of an envelope addressed to—

Madame la Maréchale Duchesse de Broglie,
Place de Vendome,
Paris.

Prince Ferdinand's object was gained of keeping open his communications with Westphalia, and relieving Hanover from menace; but his success was dearly bought. In his despatch he informed the king that "*Mylord Granby a infiniment contribué avec la Cavallerie Anglaise au succes de cette action;*" and in his thanks, issued on August 1, 1760, to the troops engaged at Warburg, His Serene Highness directed the same—

> ....to be publicly given to Lord Granby, under whose orders all the British cavalry performed prodigies of valour which they could not fail of doing having His Lordship at their head.

The prince also thanked the officers—

> ....in particular Colonel Johnston, (probably Johnston of the Blues),and the family (*i.e.* Staff), of Lord Granby, in particular Captain Vaughan, as they continually attended Lord Granby in the different attacks of the cavalry and executed His Lordship's orders in the most punctual manner.

Colonel Pierson related how Prince Ferdinand received Lord Granby after the action. The prince thanked him for the many noble actions he had performed that day, saying that he had already formed and delivered his opinion of him, and was happy to see it verified. Pierson wrote: :—

> I may speak of Lord Granby, in a way he can't do of himself. There never could be a day more for the honour of the English Cavalry of which Lord Granby put himself at the head and charged in the manner that was always expected of him. Neither foot nor horse could stand against it, and a general confusion ensued as soon as they began to act.... Col. Clinton is very well, and Gen. Mostyn likewise who charged with the cavalry.

De Mauvillon, translated by Carlyle, recorded that:—

> It was in this attack that Lord Granby, at the head of the Blues, had his hat blown off; a big bald circle in his head rendering the loss more conspicuous. But he never minded; stormed still on, bare bald head among the helmets and sabres; and made it very evident that had he instead of Sackville led at Minden there had been a different story to tell. The English by their valour, and

he, greatly distinguished themselves.

A letter from the seat of war corroborates De Mauvillon in describing how Lord Granby personally broke the French lines three times bareheaded.

Jack Mostyn, not long before Warburg, had been described as unwell from a cause so singular that Colonel Pierson could not help explaining it to the Duke of Newcastle as having arisen from "a cold caught the preceding Sunday by going to church at Lord Granby's." However, he was well enough on the eventful day, and assured the Duke of Newcastle that this time—

> The British cavalry were up time enough to decide the success and share ye Glory of ye day. . . We drove the enemy from Warburg quite over the Dymel. ("We saw our cavalry drive the French pell-mell through the Demyl."—letter from Sir J. Innes Norcliffe of the Highlanders).

Mostyn wrote this August 1—the same day that Lord Granby indited his despatch to Lord Holdernesse, to which particular attention is invited. Granby commenced—

> It is with the greatest satisfaction that I have the honour of acquainting Your Lordship of the success of the Hereditary Prince yesterday morning.

As Prince Ferdinand could not be mentioned as an actual participator in the fighting at Warburg, Granby began by crediting the success, in general, to the Hereditary Prince. His Lordship then furnished details which have already been blended, above, with those contained in Prince Ferdinand's despatches, *etc.*, in the description of Warburg. He next proceeded to say some kind things of the Infantry which could not get up in time:—

> Gen. Waldegrave, at the head of the British pressed their march as much as possible; no troops could show more eagerness to get up than they showed. Many of the men, from the heat of the weather and overstraining themselves to get on through morassy and very difficult ground, suddenly dropped down on their march.

With the cavalry fight Lord Granby thus dealt:—

> General Mostyn, who was at the head of the British cavalry

that was formed on the right of our Infantry on the other side of a large wood, upon receiving the duke's orders to come up with the cavalry as fast as possible, made so much expedition—bringing them up at a full trot, though the distance was near 5 miles, that the British cavalry had the happiness to arrive in time to share the glory of the day, having successively charged several times both the enemy's cavalry and infantry. I should do injustice to the general officers, to every officer, and private man of the cavalry if I did not beg Your Lordship would assure His Majesty that nothing could exceed their gallant behaviour on that occasion.

In other words, General Mostyn was, in effect, placed in Granby's own jack-boots, and awarded all the Warburg cavalry honours.

In a private letter to the Duke of Newcastle Granby gave a similar account, and recommended the bearer, "Capt. Faucitt, my *aide de camp*, a very deserving, worthy officer," to His Grace's notice.

★★★★★★★★★★

William Faucitt served during the "Forty-Five" in General Oglethorpe's Regiment, and as a volunteer before Maestricht in 1747-8. In 1751 bought an Ensigncy in the 3rd Foot Guards, and served through the Seven Years' War, after which he was engaged upon many military missions to the Continent. In 1766 became Military Secretary to the Marquess of Granby when Commander-in-Chief. Adjutant-General, 1778. Knight of the Bath, 1786. Colonel of 3rd Dragoon Guards, 1792. General, 1796; and Governor of Chelsea Hospital. P. C, 1799. Died, 1804; and buried in the chapel in Chelsea Hospital. He changed the spelling of his name to Fawcett, and as Sir William Fawcett, K.B., was painted by Sir Joshua Reynolds (exhibited 1895. Royal Academy Winter Exhibition).

★★★★★★★★★★

William Faucitt had been *A.D.C.* to General Elliott, at whose death, after Minden, Faucitt was attached to Lord Granby's Staff. He was a most competent and intelligent soldier, possessed, among many accomplishments, of fluency in continental languages. On this occasion he carried all the despatches, and delighted George II. by describing the battle to His Majesty in the best of German. He was awarded £500, and allowed a few days' delay, before returning, in which to recover from severe bruises arising from the overturning of a post-chaise during his journey. At a levee he was given, publicly, a gracious message from the king to the Marquess of Granby and all the troops engaged at Warburg.

Unfeigned delight was felt by all, from the king and his ministers to the crowds in the streets of London, at this wiping out of the undeserved stain which had been cast upon the British cavalry by Sackville's conduct, just a year previously, at Minden.

Lord Holdernesse conveyed His Majesty's thanks and satisfaction to Granby and the British troops:—

> He is extremely pleased with Your Lordship's behaviour in particular, and is persuaded your example will have greatly contributed to encourage others to signalize themselves as Your Lordship has done very meritoriously yourself: for though you choose to be silent upon this occasion Prince Ferdinand has been careful to apprise the king how much Your Lordship contributed to the success of the day.

The *Newcastle* and *Rutland Manuscripts* contain many letters of congratulation from the Duke of Newcastle, Lord Holdernesse, Mr. Pitt, Lord Ligonier, Duke of Bedford, and the Solicitor-General, who remarked that "the cavalry were determined to have no more questions asked at a court martial!"

Newcastle wrote to the Duke of Rutland and to Lord Granby, assuring the latter that comparisons were being made by everybody between the behaviour of our cavalry, and our general, this campaign and the last.

> The modesty of your own relation, and the generosity with which you do justice to my friend Jack Mostyn charms everybody that reads your letter. . . . Faucitt, who seems a mighty pretty man, dined with me at Claremont yesterday and said the Blues behaved remarkably well.

To Jack Mostyn the Duke of Newcastle also wrote concerning the fact of "that great, good man my Lord Granby" having given him all the credit, for which generosity Mostyn ought not to fail of showing his appreciation. His Grace need not have troubled himself: Granby and Mostyn understood one another too well for the one to require, or the other to proffer, any of the florid assurances of gratitude upon which Newcastle set so much store. Mostyn replied:—

> I hope Your Grace will do me the justice to believe that no civility, no friendship of my Lord Granby's to me can be thrown away upon me, or that I can be such a wretch as to neglect any

> occasion of showing him how sensible I am of his goodness and friendship to me. . . . I beg leave to assure Your Grace that I am most sensible of ye honour My Lord Granby does me, that I am happy in being under his command, and that I will miss no occasion of showing that I think myself so.

The only person dissatisfied with Warburg, and Granby's conduct there, was (as usual) Walpole. One turns to his letters expecting to find an acquiescence, however reluctant, in the incontrovertible fact that Prince Ferdinand's estimate of Granby, expressed after Minden, had been verified to the letter. Walpole, on the contrary, wrote in his most waspish mood to Conway, ridiculing and deriding the battle, together with Prince Ferdinand, the Hereditary Prince, and Lieut.-Colonel Johnston of the Blues.

> The *Gazette* swears this no-success was chiefly owing to General Mostyn, and the Chronicle protests that it was achieved by Mylord Granby's losing his hat, which he never wears, and then His Lordship sends over for 300,000 pints of porter to drink his own health!
> (Walpole wrote after it was known that Cassel was lost, a circumstance which, however serious, had no bearing upon the bravery of those who fought at Warburg).

Surely this was but poor fooling, and another notable instance of Walpole's bilious determination to admit no credit in the case of such as he disliked. A three-cornered hat made of beaver is not of the first consequence as a protection against cavalry sabres or infantry bullets, nor did the fact of Granby charging bareheaded in any way enhance his valour. If anything, it was a circumstance humorous rather than heroic, that his bald head at Warburg constituted itself a sort of "Helmet of Navarre," an "*oriflamme*"—a rallying-point. Nevertheless, the incident pleased De Mauvillon (in our own day it obviously pleased Carlyle—no easy task), it pleased Sir Joshua Reynolds—not to mention the king, and the British public.

But they were wrong, all of them; the incident was fit only to be sneered at, and accordingly Walpole sneered his utmost. The humour of the "300,000 pints of porter" is not traceable, unless to a gift of a butt of that liquor offered by Sir William Calvert—among the many presents sent out to Germany at the time—and which is mentioned in a letter of Mr. Thoroton's, (to Lord Granby).

One most serious modification there was of the victory; for Major-General Yorke's prophecy proved true. While the French were being hurled back across the Dymel, Prince Xavier attacked General Kilmansegge, whom he far outnumbered: Kilmansegge was forced to retire, first upon Münden, and then across the Weser; and Cassel, with its immense magazines laboriously accumulated at enormous expense, capitulated. Besides Münden, Comte de Stainville attacked the garrison, all composed of German troops, in Ziegenhayn: the garrison surrendered, after six days' siege, as prisoners of war, and Captain de Derenthal, *A.D.C.* to Prince Ferdinand, was killed. Derenthal had been a witness at the Sackville Court Martial.

Prince Ferdinand maintained silence concerning the principal disaster, possibly hoping first to win Cassel again. But Faucitt, either with or without instructions, told the Duke of Newcastle that, prior to despatching him, Lord Granby had said he believed Cassel to have fallen.

Newcastle anxiously wrote for the real facts, saying, "Silence and mystery does great harm here;" and he informed General Yorke that neither Prince Ferdinand, Granby, Mostyn, nor Pierson had alluded to a circumstance which "could not be indifferent to His Majesty's Ministers. Granby's next letter contained no news of Cassel; he wrote—

> The commissariat is going well, but I am too hurried to do otherwise than give it over to Pierson. Marches, alarms, etc., etc.,

> drive the commissariat business sometimes out of our heads or at least postpone our consultations . . . the best way, I believe, will be to drub the French in a decisive action (which it is said M. de Broglie has received orders from Versailles *coûte qu'il coûte* to attempt) as we shall then have more leisure on our hands, at present I assure Your Grace I have no time to spare. I am just setting out to visit the posts being general of the day; it is near 6 in the evening and by the duke's permission I have preferred writing letters to dining with him, a strong proof of self-denial, as I have no objection to a good dinner when hungry, and hate writing at all times. Though the enemy is so superior in numbers should they attempt a general action I hope to send Your Grace a good account, but I can't help saying I wish we had more troops.

The Guards and other reinforcements had not yet reached Lord Granby's army, which owing to much sickness was once more fast dwindling. The king again questioned the Duke of Newcastle concerning Granby's "Royal Forresters," which His Majesty intended to despatch to Germany, and was informed that, though the regiment had reached the strength originally fixed, the War Office had ordered an addition of ten men to each troop. Lord Ligonier testified to the high commendations bestowed upon this regiment, which he and Lord Barrington quickly recognised as a happy recruiting-ground from which to detach drafts to the cavalry already serving in Germany.

Granby's two requests that his army might be completed by the middle of September, and that his regiment might be among the reinforcements, were neither complied with. Ligonier maintained that considering the strain placed upon the British Army and the number of actions fought in all parts of the world, England might claim to be possessed of the finest body of troops in existence. The old commander-in-chief was very ill at this time and wrote to Granby—

> Ill as I am, I cannot forbear representing to you, my dear Lord, what should be wrote in cyphers, that we have no more than 2 regiments of cavalry, and those full of old men who, though they may serve a year or two longer here at home are by no means fit for a campaign in Germany. The rest are boys, hardly able to manage their horses. The 8 regiments of foot, two thirds of them recruits, if drafted will become entirely useless.

Dwelling upon the requirements for America, Guadeloupe, Africa, and for opposing a threatened project of the French in Scotland, Ligonier concluded:

> Do, my dear Lord, consider our circumstances, and say what you would do in our place.

Mr. Pitt assured Lord Granby that his heart accompanied the momentous campaign, and that his concern was in proportion to the impossibility of supplying all that was needed:

> May one happy day on the Dymel dissipate every cloud that for some time has hung somewhat heavily on the scene."

The Guards arrived in the Weser, and made most creditable marches. Colonel Pierson went three days' march out from camp to meet them, and reported them very tired after nine days' incessant movement. On their arrival at headquarters, they were paid the compliment of furnishing, daily, Prince Ferdinand's guard consisting of a lieutenant, an ensign, and fifty men.

Several mails were captured at this time by either belligerent, which must account for the lack of intelligence which existed both in London and Germany. The king and Newcastle were intently awaiting the truth about Cassel; the duke begging to be told everything: "not secrets, but public occurrences."

At last, the murder was out; despatches, and a belated letter from Colonel Pierson, announced that Cassel, with its immense stores, had fallen into the enemy's hands; and Lord Granby requested both the Duke of Newcastle and Lord Holdernesse to convey his gratitude to His Majesty for the messages with which Faucitt had returned. Granby assumed that the positions of the French were known from Marshal de Broglie's despatches which had been lately captured and forwarded to London. Prince Xavier's army was on the east side of the Weser, threatening to cross. Prince Ferdinand had honoured the marquess by adding to his existing command that of the Reserve then encamped at Maurode consisting of the British grenadiers, the Hanoverians, the Brunswickers, Imhoff's two battalions, and five British regiments of cavalry. Granby declared:

> Finer troops, I believe never were, and, at the head of them, I should be very happy to receive a visit from the enemy.

During this period of gloom which hung over St. James's and the River Dymel Jack Mostyn, as usual, provides a laugh—though this time at his own expense.

Lord Granby received notice that in recognition of His Lordship's high praise of General Mostyn's conduct at Warburg, His Majesty had ordered Lord Ligonier to offer Mostyn the Colonelcy of "Cope's Regiment." Newcastle added that as this was entirely the king's own idea, he thought Jack would do well to accept it; and that the vacant Governorship of Limerick, though procurable, was not worth his having. Considering George II.'s interest, and proficiency, in army matters this offer was almost inexplicable.

****

On one occasion George II. said he "would never lose a very good officer of foot by making him a very bad officer of cavalry" (*Rutland MSS.*, vol. ii. Ligonier to Granby.

****

It inflicted a hardship upon Mostyn, and placed him in a most trying dilemma; for "Cope's" was inferior in rank to the regiment he already commanded. "Cope's," or the 7th Dragoons, was absent in Flanders during the "Forty-Five;" but the term "Cope's dragoons" was associated with such as had done little at that period save exhibit a fine turn of speed in the opposite direction to the enemy.

"*Swifter than clouds before the wind, Or Cope before the Highlanders*" is a sample taken at hazard from the satires in prose and verse showered upon poor Sir John and the dragoons, which must in nowise be identified with the 7th Dragoons, who amply, and nobly, retrieved their colonel's reputation by many a gallant charge in the German War.

Mostyn wrote to Newcastle dutifully acknowledging the king's "kindness," and plaintively saying—

> My regiment is a Royal one of 3 squadrons, and ye 5th in rank; whereas 'Cope's' is not Royal, of 2 squadrons and 7th in rank. I am tumbled from a Royal Regiment to a Plebyan one: I lose my bit of Blue. Jemmy Brudenel will sing Your Grace ye song 'Oh, my bit of Blue!'

Mostyn's own wish was to wait for "Bland's" Regiment, the 1st, King's, Dragoon Guards, which his brother-officers all considered was his due so soon as old General Bland should die. A highly official reply was despatched to the Secretary at War by Mostyn, after which he took steps to ensure its being seen by the king by privately asking Colonel Pierson to press the Duke of Newcastle to bring about that result—

Mostyn said to Pierson:

You may tell His Grace, that I wrote that letter in a large black Munickhausen (*i.e.*, Münchhausen), hand on purpose that ye king should read it: you may tell him too that I wish Cope, his regiment, and Limerick all at ye Devil!

The Marquess of Granby
from a wax medallion dated 1746

Chapter 12

Personal Description

Personal description of a famous man at his most typical period is usually found at the commencement, or the end, of his biography. In neither place does it read most appositely. Coupled with his youthful doings it is anticipative—premature; and, deferred till after the chill record of his death, it comes too late to supply the requisite blending of his physical and moral attributes, except in a retrospect which not one in fifty readers is at the pains of making.

An appropriate background for a written portrayal of the Marquess of Granby is supplied by the Warburg episode which saw him approaching the zenith of his popularity, and influenced some of Sir Joshua Reynolds' portraits of him.

Possessed of great physical strength, tall, of robustly handsome and commanding proportions, fair of complexion, and with an abundance of bright healthy colouring, Lord Granby was an embodiment of precisely those characteristics which it pleases us as a nation, while it harms no other, to claim as exclusively English.

His features, though far from being classical, were well proportioned, manly—generous superlatively. They were instinct with the lovable qualities which endeared him to all classes at home, to the polyglot ranks of the Allied Army, and even to his professional enemies the French commanders.

What hair remained to him was crisply curly, and of the half-way shade which comes to most originally fair-headed men as years accumulate. Granby was bald at the premature age of twenty-four, and the circumstance was rendered doubly notable by his habit of appearing wigless, and, whenever possible, hatless at an epoch when men (though frequently carrying their hats under the arm) invariably wore wigs, or, if they possessed enough, their own hair, elaborately dressed *en perruque*; but never exposed their cranial nudity with the crude starkness of modern custom.

The older men, such as his father the Duke of Rutland, the Duke of Newcastle, Lord Chesterfield, etc., still wore long curled wigs descending to their shoulders, but the size was gradually diminished. By 1765 so many men had taken to wearing their own hair, curled in rolls at the side and tied at the back, that the master-peruke-makers petitioned the King's most Excellent Majesty to discountenance the "mode of fashion which so generally prevails of men in almost all stations wearing their own hair," thereby endangering the trade of the "peruke-makers, hair-manufacturers, ribbon-weavers, cawl-makers, etc." This was "Protection" with a vengeance.

Hence it may readily be grasped that Lord Granby's peculiarity which, in his portraits, scarcely even attracts our attention, rendered him a conspicuous figure, in or out of doors; and the close-shaven fashion of the day increased in him a smooth, bare appearance which contemporary testimony, (H. Walpole's), tells us became him by accentuating the fresh texture of his complexion, and the open sincerity of his expression.

That he was no "beauty" man, dear to a certain sticky school of fiction, will be evident if the foregoing words have achieved their main intention. The charm of his personality was due to the masculine, almost heroic, mould in which it was cast; to kindly, gracious manners; and to the unconscious nobility of his presence—to the rare circumstance, in short, of physically looking all that his most enthusiastic admirers held him morally to be. No man, we are assured, can be a hero to his valet; but that exacting critic might, haply, have admitted some claim, on Lord Granby's part, to the appellation.

Of portraits and presentments of the marquess there is a considerable abundance, in spite of the irreparable losses caused by the fire at Belvoir Castle in 1816.

Two crayon heads executed soon after he left Cambridge are at Belvoir: one is inscribed with the words "*Le Marquess de Granby, peint à Konstantinople par Liotard,* 1740," and was referred to previously in relation to his Eastern travels.

At Audley End Lord Braybrooke possesses a large full-length portrait of Granby by Allan Ramsay, painted, according to a Catalogue of 1797, before the marquess entered the army—this would fix its date between 1742-5 unless it was painted by Ramsay while studying in Italy, and during Lord Granby's tour.

At this early age Granby's forehead is represented as already growing very high. His hair is light, his complexion florid, and his tall athletic figure suggestive of unmistakable health and activity. He is dressed in a long dark blue velvet coat, a white waistcoat, and scarlet breeches; a white cravat, and lace ruffles, encircle his neck and wrists. His left hand rests on an extremely long walking-cane, and his cocked hat is carried under the arm.

A cameo-portrait, beautifully modelled in wax, comes next in chronological sequence, having been executed in 1746, just after the suppression of the Rebellion of the "Forty-Five." Though only twenty-four years of age, the marquess is represented quite as bald as in the painted portraits of some twenty years later.

About twelve years after the Rebellion Sir Joshua Reynolds commenced the first of his well-known portraits of Lord Granby simultaneously with England's implication in the Seven Years War. Eight portraits by Sir Joshua stand upon record, and, of these eight, five remain; two having been burnt, among nineteen other "Sir Joshuas," in the calamitous Belvoir fire, and a third at Messrs. Graves' Gallery in 1867. Besides these five, many replicas of them emanating from Reynolds' studio are in existence, to say nothing of copies.

Mr. Carlyle, in allusion to the Marquess of Granby's hatless charges at the Battle of Warburg, says that "the excellent Reynolds" painted him "bare and bald" solely in allusion to that engagement. This statement loses point from the circumstance that, with the exception of one of the burnt portraits (of which nothing can be asserted, since no record of its details survives, apparently), all Reynolds' pictures represent Granby not only bareheaded, but no hat appears in any of them, even as a detail of composition. Sir Joshua's pocket-books show that the marquess "sat" for two of them in 1758 and early in 1760, before Warburg was fought or dreamt of; so, it is plain that Granby's well-known contempt of wigs and hats influenced Reynolds before the date of the Warburg story, though the latter beyond doubt afterwards confirmed him in the idea, and more emphatically removed all *raison d'être* for any headgear in the subsequent portraits.

The 1760 portrait represents Granby three-quarter length in figure, and almost in profile as to the head. With his back to a column, he stands with the right shoulder thrown well forward, the right hand resting on the basket-hilt of his sword, and the left in his sash. In its best examples this is by far the most typical likeness of the marquess among the existing portraits by Sir Joshua. Vigorously firm in pose, and instinct with energy and purpose, it best accords with the written testimonies to Granby's appearance, and character. It was finely reproduced in mezzotint by Richard Houston in 1760, and the wide contemporary popularity accorded to that print endorses the above opinion.

But purely as a picture, for grandeur of conception and composition, the portrait which Reynolds exhibited in the year 1766, under the description of "A General Officer, whole length," should be awarded the place of honour. It represents Granby after he became commander-in-chief. Sir Joshua Reynolds, and Horace Walpole, both recorded the remark that the above picture was painted for the Marechal de Broglie. Though the whole scheme of this imposing canvas is on a far more magnificent scale than the 1760 portrait, the principal figure is less sturdily natural in pose, and is drawn with appreciably less vitality and vigour. Repeating the same aspect of the head Sir Joshua depicts the marquess, in this instance, standing on a natural platform of raised ground to enable him to rest his left arm on the quarters of a wondrous charger, held on the "off" side by a turbaned man.

The charger is of the conventional studio-war-horse strain, in spite of the real animal having been sent for Reynolds to study; but the fact that there is room, on this mammoth animal's wealth of back, for Lord Granby, Prince Ferdinand, and the Hereditary Prince, all three, in no way detracts from the effective background afforded by its tossing black mane to the "comely roundness" of his lordship's head. Besides the exuberant mane, a cascade of tail falls almost to the horse's fetlocks—picturesque admittedly, but uncharacteristic of "regulations" during the Seven Years War. Cavalry chargers were docked to an absurd and cruel degree, (a fashion due to William, afterwards Lord, Cadogan, Quarter-Master General in the Low Countries under the Duke of Marlborough); and, on more than one critical occasion, the consequent torment of flies came near to stampeding them.

Lord Pembroke, of Elliot's Light Horse, writing from Kalle camp said:

> Our cavalry excels them (the Hanoverians, etc.) much, when no flies make them mad; which the 'Cadogan' tail can't defend them against.

In 1747 long tails were adopted by "Cumberland's Dragoons," which followed the example of "Kingston's Horse" of the Rebellion; and they were gradually adopted by the Heavy Cavalry after the Peace of 1763. Picturesqueness is likewise responsible for the introduction of Sir Joshua's negro servant as a balance to the composition, when a trooper in the Blues, or the marquess' soldier-servant Nötzel, would have been more appropriate.

What has become of De Broglie's original picture? He later suffered many vicissitudes. After the taking of the Bastille during the French Revolution he fled, among the first emigrants, to Germany. His son was executed. Marshal de Broglie subsequently fought against France in the service of both England and Russia, and died, in 1804, at Münster, amidst the scenes of his former campaigns against Prince Ferdinand and Granby. It is probable that his property and household gods were confiscated, scattered, or destroyed; what fate befell his "Sir Joshua"? (Since the above was written, a pamphlet by Comte G. de Contades proves this picture to be at the Château de Rasnes, Normandy, and to belong to the Duc de Berghes).

The example of this portrait belonging to Her Majesty the Queen hangs in Queen Anne's room in St. James's Palace, whither it was removed from Carlton House. Another, at Trinity College, Cambridge, was presented by Charles, fourth Duke of Rutland, to his father's college, where it hangs in the principal Combination-room. As a pendant to Her Majesty's "Granby" there hangs a portrait of Count La Lippe Bückebourg, commander of Prince Ferdinand's artillery, and, during the war, known among the English Artillery as "the thundering Black Prince of Bückebourg." The head of Sir Joshua's negro peers over some battle litter in the foreground of this picture also.

Among the Duke of Rutland's collection at Belvoir is a "Sir Joshua" which, together with yet another in that at Petworth House, Sussex, appears to be a variant of the portrait of Granby last described, embodying different accessories. The Duke of Rutland's picture is a full-length practically identical with it in pose of figure. The left arm rests on a mortar in place of the horse. Lord Leconfield's picture at Petworth repeats the same pose, though the figure is three-quarter length only. The left arm is thrown over a rock, and the right hand grasps a baton to which, by the way, Lord Granby was not entitled.

Save the last, all these pictures convey suggestions of cavalry engagements in the distance. Sir Joshua painted for the fourth Duke of Rutland another portrait of Lord Granby accompanied by his *A.D.C.*s "Lord Cornwallis, General Fawcett and his hussar on horseback." This picture is not enumerated among those burnt in 1816.

A small equestrian portrait, probably by David Morier, depicts Lord Granby on a fine bay charger with an orthodox "Cadogan tail" which could scarcely hustle a midge. Granby is emerging at the head of the Blues from a wood. Again, he is bareheaded, but his Hessian servant, John Nötzel, in a blue and white hussar uniform, with busby, *pelisse*, and red hessian boots, is handing up the fugitive hat, which the marquess extends his right hand to receive. This picture represents him at the Battle of Warburg, though the wood might suggest part of the Minden story having got involved, and a cavalry encounter, on a plain adjoining, is in progress, in which the "Cadogan tails" of the horses, some riderless, are accurately depicted. Large scarlet holster-caps, richly embroidered in gold, cover Lord Granby's knees; the bridle is light and little ornamented, save by a scarlet snaffle-rein.

High up in a corner of the picture-gallery at Petworth House is another equestrian portrait representing "the Marquess of Granby relieving the Distressed Soldier," painted by E. Penny. It is a somewhat grotesque work of little artistic merit. The marquess has more the semblance of a short, rotund highwayman engaged in relieving the distressed soldier of what little he possesses. ("The sick soldier and his family are happily imagined and well executed. The officer, which seems intended for the Marquess of Granby, not so well."—Letter to the printer of the *St. James' Chronicle,* May 9, 1765). This picture, which was engraved by Houston, is chiefly notable as the sole one in which Granby appears, not only possessed of a hat, but wearing it.

These military portraits represent Lord Granby in the uniform of the Blues; a long dark blue frock (reaching to the calf of the leg) with narrow blue velvet collar, faced and turned back from the deep lapels to the extremity of the skirts with scarlet, heavily looped with gold. Over the right arm hangs a gold shoulder-knot. Lace ruffles fall from beneath wide scarlet cuffs looped also with gold. The frock is worn open over a bright steel cuirass, with gilt chasings, from beneath which appear the long flaps of a gold-laced buff waistcoat. A crimson sash is knotted loosely round the waist of the *cuirass*. Buff breeches buttoned on the sides far up the thigh are met above the knee by jack-boots furnished with small silver spurs.

In Reynolds' 1760 portrait the basket-hilted sword then worn by the Blues is represented: in the remainder a general's sword is substituted. The hat is three-cornered, of dark blue beaver, edged with broad gold lace and looped on the left side. In some of the portraits Lord Granby wears laced cambric round his throat; in others a black satin stock showing a white shirt-collar, or band.

The engravings after Sir Joshua's pictures, tine as some of them are in tone, impart a flaccid, chubby modelling to Lord Granby's features which is not apparent in the originals. An exception, tending towards the other extreme, occurs in H. Robinson's engraving of the Petworth House "Reynolds," and executed for "Lodge's Portraits." In this plate an aquiline, almost saturnine, character is bestowed upon the marquess' good-humoured face. Various small engraved heads, all after Sir Joshua's portraits, were executed for illustrated works, such as "Junius' Letters," and sundry periodicals; most of these are unintentional caricatures.

A copy of an interesting invoice relating to the 1760 portrait, by Sir Joshua, accounts for three replicas of it. The "sizes" "specified relate to the canvas and not to the figure.

The Rt. Hon: Lord Granby to J. Reynolds	Dr.
For His Lordship's picture kit-cat size, ¾ length given to Mr, Fisher,	£18. 18
D°. D°, " " Mr. Shaftoe the size between a whole & a half-length	50. —
D°. D°, a half-length sent to Mr. Calcraft	42. —
paid for miniature portrait of Lady Granby	6. 6
	£ 117 . 4

Received Jan 27th 1762 from Thomas Calcraft, Esq., the contents of this Bill, being in full of all demands

(Signed) J. Reynolds

Witness Thomas Beach.

****

Brice Fisher, Esq., M.P. for Malmesbury, and afterwards for Boroughbridge.

Mr. Shaftoe, one of Lord Granby's racing friends,

John Calcraft, Esq., of Ingres.

Lady Granby painted probably from Sir Joshua's portrait of Lady Granby, which was burnt in 1816.

****

In the Jones Collection, at the South Kensington Museum, is an oblong gold snuff-box, chased, and enamelled with groups in the Dutch style. The box is of French make, and bears the signature "*Le Sueur.*" Within the lid is a fine miniature of Lord Granby, around which is inscribed, "John, Marquess of Granby, to Brice Fisher, Esq., 1764."

Among the Franks and Schreiber Collections, in the British and Kensington Museums, Granby is represented by two similar statuettes of Bow porcelain. The Kensington example is minus the baton held in one hand, and the sword-blade. The tradition of the hat is conveyed by its position on the ground at his feet, where it lies among a flag, a cannon, a spontoon, some cannon-shot, and grenades. The companion, or pair, to these statuettes represents General Wolfe who, besides being contemporaneously famous, was born on the same day of the month as Granby, the 27th of January.

A very good likeness of Lord Granby occurs, in the same Collections, and in the Geological Museum, on some mugs, etc., of Worcester transfer-printed ware. Over his head a hovering angel bears a wreath; Fame blows the trumpet which Granby so consistently refused to perform upon himself; and Bellona, Goddess of War, presides seated on a convenient cloud. These Worcester mugs belong to pairs, of which the companion subject is, in one instance, General Wolfe; in another, William Pitt, Earl of Chatham.

All the pictures and objects enumerated, save one, represent the marquess in uniform, the one exception being Lord Braybrooke's portrait, which relates to a date when Lord Granby was yet a very young man.

His epoch is, however, so richly illustrated by the works of Reynolds, Gainsborough, Hogarth, Ramsay, Hamilton, and others, to say nothing of the actual garments which have survived, that there would be little difficulty in conjuring up Granby in his maturer years decked in the sumptuous, and stately, fashions of the decline of the eighteenth century. They are recorded by eye witnesses in many letters, and *memoirs*. Light blue velvet coats, laced with silver, with sleeves and waistcoats of brocade; coats scarlet and gold, dark blue and silver, or of light blue silk embroidered all over with gold and silver, and turned up with embroidered white satin; others of lead colour richly laced with silver, of blossom-coloured velvet trimmed with gold lace, and of yellow and silver velvet, and of white and silver, are enumerated in the *Letters* of the first Earl of Malmesbury. (October 31, 1745; December 10, 1748; December 3, 1754, etc.)

But though relations of Granby's are described, and he himself must certainly have been present on some of the occasions cited, he is not individually mentioned. A magnificent waistcoat of cloth-of-gold brocaded with flowers, which is said to have belonged to him, quite attains, however, to the highest possible limits of sartorial splendour; and Granby moreover took a large size in waistcoats. This one shows an imposing chest measurement, and is, of course, made fashionably long, with deep-flapped pockets, and an apricot-coloured satin back. These dazzling garments were reserved for important occasions, the "everyday" wear being limited to varying shades mainly of plain blue, lavender, and claret, adorned with gold or silver button-holes and garters. A capacious three-cornered hat, christened after Kevenhüller (until superseded by the small one introduced by the Duc de Nivernois), completed one, and very large shoe-buckles the other, extremity of the masculine form divine.

As a side light upon costume, an anonymous eighteenth-century begging-letter writer, signing himself "Necessitas," supplies some testimony. We know the appearance of "Necessitas" in these days as he slinks, pursuing his calling, about Belgrave or Grosvenor Squares; and this is how he appeared in 1758, when he offered to impart some priceless information to the Duke of Newcastle—for a consideration.

★★★★★★★★★★

There is a strong family likeness between this individual, Necessitas, and "Felton," who wrote asking for an interview with the Duke of Marlborough (shortly previous to his death at Münster), saying, You will not fail to meet the author on Sunday next, at 10 in the morning, or on Monday (if the weather should be rainy on Sunday), near the first tree beyond the style in Hyde Park in the foot-walk to Kensington."—See note, vol. xiii. *History of England* (Hume and Smollett). W. Barnard ("Felton") was tried for threatening the Duke of Marlborough in 1758, and acquitted.—See *State Trials*, vol. xix.

★★★★★★★★★★

Necessitas wrote:

> I shall be found, tomorrow and next day, sitting upon the nearest bench to Marlborough House in St. James' Park, between 4 and 5 in the afternoon, cracking nuts and habited in a thickset fustian frock, double-breasted, with yellow buttons and button holes.

The Duke of Newcastle was so ravenously curious that it is more than probable that he in some way gave "Necessitas" a hearing: in any case he carefully preserved the letter. His Grace's name recalls attention to the business of the war from which it was diverted by this picture gossip concerning the Marquess of Granby, whose period and relations, friends and associates—military, political, and social—were once so completely recorded upon the walls of Belvoir Castle.

A considerable number of these portraits fortunately still remain, comprising Lord Granby's father, mother, wife, and his brother Lord

BOW PORCELAIN STATUETTE OF THE MARQUIS OF GRANBY.

BOW PORCELAIN STATUETTE OF GENERAL WOLFE.

Robert Manners Sutton; his sons, John, Lord Roos; Charles, fourth Duke of Rutland; Lord Robert Manners; and his daughter Lady Tyrconnel. The Seven Years' War is illustrated by pictures of Prince Ferdinand of Brunswick, Lord Granby, the Hereditary Prince, Count La Lippe Bückebourg, General Spörcken, Lord Brome, General Faucitt, and Marshal de Broglie; and the Wilkes episode by Lord Mansfield.

Among the pictures burnt in 1816 were "the Marquess of Granby, Hussar, and Horse," Lady Granby, and a head of His Lordship, all by Reynolds; General Oglethorpe, General Lord Robert Manners, Lord Robert Sutton, Lord G. H. Cavendish, Sir Joshua Reynolds, Kitty Fisher, and John Nötzel the marquess' hussar.

The nationality of Nötzel, of the Hessian Hussars, is variously stated; Sir Joshua Reynolds called him a Swiss. He is said to have rendered some timely service, in action, to the Marquess of Granby, who, in consequence, employed and befriended him, and he accompanied Lord Granby to England after the close of the German War, continuing as his lordship's devoted attendant until the former's death. He is described as a very active, clever, handsome fellow; and on one occasion his familiarity with Continental travel caused his services to be placed, by the marquess, at the disposal of Miss Chudleigh, whom Nötzel attended on her visit to the Electress of Saxony. After Lord Granby's death his son Charles, fourth Duke of Rutland, employed Nötzel, and bequeathed him an annuity. (Six medals were struck in honour of Lord Granby in 1759, 1760, 1761, 1770 (2), and a Memorial Medal in 1774).

MEDAL STRUCK IN 1761 IN HONOUR OF THE MARQUIS OF GRANBY (*Obv.*).

Rev. A trophy of arms, flags, etc. See p. 156 (note), and Appendix VIII.

Chapter 13

1760: Zierenberg, Marburg and Wesel

After his victory at Warburg Prince Ferdinand was powerless to undertake any further offensive action, owing to his lost magazines at Cassel, and the immense superiority of the enemy's numbers. This capture, and preponderance, enabled De Broglie to continue operations with detached forces; that under Prince Xavier taking in succession Göttingen and Eimbeck, east of the River Weser, in addition to Ziegenhayn and Münden, already mentioned as having fallen to the French, on the west of the Weser.

Prince Ferdinand could merely endeavour to stem the tide, and gained a few skirmishes by a detachment under General Lückner, besides personally arresting a foraging expedition, attempted by 20,000 of the enemy, near Geismar. The Hereditary Prince crossed the Dymel once or twice to observe and harass the French movements: an attack by him near Zierenberg was repulsed with some loss to the Scots Greys; Major Scheither (who performed many dashing exploits), was wounded, and the prince himself was nearly taken.

The Allied position centred upon Warburg, near which Ferdinand's camp lay at Bühne, from whence Colonel Pierson assured the Duke of Newcastle that, though the loss of Cassel was most serious, the masterly position at Warburg would prevent De Broglie from making any forward movement. De Broglie was, nevertheless, in almost complete possession of Hesse, and threatening Hanover. Dissatisfaction is apparent, at this date, in the despatches both to and from the seat of war.

Newcastle, sore at the Cassel disaster, petulantly disputed the inferior strength of the Allied Army, in estimating which he invariably counted every man as "efficient," and made no allowances for the dead, the wounded, and thousands of sick in the hospitals. His remarks upon this topic were flippant in the extreme as addressed to Lord Granby who acutely felt, and persistently deprecated, the false situation in which Prince Ferdinand and he were placed—the situation of being dunned for bricks and denied straw. The far greater strength of De Broglie's army is attested by historians, French as well as English, and by much contemporary evidence.

Even Pitt seemed temporarily to lose faith in his scheme for conquering America in Germany, and told Newcastle that he "declared, for one, that, without a battle, he would not be for the continuance of the measures in Germany another year."

The Marquess of Granby, on his part, was depressed in the extreme by what he held to be the remediable stagnation of affairs. Since the Battle of Warburg rain had fallen incessantly, and he reported to Lord Holdernesse that the wretched weather was causing his troops "to fall down very fast." But, as reinforcements seemed unobtainable from the War Office, he wrote his views at some length to the Duke of Newcastle from Burgholtz, near Warburg:—

> I can only say, My dear Lord, that as I was convinced of the necessity there was vigorously to exert ourselves the latter end of the year, which part of the campaign has always proved fatal to the enemy, I thought it my duty to represent at home what number of men we wanted to complete us, especially as it was at H.S.H.'s earnest desire. . . . Great expenses. My dear Lord, we have certainly been at in carrying on this war in every part of the world; very great here in Germany, but they were necessary expenses calculated for the safety, honour, and interest of the Nation, and therefore readily granted by Parliament: should more money still be wanted for the same good and salutary ends I should not think that a recapitulation of the different great sums that have already been expended should in any shape be permitted to come into debate: but the only subject should be—'Can you afford, or procure, any more money; yes or no?' Just the same in regard to the sending over more troops; it is not to be considered how large a number has been already sent upon any service but, whether, if more are wanting, there is a possibility of reinforcing the service that requires it. Upon that footing, though thoroughly convinced of the great expense we have been at, and knowing the large number of Troops that have already been sent over to this country, I did not hesitate to represent what I thought was necessary for the good of the Service I was engaged in, being convinced that nothing but an

> impossibility from the situation of affairs could have prevented an immediate compliance with the request.
>
> In regard to the superiority of the enemy, it has always here been looked upon as great. When His Serene Highness talked of the 65,000 foot and 16,000 horse that were *vis à vis de lui,* he most certainly talked of effectives. Should Your Grace talk of our number of troops in the same style, from the 97,000 men I fear Your Grace must deduct some thousands. I don't doubt, however, should the enemy chuse to attack us, but we shall be able to send you some good news, as our troops are in good spirits and confident of success.

Newcastle began to realise that Granby was very much in earnest, and mortified; so he quickly changed his key, and sent congratulations on the extension of the marquess' command, which the king was equally pleased about:—

> You cannot conceive how happy we all are at the figure you make at the head of our troops; and what, if possible, pleases me still more, the king told me this day that the English and the Hanoverians lived like brothers; and that Lord Granby and Spörcken were the best friends in the world! . . . We hear the French are much discontented and disconcerted; they say the campaign and the opportunity are lost. ... Be as active a general as you wish to be, and a good one I am sure you are and will be, but don't quite forget our money affairs. . . . . I dined today at Greenwich with Lady Katherine (Pelham), and drank your health.

With reference to this letter, Granby replied—

> I most sincerely honour and love that brave, honest, and good general (Spörcken). I can assure you that there is the greatest harmony amongst the troops. I have heard of no complaints, if any have arisen.

Marshal de Broglie was threatening, Granby added, to pass the Weser, and was sending off his heavy baggage, and sick, to Marburg and Giessen.

Two small successes were scored by the Allies at Zierenberg and Marburg. The first was a night attack by the Hereditary Prince and Major-General Griffin with two battalions of Maxwell's Grenadiers, Kingsley's Regiment, and 150 Highlanders. (Major-General Griffin received a slight bayonet thrust in the chest from one of his own force, who mistook him in the darkness for an enemy. Lord George Lennox accompanied the Zierenberg expedition as a volunteer). Four hundred of the enemy, their two commanders, besides thirty-five other officers, were taken prisoners, and about the same number killed. The Hereditary Prince entered the town at the head of the grenadiers by the Dürrenburg Gate, and Kingsley's and the Highlanders by the Warburg Gate: the scene which ensued being "most disagreeable and shocking," wrote Colonel Pierson, as the British drove all before them to the market-place, where the French were shot or taken prisoners, and many of them were bayoneted, even in their beds.

For this, and his previous services, £5,000 was remitted to Lord Granby for the Hereditary Prince, who accomplished this attack, and returned to Warburg in a few hours, and with hardly any loss. The second arose out of a surprise march, made by Major von Bülow and Colonel Fersen to Marburg, which afforded an incident to Colonel Pierson wherewith to amuse the Duke of Newcastle. Von Bülow entered Marburg, destroyed a quantity of French stores, and took many prisoners, including sixty *commis* engaged in the bakeries. The governor of the Castle of Marburg threatened, in consequence, to commence firing on the town. "Fire away," replied Von Bülow, "and for each shot I will hang up one *commis!*" The governor changed his mind. On their return. Von Bülow and Fersen were attacked by Comte de Stainville: Colonel Fersen was killed, and eight guns and about 200 men were lost.

Complaints reached England touching various outrages and irregularities committed by the Guards on their march from the coast; a circumstance which was in sharp contrast to the conduct of the other troops, and thus lends colour to Hogarth's indictment contained in "the March to Finchley." The Duke of Newcastle requested to know the truth of these complaints, and Colonel Pierson did his best to exonerate the Guards, urging that they were raw, unused to active service, and somewhat irregular in conduct, but he did not believe the damage done exceeded 400 florin.

About September 10, 1760, De Broglie commenced retiring towards Cassel, which proved him to have abandoned his intentions upon the bishoprics. He encamped on the heights of Immenhausen, where Prince Ferdinand at once decided to attack him. The position was not a strong one, and Ferdinand knew every inch of the ground; but he was balked of his scheme, as he was twice afterwards, in 1761 and 1762, at the same place. On this occasion, just as all his plans were matured, De Broglie suddenly retreated from Immenhausen to the entrenched camp at the Kratzenberg, under the cannon of Cassel.

In consequence of this retreat Lord Granby and his Reserve, on September 14, crossed the Dymel to Hoff Geismar, and General Wangenheim, who was observing Prince Xavier's movements on the east side of the Weser, advanced to Ellershausen. Elliot's Regiment, under Major Erskine, and the Hessian *Chasseurs* were attached at the moment to Wangenheim's Corps, which De Broglie, as will be presently related, endeavoured to cut off.

Congratulations upon the Zierenberg affair reached the marquess from Lord Ligonier, and the Duke of Newcastle; but the latter returned a disheartening reply to Granby's recommendations concerning extra allowances to the troops already in Germany, and the necessity of reinforcing them. Newcastle said that, to tell Lord Granby the actual truth, his demand for recruits was not at all relished at home, or expected, and that the king was uneasy at a request for more infantry than His Majesty "had understood to be necessary." Rumours commenced to circulate in London of great hardships endured by the troops in Germany, and which, as the winter wore on, were painfully accentuated. The Commissariat Department, which had never attained to more than a hand-to-mouth performance of its all-important functions, began to fail in proportion as the Allied Army became decentralised; and the frightful condition of the roads increased the difficulties of transport to the different corps.

Colonel Pierson's appointment as Commissary General became a farce, principally owing to unopposable influences, but very largely to the self-seeking manner in which he connived at them. The king gave him the command of the 1st Foot Guards, and Prince Ferdinand attached him to his Staff: both were flattering distinctions entailing duties more congenial to a soldier than higgling with forage contractors; but, had he played less for his own hand and with more loyalty to his chief, for whom he professed so much affection and devotion, he would not have neglected a service which he had deliberately undertaken at the hands of the Treasury, and for no inconsiderable pay.

He acknowledged that his civil and military duties were clashing, to the detriment of the former, and coolly recommended his regimental promotion to the Duke of Newcastle, of all men, who had specially appointed him to safeguard the Treasury (that is to say the duke) from censures by Prince Ferdinand, if not by Pitt himself.

The rumours at home gathered strength, and were utilised in certain political quarters, which shall be explained presently, to discredit the Marquess of Granby, to whose relief—Heaven save the mark! Colonel Pierson had been despatched to head the Commissariat Staff.

Lord Granby described to Newcastle how a decisive action had again been prevented by the retreat, to the Kratzenberg camp, of the French, and he then spoke his mind freely on affairs both in Germany and London, from which latter place he showed himself to be well informed. Firstly, the employment of Colonel Pierson as a Major-General was entirely Prince Ferdinand's affair:—

> I had nothing to do with it, should the king disapprove, though I have every reason to think, from repeated advices, that every opportunity will be taken to insinuate privately everything to my disadvantage. I have been informed, My Dear Lord, that in many places my conduct as commander-in-chief has been found fault with, that I am said to have done many irregular things; that I suffered myself to be imposed upon; that I was 'too good-natured' to be entrusted with such a command, etc., etc. I must expect these private attacks. The great honour His Majesty has done me will subject me to envy, and many people, for different reasons, would be happy to see His Majesty discontented with my conduct and displeased with my actions. Should that happen, I must be most unhappy. I should only have one comfort, the consciousness that my intentions were to serve His Majesty faithfully to the best of my abilities in the great and important trust His Majesty has done me the favour to confer on me.

Lord Granby then referred to certain allowances to the troops recommended by him, saying that, as the Duke of Newcastle had practically placed him where he was, His Grace must now support him, or he must resign his command:—

> I flatter myself I am not ill with the troops, but should it appear I have no interest at home; that nothing I propose is granted, or at least with the greatest difficulty, they will think that His Majesty and his ministers must have some good reason to distrust my heart or at least my head. They must either think that I care little whether what I recommend for the good of the service succeeds or not; or that at home they don't think me capable of judging what is for the good of that service; and it will be nei-

ther for my honour and happiness nor that of the service that I should remain at the head of the British troops. If I can't be trusted with the disposal of five or six thousand pounds among the troops under my command as I think necessary, I am sure I ought not to have the disposal of a million and a half of public money which I am afraid will be the case."

Newcastle's answer to this letter assured the marquess he was utterly mistaken in feeling that confidence in him was wanting; with the king it increased, and he also could answer for Lord Barrington—

> If I were to mention seriously to any one man of consequence in this kingdom that Your Lordship thought yourself slighted, and were for that reason uneasy in your present situation, he would laugh in my face; for to be sure no man ever had more friends, or more universal approbation than yourself.

Major-General Yorke, at the Hague, now took a sanguine view of Prince Ferdinand's strategic position; but Newcastle, adopting a totally different tone to that he had, till lately, held, said he wished *he* could see Prince Ferdinand's prospects in so favourable a light. The duke maintained that all the prince could possibly do was to *tenir tête* against De Broglie and Prince Xavier. Whilst, should the Comte de St. Germain be despatched with 15,000 men (as was rumoured) to penetrate the king's dominions by way of Westphalia, the success of such a scheme was certain.

> How could Prince Ferdinand, already so inferior in numbers, detach 10 or 15 thousand men against the count and yet hold his own against De Broglie?

Read side by side, Newcastle's sanguine letters to Lord Granby, and the above opinions addressed to Joseph Yorke, contradict one another with remarkable flatness.

On September 27, 1760, Lord Granby reported himself and his Reserve once more encamped at Warburg, and described De Broglie's attempt to cut off Wangenheim's Corps beyond the Weser. De Broglie and Prince de Condé with a force from Cassel crossed the river and joined Prince Xavier's Corps, from which the strength of the expedition was increased to thirty battalions and sixteen squadrons. Granby's account was that De Broglie and Condé acted as "volunteers" with the above, which was under the command of M. de Luzace (Prince Xavier). General Wangenheim gained early information of the approach of this expedition, and decided that a retreat over the Weser with his little force of four Hanoverian infantry battalions, Elliot's, and the *chasseurs*, was inevitable.

He made for a pontoon bridge, thrown by the Allies over the river, closely pursued by the enemy, with whom he was meantime desultorily engaged during eight hours. Arrived at the bridge the Hanoverian infantry crossed, one squadron each of "Elliot's" and the Hessian *Chasseurs* forming the rearguard.

The cavalry forded over. The infantry formed on the west bank and, breaking the bridge, endeavoured to save the pontoons, but the enemy now opened a severe fire from the opposite side, and Wangenheim had to abandon a few pontoons.

He lost 92 men killed, 158 wounded and missing, and 4 pieces of cannon, which were declared useless owing "to the touch-holes having run with the extraordinary fire." The French loss was stated variously at from 800 to 1,250. "Elliot's" joined Granby's Reserve after this affair; and on September 21 Wangenheim once more crossed the Weser to Uslar, Prince Xavier being near Göttingen.

Colonel Pierson's account of this described De Broglie as having intended annihilating Wangenheim's Corps as a revenge for the Hereditary prince's *coup* at Zierenberg. The Guards Pierson reported as very sickly, but Lord Granby "was very well, and making all under his command extremely happy."

De Broglie was now busily occupied in repairing the fortifications at Cassel, and strengthening Göttingen, which confirmed Prince Ferdinand's suspicions that the French intended remaining in those places during the winter.

Consequently, Ferdinand decided upon sending an expedition against Wesel on the "Lower Rhine," which fortress had, from the first, been a thorn in his side, and an attack upon which might be successful, or at least oblige De Broglie to detach a considerable force from Cassel to its assistance.

The expedition was commanded by the Hereditary Prince with Count La Lippe Bückebourg, and consisted of 5 divisions, amounting in all to 47 infantry battalions, and 30 squadrons of cavalry, of which an important number were English.

The 1st Division was commanded by Lieut.-General Hardenburg, and the 2nd by Major-General Breidenbach, and both were entirely German. The 3rd Division was commanded by Lieut.-General Waldegrave, and consisted of—

1 battn. of "Kingsley's" (20th Regt.)	2 squads. of "Conway's" (1st Dragoons)	under Major-Gen. Elliot.
1 " "Homes'" (25th)	2 " Inniskillings	
2 " Hessian Infantry		
2 " British Grenadiers	2 " German Cavalry	under Major-Gen. Griffin.
2 " Highlanders (87th and 88th)		

The 4th Division was commanded by Major-General Howard, consisting: of—

1 battn. of "Griffin's" (33rd Regt.)	2 squads. of "Mordaunt's" (10th, Prince of Wales's, Dragoons)
1 " "Brudenell's" (51st)	
1 " Welsh Fusiliers (23rd)	
2 " German Infantry.	

The 5th Division, commanded by Lieut.-General Kilmansegge, was entirely German.

Lord Downe, and Lord Fitzmaurice, joined the expedition as volunteers, and among the officers were "Irish" Johnston of Conway's Dragoons, "Ned" Harvey of the Inniskillings, Sir J. Innes Norcliffe (afterwards fifth Duke of Roxburghe), of the Highlanders, and Lord George Lennox, (Lieut.-Colonel of the 33rd Foot; he was now acting with the grenadiers), who have been mentioned in preceding pages.

The route was *via* Lippstadt and Münster; and the 1st Division, which the Hereditary Prince and Count Bückebourg accompanied, left camp September 23rd, and arrived before Wesel on September 30th; the other divisions arrived later; the 5th, under Kilmansegge, on October 16 only.

Prince Ferdinand and Lord Granby remained on the River Dymel; the Allied position extending from Warburg, along that river, to beyond the River Weser, where Generals Wangenheim's and Lückner's Corps held the district between Eimbeck and Uslar. The departure of the Wesel Expedition was kept very secret, and Lord Granby wrote that the general outlook was extremely gloomy. Frederick the Great had lost Berlin, and was asking for assistance from the Allied Army which it could not afford to render; and Prince Ferdinand was entreating Granby to urge, either a reinforcement from England, or a separate expedition from thence to create a diversion in Flanders, or on the French coast.

The attention of the home authorities was implored to anything, in fact, which might tend to drive De Broglie from Cassel and Göttingen, or prevent reinforcements from France being perpetually drafted to his already overwhelming armies. Lord Granby repeated and emphasized his own views on the subject, "at the risk of being found fault with."

****

Newcastle Papers, October 13, 1760. Smollett records the opinion that had an expedition of 10,000 men been despatched from England to co-operate with the Hereditary Prince's attempt upon Wesel, the war might have been advantageously transferred to Flanders. Smollett does not say whence the 10,000 men were to be procured!

****

Without knowing its destination, though suspecting designs upon Wesel, De Broglie became aware, about September 26, of the Hereditary Prince's march, and despatched M. de Castries in pursuit, towards Cologne, with 31 battalions and 32 squadrons.

Arrived before Wesel, the Hereditary Prince proceeded at once to invest it, on both sides of the Rhine which part of his force crossed at Rees, and forced the French garrison of 500 men in Cleves to surrender as prisoners of war. Rheinberg and Emmerich were also taken and occupied, and the various siege works before Wesel actively entered upon, but which the prince never had time to complete.

The Rhine, and the Lippe which flows into it at Wesel, had to be bridged; across the latter two wooden bridges were thrown, but considerable delay ensued in procuring from Holland sufficiently large boats wherewith to form a boat-bridge across the Rhine, below Wesel at Carthauser Island, where a battery was established to defend the bridge which was completed by October 14 only.

Above Wesel a boom was to have been fixed across the Rhine to prevent reinforcements, or supplies, from being floated down stream to the garrison; but this remained unaccomplished, from lack of time, among the innumerable preparations: the weakness of the chain of blockade (caused by its extreme length) necessitated its being strengthened with earthworks and batteries, while precautions had to be taken respecting the innumerable canals and streams to prevent the enemy from flooding the land in front of Wesel. On the night of October 10-11, the trenches were opened, upon which 2,000 workmen were employed; and some sallies on the part of the garrison were repulsed on the 11th and 12th.

The Hereditary Prince has been twitted by his critics with undertaking the siege too much *selon les règles* when time was so precious, and M. de Castries praised for the speed with which he arrived to the relief of the besieged garrison.

De Castries crossed the Rhine at Cologne, collected his force on October 13 at Neuss, from whence he marched to Meurs; thus, arriving within striking distance of the besiegers long before their batteries and earthworks were completed, or the boom thrown across the Rhine above Wesel. On October 14 the boat-bridge was finished, and on the same day the Hereditary Prince, being on the west side of the river, was the first to perceive De Castries' vanguard, under the command of De Chabot, approaching.

★★★★★★★★★★

> The Wesel garrison commenced a boat-bridge, which they kept hauled up under the fortifications. Two Hanoverian and three Brunswick soldiers paddled across the Rhine, from the west bank, burnt the bridge, and returned safely under a heavy fire.—*Newcastle Papers,* October 11, 1760 (Granby to Newcastle).

★★★★★★★★★★

De Chabot drove in and occupied the prince's post at Rheinberg, and in the evening the Allied position on that side of the Rhine was strengthened by the prince's 3rd and 4th Divisions under Lieut.-General Waldegrave, and Major-General Howard. The 5th Division, under Kilmansegge, had not yet arrived at Wesel. De Chabot's success enabled De Castries to send a reinforcement of 700 men into Wesel, down the Rhine.

On the 15th skirmishes between De Castries' and the prince's outposts lasted the greater part of the day, at the conclusion of which De Chabot remained in Rheinberg, and De Castries encamped behind the Rheinberg Canal (leading to Gueldres), and the Convent of Campen—"*Kloster Campen*"—the convent itself being held by Fischer's Corps.

★★★★★★★★★★

> Johann Christian Fischer was a *protégé* of Marshal Saxe. His corps of Mounted *Chasseurs* was the origin of all the modern regiments of similar character in the French Army. His *chasseurs* wore a green tunic laced with gold, a scarlet *pelisse* trimmed with gold lace and edged with grey fur, a black busby with white cockade and plume, and scarlet overalls. Fischer adopted a curious device of three fish arranged in a triplicate design closely resembling a *fleur-de-lis.* This device, surmounted by a crown and flanked by *fleurs-de-lis*, was worn on sabretache, *shabraque*, and holster-cap.—*Uniformenkunde* (R. Knötel), Band 5, No. 59.

****

Meantime rumours of reinforcements marching from various points to join De Castries reached the Hereditary Prince, and he resolved to attack before their arrival, being already outnumbered on the west side of the Rhine, and unable to transfer more troops over the river from the east side without placing his bridge, earthworks, and batteries at the mercy of the Wesel garrison.

The prince, leaving the Campbell Highlanders to guard the bridge, marched at 10 o'clock on the night of October 15, the strictest silence being preserved; his first object being to secure Fischer's Corps at the convent, if possible, without any firing. At this stage occurred a much-disputed episode of which one version is that the Chevalier d'Assas (Captain of the French Regiment of Auvergne which was on outpost duty) having strayed outside the lines, was surprised, and taken by some of the prince's advanced guard, who, with their bayonets at his throat, promised him instant death if he uttered a sound. "*A moi! Auvergne!*" promptly shouted D'Assas, and was a dead man the same instant that his voice gave the alarm to the French piquets.

****

There are several versions of this story. De Rochambeau (in his *Mémoires Militaires, Historiques, et Politiques*), who commanded the regiment of Auvergne, says the first alarm was given by a corporal; the regiment began to fire at random, when suddenly one of its officers called out that the alarm was a false one, and that they were firing upon friends. The Chevalier d'Assas coolly walked out of the ranks right up to the troops advancing in the thick darkness, and, before being bayoneted, shouted, "*Tirez Chasseurs! ce sont les ennemis!*" Whatever the literal facts were, *somebody* appears to have been a hero, and the evidence tends to prove D'Assas to have been the man.

****

All chance of a surprise was now lost: Fischer's Corps was presently dislodged, but with an attendant musketry fire which warned De Castries in his camp beyond; and he had time to make his dispositions for defence. The Hereditary Prince's attack on De Castries occurred an hour before daylight, he personally leading his right wing consisting of Infantry. Of the main engagement of *Kloster Campen* no explanation is given by any of the ordinary sources of information. The affair, beyond all dispute, appears to have been a "bad business" from beginning to end so far as the Allies were concerned. The Hereditary Prince's horse was shot under him, and he was slightly wounded in the leg. Mistakes arose in the darkness, and friends were mistaken for foes. In spite of a great deal of individual bravery, and a determined attack of many hours' duration, the Allied infantry was driven back with heavy loss.

The *Brigade de Normandie* pursued, as the Allies retired, and was sabred by the Hereditary Prince's Cavalry, under cover of which a retreat commenced. The Hereditary Prince's wound was received, and his horse shot, at this moment; he could not walk, and Lord George Lennox and Captain McLean carried him out of action. After bivouacking near the scene of the fight, the prince continued his retreat towards the Rhine, at the banks of which a scene of the most dramatically critical nature ensued on October 16-17.

The weather was stormy, the Rhine was in flood, and the boat-bridge had not only become badly damaged, but the engineer in charge announced that it could only be made available by readjusting it at a point lower down the stream. Dead tired, with a large number of wounded, and almost without ammunition, the Hereditary Prince's ill-fated expedition, with its back to the river, awaited the inevitable arrival of the victorious De Castries. Lieut.-General Kilmansegge, with the 5th Division, arrived before Wesel on October 16, only a few hours after the battle, but the troops on the east bank of the Rhine were as powerless to cross over to the prince as he was to rejoin them, owing to the broken bridge.

Whatever of the failure was attributable to the Hereditary Prince, he now exhibited his usual resourcefulness and cool determination. (During three days and nights of incessant anxiety and fatigue he scarcely had a comfortable meal.—Sir J. Innes Norcliffe, *MSS.* of Duke of Roxburghe).

Granby wrote:

> The Hereditary Prince's conduct as a general, on no occasion has given him greater honour than on this very critical one.

The artillery was placed in front, so as to sweep the plain by which De Castries must approach; then the infantry, behind a slight redoubt, or *landwehr*, and the cavalry in the rear. A dam was raised in order to fill to the utmost a bit of a rivulet in front of the whole position, and two tumbrils of ammunition were with great difficulty floated over in boats from the east bank. De Castries arrived within a mile of this position on October 17, which day he passed the whole of in reconnoitring. It would appear that he did not realise the prince's real condition, or the state of the bridge: at all events he hazarded no attack.

(De Rochambeau alludes to the *hardihood* of the Allies in remaining all day by the Rhine).

The engineer announced that the bridge would be ready by 3 a.m. on the 18th, and, during the night of the 17th, the troops began to file off towards it. A number of wagons containing forage and straw were hastily formed into a *flèche* at the bridge-head, and a rearguard of infantry under Major-General Howard covered the retreat over the Rhine. First crossed the cavalry, then the artillery, which formed opposite, on the east bank, to cover the passage of the infantry. The night was intensely dark and stormy; delays occurred more than once owing to accidents to the bridge, but the transit was completed without the loss of a man.

The grenadiers, under Lord George Lennox, returned to bring two guns which had been placed to cover the bridge-head. The rearguard set fire to the *flèche* of wagons, and joined the main body on the Wesel side simultaneously with De Castries' arrival on the west bank, and the boat-bridge was broken up. (Sir J. Innes Norcliffe relates one of the last scenes to have been "a singlehanded tilt between Col. Janard, of the Prussian Yellow Hussars, and a French officer whom Janard cutt up."—MSS. of the Duke of Roxburghe).

> Our glorious retreat closed when every man and cannon was over by the setting fire to some wagons filled with straw which smoaked the French; and the boats and sloops which composed the bridge being disengaged from each other sailed up (? down) the Rhine."(*MSS.* of the Duke of Roxburghe).

De Castries opened an ineffectual fire from the west bank which was hotly returned; and the Hereditary Prince encamped at Bruynen, abandoning all further operations upon Wesel. Thus ended the unhappy Wesel Expedition.

The loss attending this disaster was—

Killed ...	10 officers,	16 non-commissioned officers,	221 men.
Wounded ...	68 „	43 „ „ „	812 „
Prisoners and missing ...	7 „	6 „ „ „	429 „

And 163 horses killed and missing.[1]

Among the wounded officers were Major-General Griffin, Major-General Elliot, Lieut.-Colonel Lord Downe (who led the 25th Regiment), Lieut.-Colonel Pitt, Lieut.-Colonel "Ned" Harvey, Lieut.-Colonel Johnson, and Captains Grey and Tennant. Major Pollock of Keith's Highlanders (87th) was killed. Lieut.-General Waldegrave was shot through the hat and coat, and escaped being shot through the body, according to Walpole, because he had none; from which it may be surmised he was extremely thin.

The Hereditary Prince continued his march, and handsomely repulsed De Castries' pursuing force at Schermbeck; after which De Castries went into winter quarters west of the Rhine, and the Hereditary Prince in, and about, Münster. "Conway's" Dragoons and the Welsh Fusiliers were the worst sufferers.

Lord Granby wrote that he had never seen Prince Ferdinand so overcome by anything as the disastrous news from Wesel which arrived while they were at dinner. Granby quickly sent off his best surgeon, Mr. P. Burlton, (Inspector-General of Regimental Infirmaries), to assist with the wounded, and at first hopes were entertained of Lord Downe's recovery, who was shot through both arms, the body, and one knee. He is described in one letter (Walpole, January 2, 1761), as having received in all twelve wounds. He then lingered for ten weeks, during which he told the surgeons "to put him to as much pain as they pleased, so they did but make him fit for the next campaign." (Walpole).

The rank of colonel was bestowed upon him, and Lord Fitzmaurice also, whose very gallant behaviour, Granby said, had done him the greatest honour; but regretfully added that he feared poor Lord Downe would not live long to enjoy his promotion.

★★★★★★★★★★

> "I speak of you, my dear Lord, from the information of those who were eyewitnesses of your behaviour on that day, and no one does my friend Fitzmaurice more justice than the Hereditary Prince himself."—Granby to Fitzmaurice, *Life of Lord Shelburne*, vol. i.

★★★★★★★★★★

Nor did he: the surgeons failed of making his shattered body "fit for the next campaign," and his brave heart ceased to beat, greatly to England's grief, where Walpole recorded that "not a mouth was opened but in praise or regret of him."

Meantime the Allied Army had remained quiet, though Marshal de Broglie's movements kept everyone in camp ready for instant service, and, since he showed no sign of marching southwards, Lord Granby thought nothing could avert a winter campaign. The troops, freshly arrived from England, were succumbing fast, the hospitals were crammed full, and the surgical staff was inadequate.

Lord Ligonier was greatly concerned at the losses sustained at

Kloster Campen, especially by the Welsh Fusiliers; and reported His Majesty's appointment of Captain Faucitt to be Deputy Adjutant-General in Germany with rank of Lieutenant-Colonel, from which date Faucitt was chiefly engaged with the Commissariat affairs. General Griffin was invalided home, and his wounds prevented his again serving in Germany.

The inactivity of Prince Ferdinand's army had afforded General Mostyn ample leisure in which to look his gift-horse, of Cope's Regiment, in the mouth. He described himself in a very racy letter as a reluctant bridegroom forced to marry Cope's widow, and said it hurt his vanity to follow "Johnny Cope," and he would much rather retain his Royal Irish nine troops until "Bland's" fell in. However, the Duke of Newcastle declared there was no help for it, and that Mostyn must accept the king's offer; so, on September 30, 1700, Lieut.-General Mostyn was transferred to the Colonelcy of Cope's, the 7th Regiment of Dragoons, an exchange which Newcastle acknowledged, after George II.'s death, that "poor Jack made to please my dear old Master, and lost near £500 a year by it."

Lord Granby wrote from Warburg—

> We have been amused for several days past, with the hopes of the enemy quitting Cassel, by reports of their baggage, hospitals and *vivandiers* of all sorts quitting the town; but still there they are! I wish they were gone, or that a hard frost would enable us to manoeuvre them out; otherwise, we must expect no settled winter-quarters.

This letter expresses all that the position, for a considerable time, demands, and in consequence the course of events in London, which Lord Granby said was being utilised to his discredit, can be now scrutinised with greater leisure.

****

In spite of the Duke of Newcastle's affected ignorance of any schemes affecting the marquess' position, His Grace's correspondence, in other directions, most vividly records their existence. The whole matter turned upon old Lord Ligonier's illness. The Duke of Newcastle was kept fully informed by Caesar Hawkins, Sergeant-Surgeon to the king, of the commander-in-chief's condition, which was very grave; and his death at this juncture would have produced an acute difficulty in the selection of a successor; and that successor certain people did not wish to be the Marquess of Granby, or the Duke of

Cumberland, who had long been suspected by "Leicester House" of desiring to retrieve his military ascendency. (The two Hawkinses, Caesar and Pennell, were the Court and "fashionable" surgeons).

Respecting this dilemma, the Duke of Newcastle poured out his heart to Lord Hardwicke. The king had said, "if Ligonier went off, the Duke of Cumberland, though not a great general, was the only man who could keep the army in order at home." Lord Albemarle had suggested to Newcastle that they should take Marshal Rich, or "one of the old cyphers with whom they might do as they liked." Lady Yarmouth (George II.'s mistress), was "for no general-in-chief at all, and that the king should do the whole with the Secretary at War." In this idea Newcastle was inclined to concur:—

> . . . but I will now tell you an extraordinary story indeed. My friend C. V.s told me that 'Leicester House' and all the Royal Family, meaning the Duke of Cumberland also, was for Lord Tyrawley. *That the man 'Leicester House' feared most, though they dared not say so, was my Lord Granby.* For they should not know what to do with him at the head of the army in case of an accident to the king, which God prevent. This I can easily believe. C. V. went further, and told me as a certain truth that Leicester House would be for the Duke of Cumberland rather than my Lord Granby. That I own seems incredible, but the conduct of that Court is so extraordinary that indeed almost anything may be true.

★★★★★★★★★★

C.V., Count Viri, Sardinian Minister. A "back-stair" politician and intriguer. "An artful, assiduous, observant, prudent man, with the greatest spirit of intrigue that can be conceived." (*Life of Lord Shelburne*, vol. i.). "He is a stupid animal in appearance this Viri" (George Selwyn to Lord Carlisle, *Hist. MSS.* Com., Rep. XV. App. 6.

"Leicester House" was contemplating, in the event of George II's death, the supreme government of his successor, and consequently a commander-in-chief who would be little more than a lay-figure.

★★★★★★★★★★

Lord Hardwicke replied from "Wimple":—

> I hope in God he (Ligonier) will recover, for if he should drop soon, it would be a hampering business for the administration. My Lord Granby has all the merit in the world, but he is very young and you must wait to see how things will turn out this campaign. If that scene closes well his great quality will stand

> for a good deal. I cannot understand so much as Your Grace does that Leicester House should pretend to be for the duke (of Cumberland) preferably to His Lordship. I dare say the bad state of H.R.H.'s health is a governing reason to abate their fears of him, and they may think that in talking so, they shall have the king on their side. (*Homme propose, Dieu dispose.* The king at the time was within seven or eight weeks of his death, and the Duke of Cumberland survived him till 1765).

Newcastle's next letter acquainted Hardwicke that Ligonier was still very ill:—

> Lady Yarmouth has endeavoured to sound the king upon a successor, but without success; and she then asked leave to use my name in the matter, which His Majesty allowed.

Accordingly, Newcastle was summoned to Lady Yarmouth's, after Court, and before he saw the king. Newcastle then told her that to reconstitute the Duke of Cumberland "Captain-General" (at present) "would be destruction to the king's affairs both at home and abroad—at home, for reasons often discussed; abroad, because the sole disposition of the armies everywhere in the Duke of Cumberland's hands would make it impracticable for Prince Ferdinand to continue his command." (Prince Ferdinand superseded Cumberland after Klosterseven). This "struck Lady Yarmouth extremely."

Afterwards Newcastle saw Pitt, who was outrageous against "Leicester House." He "*was for things, not men*:" he said a great deal in high commendation of Lord Granby, to whom he should give the 1st Regiment of Foot Guards if Ligonier died. (In point of emolument the Colonelcy of the 1st Foot Guards was the richest in the service, and was usually held by the Commander-in-Chief); that the king would not take Tyrawley, and Pitt indicated General Sinclair as the best man; "anyway he must have a general to act with in case of need." To this Newcastle "differed *toto caelo*"—he was against any Scotchman, and, if limited to those two, would be for Tyrawley.

Later, Newcastle had seen Lady Yarmouth again, who said:

> The king was quite with him and would see him on the ensuing Friday, when he intended proposing the king and the Secretary for War to manage the army. Should Lord Granby have any more *éclat* that campaign that alternative might be practicable. Sinclair the king positively would not have; and, to

meet Pitt's objection, someone from among the older generals could always be deputed to act for His Majesty.

Hardwicke's answer commented on the oddness, though truth, of the fact that Ligonier's death would constitute a great and embarrassing loss. He, Hardwicke, disapproved of the king taking the army, and quite agreed as to Cumberland and Prince Ferdinand. Granby might do if the campaign went well, and that course would best suit the administration.

The letters above epitomised place the various contending interests in full view: the king; the Duke of Cumberland; the princess dowager, together with Lord Bute, and their pupil, afterwards George III.; the Duke of Newcastle; Mr. Pitt; and last, but not least, Lady Yarmouth—all appear, with "C. V." flitting about the backstairs of each with bat-like volatility.

For brave old Ligonier, personally, they most of them cared not a straw, and gazed at him, on his supposed death-bed, with surprise that so hoary a veteran could be of so much consequence; and it was the veteran himself who stayed the crisis, as he had often done on very different scenes of action. In short, he got well, and soon repaired to Court where the king cordially greeted him, saying, "How do you do; take care of yourself. I want you for many things, and in many respects."

Such were the complicated motives of the party which was "crabbing" Lord Granby's reputation at home.

"Leicester House" was soon freed from anxiety concerning his lordship, for, in addition to Lord Ligonier's recovery, the long-rehearsed policy of that Court very shortly found its fulfilment through George II.'s death, which some say was hastened by the defeat at *Kloster Campen*; others, that the news of that disaster had not arrived. Lord Holdernesse informed Lord Granby of this sudden event, and enclosed George III.'s Proclamation, and Declaration in Council, in which His Majesty resolved to support his Allies, and to prosecute the war with vigour.

Lord Granby replied:—

It was with the deepest concern that I read Your Lordship's letter of the 27th of last month informing me of the most melancholy event, the death of our late Most Gracious Sovereign. I most sincerely condole with Your Lordship and the Nation on our very great loss—a loss that would have been still much more severely felt, I may say irreparably so, had we not had a descendant of the same Royal race to take immediate possession of the throne, and the reins of government into his hands. We have, my Lord, this great consolation; and the pleasing and certain proofs, from our knowledge of His present Majesty's Royal virtues, that we shall enjoy under His government the same happiness we so long experienced under our late much to be lamented sovereign.

The task of combining condolence with congratulation is a hard one at all times; and was surmounted most creditably by Granby to whom the phrase *le Roi est mort, vive le Roi!* was rendered eminently difficult to express by the fact of his sincere personal attachment to George II. This attachment was the more genuine since it was free, on the subject's part, of sycophantic servility, and, on that of the monarch, of any consequent resentment. Lord Granby had honestly differed from His Majesty on sundry matters, but the king had appreciated him the more, and showered honours upon him with hearty goodwill.

Whatever his position in the hearts of his civilian subjects, among soldiers George II., being a practical soldier, was popular, and beloved. They remembered how with drawn sword he had gallantly ridden his white charger between the lines at Dettingen—in fact, in a private letter to the Duke of Newcastle, Granby said he believed "no king ever lived more beloved, or died more sincerely regretted;" and Colonel Pierson wrote that by none was the king's death more keenly felt than by Lord Granby, and General Mostyn.

The British troops were ordered by Lord Granby to wear mourning: the officers to cover their sword-knots with black crape, to wear plain hats with crape hat-bands, and a crape band on the arm. The colours, guidons, standards, banners, kettle-drums, etc., etc., were to be draped also with black crape. (Lord Granby's *Order-Book*).

Chapter 14

1760: The Hessian Expedition

Theoretically speaking the discordant notes which had marred the political harmony of George II.'s reign should have been silenced by the accession of his grandson George III.

The latter declared himself to be by birth, education, and sympathy a Briton; and this circumstance provided such English Jacobites as had remained in sulky retirement from George II.'s Court with a useful opportunity of taking the oaths of allegiance to his successor, of which they freely availed themselves. Having testified their loyalty, there was no logical reason for denying them Court employment, but the Pelhamites were too tenacious of their long-continued monopoly of government to be logical—much less liberal.

Lord Bute, and the young king his master, have been debited with their full share of responsibility for the stormy period of faction which so soon arose; a period illustrated by a flood of literature teeming with vituperation, recrimination, and every species of "ation" in perennial use when certain pots and kettles, called Political Parties, are busy accounting one another black.

The most fruitful source of trouble was, beyond compare, the old Duke of Newcastle. With palpable insincerity he declared to Lord Granby that he did not feel equal, at his advanced age, to undertake another reign, but that he "was being overborne on all sides." Mr. Pitt, His Grace said, was behaving extremely well, and they were most thoroughly united" he was also glad to hear that the Duke of Rutland had received a polite compliment for Lord Granby from the king.

Mr. Pitt, a little later, wrote to Lord Granby:

> His Majesty's conduct justly inspires respect, and his behaviour captivates whosoever approaches his royal person.

George III., in fact, did not at first evince any wish to change his grandfather's ministers, and Walpole insists that Lord Bute originally had no declared party.

****

> *Memoirs of the Reign of George III.*—"You will have heard that everything is settled quietly and to satisfaction in England, and that the king has been pleased, in the most gracious and friendly manner, to continue all our late Royal Master's Ministers, and has assured them that he will make their situations easy and happy to them, so that they all seem pleased, and none more so than the Duke of Newcastle."—Sir Joseph Yorke to Lord Granby, November 10, 1760, *Rutland MSS.*

****

Had Newcastle retired, Pitt's influence, and preference for an eclectic executive, might have originated a combination which would have saved all parties from excesses and mistakes, and the Whigs from the egregious conviction that they alone should govern in perpetuity. But Newcastle was incorrigible. He, and his immediate supporters, shortly became furious at the appointment of Lord Fitzmaurice to be an a*ide-de-camp* to the king, in recognition of his gallantry at *Kloster Campen*. Lord Fitzmaurice was considered to belong to the "country party," and to be a Tory in disguise—more or less. But Fitzmaurice's politics did not prevent Lord Granby from valuing his friendship, and rejoicing in his promotion.

The presence of Lord Bute about the throne exasperated these self-seeking place-jobbers to the point of achieving their own ruin, and his triumph, when a compact front and calm measures would have soon grounded him on the shoals of mediocrity. George III.'s opinion, learnt at Leicester House, was that a king should govern personally, and choose his own ministers: His Majesty saw through Newcastle's intentions and schemes; so determined to rid himself of the "Pelham bit" upon which the sovereign had so long been quietly driven.

Newcastle soon began to complain:

> For myself I am the greatest cypher, the young king is hardly civil to me, talks to me of nothing, and scarce answers me on Treasury matters.

The Duke of Devonshire, Lord Chamberlain, who also assumed an attitude of incipient opposition, requested, and obtained leave to absent himself from the Councils.

Newcastle communicated his great dissatisfaction to Lord Granby who merely replied that he was sorry to hear His Grace was uneasy; but he in no way touched upon the political situation, and quickly reverted to purely military matters.

The Duke of Rutland, *having declined entering any faction*, was a calm spectator of the Court drama. Neither he nor his son had ever been numbered among "Newcastle's footmen," as George II. derisively called the regular Pelhamite supporters, but both had been, and were still, anxious to maintain a *modus vivendi* between Newcastle and Pitt. This Alliance was singularly like that between Jack Mostyn and Cope's Dragoons; sheer necessity, ungraced by a grain of sympathy, had brought Pitt into union with Newcastle, and the ducal schemer soon undermined Pitt's prospects of defeating Lord Bute by commencing a political flirtation with that nobleman himself.

For a space Newcastle still clung to the hope of remaining in office, though subjected to innumerable shocks and surprises:—

He wrote to Lord Hardwicke:

> A most extraordinary Phenomenon, appeared yesterday, of which I had the first notice by an accidental information from Ned Finch at my Lady Yarmouth's. Five Tory Lords and commoners added to the lords and grooms of the bedchamber!

These five Tory intruders in the bedchamber might have belonged to a class of "intruder" which modern civilization combats with patent insect-powder, so inveterately were they loathed by the Pelhamites who, with fastidious horror, watched their entry into the Royal household. This move on George III.'s part marked the opening stage of the struggle.

Newcastle declared his sole reason for retaining power had been to "secure a Parliament;" but, as events afforded a greater likelihood of "an inundation of Tories and Stuarts in every County, he should probably go out that week." His Grace did nothing so salutary; and, pending the further development of home affairs, the thread is resumed in Germany.

****

November and December, 1760, found the belligerents still trying to tire one another out in their endeavours, the one to regain, the other to retain, Hesse. The Allied Army was considerably scattered in different camps; the roads were impassable for heavy artillery, so that Prince Ferdinand was powerless to commence besieging the several French garrisons of Göttingen, Münden, Cassel, and Ziegenhayn. Frederick the Great's hardly earned victory at Torgau had raised the prince's hopes of Prussian reinforcements, a body of which was already reported on the march. The Allied Army was mostly in cantonments behind the Dymel; General Lückner's detachment blockading Göttingen beyond the Weser. In spite of the rigorous season, a force under General Oheim remained in bivouac near Cassel, to observe that garrison; and two battalions of each division of the Main Army bivouacked, in turn, along the Dymel.

Once winter quarters became practicable, Lord Granby desired the king's leave to come home, bringing Pierson; and owned that he "was most sincerely tired of this long, uneventful campaign on the Dymel." In consequence of the non-arrival of remittances at this period, Lord Granby had to commence availing himself of his authority to draw upon the Treasury, and advised twenty bills, amounting to £100,000, at two months' date.

The monthly instalment of £150,000 no longer met the expenditure, and Granby wrote—

> I fear very much when all the Bills come to hand already drawn by me, with those I must necessarily still draw, however backward I might have been formerly, I shall be allowed to have been ready enough with my name of late. However great the sums have been I have the satisfaction of being conscious that, as far as depends on me, the public money has been disposed of according to my instructions."

An utter weariness of the war was evident on the part of both English and French; and Frederick the Great at this moment petitioned Pitt to gain them a peace.

"Everybody seems to wish for peace in England," wrote Sir Joseph Yorke, who had just been knighted, to Granby. The Duke of Newcastle declared that, after 16 or 17 millions spent, the aspect of the war on the Continent was scarcely changed; but "*how could it be otherwise when the enemy was so superior to us in all places*." At the seat of war itself, Colonel Pierson said "he doubted the existence of a single man, civil or military, who did not earnestly wish for peace."

Prince Ferdinand shifted his army further east, increasing the detachments beyond the Weser, and Lord Granby was, in December, 1760, and January, 1761, quartered in the palace of the Prince, and Bishop, of Corvey, on the River Weser, which he had substituted for his old position in order to be more in the centre of his troops. His letters were full of gloom, expressions of weariness, and concern for the great sickness prevailing among the British troops, and the high percentage of deaths in the hospitals.

Though at first confined to the infantry this mortality, Granby announced, was spreading to the cavalrymen, "who began to fall down very fast with inflammatory disorders."

"It is very melancholy to see how fast our men die here," added Colonel Pierson to the tale of misery; "there is a contagious fever that carries the stoutest men off in 2 or 3 days."

The Duke of Newcastle, to whom such things were of little interest save as affecting home politics, expressed his hopes of seeing Lord Granby soon in England, when he trusted His Lordship would explain, verbally, what he would not do by letter—"*viz.* the cause of what was amiss with him."

Part of what was "amiss" His Grace was apprised of in the manner which invariably reduced him to a moral pulp. He received at the Treasury, from Baron Münchhausen, two memorials framed by the Hanover Regency, and "backed" by Prince Ferdinand, complaining of the inadequacy and irregularity of the supply to the army, and of the inefficiency of the Commissariat Staff. This in itself was enough to alarm the duke; but, in addition, a certain number of officers on leave began spreading reports of the extreme distresses and hardships which the troops in Germany were suffering. These rumours took shape, and the *London Chronicle* (1760), affirmed that a growing discontent prevailed against Prince Ferdinand, who was intercepting the full credit due to the British generals by never allowing them completely independent commands, though the British troops were invariably placed in the most arduous positions.

Forage and provisions were scarce, and the impression gained ground that Prince Ferdinand was benefiting pecuniarily by the chicanery of the Hanoverian contractors, and officials. Newcastle at once made for stopping the rumours rather than for seeking the causes of them. He was amazed, he informed Lord Granby, that so many gentlemen had been allowed to come over who were doing incredible mischief with their imprudent discourses: it was true Lord Pembroke and General Waldegrave, who were home on leave, "held very different language from the rest," but the distress of the army formed the universal topic in London.

Lord Granby proved that, except those on sick leave, and such officers of the Guards and cavalry who had been despatched on regimental business, only *some seven or eight officers* out of the whole infantry force were at home. The want of forage and regularity of supply had, said His Lordship, never been disputed; and the answers to his strong representations made to the Commissariat Department, were the difficulties presented by the navigation of the River Weser, the scattered positions of the troops, and the infamous roads, which all but paralyzed the transport service: "that the German War was becoming unpopular he knew; and of this last campaign he was personally heartily sick." Granby's impression was that, great as the distresses were, the more exaggerated accounts of them were being circulated, for political purposes, by enemies at home, and saddled upon the officers on leave.

The unhappiness which the marquess endured throughout this wretched winter was deep enough; yet it never led him, in any moment of impatience or provocation, to breathe or write a word concerning his own extraordinary personal endeavours to reduce the widespread privations. His effort was none the less grand that, at best, it could but soothe, without removing, the distresses of a great army. He placed his purse, his quarters, anything and everything that he possessed, unreservedly at the disposal of all whose wants he might, happily, succeed in reaching; and, by his cheery power of conciliation and wealth of generous sympathy the smouldering ill-humour of the troops was stayed from bursting into flame. (Account of an eyewitness in *Lodge's Portraits*).

The meanest camp-follower never sought his assistance in vain, much less a soldier; and his own table was open to all officers, British and foreign, who would afford him the privilege of showing them hospitality amidst the prevailing scarcity. This solicitude for the miseries of others bore fruit, for his example spread, and "officers of different nations emulated the social virtues of the British chief. By such means he gained the hearts of the whole army: they followed him with confidence, and fought under him from attachment."

Yet all the sympathy accorded him by the Duke of Newcastle was the querulous inquiry why the existence of distress had been allowed to leak out at home by the granting of leave "to a glut of officers who had nothing to do but grumble!" Sir Joseph Yorke and Lord Hardwicke were each appealed to on the subject by the duke, and both agreed that at any rate Lord Granby was the last man to blame. Sir Joseph urged that the general commanding-in-chief personally issued no money, and could not possibly be answerable for the commissariat of the various corps. Lord Hardwicke blamed the home authorities for not making better arrangements for the supply of the army:—

My Lord Granby, with the best heart and the most upright intentions in the world, must necessarily be ignorant of everything relating to contracts and accounts; and Colonel Pierson may not know enough to match him against the knaves and cheats he may meet with.

★★★★★★★★★★

A want of organisation in commissariat matters seems to have been a general fault from the very outset of the war. Lord Barrington wrote to the Duke of Marlborough expressing surprise that the expedition against the French coast (in which the duke served) should have started from Spithead without any commissary of stores.—*Political Life of Lord Barrington,* Letter, May 30, 1758).

★★★★★★★★★★

Newcastle was further perturbed by rumours that Lord Granby intended resigning his command at the close of the campaign; so, His Grace now prattled quite freely about reinforcements, and devoutly hoped that "all possible attention would be given, by *those responsible,* to Lord Granby's representations; but, for his (the duke's) part he no longer had any credit in army affairs." "C. V." was again put on the scent of affairs at Court to ascertain "how Lord Granby stood." "C.V." thought that His Lordship stood well, but that the wish was still, in the event of Lord Ligonier's death, to make Lord Tyrawley Commander-in-Chief, and Lord Granby Master-General of the Ordnance.

Upon this Newcastle informed Granby that he had every reason to think there was no important faction opposed to him at Court—

> . . . the king and Lord Ligonier have a scheme for recruiting you with drafts from Ireland and the Guards. . . . Drive the French from Cassel and Göttingen, and then we may be able to make our party good.

Newcastle's first and last consideration was "party"; it was Granby's last consideration—or, rather, it never entered his head at all.

The money instalment due November, 1760, Lord Granby acknowledged as having arrived in Holland January 11, 1761, only, and "which came very seasonably as we were in the utmost distress for the want of it." In reference to any feather-bed warriors, who might have spread over-coloured reports, Granby assured the duke that—

> A German Campaign was not like a Flanders one—one battle, tranquillity for the rest of the campaign with great plenty of all sorts of wine, &c.; and good and early winter quarters. ("As

R. Lippe
Neuhaus
Paderborn
Berchem
Gesecke
Lichtenau
Haaren
Büren
Brakell
Hoxter
Corvey
Beverungen
Burgholtz
Korbeke
Dossel
Ossendorf
Desenburg
Warburg
R. Dymel
Liebenau
Hoffgeismar
Volksmissen
Grebenstein
Kalle
Wilhelmsthal
Fürstenwald
Zierenburg
Dürrenburg
Weimar
Mariendorff
Immenhausen
Holzhausen
Hohen-
kirchen
Wolfshangen
Weissenstein
Hoff
Corbach
Sachsenhausen
Niedenstein
Waldeck
Gudensburg
Fritzlar
Felzburg
Altenberg
R. Eder
Wildungen
Waverno
Frankenburg
Eimbeck
R. Ilme
Salzderhelden
Uslar
R. Weser
Sababourg
Northeim
R. Leine
Göttingen
Düderstadt
Heiligenstadt
Münden
Lütternburg
R. Werra
Cassel
R. Fulda
Lichtenau
Heiligenberg
Melsungen
Elphershausen
Falckenberg
Langensaltza

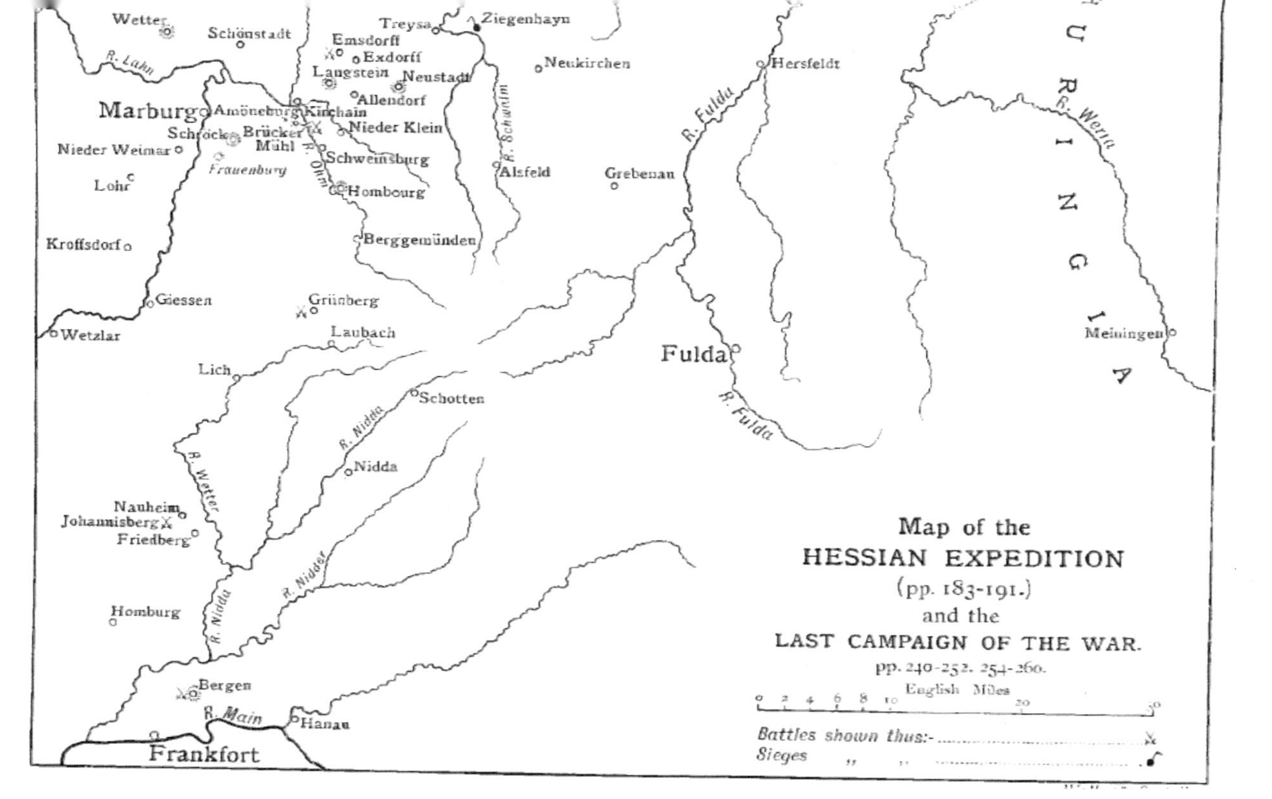

Wetter
Schönstadt
Treysa
Ziegenhayn
Emsdorff
Exdorff
Neukirchen
Hersfeldt
Langstein
Neustadt
Allendorf
Marburg
Amöneburg
Kirchain
Schröck
Brücker
Mühl
Nieder Klein
Nieder Weimar
Schweinsburg
Frauenburg
R. Ohm
R. Lahn
R. Schwalm
Alsfeld
Grebenau
R. Fulda
R. Werra
U R I N G I A
Lohr
Hombourg
Kroffsdorf
Berggemünden
Giessen
Grünberg
Wetzlar
Laubach
Lich
Fulda
Meiningen
Schotten
R. Nidda
Nidda
R. Wetter
Nauheim
Johannisberg
Friedberg
R. Nidder
Homburg
Bergen
R. Main
Hanau
Frankfort
Map of the
HESSIAN EXPEDITION
(pp. 183-191.)
and the
LAST CAMPAIGN OF THE WAR.
pp. 240-252. 254-260.
English Miles
0 2 4 6 8 10 20 30
Battles shown thus:-
Sieges " "

> for the wars formerly in Flanders, I don't suppose half the difficulties existed."—Lord Pembroke to Lord Charlemont, from Kalle Camp). People that love their ease won't love a German Campaign, which certainly is not a party of pleasure, and may not have agreed with every officer's constitution or inclination. I hope, however, that those officers who are determined to see it out will not be entirely forgot, especially Jack Mostyn, whose zeal and gallant behaviour certainly merit some mark of His Majesty's favour. I fear a thaw is coming, which may perhaps put a stop to all operations, which God prevent, for I should be very sorry to return to England and leave the enemy in possession of Göttingen.

When the campaign should close, and the fate of Cassel be determined, Granby assured the duke his reticence should cease, and he would, in person, speak his mind upon every point, and very freely. Agreeing with opinions put forward by the commander-in-chief, Lord Ligonier, Granby expressed his grave doubts of the propriety of undertaking, in winter, siege-operations against an enemy "so skilled in that art," and he sincerely hoped some other means could be found to drive the French from Cassel, and Göttingen.

Prince Ferdinand at last decided upon a sudden, and somewhat desperate, attack upon the French quarters along the Rivers Fulda, Werra, and Eder, in the depth of winter, as a final endeavour to clear the Cassel district, and drive the enemy out of Hesse, south, to Frankfort. After having given his troops a short rest in their cantonments he formed a great magazine at Warburg, where he left a battalion to guard the magazine and bakery.

To act in concert with this "Hessian Expedition" Frederick the Great contributed a corps of some 6,000 Prussians, under General Sybourg.

The Hereditary Prince had rejoined the Allies; and part of the Wesel Expedition which was still in, or near, Münster, was moved to Lippstadt: the rest remained at Münster, under Generals Waldegrave and Hardenburg.

Before Ferdinand commenced his march, some fighting occurred around Göttingen, incidental to some efforts made by De Broglie to get rid of Generals Lückner, Mansberg, and Kilmansegge, who were stationed between Heiligenstadt and Düderstadt, near the River Leine. One affair, at Düderstadt, was won by the marshal's brother, Count

Broglie, who took 200 prisoners, on January 2, 1761; but, on the 3rd, this defeat was reversed by Lückner, with the aid of Kilmansegge. They took prisoners three complete companies of the Grenadiers of France, "who bitterly reviled Count Broglie for the ill-planned manoeuvre", (Granby to Duke of Newcastle), which led to their capture.

A somewhat "sporting" sally was made by M. de Belsunce, from Göttingen, with 300 cavalry, 100 of whom carried, each, a grenadier mounted behind him. De Belsunce took prisoners 4 officers and 100 men, but the principal result of his exploit was getting a convoy into Göttingen, which garrison the Allies were hoping to starve out; but, defeated by heavy rains and bad roads, they raised the blockade.

On February 11, 1761, Prince Ferdinand issued his orders of battle: his right, commanded by the Hereditary Prince, was to attack Fritzlar; his centre, commanded by himself and Lord Granby, the Cassel district, and the French posts on the Fulda down to the River Eder; and his left, under General Spörcken, was opposed beyond the Weser to the French right, under Prince Xavier and the Comte de Stainville, in the neighbourhood of the River Werra. The Prussian reinforcements, now advancing into Thuringia, were to act in concert with General Spörcken against Prince Xavier, and De Stainville.

Lord Granby commanded the 1st Column, Prince Ferdinand's van-guard, consisting of—

3 battalions of British Guards.	3 squadrons of Blues.
1 battalion of Grenadiers.	Elliot's Regiment.
7 battalions of Hanoverian Infantry.	The *Chasseurs*.
1 battalion of Hodgson's (5th Reg.).	2 squadrons of Hanoverian Cavalry.

The whole British Artillery, and 1 Brigade of Count Bückebourg's Artillery.

Lieut.-General Mostyn, and Major-General Julius Caesar, were attached to Lord Granby's Column, which crossed the Dymel February 11.

The remainder of the Allied Army followed in three columns, and on February 12 lay with its right to Wolfshangen, and its left to Wilhelmsthal.

Lord Granby advanced to attack the French post at Weissenstein, on the heights due west of Cassel, in which attack, if unsuccessful, he was to be supported by the whole Allied Army. Before marching he wrote to the Duke of Newcastle a letter which shows the low condition of spirits to which the anxieties of the tedious campaign on the Dymel and Weser had reduced him.

Granby wrote:

> Should the French be prepared and determined to maintain the post, I believe it will be warm work, and should anything happen to me in this affair I hope I need not remind my friend the Duke of Newcastle to endeavour to procure a pension for Mrs. Mompesson (widow of one of the Mompessons frequently mentioned in the *Rutland MSS.*), and her 2 children, and I flatter myself His Majesty would not refuse this mark of his favour on such an occasion. I don't recollect I have any more requests to trouble Your Grace with, except that you will take the first opportunity of providing a king's living for Storer, who has been with me from my first coming to Germany; and will use all your interest in behalf of my friend Dr. Ewer. (Ewer was not yet made a bishop).

Bennet Storer accompanied Granby, and, in a letter to Thomas Thoroton, prayed that "Providence might preserve so good a man" as His Lordship in an undertaking which was on all sides considered very formidable.

Colonel Pierson likewise wrote—

> The morrow may teem with events . . . the prospect of fighting has put Lord Granby in better spirits . . . the infantry marches out weak through sickness; the Guards are the strongest brigade of the whole, and will do their duty.

After this solemn prelude the French, to Granby's surprise, retreated before him, ceding the post of Weissenstein without offering the smallest resistance. Granby then bombarded Gudensburg, which surrendered February 16. On the same day Fritzlar surrendered to the Hereditary Prince, the garrisons of both places being allowed to march out after signing agreements not to serve again during 1761. General Zastrow drove the enemy from Felzburg and Alsberg; and General Spörcken, aided by the Prussian contingent, defeated Prince Xavier and De Stainville at Langensaltza, taking five battalions prisoners, in addition to capturing seven colours, and large quantities of forage.

The Prussians, after this engagement, appear to have retired, and rendered no further assistance to the "Hessian Expedition." The Allies having secured the River Eder, the Hereditary Prince, with Major-

General Howard and General Zastrow, advanced to Homberg, to the Heights of which Prince Ferdinand shortly advanced the Main Army after crossing the River Eder, at Felzburg, on February 18.

★★★★★★★★★★

There are several places of this name. Homburg, the fashionable health resort, we have nothing to do with. Homberg, with the adjacent Heights, is eight miles south of Felzburg-on-the-Eder. Hombourg, with the adjacent Heights, is on the River Ohm, twelve miles south-east of Marburg, and due south of Schweinsburg.

★★★★★★★★★★

All these successes had happened so unexpectedly and simultaneously that De Broglie had not realised the extent of the enemy's intentions until the whole of his cordon had been driven back. Leaving his brother, Count Broglie, in Cassel, the marshal took the field and proceeded to Hersfeldt, from whence the Hereditary Prince (February 20) forced him to retreat towards Fulda, leaving behind him immense stores of meal, oats, and hay. Count de Stainville, after his defeat at Langensaltza, likewise retreated to Fulda, pursued by Spörcken and Lückner.

Prince Ferdinand made direct for Cassel, the siege of which was to be commenced at once, directed by Count La Lippe Bückebourg with a purely German force. Bückebourg's force, Frederick the Great computed at 15,000 Hanoverians, and the Cassel garrison at 6,000 French. Lord Granby was now speeding on towards Kirchain; Colonel "Ned" Harvey, with a Brigade of English cavalry, was scouring the neighbourhood of Ziegenhayn prior to its investment by General Schlüter. The Castle of Marburg was already invested by Major-General Breidenbach, and before it he was killed. He was a popular and able officer, who had commanded the 2nd Division of the Wesel Expedition; he was succeeded by Major-General Oheim, who was instructed to place himself under Lord Granby's orders.

The Hereditary Prince, and Major-General Elliot, next forced De Broglie, and Stainville, from Fulda, from whence the French retreated towards the Main, having previously burnt their magazines in Fulda.

Lord Granby continued advancing (together with his additional corps under Oheim) towards Marburg, which M. de Rougé evacuated (after burning his magazines) with some 6,000 or 8,000 men, and retreated to Giessen, leaving a small garrison, formed principally of the "Irish Brigade," in the Castle of Marburg. Granby later took Marburg as well as the Castle of Amöneburg, also garrisoned by the

"Irish Brigade," and, crossing the River Ohm, advanced to Schrock, upon the Heights of which he encamped.

Prince Ferdinand followed, and on March 2, 1761, the main Allied Army was stationed on the Heights of Hombourg, with its right at Niederklein; and eight battalions of General Spörcken's Corps were ordered back to join Count Bückebourg's division before Cassel. General Spörcken, with his remaining troops, together with Kilmansegge, Wangenheim, and Lückner, rejoined Prince Ferdinand. Thus, since February 11, the Allies had driven the French fifty miles southwards from Cassel towards the Main, together with all their posts on the Rivers Fulda, Eder, and the Ohm, and were now covering the sieges of Cassel and Ziegenhayn, which were both commenced with great energy.

★★★★★★★★★★

> Being sent back to Warburg on business by Lord Granby, the Rev. Bennet Storer, on his return, passed Cassel and Ziegenhayn. He reported "a most infernal fire kept up on both sides" at Cassel, whilst at Ziegenhayn "the enemy's fire was not so hot as ours, deserters said from lack of ammunition."—*Rutland MSS.*, vol. ii.

★★★★★★★★★★

Colonel Pierson might well write—

> This campaign, which with our whimsical countrymen seems to have put the duke (Ferdinand) a little out of fashion, will probably be the greatest yet made, and then I suppose he will again be thought a general. I wish success alone did not always direct our judgements.

Lord Ligonier was delighted at Granby's accounts of these events, and replied:

> Only let us get them out of Cassel, and I think our affair is finished.

Brilliant as Ferdinand's movements had been, a Nemesis in the shape of the old commissariat inefficiency followed closely upon them. General Hardenburg, with a small portion of the Wesel force from Münster, was watching on the right of the Allies, to whom it was now a matter of the first importance to prevent a junction of De Broglie's reuniting forces with those he could draw from the Lower Rhine, from the French Army of Reserve. A turn in the tide became perceptible early in March. Roads, owing to alternate frost and thaw, and the ceaseless passage of troops, were in such condition as almost to cancel any claim to the term "roads" at all, and to bring all locomotion to a standstill. Artillery and transport horses were dying in such thousands that the Board of Ordnance at home was filled with dismay.

The roads between Beverungen (where the cargo-boats from Bremen discharged their freights), Warburg, and the various scenes of the Allied sieges, and manoeuvres, were "paved with dead horses." The commissariat—lame at the best of times—became absolutely paralyzed under the scattered condition of the various corps, which the commissaries declared they sometimes could not even find; and their director-in-chief, Colonel Pierson, was unconcernedly commanding (under the king's orders, and with Prince Ferdinand's sanction—not Granby's) the battalion of the 1st Foot Guards in Lord Granby's Corps.

★★★★★★★★★★

In acquainting the Duke of Newcastle of the prospect of fighting (after the march of the Hessian Expedition), Colonel Pierson frankly stated his inability to attend to commissariat details.—*Newcastle Papers.*

★★★★★★★★★★

Excepting for what stores they captured, and which the French left unburned, the Allied Army must have come near being starved outright.

The French, on the other hand, were being driven towards their important magazine in Frankfort; while their various detached corps, up till now well-nigh hustled out of their senses, were beginning to acquire the strength which comes of union. De Broglie was adding defensive works to Bergen, and the corps under Prince Xavier, De Stainville, and De Rougé, were drawing together about Frankfort, and Friedberg. Moreover, the Chevalier de Muy, with 14,000 men from the Lower Rhine, got past General Hardenburg and the Hereditary Prince, and joined De Broglie.

In consequence. General Hardenburg, with eight British battalions, (of the Wesel force, 2 battn. British grenadiers; 2 battn. Highlanders; 1 battn. Barrington's; 1 battn. Kingsley's; 1 battn. Home's; and 1 battn. Welsh Fusiliers), and two squadrons of Conway's Regiment, which had been resting since *Kloster Campen,* joined the Allied Army at Kirchain, as De Muy's march from the Rhine had relieved the Münster garrison from risk of attack. The main body of the Allies remained on the Heights of Hombourg on the Ohm, where Prince Ferdinand was erecting huts, and placing many of his troops in cantonments in the adjacent villages.

Lord Granby passed the River Lahn below Marburg, and pushed on to Lohr, from whence he patrolled the country towards Wetzlar with the Hessian Hussars, and towards Giessen with Elliot's Light Dragoons. On the 16th and 17th March the enemy began to advance towards him in such force, on both sides of the Lahn, that Prince Ferdinand recalled him to the Heights of Langstein, near Kirchain. Granby's letters to the Duke of Newcastle, Lord Ligonier, and Lord Holdernesse, plainly show his opinion of the turn matters were assuming—

> The bad weather, by making the roads almost impossible for our artillery, has prevented our pushing the enemy so rapidly as we could have wished, and thus afforded them a breathing-time which they have employed in collecting their whole force. . . . All the troops from the Lower Rhine have now joined them. . . Ziegenhayn has been vigorously bombarded, but, . . . as we are wanting in battering cannon and ammunition, and, as we don't hear that the garrison are distressed for provisions, or any other necessaries, I begin to look upon our acquisition of the place as a very doubtful circumstance. The enemy have made two sorties from Cassel, but were repulsed by Count Bückebourg each time with much loss on their side.

From this moment ensued a period of "pull Devil," or rather, "push Devil, push Baker." A multitude of movements forwards and backwards ensued, during which the weight of numbers told slowly, but surely, against the Allies. De Muy, and Comte de Stainville, crept up to Marburg, and Grünburg. Lord Granby was now one side of the River Ohm, now the other. Prince Ferdinand on one occasion was with him reconnoitring at the old Castle of Frauenburg (on the enemy's side of the Ohm). Both Generals, and their suites, were dismounted, when suddenly a detachment of Fischer's Corps, led by an *aide-de-camp* of De Broglie's, appeared within some forty or fifty yards' distance, and opened fire upon them. Some of their horses galloped off riderless, and after a brief scene of hurry, confusion, and holding on to stirrup-leathers, the reconnoitring party made its escape, leaving various articles behind. Prince Ferdinand's spy-glass, which was among the latter, was sent back the same evening by De Broglie.

The Hereditary Prince and General Lückner were still on the enemy's side of the Ohm; the former behind Grünburg, the latter at Laubach. De Broglie ordered De Stainville to attack; Lückner was compelled to retire, and the Hereditary Prince also, to Berggemunden, after a sharp engagement on March 21, in which he lost 4 battalions (taken prisoners), 18 cannon, and 19 colours. Major-General Rheden was wounded, and subsequently died.

This defeat, and the raising of the siege of Ziegenhayn from want of ammunition, settled Prince Ferdinand's chances of remaining in his position on the Ohm which he had retained for a month, after destroying all the French magazines from the River Eder to the Main. The effectives of his Infantry Battalions had dwindled gradually to little more than one-third of their paper establishment: "Hodgson's" Regiment (5th), after detaching a piquet of 50 men, had only 5 men left with the colours; "Carr's" (50th) was little better, and, one battalion with another, did not exceed 200 men each.

The cavalry was equally weak, and the commissariat was stuck fast in the mud. On the 23rd of March, 1761, the retreat began from the River Ohm, the Allies marching in six columns to the Neustadt Heights, the Hereditary Prince forming the rearguard. Lord Granby, having to secure Count Kilmansegge's retreat, remained on the Heights of Langstein till the 24th, when he marched at 3 a.m. by Emsdorff and Gilsenberg, being joined by General Hardenburg's Corps.

De Broglie's van-guard followed in pursuit in two columns; one, making in the direction of Ziegenhayn, fell (March 25) upon the division of the Allied Rearguard, under Major-Generals Schlüter and Zastrow. Both these officers were taken prisoners, with 10 or 12 others; Schlüter was wounded, 100 men, 2 cannon, and 3 colours were lost. The enemy retired to Ziegenhayn, pursued by the left wing of the cavalry under Oheim. All that night the Allies remained under arms, marching the 26th at daylight, crossed the River Schwalm, and bivouacked at Branau.

Near Fritzlar the Hereditary Prince was joined by Colonel Harvey with 2 squadrons of the Greys, 2 squadrons of Inniskillings, 2 squadrons of Ancrams, and the Prince of Anhalt with 6 Hanoverian battalions. De Rochambeau, who was harassing the prince's rear, was repulsed, and Colonel Harvey's Cavalry took 30 or 40 prisoners. Thus, with various skirmishes, and incessant anxieties and fatigues, the retreat continued across the River Eder to Corbach and Wolfshangen; the Allied Army crossing the River Dymel and taking up its old position at, and near, Warburg, on the 31st of March. Count Bückebourg raised the siege of Cassel on the 27th, and reached Warburg unmolested. ("That same retreating is a very comical, ugly operation; being kicked, then turning about again to snarl, shew your teeth, and walk on again."—Lord Pembroke to Lord Charlemont from Kalle Camp, July, 1760).

Lord Granby wrote to the Duke of Newcastle:

> It is with concern, that I am obliged to acquaint Your Grace that, from the superiority of the enemy and the want of forage to subsist our troops, H.S. Highness found it impracticable to penetrate any further, or even to maintain the ground he held longer than the 22nd (March). On the 23rd, therefore, he commenced his retreat, and the same day the Hereditary Prince, attacked by a superior force, suffered some loss. In consequence of this and the immense superiority of the enemy the siege of Cassel was raised, and the army, after constant marching and lying in Bivouac, has this night gone into winter-quarters, the major part on the other side of the Dymel. . . . The duke made this retreat *pas à pas*, and did not relinquish the siege of Cassel till the very last moment. However, at least we have destroyed their Magazines and lived upon them for 2 months. So soon as I have seen the duke and made the necessary arrangements for the Cantonment of the troops, which I believe will be in the bishoprick of Paderborn, I propose setting out for England.

This retreat of the tired army left the whole of Hesse in the hands of the French, a circumstance which they celebrated with a *feu de joie,* and a *Te Deum.* De Broglie reinstated his army in cantonments in, and about, Cassel, and repaired to France to await overtures for peace. Sir Joseph Yorke reported that opinion at the Hague attributed Prince Ferdinand's failure to the King of Prussia having thwarted his plan by not sustaining the promised assistance upon which it was largely based. Frederick the Great maintained he promised assistance as far as the River Werra only. A memorandum of Prince Ferdinand's, dated Neuhaus, April 4, 1701, says—

> It is deputed to the discretion of My Lord Granby to determine the difficulties which have till now hampered the operations of the commissariat, and to effect such changes as shall be judged the most proper to ensure the army being better provided than heretofore.

To Lord Bute Prince Ferdinand reported his late movements, and the condition of the Allied Army, summing up the future position as follows:—

> If we are not considerably reinforced, or, if France be not obliged to call off a large portion of her troops, we have noth-

ing to expect save from a stroke of luck, or from any faults the enemy may commit during the campaign.

Thus, ended this long and exhausting effort, occupying the winter of 1760-61, during the whole of which the Marquess of Granby spared himself no effort, or outlay, which could diminish the sufferings of the private soldiers. Frederick the Great described it as "*Une Campagne où, ne respectant point les hivers, on affrontait toutes les saisons.*" The troops gained their winter quarters in the first days of April only, after which they enjoyed a hardly earned repose of nearly three months.

Chapter 15

1761: The politics of high office

Lord Granby started for England; but, pending his arrival, the current of events must be resumed at a slightly earlier date.

Both the Duke of Newcastle, and Lord Ligonier, had been endeavouring to comply with Lord Granby's recommendations respecting General Mostyn. The Military Governorship of Jersey had become vacant and was mentioned to Mostyn, though never actually offered to him. Mostyn wrote—

> I have been consulting the *Red Book* (poor Downe's oracle and *vade mecum*). There I find, in the List of His Majesty's Garrisons, Plymouth set down as £1,289. 2. 6 *per annum,* and that of Jersey as £0. 0. 0 *per annum.*

Mostyn made a signal mistake here, for, though no fixed salary was attached to the Jersey appointment, it was worth in certain fees and dues some £1,200 a year. His error, however, was immaterial, as the post was given to Lord Albemarle, the Duke of Cumberland's Lord-in-Waiting and friend. But poor Mostyn was doomed to still further disappointments, instead of merited rewards.

The rumours of Lord Granby's intention of quitting his command had led to the consideration of a successor. Lieut.-General Mostyn was not considered equal to the command-in-chief, and yet he could not have been passed over by the other Lieut.-General in Germany, Waldegrave, who was his junior. At home the only available man was General Conway, who was a few days senior in rank to either of them. Conway's name first appeared in the matter February 16, 1761, upon what it must have been gall and wormwood for the Duke of Newcastle to head with the words "Memorandum for Lord Bute," through whom all official matters now reached the king.

After so long a time passed in the cool shade of royal displeasure

General Conway's appointment to serve in Germany was decided on to the intense delight, as may be imagined, of his cousin and mentor Horace Walpole, who in high excitement wrote to Sir Horace Mann—

> Mr. Conway is going to Germany to his great contentment, as his character is vindicated at last.

Mostyn lost no time in expressing his opinion on the measure, couched in his customary Saxon-English—

> I certainly do run downhill at home at a dam'd rate; however, I comfort myself that here, with ye army, I am not in so retrograde a march. As to Bland's Regiment, be that as it may. It is my duty to wish ye king's will be done . . . but what can I say in regard to ye pleasure of it if Mr. Conway, a lieut.-general six short days senior to me, comes over to this army only to wipe my nose? What other use can his coming be of? We are already (under ye command of Lord Granby) one lieut.-general for ye cavalry, and one for the infantry.

Offence in other quarters was caused by this move, and the Duke of Bedford's faction took up the cudgels in defence of Lieut.-General Waldegrave who had served all through the war, with the infantry, as Mostyn had with the cavalry.

The Duke of Newcastle, while acquainting Lord Granby of these circumstances, took the occasion of sounding him as to his own intentions—

> Idle stories are spread of your design to quit the command. I hope in God, for your own sake and the publick's, that you will not think of it. By all I can learn you will be received with the utmost grace and favour. General Conway's friends have procured him a promise to serve the next campaign, but Johnny Waldegrave has made such a clamour about it that it is declared that, should Your Lordship not be disposed to return to Germany, in that case Conway should not go.

Conway himself, honourable always, and free of any personal greed, sought to remove this friction by applying for leave of absence from Germany so long as Lord Granby might remain in England.

Newcastle wrote what comfort he could to Mostyn, suggesting his return home on leave, saying—

> There was an idle rumour from Brussells that dear Lord Granby was taken prisoner by the French, to which we don't give the least credit.

From Hanover Mostyn replied—

> I had my foot in ye stirrup to start for England when I received word that my remaining with ye army would be agreeable to H. S. Highness, which being an honour I could not disregard. I hear of Gen. Conway, Lady Ailesbury, and Lady Mary Cook, and other great personages on Your Grace's side ye water on their way to the army. Your Grace long before you see this will have seen that best of men, Granby, so I need say nothing to you of him, or the stuff of his being prisoner.

****

> Report says that the Duchess of Richmond and some other ladies whose husbands are going, or gone, to Germany, are going there likewise, and are to be at Brunswick. I much question whether their husbands will rejoice in their company, but certainly Prince Ferdinand will not be fond of such auxiliaries.—*A Lady of the Last Century* (Mrs. Montagu).

****

Mostyn repeated that he could not, and would not, serve under General Conway—

> I have been prouder than any man in my command, and happy in it; happy in ye sincerest friendship and love of our commander, my Lord Granby, and honoured with the approbation of our commander in chief, H.S.H. Duke Ferdinand, beyond doubt the greatest soldier in Europe. (The superiority implied here of Prince Ferdinand's military genius to that of Frederick the Great is still maintained in some quarters). I had intended remaining permanently in England had not the duke prevented my coming; but I shall take the first opportunity, though I could not sham sick, nor would I desert.

All possible pressure was brought to bear against any rash resolves on General Mostyn's part, and that ever cheery soldier consented to await the possible shaping of events to everyone's contentment.

Jack wrote:

> I wish, as we toast in Germany, 'Success to all Good Things,' and if a *suspension d'armes* should take place I conclude I may come

with Duke Ferdinand's and Lord Granby's leave.

The Rev. Dr. Ewer's preferment, previously touched upon, at this time became possible, and a word or two concerning it will tend to show, from George III.'s attitude towards the Rutland family, that His Majesty was very far from including it in the Duke of Newcastle's personal clique which was so obnoxious to him. The Bishop of St. David's being dead Ewer's name was at once put forward by the Duke of Rutland. Lord Bute one day was discussing the vacant See with the Duke of Newcastle, in whose hands the ecclesiastical patronage had so long been placed, and asked His Grace's opinion.

Newcastle answered:

> If you have a mind to oblige the Duke of Rutland and my Lord Granby, you can't do it more effectually than by giving this bishopric to Dr. Ewer.

A little later the Bishop of Winchester died, upon which Newcastle suggested to Lord Bute some translations by which the See of Llandaff might be rendered vacant for Dr. Ewer, but concerning which neither the Duke of Rutland, nor Lord Granby, had yet made any application. Lord Bute replied that, before the receipt of Newcastle's letter, the plan suggested in it had been already carried out. Thus, Lord Granby's earnest wish was at last fulfilled, and Dr. Ewer became Bishop of Llandaff.

The Duke of Newcastle's "flirtation" with Lord Bute was assuming developments of which His Grace has provided the key. In a private Minute describing a secret audience held with George III. Newcastle relates how he suggested to the king, with the concurrence of the Duke of Devonshire and Lord Hardwicke, that Lord Bute should be made a Secretary of State. Newcastle urged:

> In any case, Mr. Pitt must not be offended, although I have no reason to be partial to him.

His Majesty consented, and Newcastle then proclaimed Lord Bute's promotion to Sir Joseph Yorke at the Hague, slightly varying the circumstances under which it was effected. His Grace coolly declared "*it was entirely a measure of the king's own*, though he (Newcastle) had reason to suppose H.M.'s Ministers approved it."

The Duke of Devonshire was deputed to convey the intelligence to Mr. Pitt who does not seem to have made any objections. The argument used was plausible enough that, as Lord Bute wielded so much influence in a totally unfettered position, it would be just as well to weight him with the wholesome responsibility of the Secretaryship of State for the Northern Department, which was rendered vacant by pensioning the Earl of Holdernesse.

Had Newcastle been loyal to his political Alliance with Pitt there had been nothing to deprecate in this arrangement. But he was not. His object was to place himself unreservedly at Lord Bute's disposal, and thus gain George III.'s confidence; which done Mr, Pitt might, for all Newcastle cared, have sunk to the remotest depths of the political sea.

So far Newcastle was getting quite confident again, and proceeded with his plans "to secure a Parliament." Among the many borough seats which he could command was one at Newark-on-Trent, the second seat for which was held by the Rutland interest. In the latter Mr. John Manners, of Grantham Grange, (later of Buckminster), was put forward, and the Duke of Newcastle, on his side, asked to be allowed to nominate Mr. Thomas Thoroton, M.P. for Boroughbridge. Many letters appear among the *Newcastle Papers* touching this election, at which Lord Robert Manners Sutton went to assist, and was taken ill at Stamford with an attack of ague, from which he suffered chronically since his soldiering days. Mr. Thoroton wrote:

> The fitt was regular, and I gave him some bark, and thank God he has missed his fitt, and is very well again.

After various rumours of opposition, and an incidental row over the election of churchwardens, which during several years caused a free fight, and many broken heads, in Newark, John Manners and Thomas Thoroton were declared duly elected. Thoroton was succeeded in the representation of Boroughbridge by Brice Fisher, whose name appeared earlier as the recipient of a portrait, and a snuff-box, from the Marquess of Granby.

A hitch now occurred which set Newcastle once more upon thorns. He wrote to the Duke of Devonshire:

> Yesterday, Lord Bute told me the king wished to give the Gold Key (Groom of the Stole) to the Duke of Rutland and the Staff (Lord Steward of the Household, which office the Duke of Rutland then held), to my Lord Talbot. Your Grace may imagine this has surprised, and not a little, embarrassed, us. I believe it is feared if the staff is not made vacant the key may be given that way. We have delayed it a little, and I hope shall suspend it

at least till Lord Granby's arrival.

The Earl of Talbot was a young man, belonging to the "country party," who had been much identified with Leicester House. He was a sportsman, a bit of a "bruiser," and held a reputation for adventure and free living which scarcely fitted him for the dignified office of Lord Steward, though he was by no means devoid of talent. In discussing the probability of this appointment. Lord Bute said that they would not, on any account, do the least thing that might offend the Duke of Rutland.

"C. V.," whom Newcastle instantly put on the trail, declared his conviction that "the king would have Lord Talbot in a great employment," and that, should the Duke of Rutland decline to make the necessary change, alterations would be made in the Lord Steward's office which would render it disagreeable to him.

The fear that Lord Talbot might be made Groom of the Stole arose in the minds of Newcastle, Devonshire, and Hardwicke, from the fact that this office conferred on its holder the power of constant private communication with the king through the nominal privilege attaching to it of handing His Majesty his shirt. This means of access to the king's ear was not deemed as befitting one professing political views such as Talbot's.

The Duke of Newcastle was commissioned by Lord Bute to sound the Duke of Rutland on the subject; and communicated the result of his interview, hoping he had executed Lord Bute's commands satisfactorily. The term "commands" shows the position which Newcastle had already assumed in regard to Bute.

> I took down the following words from the Duke of Rutland which I think is a full answer to my question of the Gold Key. The duke is very sensible of the king's goodness and attention to him, but in answer to my question His Grace assures me that his present Office is the only one about Court which would be perfectly agreeable to him. His Grace would not say anything that could sound like underrating the great honour of the Gold Key, but I think I can observe that, in his present circumstances, it is an Office which would not be agreeable to him.

The Duke of Newcastle then communicated the above to Lord Hardwicke, who said the appointment of Lord Talbot was still "talked about," and he wished the proposed change could be made palatable to the Duke of Rutland, as the motives for it were so obvious.

Having got matters thus far, Newcastle then wrote one of his flattering, repellent effusions to Lord Granby, informing him of Lord Bute's promotion to be a Secretary of State, *vice* Lord Holdernesse, which change "*was approved by all. . . .*"

> I wish you may be able to come over for a few days. . . . I shall want to settle something with you in regard to yourself . . . you are in the highest light that ever young man of quality was. You have attained it by your merit. You will maintain it by the same—(and so on, *ad nauseam.*)

This letter may not have reached Lord Granby in time to be replied to before leaving Germany: no answer to it appears in the *Newcastle Papers*. News of his lordship's landing, and of his having slept at Colchester, April 13, 1761, reached the Duke of Newcastle, who at once informed the Duke of Devonshire, and hoped that our separate peace with France could be completed before another campaign should commence.

On April 14 Lord Granby arrived in London, and Lieut.-General Conway started for the Hague to assume the command in the former's absence.

Before Conway's departure, Horace Walpole wrote to him, "I do not at all lament Lord Granby's leaving the army, and your immediate succession," in which sentence, and sentiment, the whole foundation of Walpole's animosity to Granby lies compactly enshrined.

Upon arrival Lord Granby was unwell, so that his intercession concerning his father's office could not directly be obtained. Mr. Jenkinson, Lord Bute's secretary, in a letter to Mr. Grenville, thus touched upon the subject:—

> Granby continues indisposed, so that he has not been with Lord Bute. Shelburne, (first Earl, father of Lord Fitzmaurice then serving under Granby), has given hopes that by means of some little agents he can employ he shall be able to make the Rutland family acquiesce in some expedients between what he desires and what is offered. I have in general but little opinion of these operations, though they often have more success upon a necessitous man, as Granby is, than others. I am convinced, however, that neither party will push affairs to extremities.

As the above letter reflects discredit upon no one save Lord Shelburne it might have been omitted, save that such omission might be attributed to misgivings as to Lord Granby having acted, on this occasion, with his customary good faith and disinterestedness.

The only difficulty in the matter was that, the Duke of Rutland having accepted the office of Lord Steward with reluctance, and on the distinct understanding of being pledged to support nobody save the king, it became a peculiarly delicate task to disturb him; especially as George III., Lord Bute, Pitt, and the Duke of Newcastle, all wished His Grace to remain a member of the Ministry. Walpole, naturally, said that His Grace disliked the office of Groom of the Stole because it had fewer employments in its disposal.

The reason would more probably have been found in the comparative periods of absence from Belvoir incidental to the necessities of each office. After Lord Granby had been consulted on the difficulty, it resolved itself into the following solution. The Earl of Huntingdon resigned the office of Master of the Horse, which was accepted by the Duke of Rutland; Lord Huntingdon becoming Groom of the Stole. Lord Talbot thus became Lord Steward, *vice* the Duke of Rutland.

All these political changes, involving the return to Court employment of so many who had been previously ostracised, provided mines of wealth to Walpole's pen. At the change above described he fairly whooped again!

> If my last letter raised your wonder, this will not allay it. Lord Talbot is Lord Steward! . . . As the Duke of Leeds was forced to give way to Jemmy Grenville, so the Duke of Rutland has been obliged to make room for this new earl. (To Sir H. Mann).

This is Walpole's reading of this change; but a different version may, perhaps, be founded upon a side light afforded by another chronicler—Bubb Dodington. Three months previously Dodington recorded that—

> Lord Bute came to him and said . . . that he was uneasy about Talbot, as he would put the Steward's Staff in Talbot's hands the first day if he could. That he (Bute) heard that Talbot thought Granby could persuade his father to quit it, and that otherwise he would not accept it on account of the friendship between him and Granby.

Really this Granby must have appeared to Walpole's eye as too genial by half! He could create harmony in an Allied Army, when the first thing both of his predecessors, the Duke of Marlborough and

Lord George Sackville, had done was to get at loggerheads with their German comrades; he could frequent the Court, and Leicester House as well; he was the strongest link in the chain which held together Newcastle and Pitt; and, "Revolution Whig" though he was, he could extend friendship, and confidence, even unto repentant Tories. How could he hope to be spoken of favourably by such as hugged their hatreds, and unfailingly made principle subservient to prejudice?

Did the part, enacted by Lord Talbot a few months later at the Coronation, belong to the Steward's department the Duke of Rutland may well have congratulated himself on his change of office, and that his part at that ceremony was merely to bear "the Sceptre and Cross in his Robes of Estate."

Lord Talbot, the new Lord Steward, aspired to play an equestrian role on the occasion as Lord High Constable, (an office occasionally revived at coronations, etc.), with Dymoke, the champion; to which end Westminster Hall was lighted up on September 18, 1761, and placed under a Captain's guard whilst a rehearsal took place. Talbot's intention was to teach his horse, after entering, to retire, courtier-wise, backwards from the royal presence.

On the eventful day, September 22, 1761, Dymoke performed his part admirably well, riding George II.'s old white Dettingen charger; but Lord Talbot's mount, either from fright or "cussedness," *approached* Their Majesties tail first, while the Lord High Constable performed prodigies with hands and heels in the endeavour to reverse the order of his going.

So, the story ran in the collective versions told by Horace Walpole, and others, and it is too harmlessly good to wish it untrue. An alleged eye-witness, however, quoted in a note to Churchill's Poems, makes no mention of the circumstance, and says that Lord Talbot acquitted himself very well. At the subsequent banquet certain economies instituted by Talbot had curtailed the number of tables, including one which had on former occasions been allotted to the Barons of the Cinque Ports. The barons expostulated, upon which Lord Talbot replied that "if they came to him as Lord Steward their requests could not be granted; if as Lord Talbot he was a match for any one of them!"

The office of Lord Steward did not apparently gain in dignity or courtesy by leaving the Duke of Rutland's hands, after an administration of seven years, commencing 1754.

CHAPTER 16

1761: Belleisle

Immediately upon hearing of Lord Granby's arrival, the Duke of Newcastle drew up a long *Memorandum* of questions to put to him:

> To enquire into Prince Ferdinand's character, manner, and conduct. His behaviour towards the officers and troops, especially the English; and the particular officers who are most in his favour among the English, Hanoverian, Brunswick, and Hessian forces. His conduct as a general. His plan at the opening of the campaign, and at the conclusion. The reason of his not coming to an action earlier in the campaign, and the *suspicion of his having received private orders to decline an action in order not to endanger the king's country.* State of the commissariat; and why the expense six times that of the French Army, *etc., etc., etc.*

The allusion to the "private orders" had its origin in Prince Ferdinand's practice, as a relation of the British king, of corresponding directly with His Majesty, a circumstance which originated a great deal of jealousy and suspicion in Newcastle's mind. At this particular moment the duke was placed in a worse fright by a communication of Count Viri's, who declared that Mr. Pitt was displaying a marked inclination to attack the Treasury on the breakdown of the supply to the army, and the consequent failure of Prince Ferdinand's Hessian Expedition.

At the Treasury, Newcastle gave "check" to Prince Ferdinand by writing a letter to the Marquess of Granby, informing him of the roundabout manner in which the prince's accusation had been made, instead of through the British commander-in-chief, or Colonel Pierson. The Treasury therefore had desired that Prince Ferdinand should acquaint Lord Granby, specifically, with the details of mismanagement, in order that *Lord Granby* might advise the board as to the future needs of the commissariat, and a successor to Colonel Pierson, who desired to retire.

That the prince was acting quite a single-hearted part there is good reason for doubting. He denied to Colonel Pierson that he had made any accusation against the Treasury, whereupon Pierson showed His Serene Highness the extract from his own letter embodying the charge, which extract had been sent to the colonel for investigation. Prince Ferdinand then maintained his letter had been misunderstood; and that he was complaining of the structure of the Commissariat Department—not of its good faith; he recommended that Mr. Hatton should proceed to England to give evidence before the Committee of Inquiry.

Mr. Hatton, the "intolerable plague," and impertinent upstart, of Newcastle's earlier correspondence, arrived, and denied that the prince's operations had been hindered by the commissariat, but by the insurmountable difficulty of impassable roads. Thus, the same Mr. Hatton whom the Duke of Newcastle had done his utmost to recall and disgrace, and who was saved by Lord Granby's interposition, now became quite a nice, trustworthy man since his evidence aided His Grace's political cause and credit.

The actual constitution of a Committee of Inquiry that was appointed is not obvious; but Lord Mansfield, Chief Justice of the King's Bench, seems to have been much occupied with it.

Some memoranda supply the following details elicited by the inquiry:—

Colonel Pierson was declared to be quite incorrupt. He had not profited by a single farthing; but either he was not invested with adequate authority by his commission, or did not exercise it. When regular supplies failed, the troops foraged the country, giving recklessly to the farmers, and others, receipts for more produce than was actually supplied.

****

In a letter written by Lord George Sackville, when commander-in-chief, he said nothing should be neglected, in relation to supply, which obviated the necessity of a general forage by the troops. It annihilated military discipline, and afforded opportunity for license and plunder which alienated the good will of the country occupied.—September 15, 1758, *Chatham Correspondence.*

****

The contractors bought up these receipts from the farmers, whom they beat down to a price considerably below that represented by the paper vouchers. The contractors then delivered the vouchers to the commissariat against payment in full.

Sooner than offer their produce on these terms, which placed the profits chiefly in the hands of the eternal "middleman," the inhabitants of the country, in which the troops were quartered, concealed their stores; scarcity ensued, and the supplies had to be obtained from outside at great expense and delay, in proportion to the distances involved. The Committee, further, came to the conclusion that the Prussian officials usurped authority, which should belong to the British Commissariat Staff, and omitted no means of defrauding the British Government. (Evidence of J. P. Fuhr).

Lord Mansfield gave the Duke of Newcastle another shock, by saying he considered the matter "very menacing to His Grace," and then dealt with Lord Granby:—

> The post assigned to Lord Granby is cruel to him. He commands our troops, but he is not commander in chief. He is not in the situation the Duke of Cumberland, or John, Duke of Marlborough, were. He has no control, he can't exercise his judgement upon the utility or necessity of the service because he don't command in chief: therefore he can do no service but in the capacity of an intendant. Such a duty is inconsistent with his station, and not to be expected from any man of his figure and rank. . . . I am told Lord George Sackville avoided having anything to do with it. So much for theory. As to facts, the result of my enquiry is that there never was such a scene of abuse, cheating, mismanagement, etc. All agree that Pierson is most incorrupt, but he hates the business, don't understand it, and refers people to Massowe.

★★★★★★★★★★

> The army finds, and finds most sensibly, that Massowe was charged with the whole conduct of the supplies, and the British Director merely the power to pay for them.—1761, *Anonymous Letter, Political Tracts,* British Museum.

★★★★★★★★★★

Lord Mansfield dealt in detail with the various abuses, one of which was the giving of gratuities to foreigners already in British pay. "Lord Granby was the last person likely to know of these abuses, and, even if he suspected them, it would be very ticklish for him to mention them" in the position he occupied towards Prince Ferdinand. An analysis showed that, at the moment the army was in its worst straits, the paid receipts represented the troops to have consumed ten times their proper allowances. It would be small satisfaction for anyone, Lord Mansfield added, even though the whole disgrace might ultimately fall on Prince Ferdinand.

Prince Ferdinand addressed another letter to the Treasury, which the latter maintained bore the appearance of being an after-thought, or change of front. A copy of it was submitted to Lord Hardwicke, (the original and copy are both wanting), whose comments show that Prince Ferdinand was pleading want of summary jurisdiction over fraudulent British commissaries and contractors.

Lord Hardwicke demanded:

> How can Prince Ferdinand's suggestion, based upon the Prussian plan, succeed with us? I suppose the King of Prussia secures the due execution of his commissariat by his arbitrary, despotic discipline; and probably instantly hangs up a commissary by martial law if he catches him in a fraud, But I fear nobody can give that power either to Prince Ferdinand, or my Lord Granby, over British subjects,

That Prince Ferdinand pursued, in the German section of the Allied Army, Frederick the Great's policy for ensuring probity and punctuality, appears certain from a letter of Lord Pembroke's, who was now appointed to Lord Granby's Staff—

> These contractors dare not use the foreigners as they do us, for, if they fail, they good-naturedly hang them, while ours scarcely keep to their engagements, by which our sick and tired perish.

****

Charlemont MSS., July 28, 1760,—"Our commissaries returned from the camp of Ferdinand to buy boroughs, to rear palaces, to rival the magnificence of the old aristocracy of the realm,"—Macaulay's *Essay on the Earl of Chatham.*

****

To the ordinary mind, Frederick the Great's treatment of fraudulent contractors and commissaries, if anything, appears too merciful fur such as can pilfer taxes, paid by a public half ruined by war, and at the same time swindle, defraud, and rob a bravely suffering army, notably the "sick and tired," of the commonest necessities of life. Yet these sordid robberies were repeated as lately as during the Crimean War; and would occur again on the first opportunity which offered to such commercial *canaille* of "doing business," as they would style it.

The inquiry proceeded, and, as regarded the rumours of discontent spread by the officers on leave, and which Lord Pembroke and General Waldegrave had endeavoured to silence, Lord Granby stated that "such matters had been discoursed in the army, but in a general way only, which did not constitute any specific charge against anyone." Since then, the whole spleen of the British Army was falling upon Herr Massowe, (apparently the Chief of the Prussian Commissariat Staff), whose dismissal would lead, Lord Granby was convinced, to Prince Ferdinand's resignation.

Prince Ferdinand repeated his statement that it was the construction of the Commissariat Department that he deprecated (though as commander-in-chief he should, surely, have been able to alter it had he wished); and, in the end, no special result was attained to by the Committee of Inquiry. It pronounced that so long as the army was concentrated and the weather fine, the commissariat, though extravagant, had met its duties; but that it broke down when winter rendered the roads impassable, and the army was scattered in four or five detachments. (Mr. Peter Taylor, Commissary, wrote, February 20, 1761, to Lord Granby: "The British troops under your command are so divided that I cannot find them."—*Rutland MSS.*, vol. ii.)

Lieut.-Colonel Pierson was to be assisted by Lieut.-Colonel Boyd, in spite of Lord Hardwicke's insistence that civil and military duties were incompatible, as Pierson had proved and pleaded. Later, Colonel Howard was sent to replace Colonel Pierson.

Prince Ferdinand was warned that the war was so unpopular in England as to necessitate the utmost economy; and, as the Treasury could not adequately investigate the alleged frauds, it did not touch upon them, in the full conviction that no one was more anxious to discover, and punish, the perpetrators than His Serene Highness himself.

In allusion to this breakdown, and the feathering of nests incidental to it, Smollett discreetly declined to give an opinion, saying: "it may be the province of some future historian, when truth may be investigated freely, without any apprehension of pains and penalties." That many fortunes were made by those who catered for the army is certain; but even that conviction fails to account for the stupendous outlay, which during the winter of 1760-1 exceeded the monthly remittance of £150,000 by a like sum, and even by £190,000; or, in other words, the monthly expenditure sometimes amounted to £340,000.

Chroniclers all pronounce Prince Ferdinand to have been a man of exceptional integrity and honour, who quitted his command as poor as when he assumed it; and it is positively known that Lord Granby was brought to the verge of ruin by his. Can it have been that, acting upon the shady code of ethics which holds all to be fair in love and war, some of Frederick the Great's "little bills" were smuggled by the Prussian officials into the British accounts, over and above his subsidy of £670,000 *per annum?*

Certain it is that his financial position at the conclusion of the Seven Years' War was a most remarkable one, considering the small resources at his disposal, and the magnitude of the struggle he maintained. Yet he sheathed his sword free of debt, and commenced compensating towns in the Westphalian war-area, and resuscitating agriculture and trade by bounties. But, for the general reader, the interest in the matter has lapsed, and no historian will probably now awaken those "sleeping dogs" which Smollett deemed it prudent to "let lie."

The condition of the British Army in Germany on March 1, 1761, is shown by a *Memorandum* which Lord Granby furnished to the Duke of Newcastle:—

The Guards were short of their full strength by				559 men, and had			972 sick.
,, Infantry	,,	,,	,,	2978	,,	,,	3500 ,,
,, Cavalry	,,	,,	,,	504	,,	,,	489 ,,
				4041			4961

The horses were short of their full strength by 1430, and 1560 were lame or sick.

On paper, its total strength would appear never to have exceeded about 25,000, to which number it was increased when Generals Griffin, Caesar, and Elliot, successively joined it with reinforcements; so that the British efficients on March 1, 1761, were 16,000 only. It was small wonder that the Marquess of Granby should have asked for either reinforcements or peace. To consider the preliminaries of the latter Mr. Hans Stanley was despatched to Paris, and M. de Bussy arrived from thence, though the prospects still savoured of war.

★★★★★★★★★★

General Mostyn wrote concerning this selection: "After Hans Stanley's being made a Minister at the Court of France, I can have no notion of any difficulty in making *anything*; therefore, why not make a peace as well as anything else?"—*Newcastle Papers*, June 20, 1761.

★★★★★★★★★★

France was becoming apprehensive of an expedition which was now made upon Belleisle by England, and which General Kingsley was to command, (he had returned, owing to ill health, in 1760. He did not in the end go to Belleisle, and was later appointed Governor of Fort William); and the Hereditary Prince had already commenced harassing the French outposts. Mr. Pitt, moreover, had declared to the Duke of Newcastle:

"I will make war for Hanover as long as you please, but never make peace for Hanover."

During the General Election of 1761 Lord Granby was returned for the county of Cambridge with Lord Royston, who informed the Duke of Newcastle of their unopposed election, and that Lord George Manners had attended as Lord Granby's representative. Lord George succeeded to Lord Granby's vacated seat for Grantham.

★★★★★★★★★★

A List of the Parliament elected after George III.'s accession contains the following names of incidental interest:—

Cambridgeshire, Marquis of Granby
Grantham, Lord George Manners.
Nottinghamshire, Lord Robert Manners Sutton.
Newark-on-Trent { John Manners. / Thomas Thoroton.
Kingston-on-Hull, General Lord Robert Manners.

Bath City { William Pitt. / Viscount Ligonier.
Malton, General John Mostyn.
Appleby, General Stanwix.
Aylesbury, John Wilkes.
East Grinstead, Lord George Sackville.

★★★★★★★★★★

On the 1st of May, 1761, Lord Granby had, by His Majesty's command, been sworn a member of the Privy Council and taken his seat at the Board; and, at the end of the month, prepared for his return journey, leaving a Memorandum with the Duke of Newcastle requesting that his Staff might be paid up as soon as possible, and Bennet Storer not forgotten.

Arrived at Harwich he was tediously delayed by contrary winds, but wrote, the 1st of June, that "the wind had come about, and he was that moment going on board." In a few days he was followed by Lieut.-General Waldegrave, Lords Hinchinbroke, Suffolk, Abingdon, and Brome. (All acting as *aides-de-camp*: Lord Hinchinbroke was an *A.D.C.* to Lieut.-General Waldegrave).

Chapter 17

1761: Vellingshausen(Kirchdenkern)

Lord Granby left Harwich June 1st and, on arrival at the Hague, was warned that the route skirting Wesel was no longer safe: he was obliged, consequently, to make a long detour by Zwolle, the Bourtange Fort, and Osnabruck, arriving at Paderborn on the 13th of June only. He found the British cavalry in fine order, but 12,000 were reported sick throughout the Allied Army, which Prince Ferdinand had already commenced reviewing.

The prospects of the dawning campaign were still less reassuring than those surrounding the close of the last; France having despatched Prince de Soubise, to the Lower Rhine, at the head of another considerable army to co-operate with that under De Broglie. Already General Conway had, upon arriving in Germany, complained to Lord Ligonier of the health, and size of the recruits sent out. Ligonier reported the complaint to Lord Granby with his stereotyped answer to all criticisms on the quantity, or quality, of the fighting material supplied to the German War; concluding—

> In short, my dear Lord, you must make the best of what you have. You know how impossible it is for us to send you one man more; and that the king made Your Lordship sensible that on the 1st May last there were 270 men in Germany more than complete, and therefore Conway's computation must go to sleep till next year."

In other words, a fixed number was insisted upon, by the king and the War Office, at which the British Army was held to be "complete;" despite the fact that Louis XV. despatched marshal after marshal, with fresh armies, to avenge his colonial disasters by taking Hanover. That Hanover was not conquered; that the armies of France were worn down, blockaded, out-manoeuvred, and, whenever chance offered, defeated by Prince Ferdinand and Lord Granby with far inferior numbers, should be more generously recognised by us when we read of Pitt's Wars, and his increase and consolidation of our Colonial Empire.

Imagine for a moment Prince Ferdinand disastrously defeated, the Allied Army surrendered to De Broglie, and a tremendous force thus liberated from Germany to oppose England elsewhere, and to invade her at the time when Lord Ligonier owned to Lord Granby—"*what should be wrote in cyphers*"—that the troops at home consisted of two regiments of cavalry composed of old men and boys, and eight of Foot, two-thirds of which were recruits! The French fleet, it is true, had been shattered in 1750 by Sir Edward Hawke; but one has always to reckon with the accident, the stratagem, and the unexpected which respectively, occurs, succeeds, and happens.

France had a talent for blinding us as to her intended striking-point, and was airing a project upon Scotland in August, 1760, the very date at which Ligonier enumerated our burlesque home-garrison in the above epistolary whisper, which he pronounced himself unwise in committing to plain writing. These conjured-up complications did not arise, fortunately for England, (Lecky says the German War involved the greatest dangers to England.—*History of England in the Eighteenth Century,* vol. ii.); yet those who averted them remain—Prince Ferdinand, an obscured character in English history; Lord Granby, an amiable, bald-headed personality who, no one exactly knows why, furnished a most popular subject to public-house sign-painters—and to Sir Joshua Reynolds, who painted more portraits of him than of any other "sitter."

Directly after his return, the Marquess of Granby reported the British cavalry and the Brigade of Guards to be leaving winter quarters for a camp near Paderborn, which he intended making his headquarters until the enemy's intentions were more defined, and some idea were gained "*où la bombe crévera.*" General Spörcken with about 20,000 men was on the River Dymel; General Conway with the British infantry battalions was near Soest and Hamm; while the Hereditary Prince was at Notellen watching for the approach of Prince Soubise, who was supposed to have passed the Rhine, and to be delayed, somewhere between that river and the Allies, by rain which hindered the advance of his artillery. General Lückner was stationed at Eimbeck, beyond the Weser.

Marshal de Broglie had not yet returned to Cassel, where his army still remained in cantonments.

The fighting strength of the Allied Army Lord Granby maintained was not more than 60,000, in round numbers—not 78,000 as the Duke of Newcastle was still tiresomely insisting—

> . . . .so, that considering the immense force we are opposed to—though our troops are in excellent order and good spirits—everyone with whom I have conversed wishes the war *concluded with a good peace.*

The term "everyone" can unhesitatingly be read as including Prince Ferdinand, the first person with whom Granby was likely to converse; and this desire for peace on his and Lord Granby's part will be recalled to the reader's mind later, when it bears most cogently upon Lord Granby's political conduct.

Prince Ferdinand and Lord Granby commenced the fourth campaign against an enemy considerably reinforced, and still in possession of Cassel, Göttingen, and Ziegenhayn. One French Army was superior in strength to that of the Allies; the other fell short of it by no considerable number. Yet Prince Ferdinand's opening movements were characterized by an energy, and confidence, which augured ill for the French Marshals should they commit any of the blunders upon which alone, he had assured Lord Bute, rested his one chance of success. The French Marshals, on their side, from the moment of Prince Soubise's arrival at the scene of war, were drawn by their mutual jealousies into playing their best for Prince Ferdinand's hand.

Ferdinand maintained a central position from which to watch the enemy on his right and left, and to strike at whichever foe offered him the likelier prospect.

Prince Soubise was ready ten days before De Broglie, who had been replenishing his ruined magazines in Hesse, and assembling his army between Cassel and Corbach. Soubise advanced to Dortmund which caused the Hereditary Prince to march to Hamm, where his outposts were attacked with some loss. This was amply compensated by the Hereditary Prince. He detached Major Scheither with fifty Hussars who reached, and crossed, the Rhine at Bistick: in ninety-three hours they destroyed at Xanlen, Aarsen, and Gennep (between the Rhine and the Meuse) magazines estimated to have contained over 1,000,000 rations of forage, 14,000 sacks, and several boat-loads, of oats.

****

Captain George Albrecht H. von Scheither raised a Free Corps of

Carabiniers and Foot in 1757, the same year that Lückner's Hussars came into being. Scheither's Carabiniers wore a long pale buff frock over a green waistcoat edged with white; black three-cornered hat with green cockade, and green sabretache and shabraque bearing a crown, "G. R," and White Horse of Hanover, in white.—*Uniformenkunde* (R. Knötel), Band 4, No. 24.

★★★★★★★★★★

They returned without the loss of a man, though hotly pursued, and with thirty prisoners!

Soubise continued on to Unna, and as De Broglie was still unprepared to march, Prince Ferdinand made the most of his time against Soubise, who was acting without any attempt at concert with his brother marshal.

The Allied Army marched from Paderborn on the 21st of June, 1761, proceeding westwards by Gesecke, Soest, and Wippringshausen. Lord, Granby led with the British grenadiers, Highlanders, Hodgson's (5th), Napier's (12th), Cornwallis' (24th), Stewart's (37th), and Mansberg's, Infantry; and the Greys, Mostyn's (7th Dragoons), and Ancram's (11th Dragoons), under Colonel Edward Harvey. These he posted on the Heights of Rhüne to cover the forming of the main army. (On June 25 the Allies fired a *feu de joie* for the taking, by the British Expedition under Commodore Keppel and General Hodgson, of Belleisle and the Citadel of Palais). On the 27th at 12 p.m. the army moved on in seven columns, each of which was preceded by pioneers and carpenters, to Werle, (Castle of Werle figures in Turenne's Wars), whither the Hereditary Prince had already retired before Soubise's advance.

Lord Granby's column was thus composed:—

Advance-guard under Colonel Harvey { 3 squadrons Prussian Black Hussars. / 3 ,, Elliot's. / The Piquets of the Infantry.

2 battalions Mansberg's (Hanoverian), 3 Hanoverian 6-pounders.

1 battalion Napier's, 1 Stewart's, 1 Cornwallis'.

1 Hodgson's, 2 Hanoverian 6-pounders, 2 battalions Highlanders { Keith, / Campbell.

2 battalions British Grenadiers { Maxwell, / Walsh.

Remainder of Artillery.

2 squadrons each of Mostyn's, Ancram's, and Greys.

Prince Ferdinand was anxious to engage Soubise's advanced troops, under the Prince de Condé, who retreated on being cannonaded by the head of the Allied columns, and fell back upon the right and left of Soubise's camp at Unna. Ferdinand persevered in his endeavours to

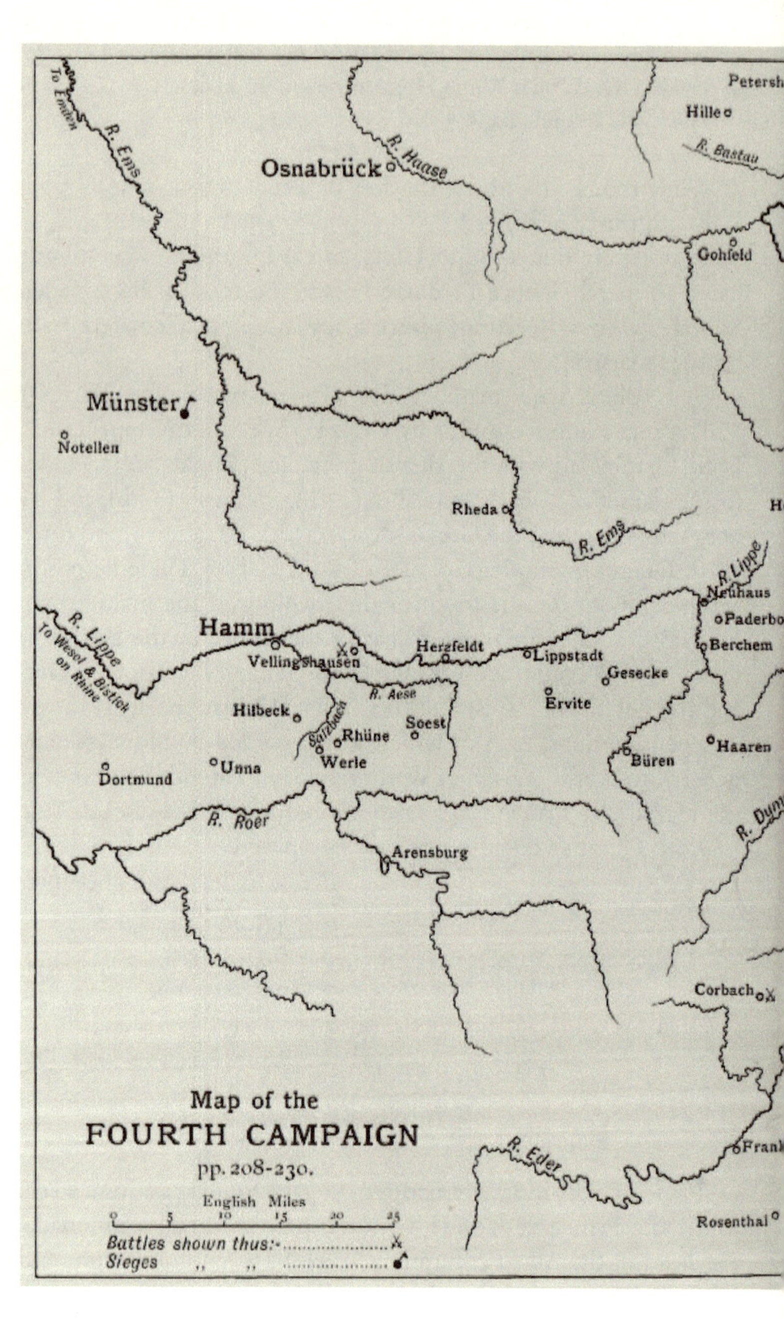
To Emden
R. Ems
Osnabrück
R. Haase
Petersha
Hille
R. Bastau
Gohfeld
Münster
Notellen
Rheda
R. Ems
He
R. Lippe
Neuhaus
Paderbo
Berchem
R. Lippe
To Wesel & Bistich on Rhine
Hamm
Vellingshausen
Herzfeldt
Lippstadt
Gesecke
R. Aese
Hilbeck
Soest
Ervite
Salzbach
Rhüne
Werle
Unna
Dortmund
Büren
Haaren
R. Roer
Arensburg
R. Dun
Corbach
R. Eder
Frank
Rosenthal
Map of the
FOURTH CAMPAIGN
pp. 208-230.
English Miles
0 5 10 15 20 25
Battles shown thus:-
Sieges ,, ,,

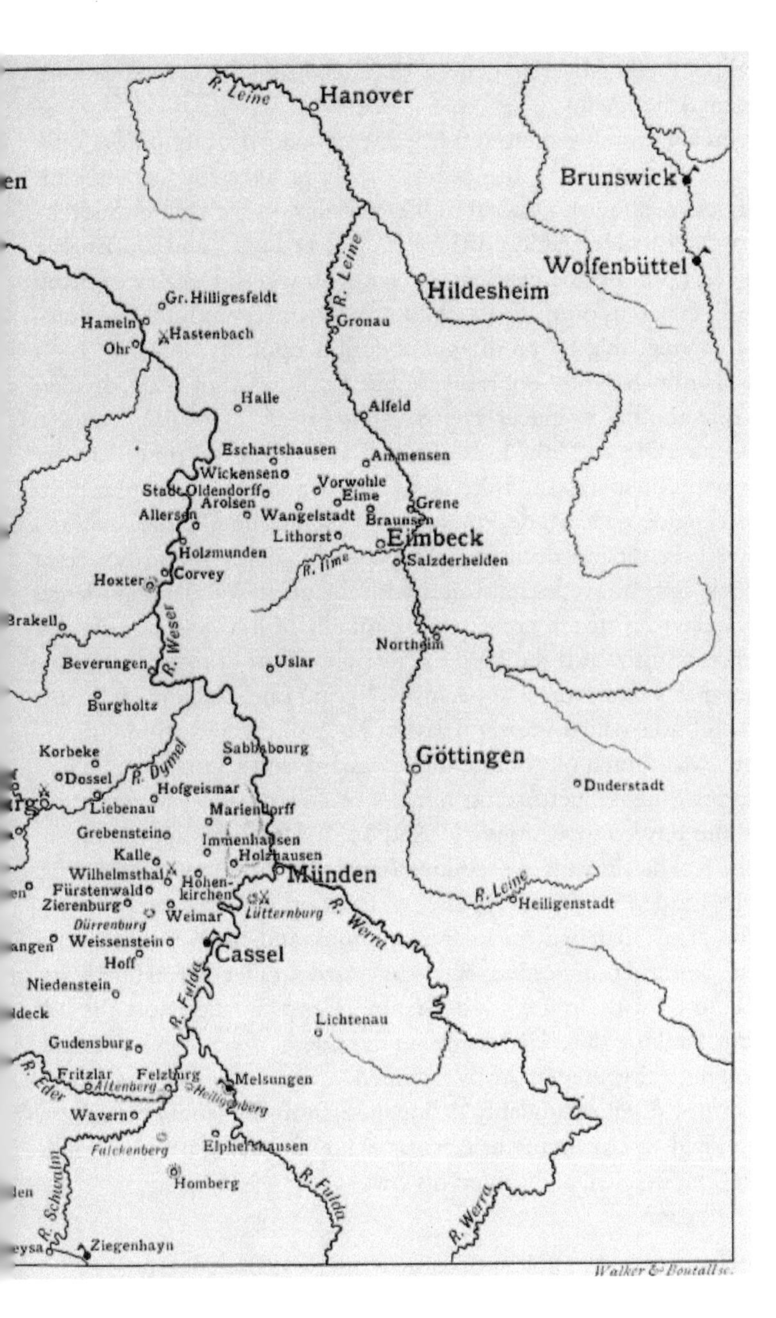

Hanover
R. Leine
Brunswick
Wolfenbüttel
Hildesheim
Gr. Hilligesfeldt
Hameln
Hastenbach
Ohr
Gronau
Halle
Alfeld
Eschartshausen
Ammensen
Wickensen
Vorwohle
Stadt Oldendorff
Eime
Grene
Arolsen
Allersen
Wangelstadt
Braunsen
Lithorst
Eimbeck
Holzmunden
Salzderhelden
R. Ilme
Hoxter
Corvey
Brakell
Northeim
R. Weser
Beverungen
Uslar
Burgholtz
Korbeke
Sabbabourg
Göttingen
Dossel
R. Dymel
Hofgeismar
Duderstadt
Liebenau
Mariendorff
Grebenstein
Immenhausen
Kalle
Holzhausen
Wilhelmsthal
Münden
Hohenkirchen
Fürstenwald
Zierenburg
Lütternburg
R. Leine
Heiligenstadt
Weimar
Dürrenburg
R. Werra
Weissenstein
Cassel
Hoff
Niedenstein
R. Fulda
Lichtenau
Gudensburg
Fritzlar
Felzburg
Melsungen
R. Eder
Altenberg
Heiligenberg
Wavern
Falckenberg
Elpherhausen
Homberg
R. Fulda
R. Schwalm
R. Werra
Ziegenhayn
Walker & Boutall sc.

provoke an engagement, but with no result. His own predicament was meantime becoming difficult. Marshal de Broglie had at length left Cassel, and had marched in such force against Spörcken at Warburg as to compel the Hanoverian general to retreat from the Dymel towards the main Allied Army.

Spörcken lost 300 men, and (the French said) 19 cannon; we only owned to 10, declaring the other 9 to have been old useless guns which had been purposely left in the redoubts on the Dymel. Spörcken marched to Herzfeldt, north of the River Lippe; and De Broglie advanced upon Prince Ferdinand's rear, who was still unable to bring Soubise out of his camp, or attack him in it, which was rendered practically impregnable by prodigious redoubts upon its front and both flanks. Ferdinand and Soubise were but a cannon-shot apart, divided from one another by a deep ravine.

On June 30, and July 1, the French attempted to cannonade the Allies without success; and the position became hourly more critical as De Broglie, with M. de Poyanne and Comte de Guerchy, fast approached. Ferdinand decided on an attempt to get round Soubise's left flank, since move he must, and with the greatest order and silence commenced his march at 11 p.m. the night of July 1-2, in a northerly direction towards the Lippe. A terrible storm of tropical severity rendered this night march a peculiarly trying one, and reduced roads to a condition which greatly delayed the Artillery and ammunition-wagons. Morning broke before the rearguard, under Lord Granby, had left camp. Soubise, persuading himself that Ferdinand was retreating across the River Lippe, simply looked on, and took no steps to ascertain the real destination of the Allied Army, which, as soon as it got out of sight, headed westwards for the left flank of Soubise's camp.

The army marched on in five columns, and three hundred unarmed workmen preceded the van-guard, under the Hereditary Prince, to clear the route. Lord Granby's Corps formed now the left column, flanking the Allied Army on the side of the enemy's position. Thus, while the French Army retained a fatuous sense of security, the van of the Allies suddenly debouched, from the close country, on to the Plain of Dortmund at 6 p.m. on July 2, having marched right round Soubise's left, and gained his rear.

Granby wrote:

> There never was a bolder or more masterly stroke attempted by any general. To march round so numerous an army through the

> strongest country, and at so small a distance that the left column (the corps which I commanded) was during the whole march within 2 or 3 miles of their camp, and by thus gaining the rear of their left flank to force them to quit their strong position or risk an attack—is a manoeuvre that must amaze everyone.

After recovering from their astonishment the French made an attack upon General Wutgenau, which he repulsed, with the aid of a reinforcement of four battalions from Granby's Corps.

On the night of July 2, the Allies bivouacked, and at daylight, July 3, formed on the Plain of Dortmund; the troops being still too tired for Prince Ferdinand to hazard an action. Soubise commenced sending off baggage, etc., to Werle, and on the 4th the Allies advanced to attack him, the Hereditary Prince's Corps leading on the left, and Lord Granby's on the right. Soubise retreated again at night, so that the Allies arrived in time, only, to cannonade his rear and take up his ground.

Soubise continued retreating, with his rear in considerable confusion, and at last halted, and faced about, with the Castle of Werle (in which there was still a small detachment of the Allies) behind his right flank. Soubise was now occupying the identical camp which the Allies had vacated a few days previously. Before him was the ravine, and he threw up redoubts along the entire length of his front.

A few outpost affairs resulted about equally for either side; and, on July 5, Ferdinand advanced in six columns, more as a feint to draw out Soubise than to attack; but finding Soubise (in Granby's words) "so strongly posted in Maréchal Turenne's famous camp, thought it imprudent and impracticable to persist:" after a mutual cannonading of some duration the Allies returned to their camp, the left of which was formed by Granby's Corps at Hemmeren, and the right by the Hereditary Prince's, within cannon-shot of the enemy.

Barren of opportunity for distinction as this last affair had been, "Elliot's Light Horse" managed to add something to their record which Lord Granby did not allow to pass unnoticed. A detachment of twenty men, led by Serjeant Hopkinson, was ordered to attack a French infantry piquet of about fifty men of De Clermont's Regiment, stationed in a copse surrounded by a ditch and fence. "Elliot's" rode at the fence, and, as they topped it, the French officer in charge of the piquet took a sort of partridge-driving shot at Sergeant Hopkinson. The officer's *fusil* missed fire and Hopkinson took him prisoner, much to the Frenchman's astonishment, who expected to be

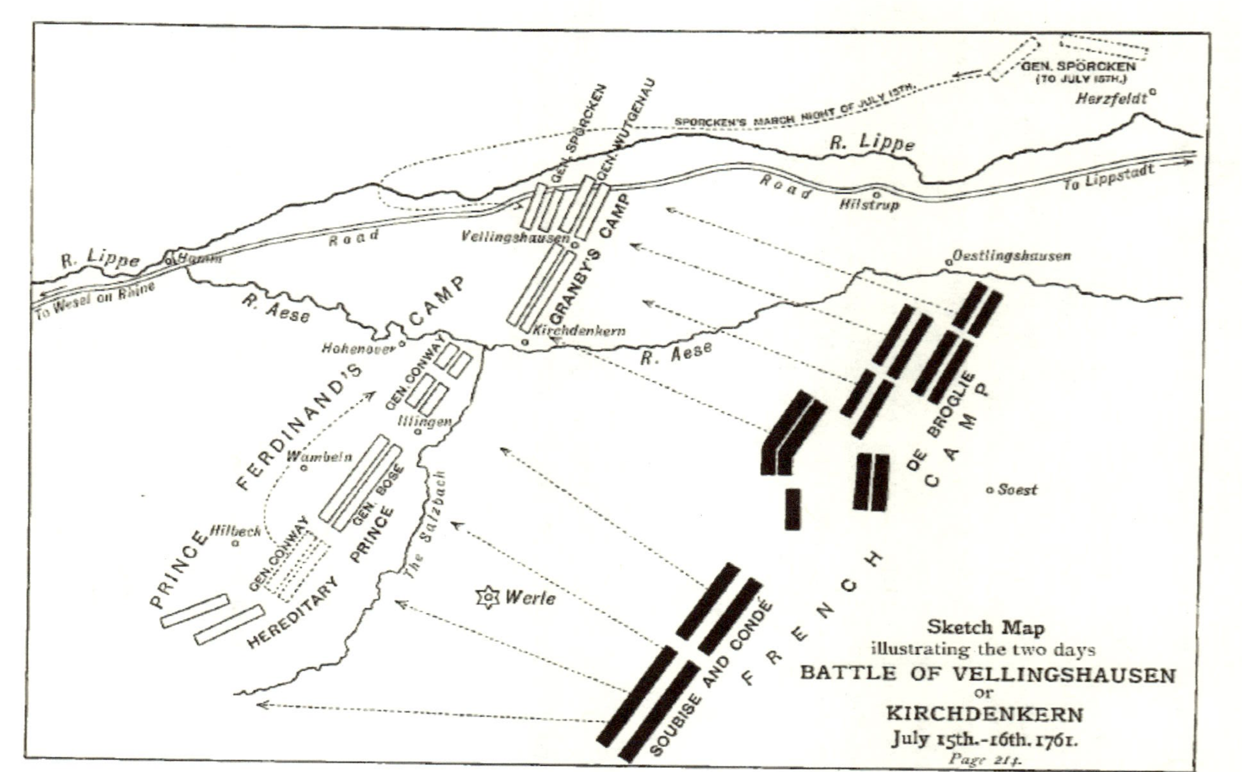

Sketch Map
illustrating the two days
BATTLE OF VELLINGSHAUSEN
or
KIRCHDENKERN
July 15th.-16th. 1761.

Page 214.

cut down on the spot, while the rest of the piquet was chased across a ravine into a wood, where most of it surrendered.

Prince Soubise retired from his strong position at Werle (why or wherefore is not patent to the lay mind, unless from lack of food by Rhüne to Soest; and the Allies followed to Hilbeck, forming along the Saltz-brook which flows into the River Aese, a tributary of the Lippe.

★★★★★★★★★★

Frederick the Great says that "*un partisan nommé Freytag*" about this time took three convoys of flour, which upset the French Commissariat for some days. The "partisan" was the leader of Freitag's *Chasseurs*. G. M. Withelm von Freitag (or Freytag) commanded a Free Corps consisting of both mounted and foot *chasseurs*. The former wore a green frock and waistcoat, buff overalls, and black three-cornered hat with green cockade, white belt and buttons. The foot the same, with white breeches and high black boots. The Grenadier Company wore grenadier caps, bearing the Hanoverian arms.—*Uniformenkunde* (K. Knotel), Band 5, No. 42.

★★★★★★★★★

Marshal de Broglie had now arrived, and joined Prince Soubise at Soest. A series of skirmishes followed upon De Broglie's efforts to advance to Hamm at the confluence of the Rivers Aese and Lippe. An attack upon his outposts, July 10, at Oestlingshausen was repulsed, but, following up his advantage too closely. Marshal de Broglie himself was nearly taken, as were seven of his officers, and many dragoons. De Broglie on this occasion dropped his spy-glass, as Prince Ferdinand had done near the Ohm, and it was similarly returned to him.

On July 12 the Allied Army extended itself towards the Lippe, Lord Granby leading, and encamping at Kirchdenkern, with his left towards Vellingshausen, on the main road to Hamm. The main army lay between Hilbeck and Hohenover; and the Hereditary Prince, from Wambeln to Hilbeck, forming its right. Consecutive feints and attempts on De Broglie's part ensued, in one of which an officer, (Captain Gun was killed, and Captain Gorry wounded), and several men of Keith's Highlanders (in Granby's Corps) were lost; and Prince Ferdinand supported the right and left flanks of the Allied Army as they were alternately threatened.

The turn of events was so constantly shifting that Granby wrote he was at a loss which to expect first—"the siege of Lippstadt, a battle, or a suspension of arms."

One point was clear, that Granby's strong post was the key of Prince Ferdinand's position, and that which De Broglie showed most inclination to attack. On July 14-15 Lord Granby was busily employed strengthening his front with *flèches* and *abatis*, and felling trees to place across the road to Hamm—upon which town he was to retire if compelled. All this movement and work took place, it must be remembered, in the dog-days, during which Lord Granby enjoined "all the butchers of the army to keep their dogs tied up, in order to prevent any bad accident happening in case any of them should go mad."

All the morning of the 15th of July Marshal de Broglie had been intently reconnoitring, and some skirmishes occurred on the outposts; but, as the day wore on, the French retired, and the Allies imagined all, for the time, to be quiet. About four in the afternoon De Broglie suddenly commenced a most determined attack upon Granby's camp, without informing Prince Soubise, whom it is supposed De Broglie wished to exclude from all share in his exploit. De Broglie advanced in three columns, and his van-guard, pushing along the Hamm road, drove in Granby's German light troops, while his centre advanced upon Vellingshausen.

Lord Granby dashed up from his quarters, and himself ordered all his troops under arms, extending his left wing obliquely towards the Lippe to protect the Hamm road.

Almost before his troops were out of their tents, the enemy's cannon-shot reached his camp; but his light troops, sustained by the two battalions of Highlanders, rallied, and repulsed the French outposts, of which about a hundred men and several officers were taken. Granby's left had, for the time being, been turned. Prince Ferdinand hurried to Granby's camp, where he found every disposition already made which he considered necessary; and, enjoining His Lordship to defend Vellingshausen to the last extremity, the prince galloped off to redispose the right so as to move up some troops in support of the sorely pressed left. General Wutgenau, to whose command three squadrons of Carabiniers were attached, was ordered to Granby's left, on the Hamm road; the Prince of Anhalt, whose command included Conway's, Mordaunt's, and the Inniskillings, under Major-General Elliot, to his right; and Count La Lippe Bückebourg, with the artillery, was placed in front of the left of the centre of the army.

Granby's Division, consisting of the British grenadiers, the Highlanders, Mansberg's, Hodgson's, Napier's, Cornwallis', and Stuart's; the Greys, Mostyn's, Elliot's, and Ancram's, and the Hanoverian Artillery, fought, as De Mauvillon enthusiastically records, "with indescribable bravery." Before Wutgenau's arrival Granby had gradually made head against the attack, and driven the French back until all his outposts were regained, and Wutgenau's, and the Prince of Anhalt's, reinforcements completed the repulse of the French, who had been likewise reinforced by the regiments of De Rougé, Acquitaine. Champagne, Auvergne, and Poitou, under the Duc d'Havre, the Duc Duras, and the Comte de Vaux.

The attack lasted till about six, but desultory firing continued till ten p.m.; and the French on retiring occupied, with a picked force, a little wooded height just outside Lord Granby's lines.

Night brought little rest to the Allied Army. Prince Ferdinand continued to strengthen his centre—in which were the 1st, 2nd, and 3rd Foot Guards, and the Grenadiers of the Guards, under General Conway—and especially Lord Granby, on his left, who was reinforced by Major-General Howard, with Rockland's, Griffin's, Brudenell's, Welsh Fusiliers, Blues, Honywood's, two squadrons of *carabiniers*, and the Light Artillery; Lord Frederick Cavendish's Brigade of Hanoverian *Chasseurs* and Hussars; and Lord Pembroke with a brigade of cavalry, consisting of three squadrons of Blues, two of Mordaunt's, and two of *carabiniers*.

★★★★★★★★★★

The Brigade of Guards was not in the centre of Lord Granby's position as stated, in the *History of the First or Grenadier Guards*, by Sir F. W. Hamilton. On the 15th of July the Guards were on the extreme right of the Allied Army, and were moved up to the left of the centre to replace the troops withdrawn to reinforce Lord Granby.

★★★★★★★★★★

In addition. General Spörcken, who had remained beyond the River Lippe since his retreat from Warburg, was ordered to cross and join Wutgenau's Division on Granby's extreme left. Granby's much-diminished ammunition was replenished, and every preparation made for the expected fresh attack at daybreak. The English and French advanced sentinels were separated from one another only by a little ravine and a field or two, and the patrols fitfully skirmished throughout the night.

De Broglie informed Prince Soubise that the battle would be resumed on the 16th, but the prince's co-operation did not amount to anything formidable; and soon after dawn De Broglie again advanced towards Granby, commencing on Wutgenau's position, and reopened a terrific attack. Prince Ferdinand pronounced that the little height, of which the French had retained possession from overnight, and from whence the hottest fire was maintained upon Granby's left, must be "rushed." Granby had his artillery posted on an eminence in front of his centre, and with it he first played tremendous havoc with the French post, as the British grenadiers under Lieut.-Colonel Maxwell, the Highlanders under Colonel Campbell and Major Keith, and two battalions of Hanoverian Guards, two of Imhoffs, and Bock's advanced to the assault; the whole commanded by Lieut.-Colonel Beck with. (The king, at Prince Ferdinand's earnest desire, bestowed a brevet Lieut. Colonelcy upon Major Maxwell for his distinguished services.—Viscount Barrington to Lord Granby, *Rutland MSS.*, vol. ii.)

They soon carried the height after a short, but extremely bloody affair; and General Spörcken having reached Wutgenau's division on Granby's left, De Broglie desisted, and the French retreated covered by a rearguard of the *regiment de Rougé*, the *grénadiers de France*, and the *grénadiers Royaux*, under the Comte de Stainville, the Comte de Sey, and the Chevalier de Modéne. Lieut.-Colonel Maxwell with the grenadiers cut off the *regiment de Rougé,* with its colours and cannon, and took the whole, including the Comte de Rougé, prisoner.

Lord Granby despatched Lieut.-Colonel Beckwith with some grenadiers and Highlanders, who harassed the rear of the discomfited enemy for some two miles on its retreat which commenced about 10 a.m. Seeing that Lord Granby had silenced and beaten off De Broglie, Prince Ferdinand drew off half the British Artillery and Lord Frederick Cavendish's Hanoverian Brigade from the left to sustain the Hereditary Prince on the right, which was attacked by Prince Soubise's main army and a Reserve under Prince Condé.The Hereditary Prince was not however in any straits; and Soubise, learning that De Broglie was repulsed and had retreated, commenced his retreat likewise to Soest. De Broglie encamped at Oestlingshausen.

The second day's Battle of Vellingshausen, or Kirchdenkern, July 15-16, 1761, was all over by 11 a.m. (De Mauvillon pronounced Vellingshausen to have been the most dangerous battle Ferdinand experienced during the war.The camp was a very critical one, save for Granby's position, the taking of which would have been fatal to the Allies). The French loss in killed, wounded, and prisoners was 6,000, together with 9 cannon and 8 pairs of colours. A letter of Lord Granby's later said that this first estimate was declared by further information to be more like 8,000. Altogether 63 French officers were taken prisoners, and Colonel Pierson invoked the Duke of Newcastle's indulgence upon a letter which he wrote in a room containing thirteen of these voluble captives, who were all to dine with Prince Ferdinand on the evening of his victory.

Among the killed were the Duc d'Havre, the Marquis de Vérac, and the Marquis de Rougé, who, all related, fell victims, as they were sitting under a tree, to the same cannon-shot. One is tempted to credit this shot, which wrought such havoc among the French aristocracy, to a sergeant of Campbell's Highlanders whom Sir James Innes Norcliffe watched serving a "long 6," which the sergeant had carefully masked with boughs. The Highlander surveyed the effects of his excellent practice, ejaculating, "Now a round!—Now a grap'!" at intervals, as he varied his load. Sir James added that after the action he noticed grape-shot sticking in some of the dead Frenchmen like grains of Indian corn in the cob, and the round-shot had occasionally taken two or three of the enemy in a line.

The Allied loss was about 1,600 killed, wounded, and missing. Among the killed were Lieut.-Colonel Cook and Major Campbell. Captain H. Townshend, one of Lord Granby's *aides-de-camp*, was wounded, "not dangerously," Jack Mostyn announced, "unless from the circumstance of Harry being rather too fat." Poor Townshend recovered, but only to meet his fate a little later at Wilhelmsthal. The Grenadiers, and the 87th and 88th Highlanders, though covered with glory, suffered terribly. Sir James Innes Norcliffe, who served with the 88th, was introduced after the battle to General Spörcken, who exclaimed, "*Ach! pover Bergschotten*," as he gazed compassionately upon the popular kilted heroes.

Though comprising all sizes, from six feet to "five-foot nothing," the Highlanders were small on the average; Marshal de Broglie said that, often as he had regretted not being tall, he became reconciled to his moderate height when he saw what those little Highlanders could do. Major Robert Murray Keith described, in a letter to his father, how Prince Ferdinand embraced him before the assembled generals, and spoke also many flattering words of regard "for the brave little bodies:" Keith added, "I am every day more obliged to Lord Granby's goodness."

Ferdinand ordered a *feu de joie*, and remained in much the same position, which he continued to strengthen. General Spörcken recrossed the Lippe to Herzfeldt. De Broglie retreated to Erwite; Soubise remained at Soest, while the Prince of Condé maintained the communications between the two armies.

The Hereditary Prince attacked their outposts at Rhüne, and the busy "Elliot's" captured some forty Hussars; but the young Prince Henry of Brunswick received a dangerous bullet-wound in the throat. He was attended by the best French surgeons, as well as the English, but died on August 8 at Hamm.

During the course of these events. General Lückner had been fencing with Prince Xavier beyond the River Weser, across which he succeeded in forcing him, and from thence to Paderborn.

So far, of this campaign, the opening advantage remained with the Allies. Dc Broglie had intended driving them across the River Lippe, and besieging Lippstadt; whereas Prince Ferdinand succeeded, by his celebrated march to Dortmund, in getting between Prince Soubise and his battering train which was still in Wesel. Ferdinand then forced both the French Armies together, and drove them into a district already denuded of food by the Allies. Such a position was untenable, and it behoved the French marshals either to force Ferdinand out of his Kirchdenkern camp, or to divide and retreat. They adopted the latter alternative, and De Broglie took the Paderborn route, and Soubise crossed the River Roer near Arensburg.

Lord Granby wrote that, in the difficult task of selecting names for mention, when all had done well, he desired to recommend those of Waldegrave, Sandford, Mansberg, Beckwith, and his *A.D.C.* Captain Broome, who, with Captain Bathurst, carried his despatches home. Captain Beckwith brought the captured colours, and Colonel Fitzroy Prince Ferdinand's despatch to the king. (The Duke of Newcastle wrote: "You have sent us over no less than 4 great officers. This affects our pockets deeply."—*Newcastle Papers,* July 31. 1761).

In his despatch to Lord Bute, Granby asked that any deficiencies might be overlooked, as for some time he had been entirely without rest.

Upon this specially important battle, as regarded the credit of Granby and the British troops, a flood of congratulation poured in from Bute, Newcastle, Ligonier, Sir Joseph Yorke, etc. The first announced—

> The king's satisfaction at Lord Granby's very able conduct and gallant behaviour of which all accounts were full; and at the signal bravery and spirit of the officers and troops under his command.

Colonel Fitzroy, Prince Ferdinand's *aide-de-camp,* was instructed to inform the king that the prince avowed himself to have been a mere bystander at Kirchdenkern, since Lord Granby had made a disposition of his troops which left nothing to be changed, and had conclusively proved his possession of the knowledge and conduct of a general. (Newcastle to Sir J. Yorke, July 24, 1761).

After the late outburst of feeling against Prince Ferdinand in England, his pains on this occasion to award to the English commander-in-chief the honours which were so justly his due, made a very favourable impression. The Duke of Cumberland expressed his high commendation of Lord Granby's conduct, and Lord Kinnoull wrote—

> It is fortunate the attack was begun upon Lord Granby's Corps, and that it lay upon him to make the disposition which has so greatly illustrated his character as a general in a point which had not been so much tryed, and was consequently hitherto less conspicuous, than his spirit and bravery. (Newcastle to Sir J. Yorke, July 30, 1761).

This tribute to Lord Granby was, in fact, endorsed by Prince Ferdinand and the army, by the king, by civil, military, and diplomatic officials, including ex-Chancellor Hardwicke; and, what is more significant, the ex-commander-in-chief, the brave, but ill-starred Duke of Cumberland, who might well have felt a passing pang of bitterness in his retired obscurity.

But what avails the opinions of such nonentities when the Oracle, Horace Walpole, holds another and an adverse one? His attitude towards the war had undergone a marked change since General Conway's appointment; and hopes that his gallant cousin might distinguish himself were interspersed with fears of battles lest he might be injured. The first rumours of Kirchdenkern were disquieting; but so soon as the despatches were published, and the fact transpired that General Conway was not only safe, but had scarcely been engaged, Walpole was quickly himself again:—

> Lord Granby, to the mob's content, has the chief honour of the day—rather of the two days. The French behaved to the mob's content too, that is shamefully, and all this glory cheaply bought on our side . . . if the mob have not much stronger heads and quicker conceptions than I have, they will conclude My Lord Granby is become *Nabob*! (*Letters*, July 22, 1761: to Lord Strafford and Geo. Montagu).

(Conway was in the centre of the Allied Camp, between Illingen and Hohenover).

Of one "damning circumstance" Walpole was mercifully not aware at the moment, or he would assuredly have utilised it in his usual fashion for the conveying of disparagement, and innuendo. Hans Stanley, whose time in Paris was, so far, not much encroached upon by any progress in pacific negotiations, disclosed to the Duke of Newcastle his discovery in Paris of a very choice and special parcel of champagne:—

> I have sent our most dear and respected friend Lord Granby a provision of it: no man more than myself rejoices in seeing the advantages and glory which my country derives from Your Grace's nephew."

At the same time Messrs. Pye and Cruikshanks advised Lord Granby of a consignment "of 6 Hogsheads of the best claret."

After Warburg, Sir William Calvert's butt of porter provided Walpole with a satirical shaft; but Hans Stanley's parcel of champagne, and the hogsheads of the best claret, providentially escaped the moral exciseman of Strawberry Hill. Otherwise, we should probably have been assured that, at "Vellingshausen," Lord Granby, Prince Ferdinand, and everyone else, excepting Conway, were all as drunk as traditional Lords, or proverbial Fiddlers.

À propos of Conway it seems clear that Lord Granby's unfailing tact soon soothed Mostyn's irritated feelings. General Conway's appointment to serve in Germany does not appear to have cost Mostyn any further annoyance, and the latter's correspondence regained its contented tone, he assured the Duke of Newcastle:—

> All your friends are very well—Lord Granby (very happily for them) at their head. He is, as he ought to be, better loved and more honoured every day he lives.

Chapter 18

1761: Skirmishes and Manoeuvres

Soon after Kirchdenkern, a matter was entrusted to the Marquess of Granby's discretion which drew from Lord Hardwicke the remark, that:

> He rejoiced in the glory My Lord Granby had gained, and in this honourable mark of confidence which the king had just now placed in His Lordship.

The mark of confidence consisted in deputing to Lord Granby the delicate, and secret, mission of offering George III.'s sister, the Princess Augusta, in marriage to the Hereditary Prince of Brunswick. On this topic Lord Bute addressed two letters, an official and a private one, to Lord Granby, as follows:—

> My dear Lord,—Your character and generous sentiments are so well known to me, that I am certain the high approbation of Your Lordship's conduct, expressed by His Majesty's order, in my last letter, will not affect you deeper than the great confidence the king is pleased to place in you, by committing to your care the delicate business I am now commanded to write to you upon. Your Lordship may recollect that, at our last meeting, I mentioned the king's great esteem for the Hereditary Prince, something also passed with regard to Lady Augusta. Since that time events have happened that endear the prince still more, if possible, to His Majesty; the king does ample justice to all this illustrious family; to the superior capacity of Prince Ferdinand, to the rising genius and intrepidity of the Hereditary Prince, to the generous ardour of his younger brothers, to the firm and steady friendship of the duke their father, and to the constant attachment and distinguished merit of Prince Lewis; but not

> satisfied with this, the king wished to show Their Serene Highnesses the strongest proof of his esteem and affection by adding another tye to all those that have hitherto formed the bond of union, the Princess Augusta's hand is that pledge of friendship His Majesty inclines to give the Hereditary Prince, a nobler is not even in the king's power to offer; his favourite sister, the first daughter of England; the most beautiful and accomplished princess in Europe, leaves the truth of this beyond a doubt.
> It is the king's pleasure therefore, My Lord, that you should communicate these his ideas to the Hereditary Prince and Duke Ferdinand, and that you acquaint me with their sentiments, on which will depend the more solemn steps to be taken with the Duke of Brunswick. . . (*From this point the private letter commences).* The king, my Lord, would think it beneath his dignity to offer his sister to France or Spain, hut to this gallant family he looks upon it as a mark of his friendship—as a reward for their great and important services. . . . . I must observe further to Your Lordship that the king, from affection for Lady Augusta and from his knowledge of the circumstances of the Duke of Brunswick, intends to procure Her Royal Highness the full dower of Princess Royal. This will be delivered to you by Colonel Broome, for whom at Your Lordship's desire I got (though with difficulty) this rank.

The Hereditary Prince's view of this proposal seem to have been based upon very sound sense, and a determination not to be hurried. A letter from him to the Marquess of Granby says—

> You are aware that I depend upon the will of my parents, without whom I should not take any important step; and yet I confess that the point most essential for me is to know the sentiments of the princess, as to which nothing can assure me *except le bonheur de lui rendre mes devoires en personne.* You understand that I fully appreciate what you have said, and can only respond by redoubling my zeal for the service of the king, and of a family which I esteem.

Here this matrimonial project rested until the end of the war.

After the Battle of Vellingshausen the movements of the armies were, at first, not attended with much of interest. General Lückner, with whom was Prince Frederick of Brunswick, recrossed the Weser at Hameln, and General Spörcken joined the Allied Main Army.

Prince Ferdinand and Lord Granby followed Marshal Broglie's retreat by Gesecke, Buren, Haren, and Paderborn; Lord Granby commanding the van-guard and ceaselessly harassing De Broglie's rear. On August 14 a strong attack was made, at which De Broglie was present, upon the Allies' post in Horn. The garrison held out bravely, and, seeing Lord Granby strike his tents prior to advancing to its relief, the French abandoned their attempt. Lord Granby informed Ligonier how a corporal of his old regiment, "the Blacks," (4th Horse, now the 7th Dragoon Guards), who had straggled with four infantrymen into Horn, rendered conspicuous service to the garrison.

On August 18, 200 of the piquets of Beckwith's Brigade, by too zealously attacking an infantry post on the French rear, suddenly found themselves within 500 yards of De Broglie's rearguard, from which some squadrons charged them; Elliot's Light Horse rode to the rescue, and charged with such spirit, Lieut. Nangle with 60 troopers making four consecutive flank attacks, that the piquets were brought off triumphantly.

After making a pause to fortify Hoxter, De Broglie proceeded to cross the Weser; Elliot's, and the Prussian Black Hussars, making free with a good deal of his baggage. He left a force in Hoxter, and two considerable corps holding the adjoining heights. Prince Ferdinand proceeded to attack the right of these Corps, while he despatched Lord Granby against their left. The French commenced to cross the Weser, Lord Granby arriving just in time to cannonade them on the left, and General Wutgenau on the right. On August 21 Lord Granby prepared to bombard Hoxter, when, to his satisfaction, the garrison quitted it and passed the Weser, thus saving, as Granby wrote, "the unhappy consequences which must have attended the poor inhabitants."

This completed the driving of De Broglie's Main Army to the east side of the River Weser.

Prince Soubise had meantime been followed by the Hereditary Prince and General Kilmansegge, and, on August 21, invested the town of Münster where the Allied Garrison was too strong, Granby wrote, to cause them any anxieties. Soubise also despatched the Comte de Stainville on a sort of roving expedition, including the bombarding of Hamm, which failed; and Soubise on September 4 raised the blockade of Münster, and, with Condé, was shortly afterwards driven by the Hereditary Prince towards Wesel on the Rhine; and the Comte de Stainville fell back towards Cassel.

For a short time, the Allied Army remained west of the Weser, on the Heights of Hoxter; and De Broglie east of the Weser, with his centre facing Corvey. Though the records which survive of them read tamely enough, these movements had not been accomplished without continuous desultory fighting, and arduous exertion. In a short note to the Duke of Newcastle, Granby apologised for referring him to Lord Ligonier for details, as, having been continually advanced near the enemy, and consequently on horseback from morning till night, Granby had not done more than write his necessary despatches to the commander-in-chief and the War Office; especially as at all times "he hated writing almost as much as he loved the Duke of Newcastle."

Granby's reports to Lord Ligonier mention that during this march to the Weser, Lord George Lennox, with "Walsh's" Grenadiers, "Elliot's," the piquets of Lord F. Cavendish's and General Sandford's Brigades, and Colonel Harvey's Brigade of Cavalry, had done very well in an affair near the Dymel, which Prince Ferdinand had witnessed, and thanked them for. The Highlanders also had done great service throughout, but had sustained great losses.

Lord Ligonier replied that the king had read Granby's letters with the greatest pleasure, all whose friends were delighted with his large share of the laurels lately gained by the army. Newcastle represented Ligonier "as declaring in all companies" that the contents of Granby's despatches proved him to be, in all respects, what the old commander-in-chief emphatically called *an officer.*

Both Prince Ferdinand and De Broglie again narrowly escaped capture. The former was pursued by some French Hussars while reconnoitring near Hoxter, and was only saved by the devotion of his *aides-de-camp*, who covered his retreat with such energy that they beat off the Hussars, and escaped themselves. In De Broglie's case, although he got off, several of his *aides-de-camp*, and 200 of his escort, were taken. (Archenholz.)

Although both French marshals had thus been driven from place to place by such far inferior numbers. Prince Ferdinand had entirely failed to bring De Broglie to an action, which the latter declined to risk, and now showed himself bent upon another project altogether. He recommenced marching eastwards, and pushed on expeditions towards the towns of Hildesheim, Brunswick, Wolfenbüttel, and even Hanover, levying contributions, and ravaging the districts traversed. To protect the towns of Hanover and Brunswick from the horrors of siege had been a main factor of Ferdinand's operations.

De Broglie expected Ferdinand would continue his "stern chase," but Ferdinand did no such thing; on the contrary, he sent a reinforcement to the Hanover garrison (presumably from General Lückner's Division), and decided to return towards the Dymel and Cassel, in order to cut De Broglie's communications with that all-important garrison. The Hereditary Prince, leaving General Oheim to watch Prince Soubise, returned to Warburg, towards which Prince Ferdinand marched with Lord Granby; Hoxter being held by General Spörcken's Corps.

Prince Ferdinand took several posts which Comte de Stainville's Corps had occupied while the Allies were on the Weser; and, crossing the River Dymel, advanced as De Stainville retired until the Allies reached the heights of Immenhausen. Just as Prince Ferdinand expected, this movement drew large bodies of De Broglie's troops from the east side of the Weser towards the environs of Cassel; and, the enemy collecting there in considerable strength, Prince Ferdinand returned to the old strong position, so often occupied since the Battle of Warburg, north of the River Dymel.

Another series of strategic movements of troops ensued; the British Guards being withdrawn from Hoxter, and encamped at Burgholtz, north of the Dymel, with General Wangenheim's Division. The enemy took the Castle of the Sabbabourg, in the Hartz Wald, which was occupied by the French and Allies, alternately, many times during the war; and De Stainville advanced to Geismar and Grebenstein, but retired again to the heights of Immenhausen. Prince Ferdinand eagerly prepared for an early attack upon this position which he had already remarked was an inherently weak one. The only escape from it towards Cassel, once the enemy were dislodged, was through a narrow defile in its rear, marked on few maps as the Avenue of Wilhelmsthal, where a retreating army could be wedged in, and attacked at hopeless disadvantage.

The Allies marched on the night of the 17th of September in eight columns, and crossed the Dymel at 2 a.m., proceeding under customary orders to maintain the strictest silence. Their intention was to reach, with two advanced corps, points on the right and left flanks of the Immenhausen camp. Lord Granby and the Hereditary Prince led these corps. Giving them time to arrive at their respective points Prince Ferdinand advanced, with the Main Army, to attack Comte de Stainville's front, who, if driven off the Immenhausen heights, would find himself attacked by the Hereditary Prince, and Granby, as he entered the funnel-shaped gorge leading to Cassel.

Again, was Ferdinand disappointed. A remark of one writer suggests that the Hereditary Prince mistook his route and debouched at a wrong point; but Lord Granby's letter conveys no such idea. He merely wrote—

> He (Comte de Stainville) had no intelligence of our march till 7 in the morning, but still had time to retire in three columns under the cannon of Cassel. . . . We cannonaded his rear and took some prisoners.

De Stainville retreated to the Kratzenberg camp, under the guns of Cassel, and the Allied Army halted in the district. Prince Ferdinand's headquarters being at Wilhelmsthal, and Lord Granby at Weimar. The Hereditary Prince, with fourteen squadrons of hussars, started off to visit De Broglie's replenished magazines in Hesse, and took 150,000 rations of oats at Fritzlar. On the 22nd of September Granby wrote to Lord Bute—

> This day the deserters from the enemy assure us that Mons' Broglie has returned to Cassel, and reinforced Mons. Stainville with the whole picketts of his army; if this last manoeuvre of Duke Ferdinand's should have obliged Mons. Broglie to relinquish his views upon Hanover and Brunswick, and at the same time allow us to consume the forage in Hesse, which the enemy had hitherto carefully spared, 'twill certainly have had the most desired effect.

De Broglie was not yet disenamoured of his scheme in Brunswick and Hanover. Prince de Soubise and Condé once again advanced from the Rhine towards Münster, and detached M. de Conflans against Osnabrück, and Emden which, occupied only by a small garrison of Invalids (pensioners), was evacuated October 24, the garrison escaping by sea to Bremen. This had necessitated the detaching of the Hereditary Prince and General Hardenburg towards Münster; and meantime De Broglie returned to the east side of the Weser, where Prince Xavier took Meppen and Wolfenbüttel, and actually commenced the siege of Brunswick.

The extension of the war in this direction spread considerable consternation locally. The reigning Duke of Brunswick, and the Landgrave of Hesse, both left Brunswick for Hamburg which already contained some 40,000 well-to-do refugees from the war districts in Westphalia and Hesse.

Everything pointed to another long winter campaign when Prince Ferdinand and Lord Granby marched by Warburg, Brakell, and Hoxter, to Ohr where a pontoon-bridge was thrown across the Weser for the passage of the army. Near Ohr they encamped, and Lord Granby, whose corps still formed the van-guard, crossed and encamped at Gros-Hilligesfeldt (about four miles from Hastenbach the scene of the Duke of Cumberland's defeat), and General Wutgenau and the Prince of Anhalt also crossed the Weser. Prince Ferdinand was actually marching to follow Granby over the river when the good news arrived that Prince Frederick of Brunswick, and General Lückner, had most gallantly relieved Brunswick; and that, in consequence of this reverse to Prince Xavier, the French had evacuated Wolfenbüttel and were retreating from that part of the country. Granby reported Broglie's quarters to be at Stadt Oldendorff, and his troops to be at Eschartshausen, Halle, and about Eimbeck.

Prince Soubise who had succeeded in doing nothing with his 30,000 men except destroy a few stores in Westphalia, and "take Emden from 2 companies of Chelsea Pensioners," again fell back upon Wesel; and, leaving a force under General Oheim at Rheda to watch him, and support Hamm against any *coup de main*, the Hereditary Prince hurried back to the Weser, which he crossed with some reinforcements from the camp at Ohr, and marched to Hildesheim to take command of General Wutgenau's, and the Prince of Anhalt's, Corps. Lord Granby announced that they were now once more marching in combination against the enemy, and that prospects of winter quarters were brightening.

Marshal de Broglie, Prince Xavier, Comte de Broglie, Comte de Stainville, and M. de Chabot were all east of the Weser, and De Rochambeau with eight battalions, and the "Irish Brigade," remained near Cassel.

Prince Ferdinand advanced upon Eimbeck but, finding De Broglie's centre too strong, retired towards Alfeld, ordering Lord Granby to Vorwohle, and the Hereditary Prince to Ammensen. Thinking that this savoured of a general retreat Marshal De Broglie followed the Hereditary Prince, and Comte de Broglie followed Granby, attacking him (November 7) just as his troops had pitched their camp after a most fatiguing march lasting from 10 p.m. one night till nearly 6 p.m. the following evening. Granby's outposts were driven in, but his tired men had the satisfaction, in sight of Prince Ferdinand, of driving Comte de Broglie's attack decisively back, and pursuing him to his own camp.

Prince Ferdinand then proceeded to try De Broglie's left flank. General Conway with his division joined Lord Granby at Vorwohle, and Lord Granby moved (November 9) to Wangelstadt, and the Hereditary Prince to Vorwohle. At Wangelstadt Granby was attacked under the same circumstances as before, just as the troops had got into their tents. This attack was repulsed, and retaliated upon by Lord Granby as smartly as the preceding one; with the result of turning De Broglie's left so effectually that on the night of the 10th of November Marshal de Broglie, under cover of the darkness, commenced his retreat towards Cassel, abandoning all further attempt at prolonging the campaign.

The Allied Army occupied Eimbeck, Lord Granby's quarters being south of it, at Salzderhelden where he prepared his returns of the British troops, and their routes to winter quarters.

Lord Bute wrote to Granby—

> I am glad to inform you of the satisfaction with which His Majesty received your account of the gallant behaviour of the British troops under your command in repulsing the enemy, and that after so fatiguing a march, with so much resolution and vigour. I congratulate you on the success of your expedition in dislodging the enemy from so great a tract of country as they have been obliged to abandon in consequence of His Serene Highness's late operations.

To the Duke of Newcastle Lord Hardwicke wrote—

> Your Grace's friend, Lord Granby, has borne a most active, and honourable, share in this enterprise, having had three different engagements with the enemy in all of which he has distinguished himself and come off victorious. Indeed, His Lordship's whole conduct is as generous, as gallant, and as honourable as possible; and it is happy for the King's Service to have a man of his uncommon integrity, affability, and modesty at the head of it.

This sweeping of Marshal de Broglie with the flower of the French Army first over the Weser, eastwards; and from thence, where he had gained a good foothold from Eimbeck to Wolfenbüttel, southwards again towards Cassel, has been dismissed by historians in a sentence or two. The details are nearly effaced now, though vastly commended at the time, and some idea of the contemporary opinion held of the circumstances, in France, may be gathered from the following. During the above events France was carrying a high head in Paris, in order to influence in her behalf, the terms of the Peace proposals. The French Gazettes contained highly coloured descriptions of what the French Armies were doing in Germany; but a captured mail disclosed what ministers were in truth thinking of the Marshals of France.

★★★★★★★★★★

After the Battle of Warburg, the French news-sheets declared their troops had routed the British cavalry; but, overwhelmed by numbers, had crossed the River Dymel and formed in line of battle on the opposite bank. Their loss was unascertained, but that of the Allies *was much larger.* Sir Horace Mann drew Walpole's attention to the extraordinary French account of "Quebec."—See "Mann and Manners at the Court of Florence," November 10, 1759.

★★★★★★★★★★

The Allied Army must have enjoyed a hearty laugh over this capture before forwarding it to Sir Joseph Yorke, who laughed in the Hague, before re-forwarding it to His Majesty's Ministers to be laughed over in England.

The Duc de Choiseul's despatch was in cypher, but the same mail carried a non-cypher copy of it. After giving his impressions pretty forcibly, Choiseul asked the French commanders to, at least, act on the defensive since they would not, or could not, assume the offensive; and declared that he would not advise Louis XV. to sustain the expense of the war for another year. Choiseul's private letter to De Broglie contained yet better reading:—

Qu'importe que les Généraux tachent de laTi9er leur fautes ou sur les individus, ou sur la Cour? Ce qu'il y a de certain c'est que nous faisons la plus Vilaine Campagne qui ait été faite de la Guerre, même des Russes, et que le Prince Ferdinand, en nous couvrant de ridicule à la face de l'Europe, se couvre de gloire.

Prince Ferdinand's headquarters were fixed at Hildesheim, Lord Granby's at Osnabrück, the Hereditary Prince's at Münster; and the troops were quartered chiefly in Münster, Osnabrück, Paderborn, Lippstadt, Hameln, Eimbeck, and Hildesheim.

General Mostyn arrived earliest in England, announcing Lord Granby to be on the road:—

The Duke of Newcastle wrote:

Jack Mostyn, is come home very well. Not old, and in as high

> spirits as ever. He has been very graciously received, and Ligonier has most honourably recommended him for Bland's Regiment.

On December 18, 1761, the arrival at Harwich of Lord Granby, Lord George Lennox, and General Waldegrave was announced; and the Duke of Newcastle wrote to the Duke of Devonshire—

> I am sure you will be glad to hear that Granby arrived safely at Knightsbridge this evening and I am to see him early tomorrow.

Immediately after Granby's arrival several councils were held; everyone was heartily delighted to see him, and indirectly his return even occasioned joy to Horace Walpole, who wrote to Sir Horace Mann—

> Mr. Conway will get a little into the *Gazette*, though not in a light worthy of his name, as it will not be for action. Lord Granby is returning, and leaves the command to him.

Chapter 19

1761: At Home and Away Again

The victory ofVellingshausen (or Kirchdenkern), had so strengthened Mr. Pitt in his demands upon France, that he wished, by another campaign in Germany, to secure the whole of Canada, the Newfoundland fishery rights, and Cape Breton, which the Duke of Newcastle was so astonished—if the wags of the day are to be trusted—to hear was an island.

George III. was opposed to pressing these demands, against which France strongly demurred; and the Duke of Newcastle, playing for what he thought the winning side, supported the king's disapproval of them. As a counter, demand France put forward some Spanish claims which Pitt emphatically declined to discuss, except with Spain alone. France and Spain then signed the Family Compact which bound the Bourbon family together against England. Pitt's unhesitating decision was to suspend the Peace negotiations, recall Hans Stanley, and declare war against Spain.

The sequel proved Pitt's policy to be correct, (Lord Bute declared war against Spain in 1762), but his old inability to instil his ideas into his colleagues by patient, even polite, persuasion and sympathetic argument, frustrated it: as Dr. Johnson said of Swift, he "dictated rather than persuaded," The members of his Cabinet, one by one, grew tired of his bullying airs of superiority; while the Duke of Newcastle and the Pelhamites were ready for any opportunity of freeing themselves of his masterful predominance. Pitt had no one so much as himself to blame that, at length, he found himself opposed by the king and the whole of the Cabinet save Lord Temple, with whom, on October 5, 1761, he resigned.

The Earl of Egremont succeeded Pitt as Secretary for the Southern Department, and the Duke of Bedford became Privy Seal in Lord Temple's place; George Grenville assuming the Leadership of the

House of Commons, and the Secretaryship of the Northern Department.

Pitt accepted a coronet for his wife and an annuity of £3,000 a year—court favours which offended his more democratic supporters. (They dubbed Lady Chatham "Lady Cheat'em."—*Rockingham Memoirs*). However, the old enthusiasm for him was soon proved to be yet alive, for on November 9 he attended the Lord Mayor's Banquet, and received an ovation which was rendered unmistakably significant by the complete indifference accorded to the king and queen, and the open insults showered upon the Earl of Bute.

The Marquess of Granby had been duly informed of these changes officially, and privately. The Duke of Newcastle assured him no alteration would ensue towards him, and that the Lord Chancellor had just appointed Mr. Bennet Storer to the living of Hampton "in the handsomest manner towards Your Lordship." Newcastle's delight, after Pitt's resignation, at what he regarded as his own resumption of absolute power, was marred only by his fear of an attack by Pitt upon the Treasury concerning the expense of the war.

He longed, he said, to talk to Lord Granby about "their respective situations," and promised himself a greater number of friends than ever at the opening of Parliament, of whom "Lord Granby's friends and family were already in town." Having hampered Pitt's war policy Newcastle was now, himself, veering round to the war again; and the House of Commons presented an address to the king expressing its resolution to support His Majesty in the prosecution of hostilities. A copy of this was sent to Lord Granby before he left Germany.

To all these allusions to home politics, and their bearing upon the war, Lord Granby had made no reply whatever. Upon his arrival home he made his representations respecting the army, the commissariat, and schemes for recruiting, proposing that 2,000 men should be drafted from Ireland and replaced there by 2,000 or 3,000 Swiss; and that the Irish and English Cavalry in Germany should be respectively recruited from the Cavalry Regiments in Ireland and England. His own regiment, the "Royal Forresters," was as popular a nest-egg as ever, and the authorities continued to draft men from it to Germany.

Having dealt with the military details of the situation, which practically amounted to what he had long been urging, Lord Granby betook himself to Belvoir, and so far as was possible severed himself from the political discussions, into which he was determined not to enter, that were to decide the prosecution, or abandonment, of the war.

His attendance was asked at a Cabinet Council in order that ministers might have the benefit of his opinions and suggestions, and the Duke of Newcastle was emphatic in his wishes that Granby should unceasingly press the execution of the recruiting schemes upon Lord Bute. Bute was deferring these pending the conferences concerning the renewal of Frederick the Great's subsidy, and the continuance of hostilities in Germany. (Frederick the Great's own ideas were at this moment indefinite, and the plan was suggested of delaying the renewal of his subsidy in order to get him to declare positively for peace or war. Newcastle Papers. February, 1762). Meantime it was decided that 2,000 German deserters, and 5,000 Swiss, should be utilised in England and Ireland.

A letter from Lord Rockingham to Thomas Thoroton, at Belvoir, shows that Granby was soon occupied keenly as ever in his favourite sport:—

> I have received a letter from Prettel by which I find His hounds will not be able to come to Grantham. I shall therefore with great pleasure send mine, and much wish that they may contribute to Lord Granby's amusement. I should be much obliged to you to inform me whether I can have the use of Lord William Manners' kennel or where I can otherwise have convenience for the hounds, and also in regard to stable room. I should be glad that the hounds were over there a week or 10 days before Lord Granby went, that the huntsman may be a little acquainted with the country and where the deer lie. I have writ by tonight's post to my huntsman to have the hounds, horses &c. in readiness against I send him full instructions.

Newcastle fretted unceasingly at Granby's absence:—

> I know you will be angry with me, but I think in the present critical situation, after the arrival of the 3 posts, which My Lord Bute fixed for the time of his coming to a decision, you cannot excuse yourself to be absent.

Later His Grace wrote again saying he must beg Granby to be good enough to return by the following Monday, bringing Lord Robert Manners Sutton, Jack Manners, and Thoroton with him, as a disagreeable matter touching the Scotch Militia Bill was imminent in the Commons: "You can't regret being called up this weather, as the ground is covered with snow."

The 20th of March found Granby back again at Belvoir, and Newcastle announced to him the determination of the Courts of Vienna and Paris to place as large armies in the field as possible, Russia had withdrawn from the war, and Lord Ligonier said that Prince Ferdinand would have 100,000 effective men:—

> I send Your Lordship a copy I have stole of Lord Bute's letter to Prince Ferdinand whereby you will see that authentic notice is given of the recruits. . . . I wish you joy on the success at Martinico which gives me additional pleasure that it was done by your friend and relation General Monckton.

Weeks passed, and George III.'s intentions respecting the German War remained a mystery.

In April, that is to say about four months after Lord Granby's arrival in England, Newcastle informed the Duke of Devonshire that he understood Granby had seen Lord Bute on the subject of the Hereditary Prince's marriage:—

> As Lord Granby is setting out for Newmarket, he may possibly not write to me, but I wish Your Grace would ask him at Newmarket what passed with Lord Bute—especially relating to the Campaign.
>
> Your Grace will see that in my Lord Bute's last letter to Prince Ferdinand, he refers him entirely to Lord Granby who, he says, shall be fully instructed with the king's thoughts *upon everything.* I am anxious to know what these thoughts will be, I suspect they must relate to recalling our troops and putting an end to the campaign.

Newcastle then referred to a conversation with Lord Bute from which he had gathered that—

> Lord Granby will have strong instructions from the king to keep his troops in such a condition, situation, or position (I really cannot tell which) as to be able to return to England upon the *first* notice. To which, upon my making some hesitation. My Lord (Bute) replied, 'What! My Lord? Suppose this country is invaded?'
>
> I thought it right to give my Lord Granby a hint. I found him extremely alarmed, and determined. His answer to me was—'If the king gives me any orders that are inconsistent with my subjection to the commands of the general in chief under whom

His Majesty has placed me, I will not return to Germany.' The case of the Duke of Ormond was too fresh in his mind upon this, therefore I think we shall have some altercation.

★★★★★★★★★★

The second Duke of Ormond succeeded John, Duke of Marlboro', as Captain-General of the British Forces, and proceeded in 1712 to Flanders ostensibly to carry on the war against France in co-operation with Prince Eugene. Ormond was instructed, secretly, not to engage the French though to preserve the appearance of hostility towards them; to which end he entered into correspondence with the French commander Marshal Villars.

★★★★★★★★★★

The honourable spirit of the above declaration renders it superfluous to say that the Duke of Devonshire's reply contained no trace of any state secrets confided by the king to Lord Granby. Did the latter possess any Newcastle might have felt certain that Granby was the last man to disclose, even if he disapproved them. But the duke was far too anxious to be informed of what was happening to leave any stone unturned, though the conviction was slowly forcing itself upon his perceptions that Pitt's resignation had made no change in the attitude, towards His Grace, of the king and Lord Bute.

Nor was Newcastle alone in his curiosity respecting the instructions which Lord Granby might have received. While delivering a speech in the House of Commons against the abandonment of the German War, Pitt turned searchingly to Granby and said, "I know His Lordship's zeal for the service of his country is such that, if he had received his orders, I am sure he would not now be where he is."

Sir Joseph Yorke reported, in May from the Hague, that Prince Ferdinand was marching the Allied Army out of winter quarters, but that peace would be believed in so long as the English generals did not rejoin. In reply Newcastle acquainted Sir Joseph that, with the consent of the Duke of Devonshire, Lord Hardwicke, and Lord Mansfield, he had decided to retire at the rising of Parliament. His Grace entrusted two letters to Sir Joseph to forward to the Duke of Brunswick, and Prince Ferdinand, saying he was heartily ashamed of them as they contained no guarantee of the continuation of the subsidy to Frederick the Great, nor of supporting the German War.

These departures from Pitt's policy he made the excuse for his retirement after having intrigued with Lord Bute against Pitt, and embraced Bute's peace policy, carrying most of his colleagues with him: then perceiving that he was gaining no real footing in the good graces of either George III., or Lord Bute, he applied his energies to the war again.

Newcastle continued:

> I have insisted with Lord Granby that he should go to his command forthwith. His own honour requires it, and what really is the publick service; though I believe they are not in haste to send him away. You ask me why don't Lord Granby get away? I answer, first, because he has not received any directions, or answer's, to the points he is soliciting, and secondly, because he will not give that attention he ought to my frequent supplications on that head.

Newcastle's arguments fell lamentably short of explaining how Lord Granby could have returned to Germany without orders; or why he should have done more than represent what reinforcements were necessary, *should* the war be resumed, since he had long made no secret of his personal desire—under the existing condition of the army—for peace. This desire could not fail of becoming more pronounced after Granby's return to England. A new ballot for the Militia had caused riots entailing the slaughter of some forty-two persons, in addition to many wounded.

The expedition against Belleisle was unpopular, and useless; for not a single French regiment had been withdrawn by it from the German war-area; and a highly significant incident had occurred in February at a general muster of the 2nd Regiment of Foot Guards (the Coldstreams) in St. James's Park. Volunteers were called for to fill vacancies in the battalion serving in Germany, but a total silence ensued—not a man stirring. (A draft of thirteen men per company was afterwards ordered to Germany). In the House of Lords, the Duke of Bedford introduced a motion pointing to the utter impossibility of England placing an army in Germany equal to that of France, and consequently of her carrying on the war there to any good purpose.

If anything shed a ray of popularity on the war it was the Marquess of Granby's personality alone, and even that was not sufficient to counteract elements too far removed from his individual influence. His own regiment, "the Royal Forresters," continued to attract recruits, many of whom were drafted to heavy regiments on account of their size being above the average of light dragoons; but this very enthusiasm entailed its detention in England as an incentive to enlistment. Its regimental motto "*Hic et ubique*" may be said to have stopped short of fulfilment at "*Hic*," for its wanderings were chiefly restricted to the peaceful limits of Herts, Bucks, and the neighbourhood of Epping Forest. The Marching Order Books of 1762 show its presence at Epping, Waltham, Stanstead, Ware, Hertford, St. Albans, Hoddesdon, Newport Pagnell, Cheshunt, Broxbourne, Stoney Stratford, Daventry, *etc.*

At Hertford in April, 1762, the Marquess of Granby inspected it, and entertained all the officers and men at the Half Moon Inn.

Lord Granby's Bill, 'The Half Moon' at Hertford, Apl. 10, 1762.

	£	s.	d.
To 80 Ordinaries	£12		
,, Beer	1	9	6
,, Servants dinners	1	10	
,, Suppers to 20 gentlemen	1	1	
,, ,, ,, Servants, &c.		7	
,, Musicians suppers		4	
,, French wines, 5 dozen	7	12	6
,, Port wine, 2 doz. & 8	2	12	
,, Punch	5	19	
,, Pipes & Tobac		4	
,, Bottles & glasses broke		3	6
,, Carriage of French wine		8	–
,, the Cook from London	1	11	6
,, Wax candles		8	
,, Rumbo		7	
,, Oranges & sugar		4	
,, Breakfasts		14	6
,, Fireing		5	—
,, Servants	5	5	
	42	5	6
To the 6 troops at 10 gs. each	63		
	£105	5	6

Pay to Major Whiteford the sum of 100 guineas, and place it to the account of your friend Granby.

To John Calcraft, Esq. Hertford, Apl. 10th.

Received the contents, 13 Apl. 1762, John Whiteford, Major R.F.

FROM AN OLD COMMON-PLACE BOOK WHICH STATES THE ORIGINAL TO HAVE BEEN IN THE POSSESSION OF THE REV. HARRY PIERSE OF CAMBRIDGE.

The government at last decided on the prosecution of the German War, and Lord Granby received his orders to rejoin his troops. In pursuance of his recommendations the Infantry cross-belts, which had been found very fatiguing on the march, were modified, and the cartouche-boxes henceforth carried on the front of a waist-belt. New clothing, and an extra supply of linen and stockings, were distributed throughout the army.

The transports with reinforcements, provisions, etc., sailed for

Bremen, and Lord Granby took leave of His Majesty and proceeded to Harwich where he was detained several days by contrary winds. The Rev. Bennet Storer again accompanied him. Granby wrote to the Duke of Newcastle, May 28, saying that they were just setting sail, though the wind was still contrary and he expected a long passage, "which, as I am not very well, and always sick at sea, I shan't like."

Newcastle described himself happily settled, "a Whig country gentleman," at Claremont, where he hoped to receive occasional public news from his former colleagues:—

"I hope sometimes to hear from my dear and best friend Lord Granby, and good news will make me the happiest of men; but I can send you nothing now but my best wishes that everything may come to you that is happy and agreeable. . . . God in heaven preserve you, and send you back to us crowned with laurels and success such as may secure a good peace."

The Earl of Bute became First Lord of the Treasury upon the resignation of Newcastle who, after lingering so long an unwelcome and powerless actor upon the political stage, quitted it now with unquestionable dignity, and independence. The king urged him to accept a pension, which His Grace absolutely refused, though grateful, as he wrote to Granby, "for His Majesty's manner which was most polite and gracious." Whatever his faults were the Duke of Newcastle was never avaricious, personally, though he so fully recognised the power to be gained by playing upon the avarice of others.

In addition to the government patronage of which he so long had the distribution, he devoted his private fortune to the House of Hanover, and the Whig cause. At the date of his resignation the Earl of Radnor said he was confident the Duke of Newcastle "had spent £200,000 for the present Royal Family;" and at the date of the duke's death the Earl of Chesterfield declared him to be £300,000 poorer after fifty years of office—"a very unministerial proceeding."

Newcastle held a farewell *levée* at his house in Lincoln's Inn Fields which was numerously attended by all classes and professions, save the very one which owed him most. The bishops, all save two, enacted the part of so many Vicars of Bray by absenting themselves in a body from the fading presence of one to whom nearly each of them owed his elevation to the Episcopal bench.

Before leaving Harwich, Bennet Storer expressed his disgust for them to Thoroton, saying:

> *Entre nous* I own I am quite ashamed that the first men of my profession, and who certainly have greater obligations to the Duke of Newcastle than to any man, should have been so wanting in paying their last compliment to him.

His Grace wittily remarked that, after all, like the generality of mankind, the bishops were but too apt to forget their maker!

Storer also enjoined Thoroton, on behalf of Lord Granby, to trust no public conveyance for letters, and to commit nothing to writing "except what was public, and which anyone might read, for be assured all our letters are opened."

The scant regard for the privacy of written communications was notorious at this period. Any letter of special importance the Duke of Newcastle invariably delayed until an opportunity presented itself of safe, private transport. When writing to Sir Joseph Yorke the announcement of his intended resignation, Newcastle entrusted his letter to an officer appointed to the army in Germany, as he "was sure letters were opened in Lombard St."

★★★★★★★★★★

The General Post Office was then situated in Lombard Street. So general a distrust of the Post-office authorities renders the total absence of reserve in Horace Walpole's correspondence curiously noticeable. Dr. Johnson says Pope was "afraid of writing lest the clerks at the Post-office should know his secrets: "the Earl of Buckingham writing to Lady Suffolk (August 11, 1765, Letters of Lady Suffolk) alluded to "the fear, or rather the certainty," of the examination of correspondence passing through the post; and though Walpole (as he, personally, complained) became a nonentity, politically speaking, after his father's retirement, he must have been known to be an active purveyor of what people were saying, and thinking.

★★★★★★★★★★

Chapter 20

1762: Wilhelmstal and Cassel

The marquess arrived at the Hague June 1, where he was received and entertained by Sir Joseph Yorke, and Prince Lewis of Brunswick, who gave His Lordship the fullest assurances of the attachment of the Brunswick family to the cause of the King of England. On June 4 Lord Granby set out for the army by way of Münster, where the Hereditary Prince was already posted, and concerning whose matrimonial project Granby was the bearer of messages from the king. From Münster Granby proceeded eastwards to Brakell and Hoxter, Prince Ferdinand's quarters being at the Palace of Corvey on the Weser; and, on June 18, the prince reviewed the Grand Army as it marched off its ground at Brakell, after which His Serene Highness was entertained at a dinner given by Lord Granby. The next day the army, preceded by Lord Granby's Corps, marched for the old position on the River Dymel, which was reached on June 20.

This, the last, campaign of the war was fought under different auspices on the side of France. Lord Granby's victory at Vellingshausen had aroused great indignation against De Broglie, and Prince Soubise. De Broglie was recalled, and, in the feminine Court intrigues into which the matter chiefly resolved itself, he was worsted by Prince Soubise—"*Général inhabile et malheureux, Courtisan souple et adroit.*" ("Clumsy and unhappy general, Supple and skilful courtier.") De Broglie was disgraced, and, exiled in February, 1762, though according to Jomini he was the sole one among the French generals of the Seven Years' War who displayed any sustained ability.

Prince de Soubise, thanks to Mme. de Pompadour's influence, returned to the chief command of the French troops in Germany, whither also Marshal D'Estrées, (he defeated the Duke of Cumberland at Hastenbach), for the second time, proceeded. Upon leaving its winter quarters in Cassel the French Grand Army under Soubise and

D'Estrées moved northwards towards the Dymel. Its right was led by De Castries, its left by De Stainville. East of the River Weser, in the Göttingen district, Prince Xavier was posted; and Prince Condé arrived at Düsseldorf to take command of the Reserve on the Lower Rhine.

****

Soubise's and D'Estrées' Army amounted to 111 battalions and 120 squadrons; Condé's Reserve to 46 battalions and 38 squadrons: Prince Ferdinand's to 82 battalions and 82 squadrons, and 5,000 irregular troops (*Œuvres de Frédéric le Grand*, t. v.).

****

Prince Ferdinand and Lord Granby opposed the main army under Soubise and D'Estrées; General Lückner was near Eimbeck, east of the Weser, observing Prince Xavier's force; and the Hereditary Prince was stationed at Münster to deal with Prince Condé's Reserve.

With the object of clearing Hesse of the French Prince Ferdinand's plan of campaign was to cut off the main French Army, in the Cassel district, and the Cassel garrison, from their communications with Frankfort; which, if successful, rendered the fall of the Cassel, Göttingen, and Ziegenhayn garrisons a mere matter of time.

The Marquess of Granby opened the fighting, under Prince Ferdinand's orders, by crossing to the south bank of the Dymel with a portion of his corps. He then pushed on to Wolfshangen, dislodging from thence some light troops of Count de Stainville's Corps, and occupied the heights of Volksmissen. Lord Frederick Cavendish did the like towards Grebenstein, on De Stainville's right; the Sabbabourg was re-captured, and Count de Stainville, with the Duke de Cogni, and De Castries narrowly escaped being taken there. A portion of their escort was made prisoner, and a number of horses captured.

Soubise and D'Estrées advancing in force Lord Granby retired over the Dymel, having effected his object of beating up the enemy's quarters to the north-west of Cassel, and securing the debouches of the Dymel.

Prince Ferdinand having drawn the enemy into a position behind Grebenstein (though not on the wished-for heights of Immenhausen), made a third attempt to pen him up in the gorge of Wilhelmsthal. On June 23, 1762, the Allies prepared to cross the Dymel early on the ensuing morning. General Lückner crossed the Weser on the night of the 23rd, leaving a portion of his force near the River Leine to deceive Prince Xavier, and advanced in rear of the French right un-

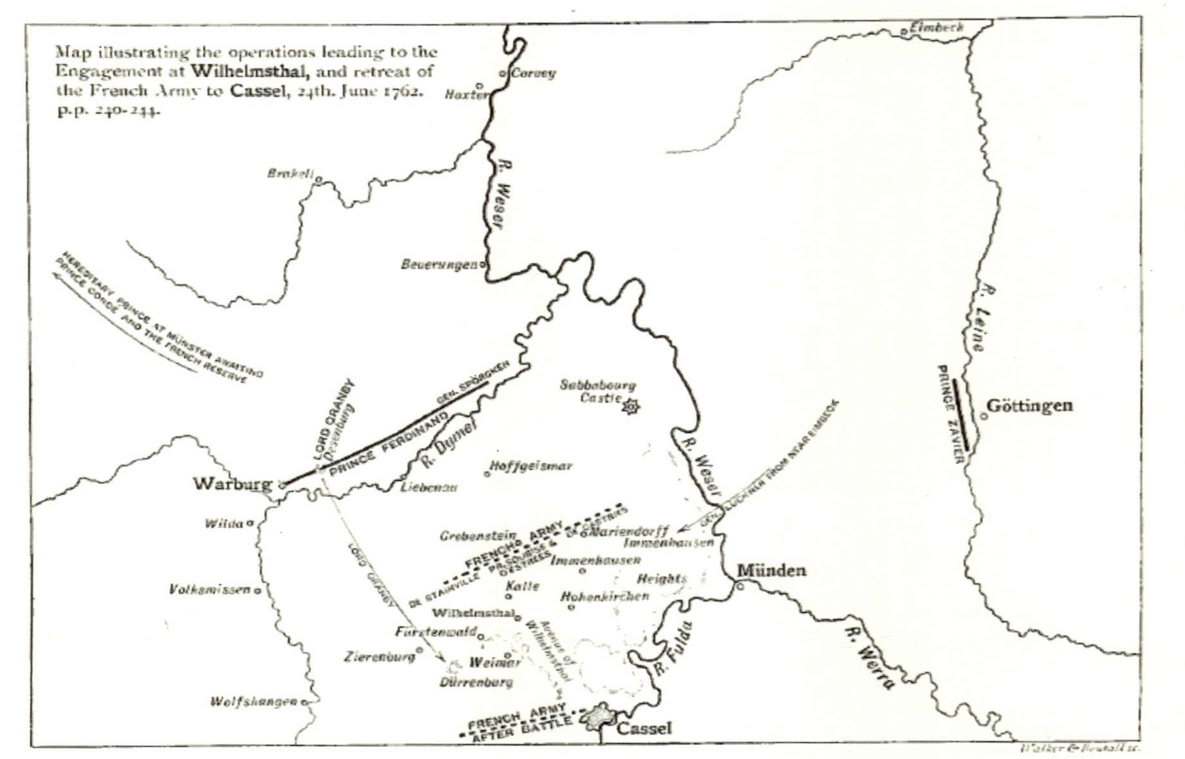

Map illustrating the operations leading to the Engagement at **Wilhelmsthal,** and retreat of the French Army to **Cassel**, 24th. June 1762. p.p. 240-244.

Walker & Boutall sc.

der De Castries. The Sabbabourg was considerably strengthened, and the Marquess of Granby, with the whole of his Reserve, crossed the Dymel at 2 a.m. on the 24th, in advance of Prince Ferdinand, and occupied a greatly important position, which the French could have prevented, on the Dürrenburg; from whence the French tents were seen still standing.

★★★★★★★★★★★

Lord Granby's troops at "Wilhelmstal":—2 battalions of grenadiers and 2 battalions of Highlanders, under Lieut.-Colonel Beckwith; 3 battalions of Foot Guards, and 1 of the Grenadiers of the Guards, under Major-General Julius Caesar; 3 Hanoverian battalions (Alsfeldt's, Rheden's, and Wangenheim's), under Major-General Wangenheim; 3 squadrons of Elliot's and 2 squadrons of Blues, under Colonel Harvey; 2 squadrons of "Sprengel's" and 2 squadrons of "Veltheim's," under Colonel Veltheim; 6 squadrons of Bauer's Hussars. Twelve six-pounders.

★★★★★★★★★★

The main army did not march till 4 a.m., General Spörcken's Corps forming its left, to act in concert with General Lückner. A fate seemed to prevail against the complete success of this favourite, and promising project of Ferdinand's, and on this occasion he himself delayed the arrival of the main army by halting at too distant a point to form line of battle. Lückner carried out the first portion of his programme and, debouching near Holzhausen and Mariendorff, attacked De Castries, driving him in upon the French right. Lord Granby continued on from Dürrenburg, arriving exactly to time at his point at Fürstenwald; and, hearing the French cannonade against Lückner's attack, believed it to be Prince Ferdinand commencing his assault on the French centre.

The French, surprised by Lückner's approach in rear of their right flank, and seeing Granby's Corps as it reached the Fürstenwald on their left rear, were now thoroughly alarmed; and commenced retreating rapidly by Wilhelmsthal, Frankenhausen, and Hohenkirchen; while the Allied centre, under Prince Ferdinand, was still too far distant to "get home." Lord Granby, beginning to fear another complete escape of the enemy, sent a detachment consisting of *chasseurs*, one company of grenadiers, Campbell's Highlanders, part of Keith's, and two guns, into the wood of Fürstenwald; and made a rapid march, by his left, with the rest of his corps on to Wilhelmsthal.

Granby made this movement quite close to the enemy's flank, the infantry of which were now running, and by it he cut off a rearguard which Soubise and D'Estrées had detached, under Comte de Stainville, to cover their retreat into the trap-like gorge of Wilhelmsthal.

As Lord Granby was preparing, in spite of his isolated condition, to charge the rear of the French, this rearguard consisting of the *Grénadiers de France*, the *Grénadiers Royaux*, the regiments of Poitou, Acquitaine, and other picked troops, made a sudden movement behind him, round the wood of Fürstenwald, and gained the flank of his Reserve (which Granby had left there), taking the two guns, and the company of grenadiers belonging to the 20th, "Kingsley's."

Granby's position was critical owing to the non-arrival of the Allied centre, which left him isolated between the enemy's rearguard and the whole of its left flank. Leaving the latter to go on with its running he wheeled to attack the rearguard; and, after a most desperate hand-to-hand fight, in which Granby again highly distinguished himself personally, De Stainville's temporary advantage was reversed; he was defeated and driven back upon the right of the now arriving main army, when such as had not already been taken by Granby's Reserve, surrendered to the 5th (Hodgson's) Regiment of Foot.

The *Grénadiers de France*, the *Grénadiers Royaux*, and the regiment of Acquitaine were taken almost entirely; De Stainville, and a small portion of his force, escaped. Soubise and D'Estrées were pursued through the gorge of Wilhelmsthal to the very gates of Cassel which they reached with a loss of 6,000 (2,700 of which were prisoners), 170 officers (prisoners), 1 standard, 6 colours, 2 cannon, and the whole of the baggage and equipages. On the left General Spörcken took 2 cannon, and hustled the Duke of Fitz James' Regiment severely, capturing a standard.

The opinion stands on record that the whole of this success, so far as it went, was due to Lord Granby; and that had Prince Ferdinand arrived with his centre in time, or had Generals Spörcken and Lückner done as much on the left as Granby did on the right, the French Army should have been destroyed.

The only officer of any note among the killed on the side of the Allies, whose total loss was very small, was Captain Harry Townshend, of the 1st Foot Guards, A.D.C. to Lord Granby. He was previously wounded at Vellingshausen, and distinguished himself at Wilhelmsthal where, in Lord Ligonier's words, "he died gloriously for his calling." (Granby to Newcastle: "My Corps was very warmly engaged. I am sorry to acquaint Your Grace that I have lost poor Harry Townshend."—*Newcastle Papers*, June 26. 1762).

Prince Ferdinand entertained all the captured French officers at a great dinner. At dessert a number of covered dishes were placed upon the table to which, just as the company was rising to leave, Prince Ferdinand drew attention, saying: "Gentlemen, there is still something left for you." The dishes proved to contain watches, rings, snuff-boxes, and a variety of valuable presents which the French officers were courteously entreated to accept as some small compensation for the looting of their baggage. (Archenholz).

Captain Boyd carried home the despatches, and told Sir Joseph Yorke, on the road, how eminently Lord Granby had distinguished himself; and how delighted Prince Ferdinand was with the confidence he had shown "in determining his movements upon the countenance of the enemy." Lord Ligonier was beside himself with satisfaction over Wilhelmsthal, the more so as an invasion by France was again talked of, and she was said to have 45,000 men encamped, ready, on the north coast. "Granby did the whole business" (declared Ligonier at dinner to the Duke of Newcastle), "than whom no man had ever acted with more courage, or more like a commanding officer, than in cutting off De Stainville's Corps from the French Army." Ligonier mentioned a slight check which had occurred owing to his own regiment, the 1st Foot Guards; but added that "Granby soon recovered it, and his Blues did almost beyond what was ever done by a regiment of cavalry."

The king's satisfaction at Lord Granby's conduct was conveyed to him through Mr. George Grenville.

An account of Wilhelmsthal manufactured for the reading of the Parisian public is too naive to pass over. The newspapers declared the whole affair to have been a deliberate attempt by the Allies upon Cassel, which was frustrated by the French *who got there first*, and repulsed the attack with some loss to the Allies!

Towards the Rhine the Hereditary Prince had bombarded the French garrison in the Castle of Arensburg; the garrison surrendered and the prince destroyed the fortifications, after which he retired to Münster.

Prince Ferdinand fixed his headquarters at Wilhelmsthal, with Lord Granby forming his right on the Dürrenburg. The French passed eastwards, over the River Fulda, on June 25, leaving a Corps in the Kratzenburg camp (at Cassel), and another at Lütternburg. Prince Xavier retired to between Göttingen and Münden; and Soubise, becoming anxious for his garrison in Ziegenhayn, detached De Guerchy and De Rochambeau to cover that place and Melsungen, as well as to threaten the advance of the Allies. Lord Granby, with Lord Frederick Cavendish, proceeded to oppose them.

Lord Frederick Cavendish successfully attacked several of the French posts. Hallershausen, Felzburg, and Fritzlar were taken; and Lord Frederick advanced to Gudensburg, and approached the Castle of Waldeck—the only post on the River Eder remaining to the French. General Lückner occupied posts along the Fulda and the Weser; and, after quitting Fritzlar, M. de Rochambeau collected what forces he could, from the French posts in the south of Hesse, and formed on the heights of Homberg, to dispute the further advance of the Allied Army.

To dislodge M. de Rochambeau was Lord Granby's next task. He advanced from the Dürrenburg to Fritzlar, on the night of June 30, to act in concert with Lord Frederick Cavendish with his German Brigade. M. de Rochambeau was to be cut off by them, on his left from Ziegenhayn, and on his right from the Fulda. The result is described in a letter from Granby to Ligonier, which also describes the various positions of the Allied Army:—

> I have not until now been able to wish you joy of the very great credit your old friends the Blues acquired on the 1st of July. I marched on the 30th (June) at night from Dürrenburg to Fritzlar with the Blues, Elliot's, Sprengel's, and Weltheim's. There I found the two battalions of grenadiers and the two battalions of Highlanders. From that point I was to proceed to dislodge Mons. de Rochambeau's Corps at Homberg by attacking his left, while Lord Frederick Cavendish with four battalions of *chasseurs* and Reidessel's and Bauer's Hussars (from the point of Feltzberg) were to attack his right.
>
> When we came near, he struck his tents and advanced a little to meet us, but when he discovered Lord Frederick's column, he began his retreat. Our cavalry pressed to engage him; Elliot's led (leaving the village of Kattsdorff on the right) through the enclosures and charged most gallantly, but Col. Harvey seeing the enemy prepared for them and that unless the regiment was instantly sustained it was undone, followed with rapidity through the village with the Blues past a rivulet that, with the narrowness of the streets and the closeness of the enemy, impeded their forming: but, as no time was to be lost, charged with them with only 6 or 8 men in front, (*i.e.* abreast).

"This had the best effect: their *déroute* was complete had not their infantry lined a little hollow way which, at the same time that it saved their cavalry prevented ours from advancing. Thus, they continued a very long time, charging and manoeuvring with such a continuance as did them an honour never to be forgot, and during this time Elliot's were extremely useful to the Blues, though their ammunition was entirely expended.

★★★★★★★★★★

The situation of the 2 regts. was at this time very critical; but the mutual support which they gave each other—Elliot's Dragoons by their continual skirmishing with the enemy; and the Blues by their manoeuvres in squadrons and by their steady countenance, kept the enemy at bay till the infantry came up.—*London Gazette.*

★★★★★★★★★★

Our infantry by this time got forward and, sustained by the cavalry, followed the enemy at least a league and a half, as did Lord Frederick's column, though it could not arrive time enough to attack them with us.

I can never sufficiently commend the gallantry and good conduct of the Blues and Elliot's, nor enough express the obligations I have to Colonel Harvey, Colonel Erskine, Major Forbes and Major Ainslie as well as the rest of the officers. Neither would I be thought to omit the infantry who showed the same readiness they have ever done.

It is now time to think of the execution of my further instructions, which were to push on with the whole corps, except the Hanoverian *Chasseurs* and Hussars, to Melsungen. I found it occupied by the enemy, but it was too late at night and the troops were too much fatigued to attack it that night, during which I received H. S. Highness's orders to return to Fritzlar.

On the 4th inst. I moved to Lohn where Lord Frederick now is with his three battalions of *chasseurs* and Elliot's. Fritzlar is occupied by his fourth battalion and 100 *arquebusiers* of Freitag's. The posts of Feltzberg and Gudensberg are likewise occupied each by 50 *chasseurs*. The rest are flung into Fritzlar. Last night (5th July) with the Blues, Sprengel's Weltheim's and the grenadiers and Highlanders I joined General Wangenheim with three Hanoverian battalions.

The Hanoverian *Chasseurs* and Hussars are on the Eder. General Caesar with the Guards and Lord Pembroke with Bland's are

> at Hoff; and Gen. Waldegrave with a brigade of British infantry at the Hercules. (The colossal Hercules near the cascade at Wilhelmshöhe). H. S. Highness's Headquarters are still at Wilhelmsthal, on the heights of which General Conway is with the right of the army. (Conway's name suggests Horace Walpole; but all he had to say of late was with reference to Wilhelmsthal (*Letters to Sir Horace Mann*, July 1, 1762): "Lord Granby is much commended. My chief joy arises from knowing Mr. Conway is safe.")

It will be observed that Lord Granby effected this dislodgement of De Rochambeau with the most complete success, except in the pursuit which was interrupted by Prince Ferdinand, on July 1, because the enemy was marching in force to Melsungen, and had already crossed the River Fulda. Granby bivouacked for the night, and then returned to Fritzlar, encamping finally at Niedenstein.

During the affair with De Rochambeau, who lost 120 prisoners, some of Lord Granby's wounded officers were taken by the French. Before retiring Lord Granby sent an English surgeon with a letter to M. de Rochambeau requesting leave to attend to the English wounded. De Rochambeau alludes to this letter in his *Memoires*, saying—

> My most intimate friend could not have written to me in terms more frank respecting the energy and precision of the movements that he (Granby) had seen executed, by the French troops under my command, to escape the triple superiority of his force.

On the 11th of July General Conway took Waldeck Castle by means of a "bluff." He invested it on the 10th, but was really without the necessary ammunition, or means, to bombard it. The garrison of 4 officers and 150 men, thinking resistance hopeless, capitulated to him as prisoners of war, and thus the last French post on the Eder was taken, and Horace Walpole at the same time much pleased.

The Main French Army was, at this juncture, on the heights of Lütternburg and Laudwehrshagen; 8,000 men were near Göttingen; Comte de Stainville was at the Kratzenburg; M. de Rochambeau and Comte de Guerchy, with 15,000, extended from Melsungen to the heights of Homberg; and a reinforcement from Prince Condé's Reserve was advancing with all haste from the Rhine.

Soubise attempted to advance on the River Eder, but was driven back towards the Fulda by Lückner and Granby, and retired to a practically impregnable camp at the Heiligenberg.

On the 13th of July Lord Granby, reinforced from Major-General Caesar's Division at Hoff, advanced to Gudensburg, bridged the River Eder, and took front before the Heiligenberg camp which was the stronghold of the French position on the heights of Melsungen. This was Prince Ferdinand's principal objective—"*Mon grand but,*" he wrote from Wilhelmsthal to Lord Granby, "*et Votre Excellence sera, en dèla, la partie principale pour agir.*" The position, besides its great strength, served to maintain the French communications with the town of Fulda, though Lord Granby's advance to Gudensburg had cut off Cassel from Frankfort.

Between the 13th and 23rd of July the pendulum of war swung to and fro. Ferdinand saw his plan of extending the French Army succeeded; and he took Amöneburg, and several small *châteaux* on the Cassel-Frankfort route, which posts harassed the French supplies. Lord Granby reconnoitred the Melsungen position assiduously for a favourable occasion of attack. The French garrison in Göttingen, fearing to be cut off, marched out on the 15th of July, but finding itself menaced by General Lückner and Prince Frederick of Brunswick, it reoccupied the town. On the 23rd of July Prince Ferdinand despatched a corps under Zastrow and Colonel Schlieffen against Prince Xavier and the Saxons' camp at Lütternburg. This was taken with 1,100 prisoners, 13 cannon, and 3 standards, at a loss to the Allies of about 200 men. During the action Comte de Stainville left the Kratzenburg camp to assist Prince Xavier, and Prince Frederick of Brunswick, during the former's absence, destroyed the defences of the Kratzenburg.

This success affected the French right to the extent of forcing it further south towards their centre; and the Main Allied Army followed up the advantage by marching over the River Eder towards Lord Granby's position. Granby carried the Falckenberg on the 24th, driving the French from the heights of Homberg, but their position at Melsungen was still maintained. At night, July 25, owing to movements of General Lückner and Prince Frederick on their rear, the French withdrew, in considerable force, across the Fulda, leaving a numerous garrison in the town of Melsungen. Lord Granby at once took the heights, and encamped there.

Prince Condé, leaving garrisons in Wesel, Coblentz, and Cologne, had advanced from the Rhine; and between the 1st, and 4th, of August detachments of his army arrived between Marburg and Giessen, on the River Lahn. Watching him, the Hereditary Prince was near Wetter; so, the whole position, at the commencement of August, 1762, was that the two main armies were opposing one another on the banks of the River Fulda; the French still retained the fortified towns of Göttingen, Cassel, Münden, and Melsungen, and were trusting to regain their footing in Hesse, and to reopen their communications with Frankfort, through the assistance of the Prince of Condé's Army of Reserve.

Lord Granby moved his own quarters to Elphershausen (some three miles south-west of Melsungen), at which place Major-General Julius Caesar, who commanded the brigade of Foot Guards, died, August 10, from the effects of a fall from his horse. (In January, 1761, Lord Granby had written to Lord Ligonier: ". . . and I must beg leave to recommend to your protection my friend General Caesar whenever a vacant old regiment shall give him an opportunity of being recommended to His Majesty's favour."—*Rutland MSS.*, vol. ii.)

On the 6th, and 7th, of August batteries were raised before Lord Granby's position at Melsungen, facing those of the enemy; and, on the 10th, a general advance was made upon the town. Lord Granby kept up a brisk cannonade all day from his batteries (using unloaded shells in order to save the town as much damage as possible), and sent, towards evening, a detachment across the Fulda to cannonade Comte de Guerchy's camp. Prince Frederick of Brunswick skirmished on the rear of the French Army towards the River Werra, and all the Allied generals were instructed to make feints from their respective positions. Granby's cannonade drove in some of the enemy's batteries, and at 10 p.m. he made an effort to get into the town; but the French stuck to their coveted post, and would neither be forced, nor frightened, out. Starvation might succeed; and the Allied detachment was recalled from the east bank of the Fulda.

Nothing of importance occurred for some days after this attempt upon Melsungen. Lord Granby repulsed, with considerable loss to the enemy, two attacks made upon his piquets, at a cost to himself of 2 officers killed, 3 wounded and missing, and 90 rank and file killed and wounded. He summed up the position, to Mr. George Grenville and the Duke of Newcastle, from Elphershausen, saying that the French were suffering greatly, cut off from their main supplies, and must soon either retire, or risk a battle. Prince Condé and the Hereditary Prince were facing one another on the River Ohm; and "all private letters, in both armies, talked of nothing but peace."

During this period of Granby's advanced position near the enemy the Allied headquarters remained at Gudensburg. Prince Ferdinand was longing to press on the peace negotiations in Paris by increased activity in the field; but the Melsungen garrison continued to defy attack. The French, it is true, were suffering severely from scarcity of food and forage, and Ferdinand tried once more to coax Soubise out of Melsungen, and from across the Fulda, to attack him. Prince Ferdinand marched from Gudensburg across the Eder to the heights of Falckenberg, behind Lord Granby's camp; and then, with His Lordship, approached, exposed to the fire of three batteries, to reconnoitre the enemy's position in and around Melsungen.

It appeared so desperately strong that the prince relinquished any idea of assuming the offensive; but, while seeking to tempt Soubise to do so, he was not without hopes that the moral effect of this approach of the Main Allied Army might induce the exceedingly hungry Frenchmen to retreat. Towards evening Prince Ferdinand withdrew to the Falckenberg, leaving a long line of advanced piquets with fires burning to deceive the French; and, later in the night, marched back to Gudensburg. Lord Granby remained to await the morning, when, had the French advanced in force against him, he was to fall gradually back upon his old camp on the heights of Homberg.

Morning proved the ruse to have succeeded: the Frenchman no more than the Englishman cared to fight without *la pièce de Roost-Béef dans l'estomac,* and Melsungen was abandoned to Lord Granby. Marshals Soubise and D'Estrées ordered Münden and Göttingen to be evacuated, leaving in Göttingen several cannon, and immense quantities of ammunition. Prince Soubise retreated towards Hersfeldt, leaving only the garrisons in Cassel (which he reinforced with several battalions) and Ziegenhayn behind him, the former of which Prince Frederick of Brunswick was detached to blockade. The Allied Army marched to Homberg, and on the 23rd of August the enemy quitted Hersfeldt (in which Lord Granby took a large magazine) for Fulda, west of which the Grand Army was soon sighted by Lord Granby, who was fast pushing on with the vanguard of the Allies.

From Fulda the French marched (August 25), and, detaching General Conway to invest Marburg on the Lahn, the Allies continued on, arriving on the 30th near Nidda. Prince Condé meantime had made unceasing efforts to pass the Ohm, and join the French Main Army. After being thrown back beyond Giessen by the Hereditary Prince, Condé tried an alternative plan of marching by Friedburg to Frankfort; thus, to accomplish the all-important junction which Soubise sought to promote by continually retiring towards the River Main.

Prince Condé's Reserve now struck a formidable blow. At Lich, on the 25th of August, he had cannonaded the Hereditary Prince who marched to Grünburg; and Condé formed on the heights of Johannisberg (near Nauheim) which command the plain of Friedburg. On the 30th of August the Hereditary Prince attempted to take the heights of Johannisberg, and was decisively defeated by Prince Condé. The Hereditary Prince in endeavouring to rally his troops was severely wounded by a bullet which passed through the top of the hip-bone, and came out at his back; his English *aide-de-camp*. Colonel Clinton, was also wounded; and the prince lost in killed and wounded nearly 2,000 men.

Except "Elliot's Light Horse," which behaved brilliantly, and Frazer, who commanded some "*chasseurs*," no English troops were under the command of the prince, who retreated towards the Allied Army; Prince Ferdinand despatching twenty squadrons of British cavalry, and the 2nd Line of Infantry, to support him. General Hardenburg assumed command of the Corps of the Hereditary Prince whose brilliant, but chequered career in the Seven Years' War ceased with this disaster.

The same excuse was made for him that he "mistook" the enemy's army for its rearguard; but it is more probable that he repeated the error which his illustrious uncle, Prince Ferdinand, never committed, of voluntarily affording the French an opportunity of profiting by sheer weight of numbers. The Hereditary Prince was far outnumbered; and his ill-timed attack at Johannisberg completed the junction of Condé with the French Grand Army, under Soubise and D'Estrées, which shortly was posted with its left at Friedburg, and its right, under Prince Xavier, on the Bergen heights—thus regaining their communications with Frankfort.

This French victory changed the whole aspect of affairs. With overwhelming odds against him Prince Ferdinand retired towards the heights behind the Rivers Ohm, and Lahn. Continued rain retarded his march to Grünburg, (Colonel Wintzingerode's *Chasseurs* were despatched to Laubach to cover the retreat of the artillery which was actually sticking in the mud), and, having raised the siege of Marburg, he crossed the Ohm September 11. The enemy harassed his rear, and took twelve or fourteen pontoons; the Hessian "Leib" Dragoons, led by Prince Ferdinand in person, exhibiting great bravery in covering the passage of the river. Lord Granby was unmolested, and the Allied Army formed with its right between Nieder-Klein and the Brücker-Mühl; its left near Schaffhoff; General Lückner encamped on the heights of Langstein; and General Hardenburg (late Hereditary Prince's Corps) at Hombourg (on the Ohm).

George III. inquired anxiously about the Hereditary Prince's wound, and desired Lord Granby to send frequent accounts of his condition. The Duke of Newcastle did the same, saying, "We talk of nothing here but Peace; the Duke of Bedford is gone to Paris to put the last hand to it."

Hans Stanley had been recalled when France put forward the Spanish claims, and the Duke of Bedford was the next envoy. France on her side sent to London the Duc de Nivernois, whom Chesterfield described as "an old friend of mine, and the most respectable man in France." The *duc* supplanted the large "*Kevenhüller*" hats, then in fashion, by a small one which was christened the "*Nivernois*" in his honour. (At Bath the Duc de Nivernois' very small hat adorned with a most splendid diamond button attracted much more attention than His Excellency did personally.—*Memoirs of R. L. Edgeworth*). He was so thin and small that Charles Townshend exclaimed the French had sent the preliminaries of a man to sign the Preliminaries of Peace. The English public seems to have been greatly taken up with the French envoy, and a Canterbury innkeeper is recorded to have been "boycotted," and eventually ruined, for having swindled Nivernois out of £35 15s. 8d. for one night's halt on his road from Dover.

England and France can scarcely be better described, as to their military and political attitude at this moment, than in the words of Jack Mostyn, he told the Duke of Newcastle:—

> The French are on one side ye Ohme, and we on ye other—our posts close to each other in many places; in short the two armies are near enough to shake hands and be friends if that be ye humour, or to go to loggerheads if that should be thought more eligible.

★★★★★★★★★★★★★★★★★★★

Leaving the armies wearily eyeing one another with a decided tendency towards friendliness which had grown out of long mutual familiarity with each other's close proximity, it is necessary to bestow a little notice upon the retired "Whig country gentleman" who had professed himself to be so happily rid of office. The Duke of Newcastle was in reality heartily sick of being "nobody." He rated people all round for not keeping him sufficiently informed upon political matters, and assured Lord Hardwicke that he was being urged to an Alliance, offensive and defensive, with Mr. Pitt; for "Lord Bute's Administration was riveted unless they did something." His Grace then scolded Lord Granby for the infrequency of his letters, declaring that he wanted to know no secrets, but merely the general trend of events, and how the commissariat trouble was resolving itself. Sir Joseph Yorke's turn came next; and, while stirring him up, Newcastle wrote—

> I have not had one word this age from my friend Granby. I shall tell him I suppose he thinks it high treason to correspond with anyone that has not the honour to be at Court.

Sir Joseph replied with his usual incisiveness—

> Your Grace knows Lord Granby too well to wonder at his not being a better correspondent. Whenever I hear him complained of, I always recollect his assuring us '*he would rather carry a letter 10 miles than write the direction*.' He has been likewise so constantly close to the enemy and hourly engaged that I really believe he has not had time for anything but fighting, in which he has done honour to his king, his country, his family, and himself; and will be loved and respected as long as he lives by both friends and enemies. (In forwarding Newcastle's letter to Granby Sir Joseph Yorke wrote: "You will see that he—the Duke of Newcastle—loves the crackle of the whip still."—*Rutland MSS.*, vol. ii.)

Lord Granby himself wrote that he should indeed be very unhappy to be suspected of any diminution of regard for the Duke of Newcastle, on account of the change in the latter's position:—

> As my friendship for Your Grace has not interest for its foundation, no alteration in your position can make any in my firm friendship for you. As to my not writing oftener, you know, my dear Lord, I hate it; and that from the moment I rejoined the army I have been fully employed. Two affairs within one week with the corps under my command is not being idle!

This was written after the Battle of Wilhelmsthal, and the affair with De Rochambeau on the heights of Homberg; and later Granby wrote again, from Nieder-Geiss at the time he was following Soubise's retreat from the Fulda, precisely bearing out Sir Joseph Yorke's letter. Granby related that he had scarcely halted since the date of his last letter, and concluded hurriedly with the words—

"I, am so near the enemy, and the alerts are so frequent that this moment, while I am finishing my letters, I hear the enemy is under arms, one of his camps being struck and a good deal of firing, on which I am just getting on horseback."

The *Newcastle Papers* record a conversation, between Lord Ligonier and the Duke of Newcastle, upon what might occur in the event of any disaster happening to Lord Granby; and rendered probable by the reckless way in which they heard he exposed himself to danger. Ligonier named General Mostyn as "the man the most esteemed, the most likely, and proper to command," which expression proves that Ligonier was not a party to the placing of General Conway before Mostyn at the moment Lord Granby's resignation was apprehended. Newcastle in consequence wrote, explaining that Lord Ligonier had evidently wished his hint should be conveyed to Granby:—

> He spoke of Your Lordship with the utmost affection and respect, but said that you exposed yourself like a Hussar; and that we could not spare you, and that you was not to be like Colonel Scheiter (commanding Scheither's carabiniers), who has got catched at last. As an old friend, servant, and well-wisher I could not forbear just repeating this to you, and adding that you ought to take proper care of yourself for the sake of the king, your country, and your friends.

Another conversation with "C. V." (Count Viri) persuaded Newcastle that Lord Bute was making great efforts to gain support in the House of Lords, and was reported to have "got" the Dukes of Kingston, Marlborough, and Portland.

Newcastle said:

> The Duke of Kingston, I am afraid, has been tampering with my friends the Manners, though I am persuaded without result. . . . The Duke of Rutland begins to be uneasy again in his Office, but he will do nothing without first consulting me.

Having cast this glimpse at the Duke of Newcastle's doings, at home, which soon expanded into more ambitious action, the scene on the River Ohm is resumed, and traced to its close.

****

Prince Soubise and Condé having succeeded in joining their armies, and reopening their communications with Frankfort, the final struggle consisted in the French Marshals' efforts to relieve the garrisons left behind them in Cassel and Ziegenhayn. Prince Ferdinand's supreme object was to prevent this by maintaining his position on the River Ohm, and frustrating all efforts of the French to circumvent him on either flank, by the Ohm, or the Lahn. Cassel was blockaded on all sides meanwhile by Prince Frederick of Brunswick.

★★★★★★★★★★

Count La Lippe Bückebourg left Germany in May, 1762, for England, after the declaration of war against Spain, and succeeded Lord Tyrawley in the command of the English and Portuguese troops. Lord George Lennox resigned his appointment in Germany, and volunteered for the same service. He became Colonel of the 25th Regiment.

★★★★★★★★★★

All the British cavalry and infantry piquets were posted in the Brücker-Holz to guard the celebrated bridge called the "Brücker-Mühl," in which name the subsequent slaughter was baptized; and the more distant bridges of the Ohm were all strongly held. The Castle of Amöneburg, on the French side of the Ohm, was garrisoned by a portion of the "British Legion" under Captain Krüse; and a redoubt on the same side, or the western extremity of the Brücker-Mühl, was held by a small detachment from General Hardenburg's Division.

On the 13th of September, 1762, this was the general position of the armies. The Main Allied Army lay with its right behind Kirchain (Prince Ferdinand's headquarters) and its left before Langstein; Lord Granby taking command, in addition to his own, of the principal portion of the corps lately led by the Hereditary Prince, occupied the posts of Schweinsburg and Hombourg. Granby's Division included—

2 battalions of British grenadiers.
3 " " Foot Guards.
1 " " Grenadiers of the Guards.
10 " " Hanoverian Infantry.
3 squadrons of Bland's.
3 " " Blues.
15 " " Hanoverian and Hessian Cavalry.
5 " " Prussian Hussars.
The *Chasseurs* of Colonels Freitag, and De Wintzingerode, and 32 cannon.

The French Army extended from Friedberg to Giessen, and Nieder Weimar, the Prince de Condé forming its left at Marburg on the Lahn; and a French detachment under M. de Lévis occupied the heights of Wetter, on the Allies' side of the Lahn, a post he succeeded in seizing when Prince Ferdinand was crossing the Ohm, about September 11. This last position, which Prince Condé had retained since his junction with Soubise, threatened the route *via* Franckenburg to Cassel; and Prince Ferdinand (September 18) moved his army in that direction, leaving Lord Granby to guard against any attempt of Prince Soubise to advance, by Granby's right, to support Lévis; or, by his left, to pass the Ohm.

General Conway and General Lückner made the attack on the Wetter heights upon which, after driving Lévis back over the Lahn, they remained encamped. The position, and nearness, of the enemy's left caused Prince Ferdinand to shift his headquarters to Wetter, and move the army by its right, so as better to cover the important route to Franckenburg; Lord Granby's division moved up to Kirchain, leaving Colonels Freitag and De Wintzingerode on his left to watch the Ohm at Hombourg, and Schweinsburg. The effect of this was immediately to encourage enterprise on the French right.

An expedition got across the Ohm and attacked the Allied bakery as it was moving from Alsfeld to Gemünden; Colonel Freitag beat back the French with the loss of some prisoners. A considerable body of French cavalry then made a more successful incursion, passing the Ohm near Hombourg, and driving back De Wintzingerode: Lord Granby had to render assistance before the enemy was finally repulsed.

The small earthwork at the "French" end of the Brücker-Mühl was captured by the enemy (September 17) together with a captain and 100 men of the Allied guard there; and, on the 18th, Lord Granby constructed a *flêche* on the low meadow ground at the end on the "Allied" side of the river, across which he had previously thrown an additional 200 men into the Castle of Amöneburg. This was done at Prince Ferdinand's request, the garrison there having been ineffectually summoned to surrender by Soubise, who then tried the effect of bribes upon Krüse, the *commandant*.

Ferdinand again moved his quarters from Wetter to Schönstadt; Granby remained encamped on the heights above Kirchain with the Brigade of Guards, Beckwith's Brigade, the Blues, and Bland's; and General Zastrow commanded the camp immediately facing the Brücker-Mühl, guarding the *flêche* at its extremity with 200 men.

Once more a lulling tendency towards peace and goodwill seemed to settle over the French and Allied camps; and towards awaiting for a while the issue of the siege of Cassel, or the settlement of the Preliminaries of Peace. Lord Granby, who had been ill with a recurrence of fever, received on September 20 a letter, or message, from Prince de Soubise, assuring him that the preliminaries were to be signed by the 25th, upon which event Soubise hoped soon to have the happiness of "embracing" His Lordship.

****

The alleged letter is alluded to both by Sir Joseph Yorke (Newcastle Papers October 1, 1762) and by Horace Walpole (*Letters*, October 4, 1762, to Rev. W. Cole), and a palpably unreliable copy of it is furnished in *Lloyd's Evening Post and British Chronicle* of October 13, 1762. The same newspaper (November 17, 1762) alludes to the *reported* letter having originated in a conversation between Prince Soubise and a British officer, who was a prisoner, and about to be exchanged for a French prisoner under the terms of *cartel*. Soubise in conversation with the former alluded to the improved prospect of peace, and expressed a hope of soon embracing the Marquess of Granby.

****

The prospect of a melodramatic embrace, *à la française*, cannot have conveyed much anticipative delight to so typical a Briton as Granby was; but the suggestion breathed pleasantly, at any rate, of peace: so, deferring to the doctor's advice, Granby took to his bed in his camp at Kirchain.

Between five and six, on the morning of the 21st of September, a startlingly sudden fire of small arms and cannon was opened by the French upon the redoubt at the Allies' side of the Brücker-Mühl. A thick fog masked the strength, position, and intention of the French attacking force; and Zastrow's guard replied with a hot fire, while guns loaded with grape and round-shot were trained to scour the bridge. This preliminary duel lasted till about 9 a.m., when the fog lifted and disclosed that the attack was also directed against the Castle of Amöneburg, and that a considerable force of the enemy, both cavalry and infantry, was formed on the skirt of the Hill of Amöneburg, just behind the mill which adjoined the French end of the bridge.

The Allied fire dispersed the cavalry, and momentarily staggered the Infantry; but a hollow lane leading from the mill to the bridge-end enabled the French to reinforce their redoubt unexposed to our guns, while there was no cover on the Allied side to protect from the enemy's grape-shot the reliefs which Zastrow marched at intervals from the Brücker-Holz to replace his 200 men behind his redoubt. Prince Ferdinand, warned by the cannonade, soon arrived from his distant quarters at Schönstadt, and the affair grew in intensity as both attack and defence became hourly more savage and obstinate. Zastrow's Division held their ground with magnificent steadiness; the 200 behind the redoubt being relieved about every half-hour, each detachment losing (according to De Mauvillon) nearly half its number in killed and wounded. (The total loss was strangely small if this phrase is accepted literally). General Waldegrave marched to Zastrow's assistance, and soon some 40 cannon on either side were concentrating their fire upon the rival ends of the bridge, at ranges varying from 500 to 200 yards. Our redoubt was some 50 yards from that of the enemy, and the mill.

Directly news of the seriousness of the attack reached Lord Granby he was quickly out of bed, and on horseback—fever or no fever; and, as he rode down from Kirchain, surely some odd thoughts must have crossed his mind concerning Soubise's dove-like letter, or message, exhaling embraces and peace.

★★★★★★★★★★

Lord Granby's letter to the Duke of Newcastle, after Brücker-Mühl, as usual so effaced himself that Newcastle actually thought he was in bed all the time, until undeceived by Thomas Thoroton who informed him that not only was Lord Granby present but "was most excessively exposed to the danger of that memorable cannonade."—*Newcastle Papers*, October 20, 1762.

Lord Ligonier wrote to Granby (*Rutland MSS.*, October 7, 1762): "I am to thank you for the remedies you have discovered for a fever; it has ever been unknown till your time, but now it is manifest, that if a man is ordered to his bed with this disorder, he has nothing more to do than jump out of it, get on his horse and fight away, and he is cured from that instant, . . . doctors differ, but my wish is that you would take care of your health, which is of so much consequence to your friends at all times, and to the king's service at this particular juncture."

★★★★★★★★★★

He arrived just as Zastrow's ammunition was approaching exhaustion, and the gallant Hanoverian general marched his division off to its quarters, having held the bridge for some eight hours.

The relief of Zastrow by Lord Granby with the Brigade of Foot Guards, Beckwith's Brigade of 2 battalions of "British grenadiers," 2 of Highlanders, and 4 battalions of Hessians, was the signal for a still fiercer fire from Soubise's redoubt, and the mill. The French artillery was reinforced, and 6 Hanoverian 12-pounders increased the fire on Granby's side. Some French magazines blew up, adding to the havoc and confusion; while, on our side the river, the Hessian Brigade, conscious that it was not the moment to indulge in sentiment, piled up the bodies of their dead comrades in their desperate need of repairing the diminishing redoubt.

The defence was continued in the same manner as before by frequent reliefs of 200 men. Seventeen battalions in turn held the redoubt from morning till evening; Lord Granby's Division maintained successfully the last fierce four hours of the defence; the Castle of Amöneburg held out; and, about 8 p.m., the French closed their attack, having succeeded in effecting no result except a most wholesale, and purposeless slaughter on both sides. M. de Castries was dangerously wounded. The loss was about equally distributed, and the total number killed amounted to 1,600—several officers of the Guards being among the 800 which this freak of Soubise's cost the Allied Army.

★★★★★★★★★★★

Edward Gibbon, writing (May 18, 1764) to John Baker Holroyd (Lord Sheffield) at De Mezery's celebrated *pension* at Lausanne said: "I heard likewise that your military list was augmented by a Hanoverian. I dare say the cannonading of Amöneburg has often been fought over."—*Letters of Edward Gibbon.*

★★★★★★★★★★

What Soubise's object was nobody divined; but the castle and town of Amöneburg were supposed to constitute the goal of his hopes, which supposition De Rochambeau confirms, stating that Soubise never expected to win the passage of the Ohm by the attack on the Brücker-Mühl. (Frederick the Great believed it was an attempt by Soubise to open the road to Cassel via Ziegenhayn.—*Œuvres de Fréderic le Grand*, t. v.) Marshal D'Estrées was understood to have had no hand in the attack, which, Lord Granby said, "was made without his (D'Estrées') knowledge, and that he was very much out of humour about it."

On the morning after, the 22nd, while Granby was visiting his outposts along the Ohm, he met Marshal D'Estrées, riding along the opposite bank, who exclaimed to him across the river, "*Milord, nous avous perdu bien des braves gens, de part et d'autre, tout inutilement hier!*"

Krüse surrendered the Castle of Amöneburg on the 22nd of September, and Prince Ferdinand was quite satisfied that he could not have held out a moment longer. The French strengthened the Mill, and constructed a "zig-zag" leading from it to the redoubt at the bridge-end; the Allies removed what remained of their old earthwork, and erected a strong redoubt in its place, flanked by *flèches* on the right and left. Prince Ferdinand removed his quarters to Kirchain, the general situation lapsing into its former condition of uncertainty. Granby wrote:

> We are in daily expectation of a cessation of arms, and in hourly of coming to blows with the enemy; I wish it were decided one way or the other.

M. de St.Victor created a little excitement by getting over the Ohm, and being chased back again by Colonel Freitag, after which M. de Poyanne stole across by Berggemünden with a convoy for the Ziegenhayn garrison. Lord Granby marched towards Alsfeldt with the Blues, Bland's, and Beckwith's Brigade to cut off this expedition by means of a concerted movement with Colonel Freitag, who failing to act quite in concert with Granby, the latter only succeeded in driving back a portion of Poyanne's Corps, part of which, with the convoy, reached Ziegenhayn. Granby returned to Kirchain September 28, and his quarters were shortly moved to Nieder-Klein. The commencement of October brought bad weather, and both the Allies and French proceeded to erect huts, and shelters for the cavalry horses. For twelve leagues round either camp foraging went on, leading to frequent skirmishes.

Between the 11th, and the 21st of October, battalions of infantry and 2 squadrons of cavalry were detached from the Allied Army to Prince Frederick of Brunswick before Cassel. Of these troops the only English regiment was the 23rd Welsh Fusiliers. The trenches were opened before Cassel on October 10; from the 17th to the 24th the garrison, which was reduced to the salted horseflesh which Comte de Broglie had stored as a final resource, (Archenholz), made sorties with varying success; on the 24th Prince Frederick unsuccessfully stormed the Reisburg redoubt, but carried it on the 29th.

Terms of capitulation were offered by General Diesbach, governor of the garrison, on October 31, which were accepted, and signed, November 1; whereupon the garrison, consisting of 10 battalions and 2 squadrons, marched out with the honours of war, and joined the Grand Army. After having been taken, and retaken, several times during the war, Cassel had been held by the French since July 31, 1700. Of the besieging force a portion left for the main Allied Army, and the remainder, including the Welsh Fusiliers, invested Ziegenhayn.

The Preliminaries of Peace were signed on November 3 at Fontainebleau, and news of the same reaching the French Army on the 7th, Soubise proposed to Prince Ferdinand a suspension of hostilities. Ferdinand had received no official intimation of the signature, so refused this proposal unless the French garrison evacuated Ziegenhayn, the position of which place in rear of the Allied Army menaced its march to winter quarters.

★★★★★★★★★★

Soubise's communications, after Brücker-Mühl, seem to have been regarded with suspicion. On the taking of Almeida, in Portugal, he wrote to assure Lord Granby that no apprehensions need be felt at the intended marching out of the French Army to fire a *feu de joie;* but this assurance prompted the issue of a general warning throughout the Allied Army.—*Entwurf des Lebens und der Thaten des Herrn Herzog's Ferdinand,* etc. Berlin, 1792.

★★★★★★★★★★

Soubise, on his side, refused; and the trenches were opened before Ziegenhayn on the 9th of November. By the 14th the mail arrived from England acquainting Prince Ferdinand of the conclusion of the Preliminaries. He and Lord Granby, attended by a brilliant staff of Hanoverian and English officers, rode down to the Ohm and requested an interview with Count de Guerchy; and at 2 p.m. on November 15, 1762, the Suspension of Hostilities was signed at the Brücker-Mühl, on the Ohm, by Ferdinand, Duke of Brunswick and Lünebourg, Marshal D'Es trees, and Marshal the Prince of Soubise.

For twenty-four hours the scene of the late butchery was transformed into one of the most genuine, uproarious happiness and excitement—both armies, French and Allied, trying to excel each other in civility, hospitality, and good-fellowship.

The French commenced their march homewards on the 16th of November; and the Allies on the 19th, to winter quarters in the bishoprics of Münster and Osnabrück, and along the frontiers of Holland.

According to the last returns the Allied Army was thus composed

The "Blues" (518), and the 3rd and 4th "Regiments of Horse" (347 each)	1212	
9 Regiments of Cavalry—viz. 1st Regiment of Dragoon Guards, 705; 2nd and 3rd ditto, each, 516; 1st, 2nd, 6th, 7th, 10th, and 11th Dragoons, each 516 (deducting 1206 for 9 Light troops of 134 each, discontinued)	3627	
1 Regiment, the 15th Light Dragoons (Elliot's)	718	
	——	5557
3 Battalions of Foot Guards (1st, 1063; 2nd, 1024; 3rd, 1024)	3111	
12 Regiments of Foot (5th, 8th, 11th, 12th, 20th, 23rd, 24th, 25th, 33rd, 37th, 50th, and 51st, each 1034)	12,408	
2 Regiments of Highlanders (87th and 88th, each 818) ...	1636	
	——	17,155
Total of the British Army, excluding Artillery and Pensioners		22,712

The Hanoverian, Hessian, Brunswick, Saxe-Gotha and Bückebourg troops, and the "British Legion" amounted to 69,061.

at the end of the war—*on paper.*

Of the British highest nominal total of 25,000 men serving in Germany, 16,000 returned home. Prince Ferdinand repaired to Neuhaus, and Lord Granby to Warburg. Against these two men with the Hereditary Prince, General Spörcken, Count Bückebourg, Lieut.-Generals Waldegrave, Mostyn, and, for a short time, Kingsley and Conway, together with an army strong in endurance and courage as it was weak in numbers, France, with an overwhelming force, had struggled in vain in order to loosen the grip of England upon the throat of the French colonial empire by conquering Hanover. With the exception of that small detached portion of Hanover lying around Göttingen, France not only did not succeed, but, at the date of the signing of the Preliminaries, her armies were swept out of Westphalia, Hanover, and Hesse back upon Frankfort, (Frankfort was not a conquest), and all her conquests retaken by the Allies with the exception of the small garrison of Ziegenhayn, which must inevitably have surrendered had the war continued a few days longer. Incredible as such a result appeared in 1757, France, with her illimitable resources, enormous army, and great Alliances, became the victim of a war which, in convulsing Europe, brought an extended sphere of dominion to Great Britain, alone, in all four quarters of the globe.

Hopes were expressed that future history would bestow upon the British troops, and their commanders, a meed of recognition adequate to their merits: if history has fulfilled these hopes their merits were indeed small. William Pitt's assertion that he won America on German battlefields is recorded distinctly enough; but how many among the modern reading public realise the full meaning of the words, any more than Pitt's public did at the date of their utterance? National pride—excusable perhaps—has not tended to expatiation upon successes which were won for us under a German commander-in-chief, in defence of the German King of England's German dominions which nobody cared twopence about; and Lord Granby, as second-in-command, has suffered proportionately in historical reputation, though his contemporaneous reputation was most brilliant, and universal.

"A Second in Service is never remembered, whether the honour of the victory be owing to him, or he killed:" so spake Horace Walpole in relation to General Conway's subordination to Lord Granby in the German War; yet Walpole, in spite of his dislike of Prince Ferdinand, and his implied sympathy with "seconds in service," never attributed a shred of the prince's success to Lord Granby's military capacity, which "the prince of letter-writers" did his utmost to deny, and with the most far-reaching consequences.

Of Pitt's own estimate of Granby's worth evidence will be afforded in subsequent pages; for the present the expression used by the great War Minister in relation to the German campaigns conveys all that is claimed here for the British commander-in-chief:

> Whoever feels for the honour of England, must think himself a debtor to the Marquess of Granby.

★★★★★★★★★★★★★★★★★★★

A gloom was thrown over the Allied Army, soon after the signing of the Preliminaries, by the desperate illness of the marquess, He was attacked by typhus fever at Warburg, and lay for weeks hovering between life and death, ignorant of the political turmoil at home, or of his brother's (Lord Robert Manners Sutton's) death, which events must be relegated to another chapter. The whole army awaited the issue with the deepest concern, attached as it was to Lord Granby by the truest affection. Alluding to the circumstance, a contemporary recorder wrote—

> Whatever could have been done to animate a soldiery, to make them cheerful in service, to alleviate the hardships of war, had been effected beyond what would be thought possible within the limits of a private fortune; and the satisfaction of a recipient always went beyond the actual benefit received, because in his greatest liberality it was evident Lord Granby wished he could do a thousand times more. By his whole conduct he inspired foreigners with a lofty idea of the English nobility. His character was, in fact, such as we, in romance, ascribe to our old English barons.

Prince Ferdinand addressed his farewell to the Allied Army from Neuhaus, and, deputing the command of the German troops to General Spörcken, repaired to Brunswick. His military career finished with the Peace of Paris, though he did not actually retire from the Prussian service until 1766; and then under a bitter sense of injustice suffered at Frederick the Great's hands. Ferdinand wrote to Lord Granby on this event—

> *J'ai résigne titres, emplois, et pensions entre ses mains. J'avais quelque droit à sa réconnoissance. Je n'ai trouvé qu'envie, mauvais traitement, aigreur, et toute sorte de mortifications pour mon salaire.*

Popular education, freemasonry, literature, and the fine arts absorbed the energies of this gallant and splendid soldier after the close of the German War, for his services in which he received from England a pension, in addition to the grants made to him during the campaigns, a Vote of Thanks from the House of Commons, and the Order of the Garter.

★★★★★★★★★★

Frederick the Great computed the total loss in this war at 888,000, of which 160,000 fell to the share of England and the German troops serving in her pay. In moralising upon the want of unanimity among the European powers, which led to this appalling sacrifice of life, Frederick wrote: "*. . . les exemples ne corrigent personne; les sottises des pères sont perdues pour leurs enfants; il faut que chaque génération fasse les sieunes.*"—Œuvres de Frédéric le Grand, t. v.

★★★★★★★★★★

Chapter 21

1762: Granby's illness

Before his illness became desperate Granby had received premonitions of the political storm which was about to burst over England. The Duke of Newcastle informed him that George Grenville neither approved the terms of peace, nor would undertake their defence in the House of Commons; consequently—

> . . . .the bold Mr. Fox is produced for that purpose, is called to the Cabinet Councils, and has the direction of the House of Commons, and the absolute disposals of all employments there.

Now, the bold Mr. Fox had long commanded the services, both in the Pay Office and in political business, of one whose name at this period came prominently forward—Mr. John Calcraft. The first step in this gentleman's career both Fox and the Marquess of Granby are alternately credited with having founded through the bestowal of a clerkship of £40 a year, from which sum, rather than upon it, Calcraft became "passing rich." He was said to be related to Fox, and his financial astuteness largely assisted the latter in rolling up the fortune which, as paymaster, he amassed. (Walpole speaks of "Fox's millions, and Calcraft's tythes of millions.")

Most self-made men acquire enemies, especially if they enter the political arena. Personal abuse is a telling weapon requiring no special skill on the part of the user; and, as material out of which to fashion it, obscurity of origin has ever been held in highest esteem. Calcraft's enemies brandished it freely. In addition, Walpole accused him of usury, and of trading in army promotion which came slowly to such as did not employ him.

An editorial note to Walpole's *Letters* traces these strictures to the circumstances of Fox having accepted office in 1754 from Walpole's *bêtes noires* the Pelhamites; after which date, he hated Fox, and his henchman Calcraft.

Through Fox's and Lord Granby's interest Calcraft obtained the agencies of many regiments, and gradually established a very large business as an Army Agent and Contractor, in which capacities he gained great popularity among the officers, his clients, on account of his liberal and friendly conduct towards them. Elsewhere it is asserted that Calcraft's probity, and punctuality, in all his pecuniary affairs were universally acknowledged; he was widely known, and entertained the leading political and literary men of his day, whilst noblemen of all shades of "party" opinion consulted him on their private affairs.

★★★★★★★★★★

> Even the person who has most to say against Calcraft records that he was known as "honest Jack Calcraft," but the authority is too palpably unreliable to be quoted to advantage on either side—*viz.* Mrs. George Anne Bellamy.

★★★★★★★★★★

With Lord Chatham he became, eventually, on terms of close political intimacy; but we shall see in due time how Walpole accounted for that circumstance.

These remarks concerning Mr. John Calcraft, of Ingres near Rochester, are pertinent owing to his having been the banker, and friend, of Lord Granby who frequently visited him; and Calcraft's name first became conspicuous during the heat and excitement which accompanied George III's struggle to free the Crown from the shackles of the great Whig families. That an event of such solemnity as a Treaty of Peace between France and England should have been constituted the peg upon which to hang that struggle, forms an instructive example of how national interests may be subordinated to party squabbles.

The Duke of Newcastle had been as busy as a bee in order to convert the Peace-terms into a petard for the hoisting of their author, Lord Bute; though no great while previously Newcastle had written to Sir Joseph Yorke: "Nothing but peace can save us, and in whatever way it is brought about I shall be very indifferent, provided the thing be done." George III. was fully aware of Newcastle's schemes, with the Duke of Devonshire and others, for frightening His Majesty with stringent opposition, and a wholesale resignation of Whig officials; and he met the plot considerably more than half way, with an energy which even dispensed with the ordinary courtesies of official etiquette.

The Duke of Devonshire, Lord Chamberlain, was summoned from Bath to attend a Council at which the final terms of peace were to be settled. His Grace replied that he begged the permission already accorded him to absent himself from the Councils might be maintained, as he could not "hold himself responsible for measures that he had no share in;" he also alluded to the desirability of his retirement. Shortly after he repaired to Court, and requested an audience with the king.

His Majesty, knowing the Duke of Devonshire had come to resign, determined as far as possible to forestall him by sending word through a *valet de chambre* refusing the audience; and, in reply to the Lord Chamberlain's question as to whom he should deliver his Staff, announced (also through the valet) that His Majesty would send him his orders. Not choosing to retain his staff for a moment after this pointed insult the Duke of Devonshire took it to Lord Egremont, (Secretary of State for the Southern Department), and desired him to give it to the king.

On either side the gauntlet was now irrevocably flung down. In excited haste the Duke of Newcastle hurried to London and begged the Duke of Rutland to fix an appointment at either Newcastle House, or Rutland House, in order to discuss the Devonshire episode and the general political outlook.

Both Pitt and Lord Hardwicke were adverse to the adoption of any vexatious, or factious, opposition to the king; Lord Hardwicke, holding that the time had not arrived for opposing Lord Bute's position as favourite, or sole minister, and that the present occasion was not a proper one. Pitt eventually opposed the Articles of Peace strenuously, but on what he held to be their demerits alone, and with no appeals to faction.

Newcastle nevertheless was bent upon the Duke of Rutland's resignation, and the reason of this selection is supplied by Newcastle himself in a "Memo, of a conversation" held with the Duke of Cumberland in which His Grace suggested that "some resignations might be beneficial." The Duke of Cumberland said he was no judge of the matter; but in the end Newcastle persuaded him that "*it might be right to have some resignations* of persons of high rank or of great distinction." (Lord Kinnoull told Newcastle that rumour attributed all the opposition to His Grace and the Duke of Cumberland—*Newcastle Papers,* December 26, 1762). The Duke of Rutland, Lord Powis, and the Lords of the Bedchamber were instanced as the most desirable for this purpose.

The Duke of Newcastle next applied himself to foster the first of these resignations by composing a most inflammatory letter to the

Marquess of Granby of which the first draft, in the duke's cabalistic handwriting, (Newcastle's handwriting was almost equivalent to a cypher code intelligible to himself, and his secretary, alone), and a fair copy, are among the Newcastle Papers, and the final letter among the *Rutland MSS.* It is of great length, but affords a most interesting account of the events following upon the Duke of Devonshire's resignation. Newcastle commenced by saying that Lord Granby—

> . . . . must know the uneasiness which had been expressed at the sole power lodged in one particular minister inexperienced in business in general and—as was universally thought, not yet sufficiently informed of the principles of our constitution. . . . . I shall say very little upon my own personal ill-treatment, in forcing me out of my office, setting up my own Board of Treasury against me, not allowing me the common power and credit belonging to my station cither in my particular office or in the general conduct of the affairs of the kingdom. The Duke of Devonshire, Lord Hardwicke, and myself were alone in Council for supporting the war in Germany and renewing an annual engagement with the King of Prussia.

The duke then passed to the Devonshire episode, of which Lord Granby was informed, describing how the king had since, with his own hand, struck the Duke of Devonshire's name out of the Council books. His brother, and brother-in-law, had in consequence resigned their offices; the king saying to Lord George Cavendish, when he tendered his staff, "that whosoever desired to quit his staff, the king did not desire he should keep it." The Marquess of Rockingham received the same reply on expressing a desire to resign his position of Lord of the Bedchamber. Other resignations were talked of, but the only one relating immediately to the Duke of Newcastle was that of Lord Lincoln which he believed would take place.

> I come now to what more immediately relates to your own family. . . . The whole town was full of it, and I believe Mr. Calcraft had declared it, that the Duke of Devonshire's Staff would be offered to the Duke of Rutland. After Court yesterday . . . the Duke of Rutland acquainted me that the king had sent for him and loaded him with compliments on his own and your account, and went through the substance of all the Articles of Peace which the king extolled mightily. . . . The king said, 'I have it now in my power to give you the first office in England

with respect to the rank, consequences, and employments depending upon it, and that is the Chamberlain's Staff.' The Duke of Rutland desired to remain where he was, and that he should do nothing till he saw his son, my Lord Granby, who was soon coming over. But His Majesty mistaking His Grace, said, 'My Lord the Chamberlain's Staff can't wait so long, and I desire you would bring me your answer tomorrow.'

The Duke of Rutland gave his reasons against accepting the Chamberlain's Staff, but, however, was this day to carry his answer, and as it will be a negative, I shall not be greatly surprised if they take the Master of the Horse from him, for I know they want it for the Duke of Marlborough.' ... As the Duke of Rutland declared both to Lord Egremont and to the king that he would do nothing till he heard from you, I took the liberty to beseech His Grace to explain his intention to the king, so that His Majesty might not think that that related to his acceptance of the Chamberlain's Office, but that, in declaring that he would do nothing till he saw you, the Duke of Rutland meant with regard to his continuance or not in his present office of Master of the Horse, and he promised me he would explain himself in that manner to the king. I hear that when one of the ministers was told that this violent measure might offend the nobility, he answered 'that it might have that effect with some few of the great Lords, but that in general it would strike terror.' What sort of comfort ought that to be to an administration in this country?

The present case is the first that has ever happened, and if some disapprobation is not shewed of it, in all probability these measures of terror will be pursued; and God knows where that will end. How can this disapprobation be shewed with the least inconvenience to the publick than by the resignation of some of the most considerable persons in this kingdom; that would strike terrors in the proper place, under the ministers who have given this advice, and prevent them from pursuing it, or put it out of their power to do it. And allow me to say, if this is a right measure for the public, and for the persons who shall think so; is there one man in this kingdom whose declaration, upon this occasion, would have more effect than the Duke of Rutland's? Who so natural as one allied so nearly in every respect, by blood, by the consequence and figure of their respective fami-

> lies, (*i.e.*, the Rutland and Devonshire families), united in the country, and always united in their sentiments and connections.

This tremendous letter Newcastle forwarded to the Hague, and enjoined Sir Joseph Yorke on no account to entrust it to any conveyance that was not positively safe.

While awaiting the result, Newcastle excitedly penned many missives to his friends—

> I hear that both friend and foe put the whole upon the Duke of Rutland's quitting, and His Grace has certainly left it with the king that he leaves that to be determined by Lord Granby. . . . That devilish Fox and Calcraft get in everywhere. The duke (of Devonshire) apprehends Calcraft will do great hurt with Granby.

With the usual tendency of sanguine partisans Newcastle stated what he *wished* as being already accomplished facts. He "gathered" from Lord Robert Sutton, Lord George Manners, Thoroton, and the Duke of Rutland, that they all felt sure Lord Granby "would show great resentment," and act upon this occasion as Newcastle wished him to do; though, in truth, they pledged themselves to absolutely nothing save to await Granby's arrival. A fresh fear seized upon His Grace that Granby was to be waylaid on his journey and entrapped into some pledge, so he decided on waylaying the Marquess himself.

The Duke of Rutland offered no objection whatever to the plan, and recommended, through Thoroton, that a letter should be entrusted to some friend at Harwich for delivery to Lord Granby on landing, desiring him, however waylaid, to give no promise, or answer, to anyone until he had seen his father. Still further uneasiness arose for Newcastle, on the receipt of a letter from Granby himself, which was not in reply to Newcastle's manifesto of November 5, but which showed that Granby was already aware of the events therein dealt with. Granby wrote:

> I am most sincerely sorry for this most disagreeable business about the Duke of Devonshire, and then—(he dropped the subject abruptly, as he invariably did allusions to party disputes! Granby continued)—I have been confined to my bed these 5 days by an attack of fever; this is the first day of my getting up, and I am taking bark.
>
> Our troops march the 19th for Münster and I hope I shall not

be left behind: this unlucky fever will prevent my being in England so soon as I intended; if it does not return, I shall arrive the first week in December. I am not certain if I shan't strike from Münster to Calais to avoid the long passage, which I should dread after my present disorder. The Hereditary Prince's wound is nearly closed.

Here was a state of affairs! Newcastle was declaring that Granby was "showing great resentment," was "extremely provoked" and "dissatisfied," and Granby personally dismissed the subject in a sentence as bald as his own head. His letter, however, answered one purpose, and that was to suggest that he might not travel *via* Harwich where Newcastle's second manifesto was awaiting him; so, His Grace indited a third, which he despatched to Dover. In it, after the usual preamble of flattery, he went on to say that Lord Lincoln, Lord Ashburnham, and Lord Kinnoull had resigned.

I have great reason to think the greatest offers will now be made to Your Lordship when the ministers are sensible how much they want you. I remember the great reason you had to complain of the neglect shewed you this last winter when for 3 months not one word was said to Your Lordship of the troops under your command, or indeed any one thing done that you reasonably recommended for the officers under your command. I have the satisfaction to know that I have endeavoured, and I thank God I have succeeded, to show the affection which I have and shall ever have, my dear Lord, for you; I have all the reason in the world to be thankful to you for your goodness and marks of affection you have always shewed me.

I am truly sensible of them. I know there are certain persons now upon the road to endeavour to surprise you. I am sure that this is impossible, and may I entreat you, my dearest Lord, to take no resolution till you have seen your best friends, and I have the honour to lay before you the state of the present question in the manner it appears to me. Forgive me, my dear Lord; a real concern for Your Lordship, your honour, your credit, and reputation, and to secure to you the continuance of the highest character that any man of your age ever had, has induced me to take this freedom with you.... Pray send me word the moment you come to London.

It is scarcely necessary to point out that in all these letters (as in a mass of others not here quoted) the real issue upon which the Marquess of Granby was coming home to vote, viz. Peace or War, was barely mentioned even. His "honour," "credit," "reputation," and "high character" were to be dependent upon his voting with a particular clique among the old, place-holding Whigs, and thus securing the reinstatement of His Grace of Newcastle in power.

But Newcastle protested too much. His very anxiety proclaimed the inward conviction that Granby would support the Peace; and, conscious of his own schemes to gain so important a vote, Newcastle commenced to attribute schemes elsewhere.

> I hear they intend to offer him the Ordnance, and to point out to him the Command of the Army. The opinion of all his friends and I think I may say of his father, his brother, and Mr. Thoroton is that he will act as I should wish him to do upon this occasion. But the means that your good friend Mr. Fox has of getting at everybody, and, by his friend Calcraft, insinuating everything that can do mischief is such that the duke (of Cumberland) fears the effect of it in this case...They talk confidently about the Duke of Rutland and my Lord Granby. I cannot believe it till I see it. My Lord Bute has certainly sent for the Duke of Marlborough to town, and it is thought upon the supposition that the Duke of Rutland at 65 years of age will take the Chamberlain's Staff"

Something trenching closely upon the lie direct is given to a portion of the above letter of Newcastle's by another of his, proving that Granby's relations pledged themselves to nothing. It is addressed to the marquess, and says—

> Lord George (Manners) was so good as to call upon me this morning, and to express himself, as he has always done, with the greatest goodness, and friendship towards me; *but, my dear Granby, your whole family will, as they ought, take your advice.* I can only add that the eyes of the whole kingdom, both friends and foes, are upon the part you shall take. I have the greatest confidence and dependence upon the continuance of your friendship and partiality for your affectionate friend.

The *denouement* of the situation as regards the Duke of Newcastle must have mortified him terribly. It was scarcely even dramatic, though it might have attained to the broadest farce but for one circumstance. The fever which Lord Granby mentioned had recurred; he had been lying most dangerously ill; and, while Newcastle had been asserting what the marquess "felt," thought," and declared," poor Granby had not even been able to read the manifesto of the 5th of November which was said to have so incensed him.

On the 12th of December the Rev. Bennet Storer wrote to the Duke of Newcastle—

> By Lord Granby's order of this day I have the honour of acknowledging the favour of Your Grace's letter of the 5th of last month which his Lordship received when he was so ill in bed as not to be able to read it: the same reason has unhappily remained ever since which Lord Granby hopes will be a sufficient excuse for his silence. Indeed, I am sorry to acquaint Your Grace that Lord Granby has been confined to his bed for near this month and of late has been in a very dangerous situation; but I have the honour and happiness to assure Your Grace that yesterday things took a more favourable turn, and last night Lord Granby slept very well.

On the same, first, day of his apparent convalescence Lord Granby called Storer, and said:

> Storer, write Thoroton that I love my friend the Duke of Newcastle, but I could wish to remain quiet in the present bustle.

During this interval of his illness Granby received the Vote of Thanks of the House of Commons, and the proposed Articles of Peace, which were read to him; but two days later he again relapsed into a still more critical condition, and consequent silence.

★★★★★★★★★★

> "That the thanks of this House be given to the Marquess of Granby for the great and important services he has performed to his king and his country during the several campaigns in which he has commanded the British troops in Germany, and that Mr. Speaker do signify the same to him."—*Parliamentary History*; and *Rutland MSS.* vol. ii.

★★★★★★★★★★

It is not plain which General Lord Granby originally intended to receive the honour of bringing home the Army, but it was certainly not Conway who had already started before Granby's first attack had shown itself to be formidable. Conway had reached Brussels when he received a request from Granby to return immediately to the army, which of course Conway did; but even so simple a circumstance as this was twisted by Walpole to suit his "history," of which hereafter.

Colonel "Ned "Harvey also relinquished his permission to leave, for which Storer, on Granby's behalf, thanked him warmly, saying:

> The troops are just now, from His Lordship's illness and from all the generals having left except General Howard, in a most perplexed situation.

Upon Conway's return to headquarters at Münster he assumed command of the British troops.

In this position matters rested: while to the additional distress of the Duke of Rutland and his family. Lord Robert Manners Sutton, after a brief illness, had died at Rutland House, November 21, 1762. (He was succeeded in his seat in Parliament for Nottinghamshire by Mr. Willoughby, and in the Colonelcy of the 21st Light Dragoons by the Lieut.-Colonel, Russel Manners). Innumerable letters of condolence passed, coupled with anxious inquiries for news from Warburg, and copies of all the letters received from thence at Rutland House Thoroton despatched to Newcastle House. Lord Granby was several times rumoured to be dead, but on December 19 his physician, Mr. Burlton, (P. Burlton, Inspector of Regimental Infirmaries), informed Thoroton that Lord Granby had been somewhat benefited by "Dr. James' Fever powders," which had brought out a series of miliary eruptions.

But the issue was still regarded as grave in the extreme. The doctors forbade Lord Granby's being told of Lord Robert's illness and death, and letters show that his own recovery was for a time despaired of. "The event is still uncertain. God grant that the next mail may remove our apprehensions for so valuable a life," wrote Valence Jones; and, Lady Katherine Pelham: "Yesterday's letters gave me some little hopes of poor Lord Granby, but I do not build too much upon them." The Duke of Newcastle—

> . . . .feared everything for my dear friend Lord Granby. Such frequent returns of these milliary eruptions give me the greatest apprehensions. I am glad they have given him James' powders: they often do good. . . . I beg my most respectful compliments to the poor Duke of Rutland, I feel for him from the bottom of my heart as well as for Lord George, and you all."

Dr. Robert Knox, who also attended Lord Granby, at last announced the possibility of recovery from "one of the most dangerous, tedious, and irregular fevers he ever remembered, and which had been borne with a firmness and composure scarce to be paralleled."

★★★★★★★★★★

A quarter of a century later Dr. R. Knox attended the "beautiful Duchess" of Rutland to Scarborough. He wrote to her husband, Charles, fourth Duke: "She is as beautiful as an angel which, as an old *Medicus*, I dare tell Your Grace."—*Rutland MSS.*, vol. iii.

★★★★★★★★★★

The Rev. Bennet Storer, after some faintly expressed hopes, grew more confident—

> Lord Granby, God be praised, continues mending. His Lordship yesterday morning ate two large slices of bread and butter with his chocolate and afterwards the same quantity with his tea. I have made his breakfast this morning, and I have the pleasure to say His Lordship's appetite was as good as yesterday. All this looks well and I flatter myself we may have the satisfaction of producing His Lordship to you safe and sound some time in February.

The Duke of Newcastle began to have hopes, and with their revival came fresh schemes. He pointed out how careless of self Lord Granby was known to be, and the desirability of his journey home being supervised by a trustworthy person. Could Thoroton be spared by the Duke of Rutland, Newcastle named him as "the properest man" for the purpose; but this ingenious plan for ensuring the safe delivery of Newcastle's letters fell through. Lord Granby was considered to be quite safe in Storer's care, and, so soon as he should land, Thoroton was to meet him with "a warm and commodious post-chaise."

One more return of the fever occurred, but of a much slighter nature: it sufficed to damp everybody's reviving spirits, and the Duke of Newcastle, under so much strain, and the irritation of being dismissed by the king from the Lieutenancies of Middlesex, Nottinghamshire, and Sussex, fell ill himself. After the manner of their day, the doctors gave him several emetics, balanced by drastic purges, and then bled him like a pig.

★★★★★★★★★★

The annals of eighteenth-century "bleeding" contain much that is now irresistibly humorous. An old family account-book contains a recurring item of 7s. 6d. "for bleeding the dogs." A note-book of General Kingsley's contains some maxims upon the subject of shipping cavalry horses. The gallant general recommends that the horses should be bled before embarkation, and again after disembarkation before commencing the march to the seat of war. (The note-book is in the possession of the family of the late Charles Kingsley.) The Bath Journal of April 20, 1772, contains the following:—

"On Sunday night as the Exeter stage was going out of town the driver getting off the box at Hyde Park Corner to take in a passenger, the horses took fright and ran away with the coach, which went over the coachman, and continued running with great speed to Knightsbridge, where the coach was overturned into a ditch. None of the passengers were materially hurt, but they were carried into the Duke of Rutland's house, and some of them, by way of precaution, were bled. The coach was broke and could not proceed any farther."

★★★★★★★★★★

Newcastle declared himself much better for this treatment, and as he was then seventy years of age, he had every right to know what agreed with his constitution.

The Warburg bulletins once more improved; and at the king's *levée* the best news circulated was the recovery of the infant Prince of Wales, who had also been unwell, and the Bishop of Llandaff's (Dr. Ewer) assurance that he had just read, at Rutland House, comfortable accounts of Lord Granby. Bennet Storer next enclosed Dr. Knox's announcement that the danger was over, and that in eight or ten days Granby would be able to take an airing, and perhaps to begin his journey.

Storer said:

> What a happy change, Blessed be God, from our late most melancholy and most distressed situation. His Lordship yesterday and today dined heartily upon tripe and chicken, drank his four glasses of claret, and found himself much the better for it!

After carefully leading up to the subject Storer, with the doctor's permission, acquainted Lord Granby with his brother's death, which most deeply affected him, they having been devotedly attached to one another. It only remained now for his lordship to gain strength to travel; and the prospect of his arrival once more revived the excitement concerning the course he should adopt in Parliament.

Chapter 22

1763: Granby Leaves the Army

On January 4, 1763, Sir Joseph Yorke addressed his congratulations to Lord Granby on his recovery, saying that the Prince of Orange, and Duke Lewis of Brunswick, both charged him to make their best compliments, and express their joy on the happy event. A severe frost at the Hague prevented the packets from getting in or out, so Sir Joseph strongly advised Granby to adopt the Brussels and Calais route.

George III. insisted, in spite of difficulties raised by the Dutch authorities, that the British troops should march homewards through Holland, and embark at Wilhelmstadt. It was characteristic of Lord Granby that in the midst of his terrible illness he bethought himself of asking the king to sanction an allowance of twopence a day, per man, to enable the troops to purchase small luxuries during their weary march. The king consented, but it is by no means sure the troops benefited by Granby's kindly forethought; for no sooner had Lord Ligonier conveyed the king's assent, than a second despatch announced that "E. Weston" begged to inform "Lord Ligonier" that "Lord Halifax" had applied to "the Earl of Bute" concerning "Lord Granby's" recommendation; and the reply was that nothing could be done without a "Board of Treasury!" Amidst such a tangle of red tape it would be rash to assert that Tommy Atkins ever got his daily twopenny worth of luxury.

The 12th of January, 1763, was Granby's last day at Warburg, and he dated from thence his acknowledgement to Sir John Cust, the Speaker, of the Vote of Thanks passed by the Commons:—

> Sir,—The honour of your letter of the 3rd of last month was not delivered to me till a few days since, the Physicians who attended me in my illness having forbid any letters being given to me in the situation my health then was: this I hope will plead

my excuse for your not having received an immediate answer. Though I cannot, Sir, be vain enough to think any services I may have done my country can have merited so high a reward as the thanks of the honourable House, yet it was with the utmost satisfaction I received them. I shall beg to look upon them as a mark of their approbation of my conduct arising, I hope, from their persuasion of my having always zealously promoted the service in which His Majesty has done me the honour to employ me, and of my having constantly endeavoured, to the best of my abilities, punctually to execute the wise and able orders I received.

I must beg. Sir, that you will, when proper, return the House my most sincere and grateful thanks for this great honour upon me, which I shall always with the utmost gratitude remember. The best return I can make will be a perpetual attention to the interests of my king and country. Give me leave, Sir, at the same time to return you my particular thanks for the obliging manner in which you communicated to me this high honour, and believe me, *&c., &c., &c.,*

Granby.

On the 13th of January he started, accompanied by the Rev. Bennet Storer, Cornet George Manners of the Blues, and servants, among whom was John Nötzel, the hussar. Paderborn was the first stopping-place, from whence they proceeded to Münster, and there halted for three days' rest, and to transact military business with General Conway respecting the march of the troops, and the disbanding of the *Légion Britannique.* A considerable portion of the latter, commanded by Colonel Beckwith, accepted service under Frederick the Great.

★★★★★★★★★★

Frederick the Great said the sole good Lord Bute's Peace did to Prussia was that it "broke" all the Light—*i.e.*, irregular, troops; and the *Légion Britannique,* Bauer's Dragoons, and the Brunswick Volunteers, to the number of about 6,000, entered Frederick's service. He sent them to Cleves, which alarmed both France, Austria, and England. Lord Bute, in consequence of fears expressed by Hanover of bad faith on Frederick's part, ordered the garrison to be doubled in Münster, and forbade the entrance of any Prussian troops into that town. Frederick declared his sole object was to attempt to regain possession of Wesel-on-the-Rhine.—*Œuvres de Frederic le Grand, t. v.*

★★★★★★★★★★

Before resuming his journey Lord Granby addressed his farewell to the British troops as follows:—

> Münster, Jan. 21st, 1763.
>
> Lord Granby has hoped to have had it in his power to have seen and taken leave of the troops, before their embarcation for England; but a severe illness having detained him at Warburg, and his present state of health obliging him to take another route, he could not leave this country without this public testimony of his entire approbation of their conduct since he has had the honour of commanding them.
>
> These sentiments naturally call for his utmost acknowledgements. He therefore returns his warmest thanks to the generals, officers, and private men composing the whole British Corps for the bravery, zeal, discipline, and good conduct he has constantly experienced from every individual: and his most particular and personal thanks are due to them for their ready obedience, upon all occasions, to such orders as his station obliged him to give.
>
> His best endeavours have always been directed to their good, by every means in his power; and he has the satisfaction to think he has some reason to flatter himself of their being convinced, if not of the efficacy, at least of the sincerity of his intentions, if he may judge by the noble return their behaviour has made him; a behaviour that, while it fills him with gratitude, endeared them to their king and country, and has covered them with glory and honour. Highly sensible of their merit he shall continue, while he lives, to look upon it as much his duty as it will for ever be his inclination to give them every possible proof of his affection and esteem, which he should be happy to make as apparent as their valour has been, and will be, conspicuous, and exemplary to after ages.

Granby was next heard of at Arnheim, on the Dutch frontier, where he halted for two days; and letters dated thence enabled Thoroton to inform the Duke of Newcastle that Lord Granby was making "short day's journies in his coach with occasional rests:" "travailing agreed extreamly well with him, he visible grew better and better every day, his strength increased very fast, and he was in very high spirits." Stoppages at Brussels, Lille, and Calais were to be made, and so soon as the last place was reached Thoroton was to start for Dover.

Bustle once more permeated the "Opposition" camp at this news, and letters prove that Pitt, in bis determination to keep clear of faction, was veiling his intentions as completely from his admirers, and would-be supporters, as from his political opponents. Newcastle hoped that the first week of February might produce some alteration, and "determine the material men in the House of Commons. . .. I mean Mr. Pitt, Lord Granby, who is expected every hour, Lord Royston, Mr. Legge, Sir George Savile, etc.;" and the Duke of Devonshire counselled "giving the Yorke family no chance" of hesitation as they seemed unsteady, but the duke thought "Pitt was safe." Newcastle then resumed his schemes: "the great card for the publick and ourselves is my Lord Granby," he wrote, and industriously set about contriving that someone should see the great card before he went to Court after his arrival. Lord Lincoln was named for this duty, but could not be implicitly depended on—

Newcastle declared:

> . . . the only person, who can do anything is my Lady Katherine Pelham. She knows as well as I do how to talk to him. These cruelties and barbarities to me and to all my friends I think will make a great impression on him.

The duke wrote a final appeal, which Thoroton was to take with him to Dover, commencing with the usual preamble of flattery, and passing to abuse of Lord Bute and Fox:—

> Your Lordship is so good-natured that, independent of the affront and indignity put upon me, such as I believe never was known in any civilized nation, I am sure your heart would bleed if you knew the distresses that many honest men are thrown into by these unheard-of practises.

Why the peace of Europe was to be postponed because Newcastle was "affronted," and many honest men thrown into distress, His Grace still failed to explain; or to be persuaded that he was mainly responsible for the whole of George III.'s relentless treatment of the Pelhamites, and their dependents.

Suddenly, at ten o'clock at night, February 6, one of Lord Granby's servants reached Rutland House to announce His Lordship's arrival at Dover, by the *Hanover* packet-boat, that day at noon. Thoroton forwarded this news at once to Newcastle House, saying he should start very early next morning to meet Granby, ". . . he purposes dining tomorrow at Mr. Calcraft's on his way to town." Newcastle and Lord Lincoln were scared at this news, and mutually exclaimed they "did not at all like the dining place," though a more natural one than an old friend's country house on the Dover road, for Granby (who was still limited to short stages) to have chosen, they would have been puzzled to select. He arrived at Rutland House, and waited on the king on the 10th of February, being most graciously received by His Majesty in an audience of unusual length. (Lord Granby left a sum of money for the poor at every place he stopped at on his journey home.—*British Chronicle,* February 14, 1763; *Royal Westminster Journal,* 19, 1763).

In what manner the fact was made known that Granby intended voting for the Peace does not appear, but it was apparently ascertained directly after Court was over on the 10th. His decision must have deprived the Duke of Newcastle of all hope of office, and added much to his fears concerning a motion proposed in the Commons by Sir J. Phillips, suggesting a committee to inquire into the present debt and expenditure of the country, and into the cost of the late war as compared with the wars of Queen Anne.

The blustering Mr. Alderman Beckford seconded this motion, stating his conviction that, by continuing the war, we might have lessened the public debt by a glorious peace instead of the infamous one proposed—a peace, in his opinion, more infamous than that of Utrecht.

Although the Duke of Newcastle was at one with the framers of this motion on the Peace question, it embodied an attack upon him and the Treasury, concerning the cost of the war, which he had long dreaded, and suspected Pitt of fostering. Several members spoke in the duke's defence: Fox did not oppose the appointment of the committee, but suggested that such matters were best adjourned until after the signature of the definitive Peace.

The Marquess of Granby then rose and warmly defended the Duke of Newcastle's integrity, saying that he could not help assuring the House that the utmost care and attention had been paid by the duke to every branch of economy in the war, the expense of which was due to the nature of that war. Speaking in general terms, the cost had been unavoidable, but whatever faults had been committed lay at the door of inferior officials abroad. The person who watched the debate for Newcastle said: "On the whole, it was a very agreeable day for Your Grace's friends."

This episode afforded Newcastle some comfort, and proved Granby's personal friendship for him to be as strong as ever, in spite of their wide divergence on the great question of the hour. The terms of the Peace of Paris were approved by the House of Lords without a division, and by the Commons by 319 votes to 65—Lord Granby and his family voting with the majority.

In a speech which is historical Mr. Pitt vehemently opposed the terms, though without associating himself with any faction of the minority. But he would have approved nothing, scarcely, which fell short of demolishing the Bourbon House; of depriving France of her last colonial possession; or of rendering impossible the re-establishment of her fleet; and the English public, delirious with loot and conquest, was with him.

It was urged that all that England demanded by the Peace was, before its signature, already hers; and that she deserved more than mere force of arms had acquired. *Soit*,—but does history leave no doubts as to France submitting to annihilation, or to such being permitted by onlooking nations whose sympathies are to the full as fickle, and as quickly swayed, as those of the ragged spectators of a gutter-fight? Before very long England stood friendless in Europe. While agreeing that England, like Oliver Twist, might have "asked for more," Macaulay and Lecky both describe the Peace of Paris as honourable and advantageous to us as a nation; and Lecky probably affords the real solution of the controversy in saying that the Peace would have been popular had it been made by other men.

The Peace of Paris was signed in February, 1763, and was ratified, in France, in March following. The arrival of the king's messenger with the news of the ratification was the signal for salutes fired at the Tower and the parks; and a Day of Thanksgiving was celebrated. May 5, throughout the country.

The above record of Lord Granby's conduct respecting the termination of the Seven Years' War is derived from such documents as have presented themselves in the course of a not inconsiderable search. Those, however, who know their Walpole will not need reminding that the occasion was the first which he adopted for an open attack on Granby's integrity. Hitherto Granby had merely been "a young man of no capacity," and "the Mob's Hero;" now his importance, and commanding influence, demanded a more definite form of detraction.

History permits of no doubt that the Court, mainly through Fox, practised the most wholesale bribery to ensure a majority on the division which was to decide, primarily, whether George III. or the "old" Whig party was to govern; and, quite secondarily, whether England

and France should continue a devastating struggle of which most were tired, and some even ashamed. Seizing this useful fact Walpole wrote:

> Whoever they could not bribe they concluded would not approve their Treaty.

And from this proposition he gives us no option of any deduction whatsoever, save the illogical one that every member of the majority *was* bribed. Out of the 319 members of the House of Commons forming the majority, not one voted according to his conscience! Accordingly, Lord Granby was bribed. The War, the Brunswick Princes, Mr. Pitt, and Lord Granby had been throughout derided and ridiculed by Walpole, and he longed for peace after General Conway's departure for Germany. But, so soon as peace became a party question, that inordinate love of faction, to which Walpole in a rare fit of frankness pleaded guilty, possessed him, and he tore up reputations like so much waste paper. (In his exceedingly flattering character of himself in *Memoirs of the Reign of George III.*)

Before Lord Granby's arrival, Walpole alluded to the impatience with which he was expected: "it is not yet certain what part he will take, and with his unbounded popularity it cannot be indifferent." Walpole added that "the most tempting honours" had been offered to Lord Granby. As to Conway, he—

> . . . .stayed in Germany to conduct home the troops. . . . I am particularly glad that he does so, for it is not every man who has resolution enough to meddle so little in affairs as I do.

This of Conway, which should be specially marked, does not suggest much confidence (on Walpole's part) in his invulnerability to temptation. The above remarks were passed while these events were in actual progress, and a fuller relation is given in Walpole's *Memoirs*, written some time afterwards, in which he adapted events to suit his own prejudices, and with a courageous disregard of dates, and facts.

> Lord Granby was waylaid on his return from the army and offered the ordnance and command of the army, setting aside the worthy old Marshal Ligonier, a bait gulped by the former without scruple. . . . Mr. Conway, to whom they did the honour of thinking they could not bribe him (and whoever they could not bribe they concluded would not approve their Treaty), was decorated with the empty honour of conducting home the army which would, and did, prevent his return before the dis-

cussion of the Preliminaries in Parliament.

It is unfortunate for the above story that we should know that Conway had already left the army in November, 1762; that he was with great difficulty, and only with Sir Joseph Yorke's assistance, overtaken at Brussels and requested to return to headquarters solely on account of Lord Granby's dangerous illness. The king's instructions, conveyed through Lord Ligonier, merely stipulated that two general officers should remain to take charge of the troops after Lord Granby's departure, but no two were specially indicated. It was therefore a matter of pure chance that the honour of bringing home the troops fell to General Conway, and one that his short service in no way entitled him to, and which would more fitly have fallen to the lot of either Mostyn, or Waldegrave.

Nevertheless, the statement made by Walpole has been copied, and recopied, by historical and biographical writers, to prove that Conway was muzzled, because known to be so immaculate and unbribeable; and that Lord Granby was waylaid with all kinds of dazzling offers for which he freely bartered his vote. Now, it is extremely curious that although the "waylaying" on the part of the Opposition, whose cause Walpole espoused, is traceable in minutest detail among the Duke of Newcastle's correspondence, there appears to be no evidence of Fox's emissaries, whose employment Newcastle merely suspected, but Walpole downright asserts.

The only communication, forthcoming, addressed by Mr. Fox to the Marquess of Granby at this date, is among the *Rutland MSS.* It is so utterly bare of suggestion, and interest, as to render superfluous here an exact copy of Fox's coy deprecation of being called "from a retirement which was most happy "to be a Cabinet Councillor and Minister, and begging the assistance of Lord Granby and his friends "to support the honest views of His Majesty, and that dignity of the Crown which every good subject must think it his duty to maintain." Nor is there a trace of any more attention having been paid by Lord Granby to this mild, conventional petition than to Newcastle's impassioned appeals.

Next, as to the alleged rewards "gulped" by Lord Granby the moment he set foot on shore at Dover, the dates and order of their offering (kindly corroborated in some instances by Walpole himself) will form part of the ensuing chapter. Suffice it to say that Granby did not receive the Command-in-Chief of the Army at this period at all. The reward which he did eventually accept was about the least, and the only one, which the king could have conferred upon a general who had seen nearly five years of continual active service, during four of which he had held the German Command with unvarying credit to himself, and honour and success to the troops he commanded. (The journals of the day spoke of considerably more important honours for Lord Granby; such as Field-Marshal, Commander-in-Chief in South Britain, or Master of the Horse.—*Lloyd's Evening Post*).

Walpole's insinuation, or rather assertion, that the Marquess of Granby sold his conscience for the Master Generalship of the Ordnance is as baseless as it is base. Granby hated languid war, and his individual desire for peace had been openly expressed again and again, as well as his mortification at the limited nature of the warfare to which Prince Ferdinand and himself were constrained.

★★★★★★★★★★

> "If there be any truth established by the universal experience of nations, it is this, that to carry the spirit of peace into war is a weak and cruel policy. . . . Languid war can do nothing which negotiation or submission will not do better: and to act on any other principle is, not to save blood and money, but to squander them."—*Macaulay, Essay on Hallam's Constitutional History.*

★★★★★★★★★★

He had, with equal consistency, during his winter leave (1761-2) studiously avoided all home controversy turning upon the questions of Peace and War (beyond stating what measures were imperative if the war were prolonged) because, already, they had become degraded into party issues. Once, however, Cassel was re-won, and the Preliminaries were signed, Lord Granby's course became fixed, and never wavered. His very arrival in London would appear to have been timed to occur at the eleventh hour for the avoidance of tiresome, because useless, personal appeals on either side. To Mr. George Grenville, he expressed himself with unmistakable emphasis on the subject of the Peace, saying—

> The Duke of Newcastle is my old friend; but His Grace shall never lead me into measures which I totally disapprove, and condemn!

Granby "totally disapproved and condemned" the opposition to the Peace of Paris; and his vote thereupon was, like all his actions, straightforward, spontaneous, and as honest as the day.

Chapter 23

1763: The Army Returns

The Peace of Paris was soon followed by Frederick the Great's separate Peace of Hubertsburg, and his extremely profitable friendship with England was succeeded by a bitter, undying hatred of her. Who was right and who wrong, as between England and Prussia, has scarcely been proved to the modern satisfaction of all parties, and the controversy is irrelevant here; but Frederick was the last man qualified to complain about "perfidy" towards allies. Frederick's hatred of England for the part she played, under the Earl of Bute, descended as a heritage to Prussia where, according to some interesting letters printed in the *Times* newspaper, it has remained a smouldering tradition ever since.

★★★★★★★★★★

January 7, etc., 1896, on the occasion of the outburst of ill-feeling between Germany and England concerning "Jameson's Raid." The experience of a year's residence, during 1869-70, in the neighbourhood of the River Lahn, upon, and near, which many of Prince Ferdinand's operations took place, corroborates the writer of those letters. Among the commonality of the inhabitants, the class in which prejudice lingers most obstinately, England and Englishmen were unmistakably unpopular. The words "*Engländer!*" and "*Stumpfschwanz*" (not infrequently emphasized by stones) were contemptuously shouted after British strangers. The term "*Stumpfschwanz*," *i.e.*, "bob-tail," was used in reference to our supposed national practice of closely docking our horses' tails. This has every appearance of being a survival of local memories concerning the "Cadogan tail" of Lord Granby's Cavalry.

★★★★★★★★★★

During the return march of the British Army through Holland the Highlanders had a most cordial reception, and were decorated with laurel leaves by the inhabitants, partly on account of their late achievements, and partly from equally cordial remembrances of the "Scottish Brigade" which had served under the Dutch. A similar reception awaited them in England after their disembarkation at Tilbury Fort, the welcome being notably conspicuous at Derby, as they marched north, which town had such a different experience of them during the "Forty-Five," eighteen years previously.

No connected march of the army into London took place.

****

The 1st Foot Guards arrived in February, and the 2nd in March. The former were billeted about Lincoln's Inn Fields, and the latter in the Borough and Spitalfields. It was observed that many of the soldiers wore breeches made of old tents taken from the French.—*British Chronicle,* March 9-11, 1763.

****

On April 5 "Elliot's Light Horse "marched in over Westminster Bridge "with every man a sprig of box in his hat in token of victory." The Royal Horse Guards (Blues) were reduced, immediately after the close of the war, from fifty-two to twenty-nine per troop; each discharged trooper, who had served at least a year, was permitted to sell his horse for his own benefit, provided he did so before embarking for England. After its five years of harassing active service (the Blues now bear the word "Warburg" only on a standard presented to the regiment by William IV.), the regiment was successively stationed at Derby, Nottingham, Leicester, Stamford, and Northampton, and exempted from its escort duties about the Court. While at Nottingham it was reviewed in the Sneinton Meadow by General Elliot in the presence of the Duke of Rutland, the Marquess of Granby, and "a prodigious number of people."

On June 4, 1703, George IIL, attended by the Duke of York, Prince William Henry, (brothers of George III.; Prince William Henry was created Duke of Gloucester), and Earl De la Warr, and escorted by the 1st troop of Horse Guards, (1st Life Guards), proceeded from the Queen's Palace, up Constitution Hill, to Hyde Park. At appointed places His Majesty was received and joined by Lord Ligonier, Commander-in-Chief; Lieut.-General the Marquess of Granby; Earl Talbot; Earl Harcourt, with their attendants and led horses; and Lord Orford, the Ranger of the Parks.

****

Soon after his return Lord Granby subscribed £1,000 towards establishing a school for supporting the orphans of subordinate officers (naval and military) who had been killed during the war. He also gave a great entertainment to the principal military officers, returned from

Germany, at the Thatched House Tavern.—*Royal Westminster Journal*, March 12-19, 1763.

****

A Royal salute from the artillery greeted the entrance of this brilliant cavalcade into Hyde Park. His Majesty then reviewed the troops assembled, including others than those from Germany which were distinguished by sprigs of laurel and oak in their head-gear. The three regiments of Foot Guards went through their "new exercises." Opposite the centre of the line an officer was placed on a scaffold and, as he alternately waved a blue or a white flag, the artillery and the infantry, respectively, fired. The troops "marched past" to the music of fifes and drums, and a grand discharge of cannon concluded the spectacle. "Elliot's Light Horse" were enthusiastically received, and the "matrosses" much admired for the "inimitable skill" with which they handled the artillery. A great number of persons "of the first distinction" witnessed this review, and about 100,000 "*others*."

The Marquess of Granby's Regiment, "the Royal Forresters," was not present at this parade, though many men were who had been drafted from its popular ranks. On March 3, 1763, it was publicly disbanded in the Market Place at Nottingham, and the officers and men thanked for their services by Lieut.-General Webbe. The officers were placed on half-pay and Lieut.-Colonel Russel Manners, who had commanded it since Lord Robert Sutton's death, was soon afterwards appointed to the Lieut.-Colonelcy of the 2nd, Queen's, Dragoon Guards; and Cornet Edward Manners to the 1st, or King's, Regiment of Foot Guards, as Lieutenant and Captain. The troopers received a gratuity of £3 per head, six days' pay to carry them to their homes, and their horse-furniture and regimentals. Their arms were returned to the Tower, and the horses sold at an average price of £7 each.

Thus was one of the finest regiments in the service, which had cost since its enrolment some £20,000, broken up and dispersed. (*Date-Book* of Nottingham).

Lieut.-General Mostyn at length got his reward for his distinguished, and patient service. General Bland died, and the Colonelcy of the 1st, King's, Dragoon Guards was bestowed upon "Jack" Mostyn in the most spontaneous manner by His Majesty.

****

General Mostyn, later, was appointed Governor of Minorca, and died February 16, 1779, at his house in Dover Street. In pursuance of

George III.'s promise, he was nominally appointed Governor of Chelsea Hospital in February, 1768, but exchanged the appointment for Minorca, in place of General Sir George Howard, K.B., who became Governor of Chelsea Hospital, March. 1768.

****

It would appear that Mostyn voted in the majority on the Peace question, as the Duke of Newcastle took an early opportunity of falling foul of him. To our modern experience the fact seems strange that nearly every officer of importance, who has been mentioned in preceding pages, held a seat in Parliament; and most of them returned home from Germany, at the close of each campaign, to vote upon matters which chiefly bore upon the policy, and conduct, of the war. Mostyn, as usual, gave as good as he got, and his pen was far more facile than that of the Duke of Newcastle, in spite of His Grace's ceaseless practice. Mostyn emphatically disclaimed any want of attention, or gratitude, in regard to the duke; to whom he pointed out that "to be represented fairly there were two essential requisites—to understand thoroughly, and to report truly."

Between the Duke of Newcastle and the Rutland family perfectly friendly relations were maintained, though the former could not always suppress the pique inevitable to one holding his convictions of the necessity of sacrificing political principle to the claims of family, or party, connection.

The Duke of Rutland refused the proffered promotion of the Lord Chamberlain's Staff, (accepted by the Duke of Marlborough), and remained undisturbed in his office of Master of the Horse. His attitude, together with a certain section of the Whigs, is touched upon, and explained, by Edmund Burke, (*Thoughts on the Cause of the Present Discontents*). To them, who had been at so much pains to maintain the Brunswick Dynasty, opposition, for opposition's sake, to George III. seemed unnatural, and even disloyal. Moreover, at this point the opposition to the king was principally due to the unpopularity of his Scotch favourite Lord Bute, against whom, in Burke's opinion, much was urged that was both unjust, and frivolous.

Consequently, when the onslaught upon the Whigs was commenced by the king, "a few individuals were left standing who gave security for their total estrangement from the *odious principles* of party connexion, and personal attachment." So far, the king had in no sense put any strain upon the Constitution; when His Majesty did eventually do so, it will be seen that the Duke of Rutland was one of its earliest and stoutest champions.

And now as to the bribes "gulped" by Lord Granby. Owing to Fox's great unpopularity some changes in the ministry became expedient, and in the April following Granby's arrival (February 6, 1763) in England, he was asked to accept the Lord Lieutenancy of Ireland. Here was a reward for a man in embarrassed circumstances as Lord Granby was, and principally through his generous endeavours to remedy departmental shortcomings!

★★★★★★★★★★

Lloyd's Evening Post recorded a letter from Germany which declared Lord Granby's expenditure during the war, for the relief of the soldiers, to have been £60,000 (November 13, 1762); and *Royal Westminster Journal* (November 13, 1762).

★★★★★★★★★★

The career of his own son, Irish viceroy twenty years later, affords a useful testimony to the value of this "bribe;" though in the latter instance the private expenditure had assumed much more serious proportions owing to the appointment having been changed to a permanently resident one. Charles, fourth Duke of Rutland, was informed by his predecessor in this office that he must count on spending £15,000 a year of private income in addition to the official salary and allowances.

In the Marquess of Granby's time this excess of expenditure over income, though greatly less than as above, was considerable.

★★★★★★★★★★

Lord Townshend, when Irish viceroy, wrote to Lord Granby: "You were wise when you refused to come here, for I have not one day in a week to myself. The air of the castle is abominably unwholesome. I often have my boots on from 7 in the morning and sit at business till near 5 in the evening. God knows whether I can succeed in the king's business or not; but my health and pocket will not, I believe, be worth a beggar's inheritance. . . . I shall most probably be £8,000 in debt."—*Rutland MSS.*, 1767-8, vol. ii.

★★★★★★★★★★

Walpole himself wrote, at the moment, that if Granby went to Ireland he would finish "his life and fortune;" yet, conscious that this admission was wholly inconsistent in regard to his bribe-gulping version, Walpole qualified it by an editorial footnote added to his published letters:

> Lord Granby drank very hard, and was profusely generous.

Lord Granby declined Ireland, and soon afterwards an unexpected event occurred, the absolute cause of which has been variously guessed at, and which thus reached the delighted ears of the Duke of Newcastle. Mr. George Onslow had the happiness to inform him "that Lord Bute resigns tomorrow morning," *i.e.,* April 8, 1763. Mr. Fox retired to the Upper House as Lord Holland, but retained the Paymastership; and Mr. George Grenville was invited to form the new Ministry, in which he appointed the Earls of Halifax, and Egremont, to be Secretaries of State.

George III. now spared no pains to induce the Marquess of Granby to accept political office, and it was not until after long persuasion that, for the first time in his life, he consented. He made it abundantly clear that he came unwillingly into His Majesty's service in consequence of the Duke of Newcastle's retirement, to whom he had been politically, as he was personally, attached. In addition, Lord Granby, in accepting the Master Generalship of the Ordnance which gave him a seat in the Cabinet, stipulated that he should support His Majesty's Government under Mr. Grenville, and in association with Mr. Grenville solely, to whom alone, among the new Ministers, he was either privately, or publicly, attached.

Instead, therefore, of Lord Granby having been given the Master Generalship by Lord Bute, and Fox, the moment he had his foot on the step of the post-chaise at Dover, as Walpole deliberately leads one to suppose, he accepted it three months later under the Administration of Mr. George Grenville, who had not approved the Peace terms sufficiently to undertake their defence in the House of Commons.

That the "worthy old Marshal Ligonier," as Walpole most justly calls him, resigned the Ordnance in favour of Granby is perfectly true. Ligonier received in recognition an English Barony; and as he was then, at the age of eighty-three, monopolising all the chief prizes of the Service, it is not improbable that he cheerfully acquiesced in this promotion of Lord Granby with whom he had been on most intimately affectionate terms, and to whose family the Ligoniers had long been attached, and indebted. (The friendship between the Rutland and Ligonier families was of old standing).

Ligonier remained Commander-in-Chief, Field Marshal, and Colonel of the 1st Regiment of Foot Guards, besides holding a lucrative Military Governorship, and various minor appointments. The functions of the Master-General of the Ordnance were to store all the Military Magazines of Great Britain with munitions of war, of which he also issued to the Royal Navy such items as pertained to his department; and he was Colonel-in-Chief of the Corps of Artillery, and Engineers. Like all appointments of the period, its value was not limited to the salary, which was moderate, as shown by an entry in the *Journals* of the House of Commons made while the office was in abeyance after Lord Granby's death—

> Saved by the vacant posts of Master General, Secretary, Under Secretary, and Clerk to the Master General, for ½ a year, £990.

This represents £1,980 *per annum,* from which has to be deducted the salaries of the two secretaries, and clerk.

The Marquess of Granby, as Master-General, appointed Mr. Thomas Thoroton, M.P., to be his secretary, and was succeeded in the Lieutenant-Generalship of the Ordnance by Lord Townshend. (The George Townshend previously often referred to). With his love of his profession, and interest in the welfare of the rank and file, no less than the officers, of the army, Lord Granby found much more congenial occupation in the exercise of his military and Ordnance duties, than in the Ministerial functions attaching to his new honour. (The evil results of the "Cadogan tail," during the Seven Years' War, caused an order to be issued subsequent to the Peace of Paris that all the Heavy Cavalry should be mounted on long-tailed horses).

As none of the old Pelhamite set was included in Grenville's Cabinet, the Duke of Newcastle soon busied himself in beating up his supporters, and ascertaining Mr. Pitt's intentions. Through the Duke of Devonshire Newcastle was assured of Pitt's friendliness towards him, though he (Pitt) would enter into no opposition. Pitt declared he should only attend Parliament on national and constitutional questions, and expressed his regard for the Tories, saying they should on no account be proscribed. He even dined with Newcastle who was specially devoting himself to organizing an opposition to the Grenville Cabinet, and to arranging a visit from Lord Granby to Claremont, where he was to be met by Lord Cornwallis, the Marquess of Rockingham, the Duke of Portland, and others who had taken part in the late struggle against the king, and Bute.

A day was fixed when Thoroton wrote from Rutland House to say an engagement had been entirely overlooked on the part of the Duke of Rutland, and Lord Granby, to attend their neighbour's (Miss Chudleigh's) fireworks at Kingston House. Miss Chudleigh was addicted to these pyrotechnic displays on the occasions of Royal birthdays, (this *fête* was in celebration of the Peace), *etc.*, and sometimes they took place from a platform erected in Hyde Park opposite to her house (which still exists) in Kensington Gore. Walpole chronicles several of them with characteristic details, such as the "pale blue watered tabby" costume worn by the Duke of York on one of these gala evenings. Newcastle replied he was so impatient of the honour and pleasure of seeing Lord Granby that he should expect His Lordship, and Thoroton, the day after Miss Chudleigh's party at about one o'clock; and that he must insist upon their staying that (Friday) night until after dinner on Saturday.

On the 21st of May, 1763, Newcastle wrote in great spirits to the Duke of Devonshire—

> Lord Granby, Thoroton, Lord Cornwallis, and Tommy Townshend are now here. I expect the Marquess of Rockingham, the Duke of Portland, and the attorney-general (Charles Yorke), tomorrow.

Prospective arrangements for "Arscotte Races" were also touched upon.

Lord Cornwallis was the Lord Broome of earlier pages, *aide-de-camp* to Lord Granby; on succeeding to the title, he had returned home, and entered vigorously into "opposition." His intimacy with Granby was the source of Newcastle's anxiety to bring his (Cornwallis') influence to bear upon Granby's political situation.

Nothing satisfactory to Newcastle came of this meeting, save the pleasure of entertaining his friends; for he was notable for hospitality in a notably hospitable age. Of eating, drinking, and eighteenth-century conviviality there was sure to be a sufficiency at Claremont; and those who are curious as to "what there was for dinner" may ascertain the fare provided by the Duke of Newcastle, whose table was reckoned a very extravagant one in his day.

During the summer and autumn Lord Granby was present at race-meetings at Nottingham, Newark, and Scarborough, besides other festive gatherings, at all of which he was welcomed with enthusiasm. At Nottingham the large attendance at the races, and Cocking, included the Duke of York, the Dukes of Rutland, and Kingston, the Marquess of Granby, Lords Byron, Strange, and George Manners Sutton.

★★★★★★★★★★

Lord George Manners assumed the name of Sutton after Lord Robert's death, and succeeded to the Lexington estates, residing at Kelham, and identifying himself with the county of Notts. He married, first (1749), Diana, daughter of Thomas Chaplin, Esq., of Blankney; and, secondly, Mary, daughter of Joshua Peart, Esq.

****

Newark Races occupied three days, and balls took place at night, one of which Mr. Thoroton is recorded as having opened by dancing a minuet with Miss Chudleigh. On this occasion Lord George Manners Sutton provided a representation of *The Jealous Wife,* which was given before the Marquess of Granby, the neighbouring nobility, the County Members, and the Borough Members, John Manners, and Thomas Thoroton.

Various songs, and poetical effusions, were written in Lord Granby's honour, such as *The British Hero,* by R. Rolt, set to music by Dr. Boyce; and one, with a refrain of *Granby O, Gen'rous Granby O!,* was a favourite with the provincials who heard from the many discharged soldiers countless stories of the conduct of their commander in Germany, and of his eagerness to share all their hardships, and dangers. That commander's reputation among his equals, and the people of England at large, is indicated by the occurrence, in contemporary pamphlets and letters, of phrases which express the warmest personal affection, as well as respect and admiration; and by the choice of his effigy for a large majority of the sign-boards throughout the kingdom.

And yet in those famous, delightful, encyclopaedic *Letters*, (Walpole's), in which nothing was too small to be recorded, from the inadequacy of Lady Backstair's bodice at the last ball, to the cut of the latest accredited ambassador's breeches—or the mode of his hat, there occurs no word concerning the suspense amid which the nation listened, with eager ears, for the slow-travelling news from Lord Granby's sick-bed at Warburg; of the delight caused by his recovery; nor of the congratulations which surrounded his return as the most conspicuously beloved, and popular figure of the day.

****

One evening Lord Granby entered Drury Lane Theatre while Mr. King was delivering the Prologue to *The Tutor.* The audience stopped the performance, and clamoured for the "Granby March." Mr. King left the stage, and the orchestra not having the music of the "Granby March "pacified the house with "Belleisle" (*Lloyd's Evening Post*, November 11, 1765). On Lord Granby's birthday, in 1764, a grand display of fireworks was given at Woolwich, concluding with a "transparency" showing "Long live Granby." Colonel Williamson and the officers of the Royal Artillery afterwards gave a dinner at the Ship Tavern . . .

. . ."the whole company rejoiced in the name of Granby" (*Lloyd's Evening Post,* January, 1764). "Junius" wrote in 1769: "Surely it was something more cordial than esteem with which you (Granby) were universally received upon your return from Germany."

****

The *Memoirs of the Reign of George III.* (Walpole's), are equally silent concerning those matters; though eloquent upon the "gulping" of "bribes" and "baits" which fade into unsubstantiality under the simplest analysis.

Jack Mostyn was indeed right in declaring that to be "represented fairly" it is necessary, above all things, to be "reported truly." The reporter par excellence of those times was Horace Walpole, who, despite his affectation of impartiality, perpetually revelled in evil rather than in good report, and sometimes would have the former, even if he went the length of manufacturing it.

****

"I am bigoted to none: Charles I., Cromwell, Whigs, and Tories are all alike to me!" (Walpole to Sir D. Dalrymple, February 23, 1764). There are several remarks of Walpole's concerning General Conway's "ill-requited services" which explain these omissions to any student of Walpole's works; a little later Walpole wrote an anonymous pamphlet in Conway's behalf, in which he directed the public to seek testimony to Conway's character from "that idol of every Englishman's affection, the Marquess of Granby".

****

RUTLAND HOUSE, KNIGHTSBRIDGE.

Marquess of Granby

By G. P. R. James

Celebrity does not always depend upon very great deeds or very splendid abilities, and the Marquess of Granby, though he himself never achieved any signal victory in the field, was as celebrated in his day as many who have personally effected more. His name was continually mingled during his life with the many important events which at that time agitated Europe; and as, in the details of the campaign and the battle, it was always spoken of with praise, he acquired a happy fame by his share in many great exploits.

John Manners, Marquess of Granby, first saw the light in January 1721. Born in the highest grade of society in England, the son of the Duke of Rutland, he received a polished and liberal education, which, working upon a kindly heart and a generous disposition, produced those amiable manners which distinguished him in after-life. A decided predilection for a military career, and considerable talent for command, induced his father to place him in the army, although fortune had raised his son above the necessity of choosing a profession.

In 1745, when the arrival of an unhappy prince, whose claims are now extinct, threw all the adherents of the House of Hanover into agitation and alarm, and raised up throughout the country a spirit of political rancour and party hatred hardly paralleled in the annals of Great Britain, the raising of troops for the service of either party became a sort of mania, and, amongst others, the Marquess of Granby levied a regiment of foot to act against the young adventurer, who was struggling to regain a crown that had been torn from his imprudent and criminal ancestor.

Little of any consequence is recorded of the life of Lord Granby from that period, till in the year 1750, he married the Lady Francis Seymour, the eldest daughter of the Duke of Somerset; an union which originating, it is said, in affection, was productive of happiness to both.

The government would have been purer than governments generally are, if the interests of two such families as those of Somerset and Rutland had not been able to raise an aspirant high in the profession he had chosen; but the Marquess of Granby had claims which his rank and connexions only served to place in a just point of view. He was active, enterprising, courageous, had exerted himself strenuously in behalf of the reigning family, and merited promotion as well by services rendered as by personal qualifications.

In 1755, the approach of an open rupture between England and France occasioned several movements in the British Army, and the Marquess of Granby was raised to the rank of Major General. During the hostilities which proceeded the declaration of war, I do not find that he was employed in any active service; and it would appear that he spent the two following years in commerce of ordinary society, and in those kindly and generous actions, which, though they sometimes in him degenerated into profusion, are, when properly regulated, fruits of the noblest virtue, and even when pushed into excess, are amongst the noblest faults.

At this period the Marquess and Marchioness of Granby, in conjunction with Lady Guernsey, another daughter of the Duke of Somerset, presented to the Senate House of Cambridge a statue of that nobleman, who had for many years been Chancellor of the university. It was executed in marble by Rysbrach, and even to the present day does honour to the genius of the artist. This fact is only worth preserving in the biography of Lord Granby, as the statue was executed under his immediate directions, and some information may be thence derived in regard to his pursuits in time of peace, and the general course of his domestic occupations.

From the society of his friends, however and the current of calmer pleasures, the Marquess of Granby, was soon called to the field by events of which some detail must be here given. The Duke of Cumberland, who had in the commencement of the war of 1756 commanded the Hanoverian Army opposed to the Duke de Richelieu, was obliged, as I have noticed elsewhere, to sign a convention at Cloister Seven, the ostensible object of which was to pacify the Hanoverian dominions, and the Allies of the Elector; and to restore tranquillity to that part of the empire.

The convention, which was drawn up with great care, seems studiously to have left so much ambiguity in the terms, that the consenting parties might recommence the war whenever it suited their convenience, and in the meantime derive what advantage they could from an unsettled state. The King of Great Britain recruited his forces, and made every preparation for breaking the convention as soon as possible; and the French pillaged Hanover at leisure, and endeavoured to fix their government upon the country they had acquired.

Everything was completed for the recommencement of hostilities on the part of the Hanoverians before the end of the summer; and the Duke of Cumberland, having resigned the command, it was bestowed upon Prince Ferdinand of Brunswick, who soon began active measures of aggression, The Duke de Richelieu remonstrated for the sake of appearances; but the German general thought it little worth his while to enter into any prolonged altercation, and consequently, after a very brief reply, marched directly to attack the enemy. The French general, who in all probability expected that long disputes would precede the rupture of the convention, and give him time to collect his troops, and press some more contributions from the country, was taken unaware by the quick movements of the Hanoverian Army.

Several of his detachments were surprised and defeated; and he himself was obliged to retreat to Zell with great precipitation. Affecting high indignation at the breach of the convention, Richelieu committed a great many of those atrocious barbarities which occasionally disgrace even the most civilized warfare. He was, however, soon removed from the command; and while Prince Ferdinand, having been joined by Prince George of Holstein and a body of Prussian cavalry, advanced upon Bremen, taking Rottenburg and Ottersburg by the way, Monsieur de Clermont, who succeeded to the station of commander-in-chief of the French, endeavoured to recruit and consolidate a sickly, scattered and dissolute army.

The Hanoverian general gave but little time for such a purpose, and, marching upon Hanover and Brunswick, took the fort of Hoya upon the Weser, after a vigorous resistance; and cleared the whole country beyond the line of Hanover, Zell, and Brunswick. The French retired from all those places with more haste than was either agreeable or glorious, and in some instances the sense of ignominy, and the thirst of revenge, induced them to ravage and waste the country they were forced to abandon. Hanover was treated with less severity; no plunder was permitted on the retreat of the army, and the provisions accumulated for its use were distributed among the poor.

By drawing his troops from all the garrisons as he advanced, the Prince de Clermont greatly strengthened his force, and more than once attempted to make a stand; but the rapidity of Prince Ferdinand's movements, gave him no time to fortify himself in any position; and, in order to check the Hanoverians, three thousand five hundred men were thrown into Minden, while the French head-quarters were formed at Hamelin. Minden could hold out but five days, and the advance of Prince Ferdinand again drove his antagonist to Paderborn, and thence to Wesel on the Rhine. That immense efforts would be made by France to retrieve her military renown, and recover the territory which had thus been wrenched from her grasp, could not be doubted; and Prince Ferdinand anxiously solicited aid from England to meet the danger by equal exertion.

The difficulty of transporting cavalry to the scene of action, delayed the movement of the English; for the Dutch treaty with France prevented the possibility of carrying the reinforcements through their country, and Embden, the only convenient port, was in the hands of the French. To remedy this, a fleet under Admiral Holmes was sent against that place; and Prince Ferdinand did not retire to winter quarters in Münster, till he had seen the French nearly beat back to their own frontier, and a port opened for his communication with England.

The Army of Hanover was soon once more in the field. Supplies for carrying on the war had been liberally voted by England; and everything promised support and success. The French were again forced to retreat, though their numbers were now very superior; and Prince Ferdinand, after having crossed the Rhine, drew the Prince de Clermont out of his entrenched camp at Rhinefeldt, and completely defeated him at Crevelt. Dusseldorf immediately surrendered; but the fruits of these victories were obliged to be abandoned; for while Prince Ferdinand was pursuing the Prince de Clermont, the Prince de Soubize had penetrated into the *Landgravate* of Hesse, had defeated the force of Prince Yssemburg, and made a demonstration of interposing between the Hanoverian Army and the supplies from England, which by this time had arrived at Embden.

These considerations induced Prince Ferdinand to retreat, and effect his junction with the British troops, which was carried into execution without loss, by the skilful manoeuvres of the commander-in-chief, and the gallant resolution of General Imhoff.

The troops sent from England consisted almost entirely of cavalry, and did not amount to three thousand men; but their presence was nevertheless of the utmost importance to the Hanoverian Army. The two officers in command were the Duke of Marlborough and

Lord George Sackville; and shortly after their arrival Prince Ferdinand found himself sufficiently strong to detach General Oberg with ten thousand men, to support Prince Yssemburg, who was opposed to the Prince de Soubize. The principal French Army still continued in the rear of the Hanoverians, and a great and advantageous change had been worked in its commanders, the chief of whom was now Monsieur de Contades, in the place of the Prince de Clermont.

General Oberg was defeated at Luttenburg; and Prince Ferdinand finding that no more could be effected that year, from the severity with which the winter set in retired to winter quarters in Münster. The Duke of Marlborough having died at that place, the chief command of the British forces in Germany devolved upon Lord George Sackville, who appears to have come over to England while the army remained in quarters at Münster. His situation as commander-in-chief having been confirmed, he returned to his post early in March, accompanied by the Marquess of Granby, by this time Lieutenant-General and Colonel of the Blues.

In the interim the French had made themselves masters of Frankfort by stratagem; and Prince Ferdinand soon found the necessity of dislodging them from that position. A diversion, however, on the side of Hesse, prevented him from making the attempt till the beginning of April, when he marched rapidly for the city, hoping to take it by a *coup-de-main*. Notwithstanding his precautions the French gained information of his movements, and on the 13th of April he found the enemy in force at the village of Berghen, between him and Frankfort. Prince Ferdinand hesitated not a moment to attack them, though they were both strongly posted, and superior in number to himself.

The French, commanded by the Duke de Broglio stood their ground; and after three successive attacks, in one of which Prince Yssemburg was killed, the Hanoverian commander found the necessity of retreating. To effect this in presence of a superior and victorious enemy was difficult; but by making fresh dispositions, as if for renewing the attack, Prince Ferdinand succeeded in amusing the enemy till night, when he fell back without molestation, gaining perhaps more military renown by the skilful manner in which he concealed his defeat from the enemy, than he would have done by success in the engagement.

The French thus maintained possession of Frankfort; their armies on the Upper and Lower Rhine, were both strongly reinforced; and in June, having united at Marburg, under the command of Monsieur de Contades, they began a plan of operations which threatened to cut off the retreat of the Hanoverians. Prince Ferdinand, forced to recede before them towards the Weser, threw every impediment in their way. But Munden, Gottingen, Ritburg, Minden, and Minister, were taken by assault or siege, and proceeding as if to certain conquest, the French forced their adversary back upon Petershagen. Here, however, having been joined by a considerable reinforcement under General Wangenheim, Prince Ferdinand made a pause, and fortified himself in a strong position, in order to arrest the farther progress of the enemy.

Various skirmishes now took place, in which the advantages fell to the Hanoverians. Osnabruck was surprised; and while General Wangenheim remained at Thornhausen on the banks of the Weser, opposed to the advance of the French Army from Minden, the Hereditary Prince of Brunswick was detached with ten thousand men to cut off the French supplies from Paderborn.

The French General Contades found that he must either retreat or attack Prince Ferdinand in position; and his determination was soon fixed by a movement which the Hanoverian general made towards Hille, for the purpose of either luring him to a battle, or attacking him at a disadvantage if he did not advance. Contades suffered himself to be deceived; and imagining that Prince Ferdinand had marched with his principal force so far to the right as to be unable to support General Wangenheim on the Weser, resolved to attack the latter immediately, and open the path into the heart of Hanover. The Duke de Broglio was accordingly directed to pass the little River Werra, and the morass which lay between Minden and the Hanoverian camp, and forcing the position of General Wangenheim early the next morning, to turn upon the flank of Prince Ferdinand's army at Hille, while Marshal Contades proceeded against him with his main body in front.

The news of the first movements of the French readied the prince at three o'clock in the morning; but his troops were all prepared to march; and in a short time, his communication with his left was completely restored. The right and left of the French Army, under Guerci and Broglio, consisted principally of infantry, while the centre was almost entirely composed of cavalry. As it was intended to turn the left of the Hanoverian Army, by driving back the corps of General Wangenheim, the right of the French under the Duke de Broglio was thrown forward, and passing the morass late on the evening of the thirty-first of July, had arrived within half a mile of the Hanoverian left before daylight the next morning. Along the whole front ran a rising ground, which covered the dispositions of the Allied Army, but was only defended by a few weak posts, which were soon driven over the hill.

Advancing to reconnoitre, the Duke de Broglio immediately perceived, to his great surprise, the whole of the Hanoverian Army drawn up in order of battle. At this moment the forces of Prince Ferdinand were all under arms upon the ground, except the detachment he had sent to cut off the French supplies. On his left were the corps of General Wangenheim, advanced so far as to be supported by a battery at Thornhausen on the Weser, and a body of Prussian cavalry under the Prince of Holstein. The centre was composed principally of infantry, with the farmhouse of Tostenhausen forming a strong post in front; while on the right Lord George Sackville, with a large body of cavalry, continued the line as far as the village of Hartum.

The Marquess of Granby commanded the second line of cavalry; and, as upon the conduct of these two bodies some of the principal events of the day depended, it may be well to notice more particularly the nature of the ground. As already stated, the cavalry was formed in two lines, the first commanded by Lord George Sackville, and the second by the Marquess of Granby. The extreme right of the right wing approached nearly to a little hamlet, with some rising ground; and its left was somewhat disjointed from the infantry of the centre, by a small open wood, beyond which extended a very narrow cornfield, having in front a wide moor, called in the accounts of the day Mindenheath. Unincumbered by any brushwood, the trees of the wood were far apart, and offered little impediment except to the sight, from which they shut out the plain. The infantry from the beginning of the action were slightly advanced; and Lord George Sackville, who was late at the head of his troops, and late upon the field, seems to have been behind the position intended for him to occupy.

As soon as the Duke de Broglio had passed the hill, he saw that full dispositions had been made for a general action; and as this state of things was very different from that which either himself or the Marshal de Contades had anticipated, he paused, and opening a sharp cannonade upon the Hanoverian line, he despatched information of the circumstances to the commander-in-chief. Contades was at this time advancing with his centre and left wing; and, as the Duke de Broglio received no answer, he rode to the centre to seek directions himself. Several hours were thus wasted, but as the French Army were now too much entangled with the morass to think of receding, the attack was continued upon the left of the Allies by a sharp cannonade from a battery now erected on the rising ground. The Hanoverian artillery, however, had been so well placed, and was so well served, that the French battery was speedily silenced, and their right wing kept in check.

In the meanwhile, in the centre, six regiments of English infantry, two batteries of Hanoverians, without waiting their adversaries' approach, advanced under a tremendous fire from two French batteries, to attack the cavalry of the enemy opposed to them. The boldness of the movement, and the success with which it was attended, did honour both to the general and his troops. The French cavalry finding themselves about to be charged by the English infantry, instantly poured down upon them; but the British regiments already had the impetus in their favour, the French were driven back in confusion, and the Duke de Broglio's corps was obliged to make a movement from their right, to cover the disarray of the centre. Prince Ferdinand instantly despatched his *aide-de-camp*, Count Wintzingerode, to command Lord George Sackville to come up through the open road to the left with the cavalry, and complete the rout of the French Army.

Whether from cowardice, or folly, or dislike to his commander, Lord George Sackville could not, or would not comprehend the order, demanded several times how it was to be executed, and at length prepared to march forward, not by the left, but in a direct line. Having seen some dispositions made towards advancing, the first *aide-de-camp* left the English commander, and in a moment after, a second messenger, Lieutenant-Colonel Ligonier, came to press the instant march of the cavalry. Still, however, Lord George Sackville was about to move straight forward, instead of to the left, which was the only spot where his presence could be useful, and new cause of dispute arose upon the arrival of Colonel Fitzroy with repeated commands for him to bring up the British cavalry.

The unhappy general now pretended to look upon the orders brought by the two *aides-de-camp* as contradictory; the one stating the cavalry, the other the British cavalry; and his unwillingness to comprehend was so apparent, that the lieutenant-colonel of the regiment at whose head he was, exclaimed aloud, addressing one of the *aides-de-camp*, "For God's sake, repeat your orders to that man, so that he may not pretend to misunderstand them." Lord George, however, would not be satisfied with the commands he received, and proceeded himself to seek for the commander-in-chief. Three quarters of an hour had now been lost, but as the infantry were still engaged, the prince, on being informed of the dispute, instantly sent off for the second line of cavalry, saying, "Give my commands to the Marquess of Granby; for I know he will obey me."

While this mismanagement had passed in front, Lord Granby had remained at the head of the second line, wondering that so strong a body of cavalry, forming nearly the whole of the right wing, should remain unemployed while a severe contest was evidently going on in the plain. In the impatience of the moment, after waiting some time for orders, he had ridden a little way in advance, to gain a sight of the battle, when an *aide-de-camp* rode up, and commanded him to bring up the second line to the support of the infantry. Lord Granby immediately asked why those orders had not been communicated to Lord George Sackville, his superior officer. In reply, the *aide-de-camp* informed him that they had been delivered, but had not been obeyed, and that the commander-in-chief had now directed them to him. Lord Granby now hesitated no longer, but putting his troops in motion, passed through the grove of trees without difficulty, and reached upon the plain.

At that moment, however, Lord George Sackville sent an order for the second line to halt till the first came up, which was so far obeyed, that the movement in advance was suspended for a few minutes; but fresh commands being received from Prince Ferdinand himself, Lord Granby immediately galloped on, and in a few minutes, the first line also appeared, forming with the second behind the infantry.

The battle was now over. So much time had been lost, that, though the centre of the French were totally defeated, their right had by this time taken measures to cover the retreat. The bridges over the stream were broken down behind them, and the passes destroyed through the marsh. Prince Ferdinand, unwilling to hazard the success of so glorious a day, abandoned the pursuit, and the enemy retired, and reposed under the cannon of Minden. The news, however, reached their camp that night, that the hereditary Prince of Brunswick, who had been detached from the Hanoverian Army to cut off their supplies, had completely defeated Monsieur de Brissac at Coesfelt, and that in consequence their communication was interrupted with the country behind them. A precipitate retreat was the consequence, and the victory at Minden was thus rendered complete and serviceable,

In the morning which followed the battle, Prince Ferdinand issued a general order of thanks to the officers who had principally contributed to his victory, from the list of whom the name of Lord George

Sackville was purposely excluded. His commendation was chiefly bestowed upon the British infantry, to whose gallant efforts, success was certainly to be greatly attributed; but at the same time, he publicly declared to the Marquess of Granby, that he felt sure if he had had the good fortune to have him at the head of the cavalry of the right wing, the victory would have been much more complete and brilliant.

Such strong expressions of disapprobation could not pass unnoticed by Lord George Sackville; and he solicited leave to resign his command, and return to England, which was immediately granted. He was instantly on his arrival dismissed from all his military appointments, and a court martial was called to try him for disobedience of orders. In the meanwhile, the Marquess of Granby was appointed Commander-in-Chief of the British forces in Germany and Master-general of the Ordnance, two posts of which Lord George Sackville was deprived. To the Battle of Minden succeeded a long train of successes against the French, in all of which Lord Granby participated. Minden and Cassel immediately fell into the hands of the Hanoverians; and the French Army was driven across the Weser into a country offering but small means of subsistence, and in which no preparations had been made for their support.

Münster also surrendered, after a short siege, and Fulda was taken by surprise. The year being now far advanced, both armies retired into winter-quarters; and Lord Granby returned to England, with the painful task before him of attending as a witness at the trial of Lord George Sackville. To aid in the condemnation of another, whatever may have been his faults, and however loudly justice may call for his punishment, can never surely be a grateful undertaking; and though, where the public weal is concerned, the least modification of truth by a witness is either weakness or crime, yet in the minute shades of human conduct we are always more pleased to see the heart turn rather towards mercy than towards severity.

In his evidence against his former commander-in-chief, Lord Granby told the truth as mildly as the truth could be told without perverting its purity. Other witnesses were more harsh, and gave importance to minor facts, by the weight of indignation and perhaps of prejudice. The evidence, however, was so strong and conclusive, taken as a whole, that notwithstanding all the interest and exertions of a powerful family, Lord George Sackville was condemned, and dismissed the service with disgrace.

During the absence of the Marquess of Granby from the scene of war, Prince Ferdinand had remained in winter quarters in the neighbourhood of Paderborn, Cassel, and Münster. Several unimportant skirmishes had taken place during the winter and spring; but the commencement of active hostilities was deferred by both armies to a late period in the year, the French pausing for want of forage for their cavalry, and Prince Ferdinand remaining inactive in expectation of the reinforcements which had been despatched from England. These reinforcements at length arrived by the way of Embden, and after various preparatory movements, and one or two serious encounters, in which the French and the Allies were alternately successful, all seemed to tend towards a general battle.

The French Army, divided into three bodies, marched forward as with the design of surrounding the Hanoverian forces. The left, commanded by Monsieur de Muy, passed the Dymel, and extending itself down the river, interposed between Prince Ferdinand and Westphalia, while their right, under Prince Xavier of Saxony, endeavoured to turn the left of the Allies by marching upon Cassel; and the main army, commanded by the Duke de Broglio, who had now been appointed Commander-in-Chief, advanced directly upon the Hanoverian position.

The situation of the Allied Army now became critical, but the Duke de Broglio had committed the common error of extending his line of operations too far, in hopes of surprising his adversary. Of this Prince Ferdinand immediately took advantage; and, paying no attention to the centre and right of the enemy, he marched to attack their left, consisting of thirty-five thousand men under Monsieur de Muy. This force was posted with its right resting on the small town of Warbourgh, and its left reaching nearly to the heights of Menne. The Hanoverian Army advanced against it in two divisions. The right commanded by the Hereditary Prince of Brunswick and General Sporken, a little in advance of the centre, proceeded round the heights on the enemy's left, and sheltered by a thick fog, contrived to get both upon their flank and rear; while the main body, under Prince Ferdinand and the Marquess of Granby, marched forward to attack the French in front.

The ground in advance was marshy and difficult, and the Hereditary Prince had reached the rise of the heights before the rest of the corps were upon a parallel with that which he commanded. At that instant the fog cleared away, and the French, who were aware of the march of an enemy, but did not well know in what direction to expect their attack, now found two columns of the Allies advancing upon them, one already in their rear, and the other climbing the heights upon their flank.

Three brigades were immediately pushed forward to oppose the ascent of the Hanoverians; but the attacking party reached the summit first, and the battle began on the flank and rear of the French left, almost at the same moment. In the meantime the centre and right of the Allies, in which were the principal force of the British troops, toiled on to come up to the scene of action; and such were the exertions made that several of the English infantry dropped down dead with the hot sun and the fatiguing nature of the ground. By the distance and the difficulty of advance, the foot were prevented from reaching the spot in time, but the British artillery was hurried up with a speed previously unknown, and the cavalry arriving, charged the main body of the French, while the Hereditary Prince upon the heights drove back their left upon their centre.

Warbourg being attacked at the same time, the retreat of the enemy was immediate; and, though there was some confusion in passing the Dymel, it was conducted in such a manner before a superior force, as to do high honour to Monsieur de Muy and the French officers under his command. After passing the river, the French once more formed on the opposite heights; but the Marquess of Granby following, with a part of the British troops, the enemy again decamped and retreated to Wolfshagen. A number of minor movements succeeded, which belong more to the general history of the war than to the biography of an individual. It is perhaps only necessary to slate that in all the events of the campaign Lord Granby played his part, and maintained his own character as a brave man and a skilful officer.

Though acting only as second in command, he acquired a high reputation as a military man; and, brave to a fault, generous and kind-hearted, he also gained the devoted love both of his soldiers and officers. Notwithstanding all the efforts of Prince Ferdinand, the immense numerical superiority of the French Army acted as a weight which he could not throw off; and, at the end of the campaign the enemy were in possession of Hesse, with a great number of fortified places, strengthening the long line on which they had taken up their winter quarters, and with the whole of Hanover open before them for the next campaign.

The fact of having during a whole year kept in check so formidable a force, was highly glorious to the Allies; but the plan laid down for the ensuing season was one of the grandest schemes of military operations perhaps ever planned. The French had hitherto never shown themselves very active in the winter season, and Prince Ferdinand resolved to put his army in motion at a time when the enemy were least disposed to act; and by attacking their line on four different points to drive them back, or so disperse them that their concentration would be afterwards both difficult and dangerous. Before each of the columns a sort of advance guard was thrown out, and in the very beginning of February the Allies were in the field.

Consternation and surprise spread through the French Army at this unexpected attack; and flight became the order of the day. The strong forts, however, with which they had furnished their line, offered secure places of retreat, and gave them the means of rallying from their first confusion. The Hanoverian forces still eagerly pursued their advantage. Fritzlar was taken by the Hereditary Prince, and the Marquess of Granby made himself master of Gudersburg. The French retired in every direction, burning the stores and magazines they had provided for the winter, and General Sporken, with a considerable body of Hanoverians, forced his way between the French and Imperial Armies, effected his junction with a reinforcement from the Prussian Army, and completely defeated the Saxon forces near Lagensaltze.

Notwithstanding the great success which attended the first operations of the Allied Army, various circumstances were rapidly combining to render their triumph short. Cassel and Ziegenhayn held out against them, the French were rapidly recovering from their first surprise, and the Duke de Broglio was collecting gradually his detachments from the Lower Rhine. At length, finding his force superior to that of the Hanoverians, he marched to the relief of Cassel, defeated the Hereditary Prince of Brunswick, forced the Allies to retire towards Paderborn, and then having recovered all that had been lost, retired again into winter quarters, nearly on the same line which he had formerly occupied.

It was sometime before either party thought fit to recommence the campaign. The French suffered extremely from the loss of their stores; and the want of forage kept them in quarters till June. As soon as they took the field the army of Prince Ferdinand was obliged to retreat before them, and fall back upon the Lippe; but here the prince took up a position, the natural strength of which gave him some hope of being able to oppose with success the superior force of the enemy.

The road from Lipstadt to Ham, for some way, ran along a sort of peninsula formed by the Rivers Aeth and Lippe, which flow side by side for several leagues, leaving occasionally less than half a mile between them. To command this road, the left wing of the Hanoverian Army, under the Marquess of Granby, was drawn up across the peninsula, with its left leaning on the Lippe, and its right touching the Aeth at the little village of Kirch Denkern, where the Aeth is joined by the Saltzback. This last-mentioned stream flows through a deep ravine at a right angle with the Aeth, and is domineered for some way by a considerable range of heights, on which the centre and right of the Hanoverian Army were posted.

The dispositions for taking up this position were hardly complete on the 15th of July, when the French appeared in superior force on the peninsula, and instantly commenced the attack upon the corps of the Marquess of Granby. The event of the war now depended upon the skill and firmness of the British general, and the courage and resolution of his small body of troops. The fire of artillery and musketry was tremendous, the attacking force overwhelming, and the charge of the French conducted with all that impetuous confidence in their own success, which has so often won them the victory.

At the same time no succour could be afforded to the British forces. General Wutgenau, destined to support them, could not reach the spot for nearly three hours; and during the whole of that time, Lord Granby resisted, without yielding a step, a force of more than ten times the number of his own troops.

The bold determined courage, however, of their general gave every support to his men in their perilous situation, and the great carelessness of his own person, which the Marquess of Granby displayed, though in general approaching to rashness, could not be blamed on an occasion when the least appearance of timidity would have been ruinous to the whole army. At the end of three hours the reserve of the left wing came up; and thus strengthened, Lord Granby renewed his efforts, and succeeded before nightfall in driving back the French into the woods.

During the night the Allies, feeling certain that the French though repelled were not conquered, employed their time in strengthening their position. The village of Kirch Denkern was fortified as well as could be effected in a few hours, and the division of the Marquess of Granby and General Wutgenau was reinforced by several fresh regiments. As this was the weak point in the Hanoverian line, in regard to natural defences, every effort was made to secure it by other means; but a high ground, commanding the front of the British troops, was left unoccupied, either by neglect or by the impossibility of embracing it within the line, without leaving the left flank exposed.

At daybreak on the sixteenth, the whole forces of France, now united, poured down again on the post of Lord Granby; but though now trebled in number, they were met by the same determined resolution which had repelled them the night before. As on the passage towards Hamm the success of the campaign greatly depended, the whole efforts of the French were directed against this point, and five hours were expended in useless efforts to drive Lord Granby from his position. At length the heights, which had been equally neglected by the French and the Allies, caught the attention of the Prince de Sobuise, and he instantly ordered a battery to be erected there, which would soon have dislodged the Hanoverians from their ground.

But Prince Ferdinand, seeing the enemy's movements to that effect, despatched information to Lord Granby, and at the same time detached a considerable reinforcement under General Sporken, to enable the British commander to charge the enemy in flank, while embarrassed with an alteration of proceedings. This was immediately effected. The British troops, supported by the Hanoverians, charged with steady intrepidity, and drove the right wing of the French back in confusion. One whole regiment of the enemy surrendered: and the rest of that division abandoned the field in haste, leaving behind them their cannon and their wounded.

The left of the French, and the centre, which had been posted to keep in check the Hanoverian divisions on the heights behind the Saltzback, now moved to the right to cover the retreat of their defeated brigades. This was done with coolness and regularity, and their force being far too strong for Lord Granby to attack, the retreat of the whole French Army was effected without much loss.

They left about three thousand men in killed and wounded upon the field; and fifteen hundred prisoners, as well as possession of the ground, attested the triumph of the Allies. This victory produced the effect of checking the French progress for the time, but that was all. The immense numerical superiority of the enemy, gave them advantages which all the activity and skill of Prince Ferdinand could not counterbalance.

The French Army now divided, and throwing out large detachments into different parts of the country, ravaged, pillaged, and destroyed as they went, waging a much more dreadful warfare than by the ordinary course of siege and battle. This continued to the end of the year, when the troops of both nations retired into winter quarters.

The next campaign opened somewhat unfavourably for the Allied Army, and after a number of skirmishes and manoeuvres from which neither force derived any considerable advantage, the French took up a position between Meinbrexen and Grebenstein, on which last named place the right rested, while a considerable body of troops was thrown out on the same side as far as Calsdorff. At the same time Prince Xavier of Saxony lay near Gottingen, keeping a large detachment of the Allies, under General Luckner, in play to watch his movements.

Notwithstanding the advantages which the French possessed in their position, which was defended by a number of streams deep and ravines, was raised upon the heights near Grebenstein, Prince Ferdinand determined to attack them. General Luckner was ordered to draw off his forces from the side of Gottingen, and to co-operate with General Sporken, who passing the Dymel was to attack the French right at Calsdorff in flank, while the former officer charged them in the rear. The Marquess of Granby, passing the same river at Warburg, was to attack the enemy's left by marching over the heights of Zierenburg, while Prince Ferdinand himself proceeded to assail them in front.

The French, in addition to the advantage of the ground, had the superiority of numbers, being in regard to the Allies as five to three; but the rapidity and precision with which the movements of the Hanoverian Army were made, took them by surprise in every quarter. Attacked at once on both flanks and in front, the French scarcely attempted to defend their position; but retreated as fast as possible under cover of a brief stand, made by Monsieur de Stainville with a part of the infantry. This gallant little corps, taking possession of the woods of Wilhelmstadt, sacrificed themselves for the rest of the army; and after fighting resolutely for some time against the Marquess of Granby, were almost all either killed or taken.

Little loss took place on the Hanoverian side; the Allies having only three hundred killed. The resistance, however, of the French infantry swelled the loss of the enemy to near four thousand in prisoners and slain.

Marshal d'Estrées immediately retreated under the cannon of Cassel; and Prince Ferdinand proceeded to cut off the French communication with the Rhine. To compensate this success, the Prince of Conde, who commanded the army on the lower Rhine, completely defeated the Hereditary Prince; and after various partial engagements, in which the Marquess of Granby continued to distinguish himself both for valour, and for conduct, the French captured the fort of Amoenburgh; but were much greater losers by the fall of Cassel, which surrendered to the Allies on the first of November 1762.

This was the last act of the war. A short time before, George II. had closed his career in death, and his grandson George III. having succeeded him, new feelings and interests were brought into play. However sad it is that the fate of nations and weal of worlds should hang upon the frail thread of one weak human life, so it has ever been, and never was more strongly shown than in the events which followed the death of George II. Mr. Pitt and Lord Temple retired from the ministry; the influence of Lord Bute became predominant, and after a struggle to maintain their places for some time, the whole of the former administration seceded also, and peace was almost immediately concluded between England and France.

Lord Granby, with the rest of the English forces returned to England, where for some time he spent his days in tranquillity, mingling but little in the political strifes of the time. Amidst the various changes, however, which took place in the offices of State, though not selected for any post of great importance, he was not forgotten, and seems to have enjoyed a considerable portion of that unsubstantial good—court favour. The want of that continual and active exertion both of mind and body, which by long habit in actual warfare becomes a necessity, has often driven old soldiers to a thousand of the minor vices, in the time of peace.

About this period of Lord Granby's life, we find him accused of too great conviviality of disposition, or to call it by a truer name—of addiction to excess in wine. His good humour also was frequently imposed upon, and perhaps deviated into too great facility; but still he retained his high character as a man and a soldier, as well as the love and respect of the men he commanded. He was a correct though not a severe disciplinarian, was minutely acquainted with every particular of the service; and, having through the whole course of a long war distinguished himself greatly as a second in command, well deserved to be tried in a still more elevated station. No officer in the British service at that time had so many recommendations to the office of Commander-in-Chief of the British forces as he had; and whether it was consideration for his great claims, or merely party influence which procured him that appointment, he received the office in 1766, and continued to exercise it under the administration of the Duke of Grafton and Lord North.

At this time a multitude of follies and weaknesses—the approaching separation of our American colonies from the mother country, the fury of party faction, and probably the disappointment of individual ambition, called up an anonymous writer, who, to the most potent virulence of invective, added the most felicitous farce of expression, the fearlessness of secure concealment, the poignancy of minute information, profound knowledge of constitutional law, contempt of every human feeling, and the gift of magnifying truth without the appearance of hyperbole. This writer on the 25th of January 1769, published a letter in the *Public Advertiser*, under the happily assumed name of Junius, in which he attacked the personal and political character of every member of the ministry.

Now that the prejudices of the parties of that time have passed away, and that we can judge the characters of the dead by facts and not assertions, abstract justice may be done to those whom Junius slandered; but unfortunately, the magnificent record of his own powers which his works afford, and the benefit which they have produced to his country, withhold us from sufficiently detesting the man who, for any motives, could make calumny a profession, and win his reputation by bitterly traducing his fellow-men.

Notwithstanding the immense and unequalled powers that he displayed in one of the most difficult tasks on which the human mind can exercise its faculties, the fame of Junius is an unenviable one; and as inferior to that of his contemporary, Howard, as the fame of Milo the wrestler to that of Trajan. Amongst the many virulent accusations and biting sneers, by which the majestic truths of his first letter are accompanied, Lord Granby, as forming a part of the ministry whom he attacked, was not forgotten by Junius. After noticing in the same manner all the other members of the administration, he proceeds:

> It has lately been a fashion to pay a compliment to the bravery and generosity of the commander-in-chief at the expense of his understanding. They who love him least make no question of his courage, while his friends dwell chiefly on the facility of his disposition. Admitting him to be as brave as a total absence of all feeling and reflection can make him, let us see what sort of merit he derives from the remainder of his character. If it be generosity to accumulate in his own person and family a number of lucrative employments; to provide at the public expense, for every creature that bears the name of Manners;

> and neglecting the merit and services of the rest of the army, to heap promotions upon his favourites and dependants—the present commander-in-chief is the most generous man alive. Nature has been sparing of her gifts to this noble Lord; but where birth and fortune are united, we expect the noble pride and independence of a man of spirit, not the servile humiliating complaisance of a courtier. As to the goodness of his heart, if a proof of it be taken from the facility of never refusing, what conclusion shall we draw from the indecency of never performing? And if the discipline of the army be in any degree preserved, what thanks are due to a man whose cares, notoriously confined to filling up vacancies, have degraded the office of commander-in-chief into a broker of commissions.

Such were the charges against Lord Granby produced by Junius; and though assertions without any proof or instance, especially from an unknown writer, cannot affect the character of any one, yet it is worthwhile to remark that the principal accusations brought by Junius, namely, the neglect of the services and merit of the army in general, the non-performance of all promises, and sole attention to the sales of commissions, is sufficiently refuted by the known and universal love of the whole army for the person of whom he spoke. The disingenuousness of attributing courage to Lord Granby, only from want of all feeling and reflection, requires hardly a comment. On the same principle, Junius, who concealed his name while he aspersed others, might argue that he himself was a man of feeling because he was a coward.

The Marquess of Granby himself, took no notice of the attack; but one of the many whom the better parts of his character had bound to him, stood forward to defend him in the eyes of the world. This was Sir William Draper, and having heard the language of party hatred, let us mark the character drawn by affectionate panegyric, first remarking, that Sir William Draper was himself a distinguished officer, a classical scholar, and a gentleman. He writes:

> A very long, uninterrupted, impartial, and, I will add, a most disinterested friendship with Lord Granby, gives me a right to affirm, that all Junius's assertions are false and scandalous. Lord Granby's courage, though of the brightest and most ardent kind, is amongst the lowest of his numerous good qualities; he was formed to excel in war by nature's liberality to his mind as well

as person. Educated and instructed by his most noble father, and a most spirited as well as excellent scholar, the present Bishop of Bangor, he was trained to the nicest sense of honour, and to the truest and noblest sort of pride, that of never doing or suffering a mean action. A sincere love and attachment to his king and his country, and to their glory, first impelled him to the field, where he never gained aught but honour.

He impaired through his bounty his own fortune: for his bounty, which this writer would in vain depreciate, is founded upon the noblest of human affections—it flows from a heart melting to goodness from the most refined humanity. Can a man, who is described as unfeeling and void of humanity, be constantly employed in seeking proper objects on whom to exercise those glorious virtues of compassion and generosity? The distressed officer, the soldier, the widow, the orphan, and a long list besides, know that vanity has no share in his frequent donations: he gives, because he feels their distresses. Nor has he ever been rapacious with one hand to be bountiful with the other.

Yet this uncandid Junius would insinuate, that the dignity of the commander-in-chief is depraved into the base office of commission broker; that is, Lord Granby bargains for the sale of commissions: for it must have this meaning, if it have any at all. But where is the man living who can justly charge His Lordship with such mean practices? Why does not Junius produce him? Junius knows that he has no other means of wounding this hero than by some missile weapon, shot from an obscure corner. He seeks, as all defamatory writers do——

spargere voces

In vulguni ambiguas,

—— to raise a suspicion in the minds of the people. But I hope that my countrymen will be no longer imposed upon by artful and designing men, or by wretches, who bankrupts in business, in fame, and in fortune, mean nothing more than to involve this country in the same common ruin with themselves. Hence it is, that they are constantly aiming their dark and too often fatal weapons against those who stand forth as the bulwark of our national safety. Lord Granby was too conspicuous a mark not to be their object.

He is next attacked for being unfaithful to his promises and engagements. Where are Junius's proofs? Although I could give

> some instances where a breach of promise would be a virtue, especially in the case of those who would pervert the open unsuspecting moments of convivial mirth, into sly insidious applications for preferment or party systems, and would endeavour to surprise a good man, who cannot bear to see any one leave him dissatisfied, into unguarded promises. Lord Granby's attention to his own family and relations is called selfish. Had he not attended to them when fair and just opportunities presented themselves, I should have thought him unfeeling, and void of reflection indeed. How are any man's friends and relations to be provided for, but from the influence and protection of the patron? It is unfair to suppose that Lord Granby's friends have not as much merit as the friends of any other great man. If he is generous at the public expense, as Junius invidiously calls it, the public is at no more expense for His Lordship's friends than it would be if any other set of men possessed those offices. The charge is ridiculous.

Such was the character of the Marquess of Granby, as drawn by the hand of friendship; and his defence by an able and intelligent officer, who farther went on to appeal to existing facts in order to prove that the army under the chief command of that nobleman, was in as good a state, if not a better one, than it had ever been. From the beauty of the portrait, as given by Sir William Draper, we must of course take away something on account of the partiality of friendship, and the desire of pleasing a person much beloved; but still such commendations would hardly have been ventured in the face of the public, had they not been founded in some degree; for fortunately, constituted as the world is at present, abuse may always be sent out into it much more safely than praise, certain that the one will always find patrons and propagators, while the other is too often suffered to drop into oblivion.

To the letter of Sir William Draper, Junius replied as a giant contending with a child. There seems to have been in his feelings a degree of satisfied virulence in the opportunity afforded him, of impaling Sir William Draper on the same stake with which he had transfixed his friend, which made the beginning of his letter almost polite. In the course of it, however, he found himself obliged to shuffle or retract, notwithstanding the immense command of language which gave him the power of rendering his attack dreadfully potent without being clearly defined. The words he had formerly used, saying that Lord

Granby had "degraded the office of commander-in-chief into a broker of commissions," could have but one straight-forward meaning; yet Junius in his second letter declares "I acquit him of the baseness of selling commissions." He is also under the necessity of receding so far from his assertion in regard to the ruined state of the army, as to acknowledge that the portion of it which was in England was "perhaps in some tolerable order."

By one of those bold falsehoods also, which generally convince the weak, and often stagger the more discriminating reader, he assumes that Sir William Draper had admitted that "Lord Granby often made promises which it was a virtue in him to violate," though his opponent had but asserted that there might be such things as promises which it would be proper to break, without granting at all, that Lord Granby was in the habit of making them.

Junius then turned his attack upon Sir William Draper personally, and the subject of Lord Granby was soon after dropped by his opponent, it is said at the express desire of the Marquess himself. On this subject it is only necessary farther to remark, that Junius, though sufficiently willing to bring forward proofs and individual instances of misconduct, wherever it was in his power to do so, confined himself to general assertions in regard to Lord Granby, though frequently called upon by Sir William Draper to substantiate his accusation. Secure in the cloud with which he had involved his person, he dared to make any charge that might injure his political opponents, certain that the powers of his mind, and the vigour of his style, would drive the dagger home even through the shield of truth; but he dared not at once be both false and circumstantial.

A degree of remorse seems to have touched the mind of Junius in regard to Lord Granby, after the death of that nobleman. In the collection of the famous letters, with notes by Junius himself, the following observation is appended by the author to the seventh letter.

> Sir William Draper certainly drew Junius forward to say more of Lord Granby's character than he originally intended. He was reduced to the dilemma of either being totally silenced or of supporting his first letter. Whether Sir William had a right to reduce him to this dilemma, or to call upon him for his name, after a voluntary attack on his side, are questions submitted to the candour of the public.
>
> The death of Lord Granby was lamented by Junius. He un-

doubtedly owed some compensations to the public; and seemed determined to acquit himself of them. In private life he was unquestionably that good man who, for the interest of his country, ought to have been a great one. *Bonum virum facile dixeris; magnum libenter*, I speak of him now without partiality: I never spoke of him with resentment. His mistakes in public conduct did not arise either from want of sentiment or want of judgment, but in general from the difficulty of saying 'no' to the bad people who surrounded him.

If *this* was the real character of Lord Granby, *that* put forth of him in the first letters of Junius was an infamous falsehood; and political writers should remember, that it is as base, as degrading, as criminal, to traduce an honourable man for the interests of party, as it is for the mean consideration of money. Had the atonement made by Junius been complete, I should have offered no further observations upon his accusation; but it was not complete, and after having attacked him as a military man, he did not do him justice as such. The conduct of the Marquess of Granby, however, while commanding the British forces in Germany, needs no defence. He gained honour in every field; in every endeavour he was successful; and when peace put a termination to the operations of the army under his command, he led it back to England crowned with glory and victory.

The letters of Junius gave him considerable pain—the more, perhaps, because he had never been strongly attached to Lord North's administration. Shortly after their first appearance, he resigned his command; and on quitting the ministry, animadverted very severely on some of their measures. This was his last public act. His health was at this time considerably shaken, and on the 19th of October, 1770, he died at Scarborough, in the fiftieth year of his age.

ALSO FROM LEONAUR

AVAILABLE IN SOFTCOVER OR HARDCOVER WITH DUST JACKET

THE FALL OF THE MOGHUL EMPIRE OF HINDUSTAN *by H. G. Keene*—By the beginning of the nineteenth century, as British and Indian armies under Lake and Wellesley dominated the scene, a little over half a century of conflict brought the Moghul Empire to its knees.

LADY SALE'S AFGHANISTAN *by Florentia Sale*—An Indomitable Victorian Lady's Account of the Retreat from Kabul During the First Afghan War.

THE CAMPAIGN OF MAGENTA AND SOLFERINO 1859 *by Harold Carmichael Wylly*—The Decisive Conflict for the Unification of Italy.

FRENCH'S CAVALRY CAMPAIGN *by J. G. Maydon*—A Special Correspondent's View of British Army Mounted Troops During the Boer War.

CAVALRY AT WATERLOO *by Sir Evelyn Wood*—British Mounted Troops During the Campaign of 1815.

THE SUBALTERN *by George Robert Gleig*—The Experiences of an Officer of the 85th Light Infantry During the Peninsular War.

NAPOLEON AT BAY, 1814 *by F. Loraine Petre*—The Campaigns to the Fall of the First Empire.

NAPOLEON AND THE CAMPAIGN OF 1806 *by Colonel Vachée*—The Napoleonic Method of Organisation and Command to the Battles of Jena & Auerstädt.

THE COMPLETE ADVENTURES IN THE CONNAUGHT RANGERS *by William Grattan*—The 88th Regiment during the Napoleonic Wars by a Serving Officer.

BUGLER AND OFFICER OF THE RIFLES *by William Green & Harry Smith*—With the 95th (Rifles) during the Peninsular & Waterloo Campaigns of the Napoleonic Wars.

NAPOLEONIC WAR STORIES *by Sir Arthur Quiller-Couch*—Tales of soldiers, spies, battles & sieges from the Peninsular & Waterloo campaingns.

CAPTAIN OF THE 95TH (RIFLES) *by Jonathan Leach*—An officer of Wellington's sharpshooters during the Peninsular, South of France and Waterloo campaigns of the Napoleonic wars.

RIFLEMAN COSTELLO *by Edward Costello*—The adventures of a soldier of the 95th (Rifles) in the Peninsular & Waterloo Campaigns of the Napoleonic wars.

AVAILABLE ONLINE AT **www.leonaur.com**
AND FROM ALL GOOD BOOK STORES

07/09

LEONAUR

ALSO FROM LEONAUR

AVAILABLE IN SOFTCOVER OR HARDCOVER WITH DUST JACKET

THE 9TH—THE KING'S (LIVERPOOL REGIMENT) IN THE GREAT WAR 1914 - 1918 *by Enos H. G. Roberts*—Mersey to mud—war and Liverpool men.

THE GAMBARDIER *by Mark Severn*—The experiences of a battery of Heavy artillery on the Western Front during the First World War.

FROM MESSINES TO THIRD YPRES *by Thomas Floyd*—A personal account of the First World War on the Western front by a 2/5th Lancashire Fusilier.

THE IRISH GUARDS IN THE GREAT WAR - VOLUME 1 *by Rudyard Kipling*—Edited and Compiled from Their Diaries and Papers—The First Battalion.

THE IRISH GUARDS IN THE GREAT WAR - VOLUME 1 *by Rudyard Kipling*—Edited and Compiled from Their Diaries and Papers—The Second Battalion.

ARMOURED CARS IN EDEN *by K. Roosevelt*—An American President's son serving in Rolls Royce armoured cars with the British in Mesopatamia & with the American Artillery in France during the First World War.

CHASSEUR OF 1914 *by Marcel Dupont*—Experiences of the twilight of the French Light Cavalry by a young officer during the early battles of the great war in Europe.

TROOP HORSE & TRENCH *by R.A. Lloyd*—The experiences of a British Lifeguardsman of the household cavalry fighting on the western front during the First World War 1914-18.

THE EAST AFRICAN MOUNTED RIFLES *by C.J. Wilson*—Experiences of the campaign in the East African bush during the First World War.

THE LONG PATROL *by George Berrie*—A Novel of Light Horsemen from Gallipoli to the Palestine campaign of the First World War.

THE FIGHTING CAMELIERS *by Frank Reid*—The exploits of the Imperial Camel Corps in the desert and Palestine campaigns of the First World War.

STEEL CHARIOTS IN THE DESERT *by S. C. Rolls*—The first world war experiences of a Rolls Royce armoured car driver with the Duke of Westminster in Libya and in Arabia with T.E. Lawrence.

WITH THE IMPERIAL CAMEL CORPS IN THE GREAT WAR *by Geoffrey Inchbald*—The story of a serving officer with the British 2nd battalion against the Senussi and during the Palestine campaign.

www.ingramcontent.com/pod-product-compliance
Lightning Source LLC
LaVergne TN
LVHW091639100826
845152LV00006B/96/J
9781916535183